The Second Martin

The Second Martin

The Life and Theology
of Martin Chemnitz

J. A. O. Preus

SAINT LOUIS

Copyright © 1994 Concordia Publishing House
3558 S. Jefferson Avenue, St. Louis, MO 63118-3968
Manufactured in the United States of America

Library of Congress Cataloging-in-Publication Data

Preus, Jacob A. O. (Jacob Aall Ottesen), 1920–
    The second Martin: the life and theology of Martin Chemnitz/
J. A. O. Preus.
        p. cm.
    Includes bibliographical references and index.
    ISBN 0-570-04645-9
    1. Chemnitz, Martin, 1522–1586. 2. Lutheran Church—Doctrines—
History—16th century. 3. Theology, Doctrinal—History—16th century. I Title.
BX8080.C47P74   1994
230' .41' 092—dc20
                                             94-15925

1 2 3 4 5 6 7 8 9 10   03 02 01 00 99 98 97 96 95 94

To Delpha, my constant helper and companion, without whose love and support I could never have written this book or accomplished anything else in this world.

Contents

CONTENTS

CONTENTS

Abbreviations

AC   Augsburg Confession

AE   American Edition of *Luther's Works* (English. St. Louis: Concordia and Philadelphia: Fortress)

Apol.   Apology to the Augsburg Confession

CR   *Corpus Reformatorum,* ed. C. G. Bretschneider *et al.,* Halle, 1834 ff., for works of Melanchthon in the original

CTM   *Concordia Theological Monthly,* St. Louis

ECT   *Examination of the Council of Trent,* 4 volumes (St. Louis: Concordia, 1971–1988)

Ench.   *The Enchiridion* (St. Louis: Concordia, 1981)

Ep.   Epitome of the Formula of Concord

FC   Formula of Concord

LC   Large Catechism

LT   *Loci Theologici* (St. Louis: Concordia, 1989)

LS   *The Lord's Supper* (St. Louis: Concordia, 1979)

SA   Smalcald Articles, including Tractate

SC   Small Catechism

SD   Solid Declaration of the Formula of Concord

TNC   *The Two Natures in Christ* (St. Louis: Concordia, 1971)

WA   Weimar Edition of *Luther's Works* (German)

Preface

About 30 years ago my uncle, Dr. Herman Preus, and a colleague of his, Dr. Edmund Smits, undertook to produce a volume that included long quotations from Martin Chemnitz (1522–86) and John Gerhard (1582–1637) showing how these two great Lutheran fathers dealt with the doctrine of anthropology. The result was a book entitled *The Doctrine of Man in Classical Lutheran Theology*, edited by the two men mentioned and translated by Mario Colacci et al., (Minneapolis, 1962). I had the honor to be one of the "et al.," having been selected to revise some material from Chemnitz' *Loci Theologici*, which had been first undertaken by a Ph.D. in Classics whose knowledge of theology was so limited that when he came to references to Peter Lombard (d. 1164), he called him Lombardi, perhaps out of a zealous but albeit mistaken identification of the "Master of the Sentences" with Vince Lombardi of the Green Bay Packers! At any rate, as the years went on, I was tagged to shore up a flagging translation of Luther's (1483–1546) *Lectures on Romans* which was first entrusted to a Roman priest who could not understand Luther and then to a Lutheran who unfortunately died before he finished the job. So the pinch hitter was called in again. This led to an assignment to translate Chemnitz' *The Two Natures in Christ*, which appeared in 1971, and his *Fundamenta sanae doctrinae de vera et substantiali praesentia, exhibitione et sumptione corporis et sanguinis Domini in Coena*, which came out in English in 1979 under the title *The Lord's Supper*. And finally in 1986 I completed the translation of his commentary on Melanchthon's (1497–1560) *Loci Communes*. This work, the next to the longest of Chemnitz' writings, was published in English in 1989. (And since no one has ever found a good English translation for Melanchthon's work, we have left Chemnitz' title also in the original Latin. Both titles refer merely to the fact that the books are summaries of the main points [*Loci* or topics] of Christian doctrine.)

All of this adds up to the fact that for 30 years I have been reading and translating the writings of a little-known but extremely important Lutheran theologian who lived in an important period of our church's history and who made great contributions to Lutheranism, many of which have been forgotten and many others misunderstood. For over 20 years I used to get up an hour earlier to translate Chemnitz. I had some of his work photocopied, and I carried it on planes all over the world, not just because I enjoyed translating Latin, but more importantly because I enjoyed and was edified by spending an hour with a magnificent Lutheran theologian. I hope by means of this little book, which Chemnitz might call a *libellum,* to stimulate in the minds of its readers an appreciation for this modest and quiet man, who was so gifted, so competent, so retiring personally, and yet who made enormous contributions to the Gospel-centered theology of our church and to the actual survival of Lutheranism itself.

One of the most impressive features about Chemnitz was the fact that although he had excellent ecclesiastical connections and the backing of none less than the mighty Philip Melanchthon, yet he left a professorship at Wittenberg (something that very few ever did) and took a position as an assistant, a coadjutor, to a none-too-prominent superintendent in the city of Braunschweig (Brunswick). At that time Braunschweig was under the harassment of Duke (Herzog) Henry the Younger (1514–68), the famous Hanswurst of Luther fame, who was trying to regain the city for Rome and for himself. Chemnitz' duties included serving as pastor to a congregation, educating young men for the ministry, supervising the work of the churches of the city in a way a modern bishop might, defending the faith throughout the entire Lutheran world, and continuing his lectures on Melanchthon's great and extremely popular *Loci Communes.* Being an assistant superintendent was not a particularly prestigious position, yet Chemnitz remained in this city for the rest of his life. After 13 years as coadjutor he became the general superintendent. During his entire career he was engaged in writing the theological treatises designed to uphold Lutheranism, and particularly through his important work on the Formula of Concord, he worked to unite the factionalized Lutherans of Germany—something that was accomplished to an amazing degree by his work.

This required extensive travel, countless meetings, and many doctrinal papers and books. But it saved Lutheranism from the inroads of a virulent Calvinism and a revived Rome with its Counter Reformation. This man, as the theological genius of his age, operating from his base in northern Germany, is the chief author of the Formula of Concord, the father of orthodox Lutheranism, and the father of what we today, 400 years later, call normative Lutheran theology. He was a scriptural theologian, cautious and hesitant about innovation, and the greatest expert on the church fathers (patristics) that Lutheranism had produced up to that point.

It is interesting to speculate on what might have happened had Chemnitz stayed at Wittenberg. Theoretically he might have succumbed to the capriciousness and weakness of Melanchthon and his dishonest supporters, in which case Lutheranism would have lost its staunchest bulwark. Or he might have been able to stop Melanchthon's drift toward Calvinism (something that Luther himself recognized but was not able to stop completely). But Chemnitz went to Braunschweig and Melanchthon continued to drift.

Along with his supervisory duties, Chemnitz remained a parish pastor, thinking and speaking in nonphilosophical and nonscholastic categories, living and working at the cutting edge of church life, not in the cloister of academia or at the heady level of the full-time church administrator. The audiences for his lectures on Melanchthon's *Loci Communes* were parish pastors and theological students. He held meetings similar to our Bible classes, where both men and women were invited to participate. He developed guidelines for the financial support of the widows and orphans of pastors. He supervised the work of almoners who took care of the city's poor. And he developed organizations like our modern young people's societies.

At the same time, Chemnitz was a remarkable student of Scripture and the early fathers of the church and a devoted disciple of Luther. He was instrumental in bringing the Reformation to areas that up to that time had been Roman Catholic. He served as a theological advisor to many churches and princes and as a leader in peace efforts among the warring Lutherans. He was a man who refused to indulge in personal attacks against his opponents in his public writings, yet he was constantly on the attack against the errors of John Calvin (1509–64) regarding the Lord's Supper and the doctrine of Christology, as well as against those within Lutheranism who supported these and other vagaries. At the same time he was the most effective opponent the Romanists had from within the Protestant ranks. The Romanists called him the "second Martin," saying that if the second Martin had not come, the first would not have prevailed.

Dr. Charles Porterfield Krauth (1823–83), one of the truly great theologians of what is today the Evangelical Lutheran Church of America (ELCA), makes the following significant statement:

> The controversies which followed Luther's death arrested the internal development of the church and brought the processes of its more perfect constitutional organizing almost to a close. The great living doctrines which made the Reformation were in danger of losing all their practical power in the absorption of men's minds in controversies. . . . The church was threatened with schism. Her glory was obscured. Her enemies mocked at her. Her children were confused and saddened. Weak ones were turned from her communion, sometimes to Zurich, or Geneva, sometimes to Rome. . . . There was the danger that the age which the Conservative Reformation has glorified should see that groundwork lost in the endless dissension of embittered factions. Hence . . . the Formula [of Concord], if not exclusively, yet in the main, was occupied in stating the truth, and defending it over against the errors which had crept into many and corrupted some of her children.[1]

Here is where Chemnitz, together with the other authors of the Formula came to the fore. Of him Krauth says specifically,

> The learning of Chemnitz was something colossal, but it had no tinge of pedantry. His judgment was of the highest order. His modesty and simplicity, his clearness of thought, and his luminous style, his firmness in principle, and his gentleness in tone, the richness of his learning, and the vigor of his thinking have revealed themselves in such measure in his Loci, his Books on the Two Natures of our Lord, and on the True Presence, in his Examen of the Council of Trent, his Defense of the Formula of Concord, and his Harmony of the Gospels, as to render each a classic in its kind, and to make their author as the greatest theologian of his time— one of the greatest theologians of all time.[2]

The modern German historian, Inge Mager, writing a century later asserts that "Chemnitz continued to be the most consulted theologian and advisor for the establishment of Reformation church-life in the land."[3] Of no theologian of Lutheranism of that era, except for Luther himself, are such wonderful words spoken—and so justly.

Yet few have ever heard of Chemnitz, and even fewer know much or anything about him. In this age of searching for closer harmony among Lutherans, Martin Chemnitz stands out like a beacon. He succeeded in uniting over two-thirds of German Lutheranism, and when everything was over and a few important funerals had taken place, nearly every territorial church in Germany subscribed to his Formula of Concord. The Church of Sweden did the same. Denmark (which at the time also ruled Norway and Iceland) gradually withdrew its objections, which had arisen mainly out of the irascibility of the Danish king, and the theology of Chemnitz and the Formula of Concord became the standard for normative Lutheran theology and remains such for large portions of 20th-century Lutheranism. Robert Preus in his *Theology of Post-Reformation Lutheranism* says,

> While attending some of the unpleasant conferences between the Philippists and the Gnesio-Lutherans, Chemnitz came to recognize the importance of Lutheran unity especially against the threat of the Counter Reformation, and he determined to do his utmost to unite the Lutherans doctrinally. In this he was eminently successful. He strengthened the theology of Jacob Andreae and was perhaps responsible for rescuing Selnecker from the compromising spirit of Melanchthonianism. He was the leading spirit in the writing of the Formula of Concord. . . . His fruitful literary output and his beneficial activity in the church made Chemnitz, after Luther, the most important theologian in the history of the Lutheran Church.[4]

And few have ever heard of him! Is not this amazing in our ecumenical age, when many Lutherans talk about nothing but ecumenism, Lutheran union, and getting Lutherans together? And yet who has ever heard of the man who was more successful in this enterprise than anyone in history? To this day many theologians and church historians, at least in North America, have very little good to say about the Formula of Concord or its authors. Yet who has ever equaled the work done by this document and its authors?

17

Very few have heard of Melanchthon either. What little work has been done on him in North America has been done largely by Reformed scholars.[5] But it might be worth the career of at least one scholar, especially in American Lutheranism—swimming as we are in a sea of liberal, fundamentalistic, ecumenical, Reformed, Calvinistic, Arminian confusion, well seasoned with liberal Catholicism, humanism, and secularism—to tell the story of Melanchthon and some of the other fathers of our Lutheran churches with our great heritage of Luther himself, the confessional writings of Lutheranism, and the struggles of countless pastors, professors, and lay people down through the centuries. History and the Lutheran church have not treated Melanchthon very well, and most of what he got he deserved, but the fact is that for a generation he was the ecclesiastical, theological, and political successor of Martin Luther and the leader of a Lutheranism that was divided theologically, politically, in language and in goals, and that was confused over almost every problem that arose in that fast-moving and revolutionary age. And there was no other universally recognized leader. On many issues he was wrong, but on many others he was correct and helpful. The divided and confused Lutherans all over central Europe looked to him. He had wide-ranging contacts with secular rulers as well as Calvinists, Roman Catholics, Eastern Orthodox, and all kinds of Lutherans. When the uproar arose over Servetus (1511–53), it was the Lutheran Melanchthon who wrote to the Senate of Venice in their murky Catholicism, warning them against harboring this dangerous unitarian heretic. The Venetian Senate very obligingly took Melanchthon's advice and expelled Servetus who then made his way to Geneva, where the senate of that city at the advice of another friend of Melanchthon, John Calvin, proceeded to burn the poor man at the stake.

Chemnitz, because he had been a co-worker of Melanchthon and had been recommended by him for a position on the Wittenberg faculty and because he spent all the years of his public ministry studying Luther and the church fathers and also lecturing on Melanchthon's great *Loci Communes* and because of his rather mild and patient disposition, was the most qualified of all the so-called third-generation Lutheran leaders to be a kind of bridge or connecting link to hand down to the Lutheran churches of his age the best of Luther, the best of Melanchthon, and the best of the theology of the period 50 years after the presentation of the Augsburg Confession. And this is exactly what he did, veering neither to the left in the direction of non-Lutheran Protestants, such as the followers of Zwingli (1484–1531) and Calvin who had such a fascination for Melanchthon, nor to the right in the direction of a return to Rome, for which Melanchthon also, strangely, had a hankering. Melanchthon was a natural ecclesiastical wheeler-dealer, but Chemnitz, like Luther, was much more theological and had much more integrity.

Related to his integrity was his courage. Chemnitz did not hesitate in the defense of the truth and of Lutheran theology to enter into theological dialogs and controversies with anyone. One of Chemnitz' first encounters, several years before his ordination or any study of theology, was with Andrew Osiander (1498–1552), a notable Lutheran who had signed the Smalcald Articles and brought the Reformation to Prussia, but who fell into error on the doctrine of justification. Chemnitz also took on the Lutheran leader in Bremen, Albert Hardenberg (1510–74), regarding the Lord's Supper. Later in his most famous work he attacked the Roman Catholic Church in what is still regarded as the most trenchant analysis ever made of Roman Catholic theology after the Council of Trent. He also carried on constant battles in defense of the scriptural and Lutheran doctrine of Christology and the Lord's Supper with Calvin and other leaders of the Reformed church and against errors on the same points within Lutheranism.

Chemnitz was a devoted father and husband, a dutiful citizen, a man of unimpeachable character (which may be one reason he is not well known). Not one breath of scandal is attached to him. He does not talk with the earthiness of Luther, nor does he possess the arrogance and petulance of Melanchthon. He remains the common man who as a boy had to scratch for money for his education. His writings breathe a pious and sincere Christian faith, devoid of pomposity. His congregation and the city council of Braunschweig loved him and would never release him to take another call. His pastors imitated him. Duke Julius (1528–89) loved and honored him, but when the two met head to head on a matter of principle, Chemnitz stood by his confession at great cost to his honor and his social and ecclesiastical position and that of his children. He was not a "court theologian."

While he was not a court theologian in the ordinary sense of that term (although he served princes), he was also not a Melanchthonian in any theological sense of that term. He was not a strident polemicist nor a compromising church politician. He was a scriptural, confessional, Lutheran theologian with the highest regard for the ancient, orthodox church and a very thorough understanding of Luther, his theology, and his place in the history of the church; a church leader; and perhaps above all a man with a pastoral heart who believed his message and his calling. For those who practice speed-reading, this is the sum and substance of this book.

It is with all of the above in mind that I, fully aware of my limitations and inadequacies, undertake to tell pastors and students, lay people, and perhaps even a few professors a few things that they might not know and that I hope some of them might appreciate knowing about "the second Martin" and his significance for Lutheranism today. Chemnitz in his will mentioned several books as his legacy to the Lutheran churches of his day, and I believe that the greatest legacy I can leave to our beloved Lutheran church is the translation of some of the writings of this great man and this *libellum* about his life and work.

Acknowledgments

Prefaces of this kind always give credits, and this book, more than most, must do the same. First there is the unending gratitude I have toward my beloved, talented, and dedicated wife, Delpha, whose help and inspiration have kept me going for over 40 years. Then to CPH, Mr. John Gerber, president, and the wonderful editorial department; to Dr. Everette Meier for his great help in deciphering German which I never truly mastered and yet without which one can never understand Chemnitz or for that matter Lutheranism; to Dr. Robert Kolb for his careful criticism; to Pastor Wolfgang Junke of Braunschweig, Germany, whose help in the weeks we spent at Wolfenbüttel was beyond calculation, as was that of the staff and administration of the Herzog August Bibliothek of Wolfenbüttel, particularly Herr Ulric Kopp; to my brother, Dr. Robert Preus, whose lifelong interest in the period of Orthodoxy and Post-Reformation Lutheranism constantly kept my interests alive; to Drs. Fred Kramer and Eugene Klug, my old and valued colleagues, of Concordia Seminary, Springfield, Illinois, and to countless more—a sincere thanks.

A very special and sincere thanks is due to Dr. Charles Arand of Concordia Seminary, St. Louis, who gave untiringly of his time and talent, helping me with the final stages of this opus, preparing the manuscript for publication, checking footnotes, bibliography, historical and theological points, and countless other details. I am deeply and eternally grateful to this fine, young scholar and student of our beloved Lutheran Confessions.

A special word of thanks also goes to certain men whom I have never met, but whose influence is reflected in this volume. In the past generation a new interest has developed in the later Luther in contradistinction to the preceding century or more in which the young Luther figured so prominently. A brief study of the Formula of Concord and the other writings of Chemnitz reveals that he and those of his age were very attached to the writings of the "old," or perhaps we should say "mature," Luther (as well as to the young Luther). They looked upon themselves as part of an unbroken continuum of Lutheran teaching and confession that began with Luther himself, starting with his Ninety-five Theses of 1517 and continuing up to the time of his death, and that continued on, with some ruffles, through the period of Melanchthon, and then resumed in full flower during their own era. To them the Formula of Concord did not represent a "new dogma" but merely the continuation of Luther's teaching and the theology of the Augsburg Confession. It appears that this same understanding entered into the thinking of some very fine young historians, such as James Kittelson in his excellent *Luther the Reformer* (Minneapolis: Augsburg, 1986). Also, I want to mention Mark Edwards' excellent *Luther's Last Battles* (Ithaca: Cornell University Press, 1983), in which among many other important points, he shows that Luther's fruitful and seminal theological thinking continued to the end of his life. Books such as these show the progress and continuity of Luther's theology through his entire career and on into the late Reformation period. The same interests seem to be present in the thinking of many in Europe also, in such writers as Gensichen, Inge Mager, Theodore Mahlmann, Jobst Ebel, and many others, including Peter Barton who has popularized the term "late Reformation" in contradistinction to the earlier "post-Reformation."[1] I hope that this little effort of mine will contribute to this trend.

Viewed from this perspective we have a span of only eight years from the death of Luther in 1546 to the beginning in 1554 of Chemnitz' professional career at Braunschweig, where, as also in other places in Germany, efforts had been going on all the time to stem the influence and effort of Melanchthon and his cohorts to water down Lutheranism. The witness to the great truths of the Reformation never really stopped until it culminated in the adoption of the Formula of Concord in 1580, which was a reaffirmation of the best of Luther, a repudiation of all of his opponents, and the dawn of a new beginning for Lutheranism on the foundations so strongly laid by Luther and continued by Chemnitz and the authors of the Formula of Concord, yet always recognizing and giving credit to Melanchthon for his many contributions. I recognize full well that

ACKNOWLEDGMENTS

there is a school of thought within and outside of Lutheranism that the Augsburg Confession is a Melanchthonian document and that both the Smalcald Articles and the Formula of Concord, and perhaps even the catechisms, are in a sense deviations from or perversions of a more correct interpretation of the Christian faith as enunciated by the young Luther and even Melanchthon. Chemnitz did not believe this, nor did the men who worked so valiantly for both Lutheran unity and solidarity in those days of the late Reformation.

J. A. O. PREUS

The Baptism Day of Martin Chemnitz
11 November 1992

So then, brothers, stand firm and hold to the teachings
we passed on to you,
whether by word of mouth or by letter.

May our Lord Jesus Christ himself and God our Father,
who loved us and by his grace
gave us eternal encouragement and good hope,
encourage your hearts and strengthen you
in every good deed and word.
2 Thess. 2:15–17

Luther: "Histories are, therefore, a very precious thing. . . .
There one finds both
how those who were pious and wise acted,
refrained from acting, and lived,
how they fared and how they were rewarded."
Luther's Works, American Edition 34:275

PART 1

THE TIMES AND CAST OF CHARACTERS

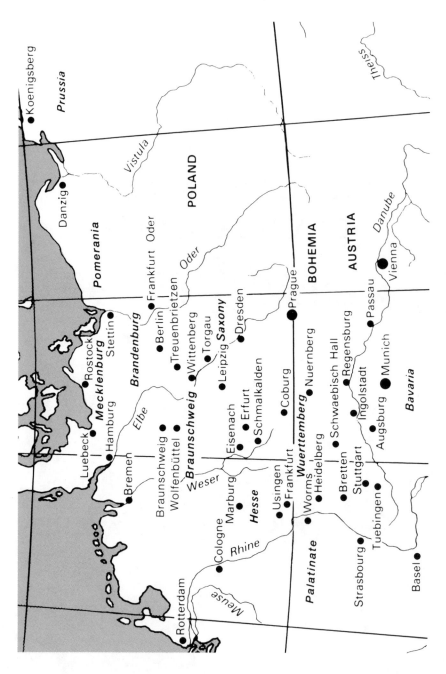

Germany at the Time of Chemnitz

1

The Political and Ecclesiastical Situation

In order to understand the life and significance of Martin Chemnitz and his theology, it is necessary to have a picture of the world in which he lived, particularly the political, ecclesiastical, and theological forces at work in the years preceding and during his lifetime.

EMPEROR CHARLES V

Charles V (1500–58, reigned 1519–56) is not of direct significance in the life and work of Chemnitz, but he laid the foundations for the world in which Chemnitz worked. He was both emperor of the Holy Roman Empire and King of Spain (as Charles I). He was the son of Philip of Burgundy, thus giving him French connections, and Joanna (known as La Loca), the mad daughter of Ferdinand and Isabella of Spain. He was born at Ghent, now in Belgium, at that time a part of the Lowlands, of which his father shortly after Charles' birth became ruler. In 1516, at the death of Ferdinand, Charles also became king of Castile and in 1518 Aragon was added to his domains. In 1519, as a Hapsburg, he succeeded to the possessions of his grandfather Maximillian and finally in 1520 he was elected emperor of the Holy Roman Empire. The Holy Roman Empire was basically a federation of several small German states together with Austria, usually under the rule of a Hapsburg with that family's wide-ranging possessions. Also included were the vast possessions of Spain in the western hemisphere.

Charles, who sometimes has been called more Catholic than the pope, was totally committed, as were nearly all rulers of his age, to the concept that there should be unanimity of religious and political beliefs in his realm. Thus it was a matter both of faith and political theory that he must bring the Germans back into the fold of the Roman Church. The empire was actually in decline and impossible to control, but Charles did not realize this when he first became emperor. Perhaps his early retirement in 1556 signalled his realization of this fact. In regard to this determination, his career is divided into three periods. From 1520 to 1529 he did nothing, disregarded the Lutheran development, and devoted his efforts to the defeat of his other enemies, using the Lutheran princes and armies to assist him. From 1530 to 1545 he tried to defeat the Lutheran movement by diplomacy and negotiation, holding the pope at bay pending the calling of a council, all the while watching the growth of Lutheranism. From 1546 to 1555 he tried war.

As early as the Diet of Worms Charles had determined to remain Catholic and that the empire should remain Catholic. It was there that Charles and the great heretic Luther first met and Luther was told to recant and get back in line. But nothing happened because the elector of Saxony, Frederick the Wise (reigned 1486–1525), protected Luther—and Charles needed the elector's help. Again, at the Diet of Augsburg in 1530 this stern monarch met the heretical princely followers of the heretic Luther, and again, despite the favorable terms of this diet, Lutheranism was still only tolerated—not considered equal or legal and was still under the strictures of the Diet of Worms of 1521. Pluralism had no part in Charles' thinking. The only thing that saved the Lutherans was that Charles was so busy with his other enemies and so needed the support of the Lutheran princes that he could not deal with them.

During this time, the Turks were on the march, particularly under Suleiman, called the Magnificent (reigned 1520–66), the sultan of the Turkish Empire. They reached their high-water mark during Chemnitz' lifetime. They could well be called the allies of the Reformation because they kept both Charles and the pope at bay, and at one point the Turks and the pope were actually de facto allies against Charles and in indirect support of the Lutherans.

In the meantime in France, King Francis I (1494–1547, reigned from 1515) did everything possible to thwart Charles, including entering into a treaty with Suleiman. For the same reason Francis was supportive of German Protestants, while persecuting French ones. In 1545 he even asked Melanchthon to draw up a formula for reconciliation between Lutherans and Catholics, thereby to produce an alliance between France and Germany against Charles. After the death of Francis I, the sympathies in France began to swing in favor of Catholicism. Chemnitz lived during the St. Bartholomew's Massacre in August of 1572, under Francis' morally degenerate grandson, Charles IX (1550–74), in which about 50,000 Protestants were slaughtered.

Because of his desire to be at peace with the Germans, Charles had tried to force the unwilling pope to call a council to settle the religious quarrels. The pope was unwilling to comply for fear that this council might do to him what the Councils of Constance and Basel had done to his predecessors, namely, strip him of much of his power. The council finally did begin to meet on Dec. 13, 1545 at Trent, but it was evident that it was going nowhere. When Charles saw this, he began the Smalcald War in 1546, shortly after the death of Luther. His purpose was to reunite the church. He used the bigamy of Philip of Hesse as one excuse to wage war upon the Lutherans. The Lutherans were defeated in the Battle of Mühlberg in 1547. The end result of the war was the Peace of Passau of August 1552, favorable to the Lutherans, which paved the way for the Peace of Augsburg of 1555. This gave them peace until the outbreak of the Thirty Years' War in 1618. The Peace of Augsburg of 1555 laid the political basis for the whole period of Chemnitz' professional career.

THE PAPACY

The most potent political as well as ecclesiastical force affecting Lutheranism during this entire period was the papacy itself. The popular historian, Barbara Tuchman, in her *The March of Folly,* goes so far as to suggest that there never would have been a Reformation had it not been for the six notorious Renaissance popes, with their corruption, their nepotism, and their venality, all of which both offended and impoverished the Germans, among others.[1] Recall the famous statement of Leo X, which was typical of the age, "Let us enjoy the papacy, since God has given it to us." Whether Tuchman is correct in every detail or not, it is certain that attacks had been made on the papacy for several centuries. Luther's were particularly effective both because of the times and because he hit at the very core of the Catholic religion, not only the papal corruptions of it. Erasmus, Valla, and the other humanists had been gadflies, but they had not done great harm. Luther did.[2]

By the time of Chemnitz, however, the morals and general atmosphere of the papacy had improved, making Chemnitz' job, in this respect, more difficult than Luther's. In some instances the Romanists in their indecisiveness simply handed over large pieces of real estate to the Reformation. For example, Pope Clement VII (1523–34) got caught between Charles V and Francis I of France. He bet on the wrong horse, namely, France, and was captured by the Spaniards. As long as the quarrel between Charles and the papacy continued, the Lutherans made headway. Clement VII could never decide to call a council, and during this period of indecision large portions of Germany, England, Switzerland, and Scandinavia were lost forever to the papacy.

To capsulize the situation that developed at the time of Luther's death: Under Paul III (1534–49) the immediate successor of the feckless Clement, things began to improve for Rome. Paul's pontificate is regarded as the beginning of the Counter-Reformation. The rise of the Jesuits to prominence may also be traced to this period. Pope Paul cooperated with Charles, and during his pontificate the Council of Trent began, the inquisition was reinstituted, the Smalcald War with its victories for the Catholics took place, the Interims were forced down the throats of the helpless German Lutherans, the mantle of leadership fell on the pusillanimous Melanchthon, and quarrels broke out among the Lutherans.

Again, under Julius III (1550–55) a man utterly unlike his notorious predecessor of the same name, the fortunes of the papacy waned. With the defeat of Charles V at the hands of Maurice of Saxony in March of 1552 and the signing of the religious Peace of Augsburg in 1555, Protestantism again forged ahead.

Then a trend set in under Paul IV (1555–59) that was never again reversed. Paul hated the Hapsburgs, the family to which Charles V belonged, but he also hated Protestantism, which he eradicated in Italy. Often the fortunes of the papacy and of the Protestants rose together over against the Hapsburgs, but when the Hapsburgs and the papacy were on the same side, Protestantism did not fare well. This was the case under Paul IV. The papacy prospered, the Council of Trent proceeded, and due to the complexion of the council as well as the general political situation, the breach between Rome and Protestantism became final and unbridgeable. The Catholic-Lutheran 1557 Colloquy at Worms only revealed the divisions among the Lutherans, and the Catholics took advantage of this to walk out, since many of them had not wanted to be there in the first place.

The next popes, Pius IV (1559–65), Pius V (1566–72), Gregory XIII (1572–85), and Sixtus V (1585–90), all contemporaries of Chemnitz, finished the job. All continued the work of internal reform in the Catholic Church, purging the church of the rank corruption that had been manifest in Luther's time. They made positive changes in the organizational or institutional and moral aspects of church life. At the same time, they worked at the task of shoring up the power and influence of the papacy itself. During this period, for example, the papacy gave aid and comfort to Mary Queen of Scots in her ill-fated efforts to regain Great Britain and supported the persecution of the Huguenots and Calvinists in France. They rejoiced at the great naval victory at Lepanto in 1571 in which Don Juan of Austria, the illegitimate and talented son of Charles V, defeated the Turks, using Catholic sailors. They also used the victory for Roman propaganda. They encouraged great mission expansion in the New World, the imposition of the inquisition wherever possible, the passage of stricter rules governing the marriage of priests, and the purification of monastic life. This spirit continued dominant among Catholics for at least 150 years, ultimately leading to a virulent Catholic triumphalism and almost a total forgetfulness that there ever had been a Reformation or the need for one. Witness the great work of the Dominican and Jesuit missionaries in Canada, the forced conversion of the Indians in Latin America, and the energy with which the successive popes and their secular royal partners prosecuted the Thirty Years' War. This was a war to the death of Protestantism—and Protestantism barely survived.

COUNTER-REFORMATION AND TRENT

The true theological and spiritual spearhead of the Counter-Reformation was the Council of Trent itself. The reforms in the papacy, the mission expansion, the moral and intellectual reforms of the church at large were important and played a major role in the revival of Catholicism, but the council—which had been so long demanded by Luther and the secular rulers and the Protestants in general, and so long denied by the popes—turned out to be the guiding principle for generations to come of a renewed and in many ways reformed Roman Church. This is strange in view of the pusillanimity of the series of popes who had refused to call the council, the overbearing and warlike attitude of the Catholic princes who demanded it, the dashed hopes and ultimate virtual exclusion of the Lutherans who had so long clamored for it. Yet this council, dominated by right-wing clerics, apparently was just what the Roman Church needed to give it unity, direction, and an attitude that either Rome would have to get its house in order or it would disappear. It got its house in order.

The council began in December of 1545, about two months before Luther's death, and it finally came to an end in December of 1563. It was never attended by any significant number of church leaders or by the pope himself. It was almost totally under the domination of Spanish, Italian, and Portuguese theologians and was never formally adopted in France (or, obviously, the Protestant parts of Germany). Still the council had an influence far beyond the caliber of people who attended and prepared its decrees and canons. It was obvious that its authors attempted to keep their language as irenic as the situation, in their eyes, permitted, avoiding the names of such arch heretics as Luther.

The council followed the historic pattern of previous councils, building on the foundations of the six ancient ecumenical councils, opening by the confession and quotation of the Nicene Creed, "the symbol of faith which the holy Roman Church makes use of as being that principle wherein all who profess the faith of Christ necessarily agree." It also described itself as "assembled in the Holy Spirit . . . with the Holy Spirit dictating . . . following the example of the orthodox fathers." It is obvious that the council looked upon itself, as did previous councils, as confessing the faith. Thus in this age of competing and conflicting confessions, the Roman Church, which had replied to the Augsburg Confession only with a hastily drawn Confutation, now, 15 years after Augsburg, decides to enter the confessional arena itself. Two points become manifest here.

The first is that Martin Chemnitz—who during his years of working on his *Examination of the Council of Trent* (1566–73) had been involved in the preparation of confessional statements for his Lutheran confreres—also developed his *Examination of the Council of Trent* as a confessional statement. Thus, while no one ever suggested that Chemnitz' *Examination* be treated as a confessional document, it is manifest that he writes it in a spirit of producing a confessional document to answer a confession, much as Melanchthon did with his Apology over against the Roman Confutation, and as Luther did in preparing the Smalcald Articles as a confession of the Lutheran party for the forthcoming council (which actually occurred, however, eight years later and after Luther's death).

The second point to emphasize regarding the canons and decrees of Trent is that the Romanists apparently felt that, perhaps after the difficulty of getting the council to meet, they might as well cover the entire waterfront. Thus, under 29 topics they cover not only the errors of their principal target, Martin Luther, but nearly every one else as well, and they undertake to defend nearly every tradition and practice that had arisen over the centuries and which various or all Protestants had opposed. The topics are first those dealing with the formal principle of theology, Scripture and tradition, followed by the most important material principle of theology, the doctrines of original sin and justification. They direct themselves to the remnants of original sin after Baptism, the immaculate conception of Mary (who was thus born without original sin), the works of the unregenerate, free will, and finally justification itself, faith, and good works. These points make up the entire first volume of Chemnitz' *Examination*. The council continues with material on the sacraments, Communion in both kinds, the mass, penance, extreme unction, holy orders, and matrimony. Thus volume 2 of Chemnitz. In volume 3 he deals with chastity, celibacy, and virginity, the celibacy of priests, purgatory, and the invocation and veneration of the saints. And in volume 4 the list gets even murkier: relics, images, indulgences, fasting, and festivals. The substance of Roman Catholicism all remained, but the council introduced a number of changes in the forms and general practices of many points in Roman theology and praxis.

Trent evoked Chemnitz' longest and most significant theological work, which established him for all succeeding generations as a first-class theologian, not only of Lutheranism but of Protestantism in general.

THE ROLE OF THE RULERS IN CHURCH AFFAIRS

As more and more the quarrels about religion became matters of political and even military action, more and more the princes, both Catholic and Lutheran, began to enter into religious and even theological matters. As a result, the dominant role previously played by the pope and his bishops in both religious and secular matters was now played by the secular rulers. European monarchies were going through a period of change, from the "medieval monarchy" of the period up to the 15th century, through the "Renaissance monarchy" of the late 15th and 16th centuries, into the "absolutist monarchy" of the 17th and 18th centuries. The Reformation coincides with the rise of absolutism. The Renaissance monarchs were determined to strengthen central government, and that included strengthening the control over the church which princes had tried to exercise throughout the Middle Ages. For example, we see such rulers as Henry VIII of England during his Catholic period and Duke Henry the Younger (Hanswurst) of Braunschweig working in defense of the Catholic position, engaging in personal literary attacks against Luther. Henry the Younger even followed the very good Lutheran practice of instituting "visitations" to restore Catholicism in his territories after they had joined the Reformation. Meanwhile, on the Lutheran side, the authorities of both church and state conducted visitations to determine not only the state of religion among the people but such matters as property ownership, salaries of pastors, and the like. In effect, the state became the partner of the church leaders and reformers in introducing the Reformation into previously Catholic areas. Thus when Duke Julius introduced the Reformation into the Duchy of Braunschweig, he used Chemnitz and Andreae as his ecclesiastical agents to accomplish this.

An account of how much the church almost begged the state to do this is described by J. M. Estes in his *Christian Magistrate and State Church: The Reforming Career of Johannes Brenz.* Estes makes the initial point that although Luther

> repeatedly called upon the secular authorities for help in reform-
> ing the church, and in so doing he contributed to the process
> which turned the German territorial rulers into the heads of terri-
> torial state churches, yet, the state was never Luther's first recourse
> and he was never comfortable with the development of state con-
> trol of the church. For while his view of the church and of secu-
> lar government made it possible for him to assign a limited, help-
> ing role to the secular authorities, that same view made it
> impossible for him to assign to them routine authority over the
> internal affairs of the church. . . . In his early reformatory writ-
> ings, such as his "Address to the Christian Nobility" of 1520, Luther
> laid down some basic principles and definitions which, as it
> turned out, could be used for their own purposes by reformers
> who, in contrast to Luther, did assign routine authority over the
> internal affairs of the church to the secular authorities.[3]

While Luther had insisted almost to the time of his death that the
Word alone should reform the church and create proper church
government, it became evident that if the papacy were removed
from power, somebody or some kind of force would have to take its
place. For example, as an indication of Luther's frustration see his
address *To the Christian Nobility.*[4]

The mantle of leadership fell, quite logically, on the secular
rulers. In England, Henry VIII became the Defender of the Faith,
while in Denmark (including Norway and Iceland) the absolutist
King Christian III in 1536 converted his realm to Lutheranism by
royal decree. In 1537 John Bugenhagen was invited by the King of
Denmark both to crown his successor and to ordain seven bishops
for Denmark and Norway. Much the same course was taken in Sweden by Gustavus Vasa. In Germany, led by the Free Cities and the
princes, there was a mass exodus from the papacy and an espousal
of the Lutheran cause. This necessitated the creation of some kind
of church government to preserve both order and orthodoxy. However, it was always Luther's position that the intervention of the
secular rulers was for the sake of emergency alone and they were
not acting out of any divinely given authority. But Luther did not
designate any ecclesiastical authority to supersede the papacy, and

the situation was simply allowed to drift and was never really faced. To this day the same ambivalence remains in Lutheranism.

Luther seems to have hoped that some ecclesiastical authority might arise in the Roman Church. However, the failure of Trent to free itself from the pope actually made the church more the creature of the pope than ever before, and it became evident to Luther's successors that any idea of a centralized church government, especially one based in Rome, was impossible. All doubts in this regard disappeared with the failure of Melanchthon, the quarreling of the theologians, and the independence and aloofness of most of the rulers from matters outside their own jurisdictions. The result was territorial or, at the best, national churches. While not much was said in terms of one, grand Lutheran church of the world, which was impossible because of the fractured nature of the German states, it became evident with the Council of Trent that reunion with Rome was impossible and that some kind of Lutheran organization had to develop, at least to maintain theological unity. Such a structure, crossing national boundaries and functioning under and with the cooperation of the various states, was developing and for reasons of protection had to develop. The international aspect must not be overlooked. Chemnitz himself, in addition to receiving calls into various German territorial states also was called to both Copenhagen and Austria and carried on theological correspondence with the Primate of Sweden regarding the Formula of Concord.[5]

The Scottish Presbyterian Andrew Drummond, in his *German Protestantism since Luther,* despite a noticeable bias in favor of the Reformed, nevertheless makes some points on the development of German Lutheran state churches and the problems this involved. He concludes,

> After Luther's death the German princes took a stronger line. Not content, like the Stuarts, with subservient bishops, they claimed the *jus episcopate* for themselves and branded those who wanted synodical government as "Crypto-Calvinists," disloyal to a fundamentally German institution. One principality after another adopted the "Territorial System." What had been improvised out of sheer necessity came to be claimed as a prescriptive right. . . .
> The German Bishops were "not called upon to exercise their prerogative of ordination, nor do they appear to have insisted on its necessity to build a valid ministry. Melanchthon, and to a certain

extent, Luther, had no objection to the Episcopate as exercising a function of supervision over the churches, if it could have been based upon human right, *jure humano* and not *jure divino.*" Passing from these suggestive speculations, we ask, what are the facts as to Lutheranism and the Episcopacy? The Swedish Church retained "Apostolic Succession" more by undesigned circumstances than by conviction. The Church of Finland possessed formal "Succession" but lost it as late as 1884. . . . The German priest Bugenhagen, ordained seven Superintendents for Denmark and Norway (1527) who afterwards received the title of Bishop. In Germany, little interest was shown in the historic aspect. In 1542 Luther instituted Nicholas von Amsdorf, nominated by the Elector of Saxony, to the See of Naumburg. He consecrated the new bishop himself, though he could easily have obtained "Apostolic Succession" through Roman Catholic Prelates who had become Protestants. Chillingworth in 1637 referred to Amsdorf, "consecrated by Luther though he himself was never a bishop". . . . In 1544 Luther instituted George of Anhalt to the Bishopric of Merseberg, as he had installed Amsdorf at Naumburg. No serious attempt was made in Germany to link up the Lutheran ministry with theories of "Apostolic Succession." This is somewhat surprising when we consider Luther's attempt to demonstrate liturgical continuity by pruning the Mass and translating it into German. The German princes, however, had no intention of allowing a uniform, reformed episcopacy to take the place of the old prelacy. Every prince wanted to be his own bishop—hence the "Territorial System," the *Summepiscopat.*[6]

The tragedy of the entire matter of state control over the church for Lutheranism does not lie in the absence of what some might have believed to be a Scripture-based form of church government, but that the form into which Lutheran church government ultimately drifted, namely, territorialism and state churchism, in the long run served Lutheranism and Lutheran theology so poorly that the damage can hardly be calculated. Those who came to America, while unable and in most cases unwilling to duplicate the system here, seem never to have regretted the change.[7]

The real losers in all this activity were the bishops. The rulers wanted to reduce the bishops' power, particularly the power of the ecclesiastical courts, and to take over their patronage privileges and property. (This was done much more brazenly in England than in Germany where church property after the Reformation was commonly set aside for religious purposes.) The pope had also wanted to reduce the power of bishops because he held them responsible for the losses of power he had suffered at the various reforming councils prior to the Reformation. Likewise, it was in the interest of many reform-minded clergy to reduce the power of bishops and work through secular authorities instead.[8] For example, it was much easier to dismiss incompetent or recalcitrant clergy using the secular arm rather than the ecclesiastical route. In short, there were few cogent reasons for retaining the episcopate in Germany, and the power of secular rulers in the Lutheran churches of Germany was an accomplished fact, which probably no one could have resisted. Pelikan summarizes thus:

> By a long and complex series of circumstances the destiny of the Lutheran Church was put more and more into the hands of the political leaders in the territories where the Reformation took over. The *landesherrliche Kirchenregiment* may have been necessary for the preservation of the Reformation against the attacks of the Pope and the Emperor and for the continuation of certain work which had previously been the function of the bishops. But it was an institution of grave consequences for the internal life of the Church as well as for the history of Germany.[9]

Pelikan continues by asserting that Melanchthon's sanctifying of Aristotle even in the Apology of the Augsburg Confession brought philosophy into the church and state to a very high degree and this in turn may have been responsible, more than anything Luther said, for the quietism and "indifference of much of German Lutheranism in political matters."[10] This point is debatable. Lutheranism can always be grateful that the rulers during the first 100 years of its history were generally speaking pious, orthodox Christians who really had the welfare of their churches and their people at heart. But we can see the seeds of church-state conflicts in contemporaries of Chemnitz such as Henry the Younger, the crusading Romanist of Braunschweig, and also in his Lutheran son, Julius, also a crusader, who brooked no opposition even from the great Chemnitz. In his altercation with his good friend and mentor, Duke Julius, perhaps Chemnitz had greater foresight into the dangers of state church entanglements than we generally attribute to him and his fellow superintendents and theologians.

THE ANABAPTISTS

The Anabaptists were convinced that reformers such as Luther, had not gone far enough. They considered themselves to be not only reformers of the old religion but also of the reformed churches—thus incurring the opposition of Romanists, Lutherans, Reformed, and Anglicans alike. Named from their practice of rebaptizing those who had been baptized as infants and their insistence on the so-called "believers baptism," their views had taken deep root among the peasantry and the poorer classes in all parts of Germany. Since Lutheranism was in many ways the peculiar possession of the royalty and the ruling classes, it was to be expected that the lower classes would be attracted elsewhere. Further, because of the Anabaptists' views on the public ministry (so vigorously opposed by the official state clergy and the rulers with reference to the lawful, public call to serve as pastor of a congregation) and the concept planted by the Peace of Augsburg of 1555 wherein each ruler determined the faith of his territories, the cleavage between the official churches and their clergy on the one hand and the Anabaptists on the other was deep and unbridgeable. Furthermore, the notions entertained by some of these sects, added to the division, for example, abolishing marriage; establishing communal and almost communistic lifestyles; refusing to take oaths, bear arms, or hold public office, together with their repudiation of an ordained and educated ministry. There were many cases of revolt and persecution over these matters in many places, and yet the movement was never entirely exterminated. This situation is often reflected in Chemnitz' *Loci Theologici* (*LT*), where of course he always maintains the position of the established church. His lengthy treatise on taking oaths in his *LT* is directed in part against the Anabaptists.[11] However, he does not enter into a direct formal attack on this movement in any of his writings, nor does he seem to regard it as in the same class as Rome and the Reformed. On the other hand, other Lutheran theologians attacked the Anabaptists vigorously, e.g., Urbanus Rhegius (1489–1541).

Particularly in his locus on the church in *LT,* we note Chemnitz' opposition to and irritation with the Anabaptists as the matter pertained to the public ministry.[12] Their ministers came under no supervision, no church order, no *corpus doctrinae,* no rules and regulations as to their theology or the conduct of their office, and they had little if any education. Chemnitz does not hold any high-church notions regarding the office of the Lutheran pastor or the holy ministry, but he does believe in decency and order, in a minister who is rightly and lawfully called (*rite vocatus*), in proper spiritual care of the flock, in good theology for all of the people, in the concept of the unity of the faith, and in peace and tranquillity in the state regarding religion and faith. All of this was, of course, violated by the very presence of the Anabaptist movement. The Formula of Concord in Article XII deals briefly with all of these concerns and concludes by saying, "The entire sect, however, can be characterized as basically nothing else than a new kind of monkery."[13]

THE REFORMED

By the time of Chemnitz' public ministry, in many ways the Reformed had become a greater threat to the Lutherans than the Catholics. While Zwingli was never highly regarded, in Calvin, Beza, Oecolampadius, Bucer, and others the Reformed movement made great strides. It was possible for the Lutherans to deal with Rome publicly under treaties and with a degree of military success. But the Reformed really had no legal rights at all. They crowded in under the rights granted legally to Lutherans by means of a questionable acceptance of the Variata editions of the Augsburg Confession. This meant that the Lutherans were not in a position ecclesiastically to defend themselves against Calvinism by either political or military power. Their theological arguments and polemics, even as careful and objective as those of Chemnitz, did not always prevail, especially if the rulers, such as the elector of the Palatinate, favored the Reformed position (often for purely political reasons). The Reformed were despised by many of the Lutheran leaders, including Chemnitz,[14] for being sneaky and dishonest and using the Lutheran flag to import error into Lutheran churches.

Because of the Crypto-Calvinists it became impossible to organize something like the Smalcald League to form a united front against Calvinism and its adherents in Lutheran territories. From Chemnitz' *LT* we also see the theological weaknesses of the Reformed position on Baptism, on aspects of justification, on the matter of the covenant, and particularly on the Lord's Supper. Nearly all of the many writings of Chemnitz on the Lord's Supper, along with his special writings on Christology, such as *The Two Natures in Christ,* derive from the conflict with the Reformed. Chemnitz wrote more on the Supper than on any other subject and probably more on this subject than any other theologian of his time, nearly all of it related to Calvinism.

Although Luther at Marburg in 1529 perhaps still entertained some hope of closer relations with the Reformed, and while Melanchthon had leaned over backwards to compromise with them, after the exposure of the Crypto-Calvinists at the very heart of Lutheranism at the University of Wittenberg in 1574, the breach with the Reformed became almost as great as that with Rome. It was even further widened by the takeover of several heretofore Lutheran territories, such as Bremen, Anhalt, the Palatinate, and Hesse. Furthermore, as the conflict over the Supper went on, the arguments became more acrimonious and the differences became greater and greater, bridging over into the doctrine of Christology, as the writings of Chemnitz testify.

As time went on certain theological emphases developed within the Reformed camp that further aggravated an unpleasant situation. Some of this can be seen in Chemnitz' *LT,* such as their erring views on the Sabbath and the third commandment, on the covenant, on the second commandment and the use of statues, and on matters of church discipline and personal piety, as well as the injection of an element of rationalism and the elevation of reason in the discussion of the Lord's Supper and Christology.[15]

THE LEGACY OF LUTHER

It is not the purpose of this book to give a life or theology of Luther. That has been done hundreds of times by people much better informed than this writer.[16] But it is not possible to ignore Luther.

He is very much involved in the life, the theology, and the entire career of Chemnitz. Much of what was important to Chemnitz had been important to Luther. We must remember that many of the controversies that had begun at Luther's time and that were still in need of settlement by the Formula of Concord dealt with issues that would not go away because they were basic to the Reformation itself. Luther's basic discovery of the Gospel, that we receive forgiveness and salvation by God's grace through faith in Christ, defined the issue for his time and for Chemnitz'. Especially after Trent, very little would change. While the terminology became more sophisticated, the issues remained, as Chemnitz' chief work, the Formula of Concord, testifies. In other words, the faces changed, but the agenda to a large degree remained the same.

Edmund Schlink observed:

> If, then, God's law is correctly understood only when we know the Gospel, i.e., the work of Christ, it follows that the rediscovery of the Gospel is also the rediscovery of the divine law. . . . one can correctly understand the second part of the Augsburg Confession and the Apology which treat of the correction of abuses, only if one realizes that with the rediscovered Gospel the rediscovery of the law and its divine glory has been given too.[17]

Here Schlink calls attention to a theological concept that was still being debated, denied, rejected—up to the time of Chemnitz. It was finally settled among the Lutherans only at the time of Chemnitz and largely through his efforts, as can been seen in his *LT* and in the Formula of Concord. Large portions of both of these great writings deal with basic questions raised by Luther, such as the nature of people, the nature of God, the Law of God and its role in human salvation and their Christian lives, the person and work of Christ, sin, forgiveness of sins, and justification. These basic issues were still crying for solution at the time of Chemnitz.

Some shifts took place in the later years of Luther's activities, due not only to his advancing age but also to the changing political scene. Luther became embroiled in controversies with secular leaders, and some of these disputes fell to the lot of Chemnitz and his associates. Fortunately for the cause of Lutheranism most of the Lutheran princes were of one mind with each other and with their theologians. The task of the theologians of the Formula of Concord was to reach agreement with as many as possible of the theologians on what Lutheran theology actually was. In this they succeeded remarkably well.

Some issues were not solved in Luther's time, partly because they had not arisen, such as the dispute over adiaphora. Others had not been definitively settled, such as the matter of antinomianism, the relations between church and state, or the ever-fluid matter of the relationships between Lutheran and non-Lutheran churches. Other issues came up because some of Luther's followers, particularly Melanchthon, put a different emphasis on certain matters or changed their minds. Still other changes were on the horizon. For example, the Council of Trent would force Chemnitz to delve into the doctrine of Scripture itself and other matters that were not paramount at the time of Luther or within Lutheranism. Luther knew of many of the problems, dealt with some of them in a cursory way, and then went on, but Trent forced Chemnitz to go deeper. Thus, while the theology of the Formula of Concord and the earlier Confessions is the same, the thrust and the emphasis of the Formula of Concord are somewhat different. Given these shifting theological winds, the bold and courageous Luther himself had fears for the Reformation. In a sermon for Invocavit Sunday, based on 2 Cor. 6:1 and following, he summarizes what he said many times,

> Secondly, he [the apostle] indicates the danger of neglecting the grace of God. Thereby he certainly intimates that the preaching of the Gospel is not a constant, permanent, and continuing proclamation. The Gospel is rather like a pelting rain that hurries on from place to place. What it hits it hits; what it misses it misses. But it does not return nor stay in one place; the sun and heat come after it and lick it up. Experience also teaches us that in no section of the world has the Gospel remained pure and unadulterated beyond the memory of a man. On the contrary, it stood its ground and flourished as long as those remained who had brought it to the fore. But after they had passed from the scene, the light also disappeared. Factious spirits and false teachers immediately followed.[18]

Perhaps part of Luther's colicky disposition in his old age was brought about by his fears as to what Melanchthon, Agricola, and other loud voices in his own camp would do, to say nothing of the encroachments of the Reformed and the Counter-Reformation.

Despite some of the unresolved issues that would be left to Chemnitz' generation, the fact remains that Luther was a remarkably strong leader for a remarkably long time and was an extremely good defender of the faith that he had restored to the church. Note the Smalcald Articles of 1537, his lectures on Galatians and Genesis, and his several treatises on the Lord's Supper as examples of the vigor and power of the old Luther. To the very end of his life he was defending and bearing witness to his most important discovery of all, the Gospel. He clung to his testimony regarding the Lord's Supper. His polemics were not, despite the works of some historians, merely the reflections of the deterioration of his liver. Mark Edwards in a remarkable historical piece concludes his entire book by saying,

> He [Luther] remained involved and productive to his death. Sustained by his faith, his trust in God as the author of history, and by his robust sense of humor, he continued to learn and grow, especially in his study of history. He was vulgar and abusive when he wished to be, moderate and calmly persuasive when it suited his purposes. And all the treatises of his old age, even the most crude and abusive, contained some exposition of the Protestant faith. Luther could never just attack. He always had to profess and confess as well.[19]

2

Philip Melanchthon

The man who played a pivotal role in the fortunes and misfortunes of the Lutheran church in the period following Luther's death, the era that would provide the setting for the work of Martin Chemnitz, was Master Philip Melanchthon. What kind of man was he and what kind of role did he play in the life of the Lutheran church? We are devoting more space in this book to Melanchthon than to Luther, not because the former was more important, but because there are a thousand more books written and available on Luther than on Melanchthon, or Chemnitz, and no one can really understand the theology or the historical development of the late Reformation without understanding a little more about Melanchthon than most people ordinarily do.

Melanchthon (1497–1560) was the son of a smith or an armorer, because of which occupation the family bore the name of Schwartzerd (black earth), a name which Philip's great uncle John Reuchlin hellenized into Melanchthon. Melanchthon was educated at Heidelberg where at 14 he obtained his baccalaureate degree after only two years in attendance. At Tübingen he received his master's degree in 1514. At that age he already was highly regarded as a classicist and humanist. Throughout his life, he possessed as great a reputation as a student of Greek and Latin as he did in the realm of theology. He was often called the Grecian. Sandys says,

> Melanchthon . . . left his mark on the history of education in Germany, not only as a lecturer on Virgil, Terence, and the rhetorical works of Cicero, and as Professor of Greek at Wittenberg, but also as a keen advocate for a thorough training in grammar and style. He produced works on Greek (1518) and Latin Grammar (1525–6), and many editions of the Classics, besides text-books of all kinds, which remained long in use . . . a series of commentaries on Cicero's rhetorical works, on Terence and Sallust, on the Fasti of Ovid, the Germania of Tacitus, and the tenth book of

Quintilian, as well as on selections from Aristotle's Ethics and Politics. The series included editions of Hesiod and Theognis and the Clouds and Plutus of Aristophanes, with translations of Pindar and Euripides, and of speeches of Thucydides and Demosthenes. Of his numerous "Declamations" the most celebrated is that on the study of the classical languages, and especially on the study of Greek, delivered as his inaugural lecture at Wittenberg (1518). He had no sympathy with the paganizing spirit of many of the Italian humanists: the principles of Christianity were part of the very life-blood of the *praeceptor Germaniae*.[1]

Melanchthon's Latin grammar was used in all parts of Europe. It ran through over 50 editions and until 1734 was used as a textbook, even in Catholic schools. Pelikan notes that Melanchthon had had as his ambition to prepare a complete edition of Aristotle's works but had been deterred from this by Luther who wanted Melanchthon full time in theology. However, as indicated above, Melanchthon did prepare material on Aristotle's *Ethics* and *Politics*, both works that fit in with the marriage of theology and philosophy that the humanistic Melanchthon was constantly trying to achieve. In preparing an edition of the *Clouds of Aristophanes*, Melanchthon was trying to demonstrate his break with philosophy, for the original is a great satire on the Greek philosophers, but it is manifest that this break was only temporary.[2]

Upon the recommendation of Reuchlin, Melanchthon accepted, at age 21, a position at the newly established university at Wittenberg. He arrived in 1518, one year after Luther's posting of the Ninety-five Theses. He was a professor of Greek, medicine, astronomy, mathematics, and philosophy and only later took up theology. He was also deeply interested in astrology. Of the 100 courses he taught during his long career, only 30 of them were in the area of theology. He thus gained great influence over a generation of students, touching the lives not only of future church leaders but of secular leaders as well, seemingly especially physicians. Among his students were princes, counts, and other members of the nobility. He never took his doctorate and was never ordained, nor did he ever preach from the pulpit. Upon his arrival this young man with his humanistic background became a fervent disciple of Luther and a dear friend. The friendship lasted during all of Luther's life, although it would cool considerably.

PERSONALITY AND LEADERSHIP QUALITIES

In personality, Melanchthon was a very amiable and popular person. He had friends, especially among the higher classes, all over Europe, with a wide-ranging correspondence that included many learned people. He was a correspondent of many kings. He was popular and craved friendship. He was a great classroom teacher, brilliant, urbane, sophisticated. He gave a certain "class" to the Reformation, to the university, and to Luther himself. He was also a contemplative scholar, an expert in his chosen areas of academic work, recognized throughout the learned world as a top-quality scholar. But like many people out of academe, he did not possess the leadership qualities necessary for the positions he came to hold or that were thrust upon him. At times, he vacillated and tried to play all sides.

During Luther's confinement in the Wartburg Castle in 1521–22 at the time of the Diet of Worms, Melanchthon was basically in charge at Wittenberg. But when the Enthusiasts under Carlstadt tried to overturn the existing social and ecclesiastical order, an action that Luther vigorously opposed, Melanchthon was unable to stop them, and Luther had to step in to quell the uprising. However, it appears that no one learned from this experience, because for the rest of his life Melanchthon found himself in positions of leadership, and he almost always found himself in difficulties over it.

Like many academics, he was thin-skinned and unable to take criticism. During the years that he and Luther worked together, Luther took most of the burden of criticism. When Luther left the scene however, Melanchthon—who by 1546 was a mature man and an honored teacher (the *praeceptor Germaniae*) and who had already spent nearly 30 years pontificating to students (and most of the ecclesiastical leaders of the evangelical movement in Germany by this time were his former students)—was not much inclined to take their criticisms, especially when they were delivered in public writings. It was Luther who took on the tough critics while Melanchthon spent his time making friends and sometimes apologizing for Luther. He seemed to have a particular fascination for John Calvin, who was much like him in several ways. Melanchthon seems to have liked traveling in the fast lane, wheeling and dealing with ecclesiastical and political nabobs. He was always very desirous of making peace, of trying to get together for military or political defense against the papists, and he was willing to compromise doctrine to do so.

ECUMENICAL INCLINATIONS

The popular and skeptical historian Will Durant has sarcastically described the Melanchthon of the period of the Diet of Augsburg as being "kept grievously busy moderating his master and finding ambiguous formulas for reconciling contradictory certitudes."[3] For Melanchthon the external unity of the church was an important part of his world view, and he fought with a passion to preserve it. We see this as early as the Marburg Colloquy in 1529. This passion never left him. That Melanchthon was interested in improving relations among the warring factions of Christendom needs no further proof or comment. Many suggest that his overarching motivation was based on his belief that the church was visible and that its visible unity had to be expressed. The only significant point here is that he never seemed to have a similar interest in improving relations among and between his warring Lutheran brethren. In interchurch relations Melanchthon looked in all directions. He carried on extensive negotiations with the Romanists and with the Reformed, both Zwinglians and Calvinists. He corresponded with the patriarch of Constantinople. He dedicated one of his revisions of the *Loci Communes* to Henry VIII of England. He was on very good terms with Calvin and many Crypto-Calvinists. He drew the line only at the Anabaptists, the Unitarians, and the Lutherans with whom he disagreed.

Rome

Melanchthon's hope for reconciliation with Rome shows up at Augsburg in 1530 and repeatedly thereafter.[4] On a number of occasions—in 1530 at Augsburg, in 1541 at Regensburg, in 1557 at Worms, and in connection with the Leipzig Interim in 1548, to mention only the most prominent meetings—whenever Melanchthon had official dealings with Romanists, almost to the time of his death, he negotiated with them in a compromising way and tried to come to terms with them. (The full story of his early efforts with Rome are recounted in Schmauk's *Confessional Principle*.)[5] Melanchthon was captivated by the emperor's call for a diet, and he felt that by diplomacy and negotiation, into which he himself entered most enthusiastically, the preparation of the Augsburg Confession could be avoided entirely and peace restored between the papal and the evangelical party.

This seemed to be one of his methods of operation all of his life—private meetings, quiet diplomacy, ambiguous statements, no real black on white documents of agreement. Kolde quotes the Romanist Cochleus,

> In the first place indeed Philippus ignores his own rudeness and tactlessness, for at Augsburg he did not only publicly pretend that he was a lover of peace and concord and zealous for the same; but he also on his own initiative kept running here and there, bursting into and entering not only the homes and entertainment places of private individuals, but also the palaces of cardinals and other princes . . . seeking by an altogether too insidious circuit those whom he might devour by his hypocrisy. And indeed, by his wiles and simulated blandishments he deceived not a few, while he affirmed here and there in conferences and meetings that he could easily restore the peace of the church, if only there were granted to him and his friends, the sacrament to the laity sub utraque [in both kinds], the marriage for the priests, and the use and communication of the mass.[6]

This statement certainly makes it appear that Melanchthon's vanity played a major role. In the meantime Luther sat in lonely isolation at the Coburg crying for information from Melanchthon as to what was going on at Augsburg. Schmauk goes on for pages documenting the duplicity and pusillanimity of Melanchthon and his virtual bypassing of Luther in these negotiations. George Fritschel adds, "His [Melanchthon's] negotiations at Augsburg became so scandalous that Luther was called upon to interfere and bring him to reason, lest he would betray the Lutheran side for a few flimsy and non-essential concessions."[7] Yet it must also be said that Luther recognized Melanchthon's ability to "step softly" and avoid extravagant language (not intended as a put down, as so often it is interpreted).[8] Melanchthon also appears to have been governed by timorousness and lack of faith. Schmauck ultimately characterizes him as having weak faith:

> On nearly every great occasion he [lacked the strong faith of Luther] . . . together with his apparent inability to trust Providence. . . . He depended too much on the opinion of others, and seemed to be unable to stand on his own feet no matter what Rome says or does. . . . Melanchthon's faith was not firm and great, because his reason was always interfering with his faith—and he, in a sense, followed his reason.[9]

Even Rogness who takes a more supportive position toward Melanchthon, in his *Philip Melanchthon: Reformer without Honor,* agrees with Schmauck and others when he says,

> Looking back we see that Melanchthon misjudged history. He feared—and being overly apprehensive was one of his life-long characteristics—that without concessions the emperor would cruelly stamp out the evangelical faith in Saxony, similar to what took place in Swabia. He therefore calculated that they might be able to preserve the chief doctrine of their faith, justification by grace through faith, if they conceded to the emperor those "external things." Under normal circumstances he would not have compromised, but he felt the very existence of the evangelical cause was at stake.[10]

The fact, of course, is that if Charles had had his way the evangelical faith would have been exterminated in northern Germany as well. What saved Lutheranism was not the compromises of Melanchthon, but rather the treachery and perhaps the bad conscience of Maurice of Saxony. The compromises were all in vain and served only to create confusion among all parties.

The Reformed

Books have been written and more could be written on Melanchthon's constant and almost career-long flirtation with the Reformed, particularly with John Calvin in Geneva and the Crypto-Calvinists in both Bremen and Wittenberg. The Reformed theologian Manschreck virtually claims Melanchthon for the Reformed church and convincingly shows that his heart was more in Geneva than in

Wittenberg in his later days. The Lutheran Juergen Neve, himself a conciliatory and moderate historian, writes,

> In this discussion we must confine ourselves to matters in which Melanchthon approached Bucer and Calvin, the Lord's Supper and the person of Christ. We have to keep in mind that Melanchthon had no doctrine of the Eucharist of his own. It was in his nature to evade the controversy rather than to solve the problem. He preferred to leave conflicting principles untouched. There is something eclectic about him. It cannot be said that he ever adopted Calvin's doctrine of the Lord's Supper, especially not its characteristic formulas of the exaltation of the believing soul into heaven and of the communication of Christ's humanity to the believer through the Spirit. Neither did he reject it. . . . We must agree when Stahl says: "Melanchthon's conception of a general presence of Christ in the Supper is after all Calvin's doctrine not openly expressed. There is no middle doctrine between Luther and Calvin. As soon as the Lutheran view is abandoned the Calvinistic view of a personal presence seems the only one that is left. Calvin, Bucer, Melanchthon mark only different theological types of Calvin's doctrine."[11]

So as not to leave the entire burden on Neve, a few lines from Jaroslav Pelikan, another Lutheran, may be helpful. He says,

> Melanchthon's somewhat squeamish nature was alarmed at the fact that Luther's reformation had split visible Christendom, and repeatedly he compromised his position in an attempt to heal that breach. More than once in his life he was drawn near to reunion with Roman Catholicism. His desire for a reunited Christendom at almost any price also lay at the basis of his watering down of the Lutheran doctrine of the real presence in an effort to conciliate Calvinism. . . . Melanchthon's attempted harmonization of Calvinism and Lutheranism on the doctrines of the Lord's Supper and the person of Christ came to naught through the theological scholarship of Chemnitz and the adoption of the Formula of Concord.[12]

Much had been said and much more can be regarding Melanchthon's dealing with the Reformed, but the above suffices to tell the story.

The Anglicans

Another interesting ecumenical connection is Melanchthon's dealings with Henry VIII of England (1509–47) and with his son Edward VI (1547–53). Henry and Luther had squared off in 1520–22, when in response to Luther's *Babylonian Captivity of the Church,* Henry had fired off a rebuttal defending the seven sacraments, his *Assertio Septem Sacramentorum Adversus Martinum Lutherum,* presumably written by Henry himself. As a token of his appreciation for this endeavor, Pope Leo X bestowed upon Henry the title that has remained with the British monarchy to this day, "The Defender of the Faith." Luther replied the following year.[13] Forever after, Henry disliked Luther—even though he tried to use Luther in his divorce case.

Although Luther was unpopular with Henry, such was not the case with the charming Melanchthon. In fact, during Henry's reign the preceptor received two calls to England, and in the reign of Henry's son Edward he received a third. Although Melanchthon declined a call in 1534, he—apparently in gratitude—dedicated the 1535 edition of his *Loci Communes* to King Henry VIII. This was done also at the request of the English Lutheran, Robert Barnes, who felt it would help relations between the two churches.[14] The king repeated his call in 1538 and asked the elector to send him Master Philip. And again, after Henry's death, in 1553, Melanchthon was appointed to the faculty at Cambridge but declined.

The English preferred the milder Melanchthonian type of Lutheranism. They did not like Luther's strong position on the real presence of the true body and blood of Christ in the Supper, and they found no problem with Melanchthon's three causes of conversion. Melanchthon had even succeeded in getting the Wittenberg faculty and the commissioners of King Henry to agree to the Thirteen Articles which he had written. Manschreck describes the close relationship between these articles and the Thirty-nine Articles of the Church of England and the Forty-two Articles of 1553.[15]

We get a little glimpse of the Melanchthon of 1535 if we take a brief look at the version of the *Loci Communes* that he dedicated to Henry, one year after his notorious divorce from Catherine of Aragon. Henry is addressed as "the most serene prince, Lord Henry VIII, King of England and France, Lord of Ireland and Prince of

Wales and Cornwall."[16] After several pages of respectful language about good and prudent kings and their concern for the faith of their people, Melanchthon concludes,

> The prophet Isaiah, when he prophesied that there would be godly kings as nursing fathers [Is. 49:23] of the church, as he calls them, demanded that the kings protect the godly against unjust severity, so that they may take care about teaching the correct doctrine. What titles or trophies are more to be sought after by great and wise kings than that a voice from heaven may attribute to them the loveliest title: the Gospel of Christ our nursing Father is proclaimed to the church? Great and fulsome are the honors and dignity of Africanus, of Macedonicus and others of this kind, to mention only a few. But it is much more glorious to be called the father of one's country (*pater patriae*). Furthermore, for us there is an eternal fatherland, the church of Christ. To be the nursing father of this true fatherland, to use the language of the prophet, is a great glory and something to be especially looked for in kings. These duties serve to reconcile kings with God; these duties are the most beautiful sacrifices to God. But those men are not nursing fathers to the church, who although they cover their cruelty under the pretense of the name of the church, yet most unjustly kill the true members of the church, that is, godly and learned men, and destroy the doctrine in which the true worship of God is manifest. And thus not only your moderation and clemency are much to be praised, but the judgment and wisdom that your majesty has exercised in caring for the peace of the church are also most praiseworthy, so that you promote zeal for piety and understand that certain abuses must be corrected. Therefore, since I know that your majesty excels in learning (*doctrina*) and since I understand that in these dissensions you are using singular moderation and clemency which befit your learning, therefore I have determined that this writing must particularly be sent to you, because although I am submitting it in its entirety to your majesty's judgment, yet, as I hope, it will demonstrate that the anger of your kingdoms against us is unjustified. I have no doubt that your majesty at the same time most anxiously desires counsel toward both the glory of Christ and the peace of the church and often deliberates about the remedies for this unrest, for which purpose it is beneficial not only to see their writings which distort our cause with most unfair criticisms, which not only certain shameless people do and men who are inferior judges but also some

others who have entered into this theatre or arena, having adopted the guise of singular seriousness and wisdom which befits their great authority, not for the destruction of good things and the inflaming of the cruelty of ignorant men, but rather to adorn the glory of Christ, to correct the practices of the church, and to turn the minds of princes toward Christian kindness [probably sarcasm]. For it is a most shameful thing for great men under the pretense of earnestness to practice sycophancy, which they do when they cleverly hide the fact that they permit abuses and artfully pervert those things which give us useful and godly advice. From my heart I honor the universal (*catholicam*) church of Christ and with all zeal I cling to its opinion. Nor would I ever dissent from the judgments of good and learned men in the church. Thus I am offering this commentary of mine to your majesty, not as a patron for myself if I err in any respect, but that in times of serious controversy I may find a censor whose judgment for the sake of correct doctrine I may establish because of the free and equal condition of your royal highness. And thus I ask your majesty willingly and in his own name to receive this writing of mine, in which I hope he will see that I have held to things which are useful for piety and that I am most desirous of the peace and concord of the church. May Christ preserve your majesty in good health and flourishing, and may He guide you to adorn the glory of Christ and to the salvation of the church. 1535.[17]

We do not know if Henry read this copy of the *Loci*, but we do know from the content that if he did so, he would find a treatment of free will that would fit in with Erasmian synergism and of the Lord's Supper that would be acceptable to the Reformed.

The Eastern Church

Melanchthon also reached out to the Eastern church. He had communication with the patriarch of Constantinople and even sent him a copy of the Augsburg Confession translated into Greek. Werner Elert expands on this point saying that "in 1559 Melanchthon expresses to the Patriarch of Constantinople the conviction that in the Eastern Church God 'is preserving for Himself an assembly which rightly worships and calls on his own dear Son, Jesus Christ.'"[18] Melanchthon went out of his way to be complimentary toward the Greek church by citing them in Apology XXII 4. In fact, in the Apology (the only Lutheran confessional document to refer to the Greek, or Eastern, church), Melanchthon is very gentle with the Greeks and cites them in a complimentary manner most of the time (cf. Apol. XXII 6; XXIV 79, 88, and 93).

POLITICAL MACHINATIONS

Melanchthon did not limit his efforts to positive dealings with theologians and church leaders, secular and ecclesiastical. He was also a passive instrument, often not by his own devising, but willingly used in ecclesio-political involvements. One instance of this occurred in his dealings with Francis I of France. Francis was a pragmatic man, not particularly pious, and noted for his womanizing, but he was a great warrior and a great promoter of France, who in the decade of the 1520s and 30s had the real possibility of becoming Protestant. Francis permitted a certain amount of Protestant activity as long as it did not upset society or cause unrest. He probably also had some doubts about Rome. Perhaps the best proof of all that Melanchthon put church unity at the very top of his agenda is demonstrated in his dealings with Francis, who himself switched support first for one side and then the other in his efforts to settle the religious strife in France and to harass and overcome the emperor. Religion played a very minor role in the entire matter; politics reigned supreme, although many of the leaders were sincere Christians and motivated by much higher ideals than mere control or military or financial considerations. But Francis does not belong to the latter class.

In 1532 he became angry at the warming relations between Pope Clement VII and the emperor and thus began making overtures to the German princes, particularly the Smalcald League. But by 1533 he was on good terms with the pope and threatened to persecute Protestantism. By 1534, when conditions again changed, Francis invited both Melanchthon and Bucer (who was a carbon copy of Melanchthon in the area of church politics) to come to France to formulate a possible reconciliation between the French Catholics and the German Lutheran princes, thus facilitating an alliance between the French and the German Lutherans in opposition to Charles V. Melanchthon complied with the request in 1534, but nothing came of it because the political climate changed. Yet before a year was out, on July 23, 1535, Francis wrote a personal letter to Melanchthon asking him and his friend Bucer to come to France and "confer with some of our most distinguished doctors as to the means of re-establishing in the Church that sublime harmony which is the chief of all my desires."[19] (Calvin was behind this invitation.) Thirteen years before the Augsburg Interim of 1548, Melanchthon already was getting practice in drawing up peace documents between Catholics and Lutherans/Reformed. He did not go, but that was not his own doing but Luther's and the elector's. Francis' peace efforts ended when he and Charles made peace in 1538.

During his career Melanchthon also received invitations to aid the Reformation in Poland and Denmark, and his influence reached even into Greece, Hungary, and Italy. Yet there is another side to the charming, ecumenical, and popular Melanchthon. He had no sympathy for the peasants in their revolt. He served as secular inquisitor in suppressing the Anabaptists in Germany. On some occasions he proposed death as the punishment for heresy. He asked the elector to ban Zwingli's books in Saxony. He upheld the divine right of kings and serfdom. Freedom and inclusiveness were limited for him. Yet in these attitudes, Melanchthon was merely reflective of the age in which he lived.

THE INTERIMS

Smalcald War

Probably no single event in the history of the era had a greater effect directly on the status of Lutheranism and the career and reputation of both Melanchthon and Chemnitz than the Interims that followed the close of the brief but tragic Smalcald War. As we mentioned earlier, the Catholic party had had great difficulty in getting its act together. The constant threat of the Turks, along with the squabbles among the papacy, the emperor, and France had actually given the Lutherans, along with the Reformed and the Anabaptists, the entire period from 1517 to the death of Luther, nearly 30 years, to consolidate their position. The Lutherans were aided in this by a succession of dedicated princes in Saxony, by rulers in other places in Germany who had religious, political, and economic reasons to support the Reformation, and above all by the dynamic and towering personality and faith of Luther himself. But on Feb. 18, 1546, the great man died. And things quickly fell apart.

On June 26, 1546, less than six months after Luther's death, the emperor and the pope formed a secret alliance to go to war against a divided and disorganized Smalcald League. Finally the pope and the emperor had joined hands and undertaken to do by force of arms what they had not been able to accomplish by any other means. Charles V who had become emperor in 1519 at almost the same time that Luther began his public career and who had been looking for the opportunity to move against the Lutheran heresy ever since the Diet of Worms in 1521 but who had been thwarted by his wars with the Turks, the papacy, and France, finally saw his opening. He made a surprise alliance with the Lutheran Maurice of Saxony. Maurice in turn used the occasion to turn on his Lutheran people and particularly on John Frederick the ruler of electoral Saxony in order to extend his own lands. Ironically, Maurice was a cousin of John Frederick and son-in-law of Philip of Hesse. With the help of Maurice, Charles attacked the Smalcald League, was victorious over it, and captured Philip and the elector of Saxony.[20]

Charles had made peace with Francis I of France, bought off the Turks, and made several secret treaties with German princes.These princes included the Catholic Duke William of Bavaria, the Lutheran Joachim elector of Brandenburg, the famous Hans (John) of Brandenburg-Küstrin (who resented the capture of his father-in-law Henry the Younger of Braunschweig), Hans' radical relative, Albert Alcibiades, and most important of all Maurice, to whom Charles had promised most of the territory of electoral Saxony. He also had his treaty with the pope. Charles had two basic purposes: to restore religious unity in his empire by force, since diplomacy had failed, and to crush the power of all the princes and make them subject to himself.

Charles was the most devious of men, surpassed in this talent only by his temporary ally, Maurice of Saxony. And by means of this secrecy plus some good fortune on the battlefield together with the disorganization of the Smalcald League he defeated the league, and the two princes were taken prisoner. Philip of Hesse was quickly released, but the elector of Saxony languished in jail. The only fly in the imperial ointment was the pope's unilateral decision to move the council out of Trent back into Italy. This thwarted Charles' plan to assure the Lutherans of something that at least looked like a square deal on the council, which now fell entirely into the hands of the most virulent and reactionary Romanists, the Jesuits and Dominicans, the Italians, Spaniards, and Portuguese.

On April 24, 1547, at Mühlberg, Charles and Maurice of Saxony defeated the armies of the Smalcald League, and on May 23 Charles stood at the grave of Luther. Romanists standing with him suggested that he dig up Luther's body and burn the heretic at the stake, to which Charles replied in probably the best-known and wisest statement of his career, "My quarrel is with the living, not with the dead."

Augsburg Interim

At the end of the war in May 1548, Charles imposed the so-called Augsburg Interim on the captured Lutheran territories. The word *interim* was used to designate a treaty or arrangement that would be in effect during the interim between the end of the Smalcald War and the conclusion of the Council of Trent, which everyone was expecting to bring final settlement to the religious problems of the empire. The Interim was first suggested at the diet in 1547 and became law at the Diet of Augsburg in June 1548. The intent was that the Interim should be in effect only until the council should make final determination, presumably very soon. Actually the council took 18 years and utterly ignored Protestant concerns.

The men designated by Charles to draw up the terms of the Augsburg Interim were two German bishops, Julius Pflug of Naumburg and Michael Helding (Sidonius) of Mainz, and tragically, John Agricola, who had recently left his native Eisleben to become court preacher to the elector of Brandenburg. Charles commanded them to prepare a draft of the agreement. Secrecy surrounded the document. The Lutherans were led to believe that this Interim would apply to all states in the empire, but Charles held the Catholic states to the old religion in toto, thus angering many princes, some of whom had signed it in the belief that the same document covered all. The Interim was published on May 15, 1548. On June 30, 1548, the Augsburg Interim became imperial law. It contained 26 articles dealing with humanity's condition before and after the fall, redemption through Christ, justification by faith, love, good works, confidence in the forgiveness of sins, the church and the priesthood, the pope and bishops, the seven sacraments, the mass, the invocation of saints, the commemoration of the dead, Communion, ceremonies, and the use of the sacraments.[21] Everything was explained in the Catholic sense, though couched in mild terms. Some concessions were made in the areas of the marriage of priests and Communion under both kinds.

In the purely ecclesiastical and theological area the inclusion of Luther's old nemesis, the leader of the antinomian movement, John Agricola, who was better known for his vanity than his theological acumen, was a calamity. He was instrumental in misleading the elector of Brandenburg into supporting the Interim for a time. Yet this antinomian "mouse-head" was so clever in his machinations, that despite his own previous errors and his subsequent betrayal of Lutheran doctrine, he still managed after the Leipzig Interim to shift all the blame onto Melanchthon and emerge as the darling and hero of the Gnesio-Lutherans, proving that his hatred of Melanchthon, due in no small part to Melanchthon's opposition to Agricola's antinomianism, transcended all his theological concerns and errors. During the heat of the fray Agricola had stated, "The Interim is the best book and work making for unity in the whole Empire and for religious agreement throughout all Europe. For now the Pope is reformed, and the Emperor is a Lutheran." This man represented Lutheranism at this dark hour!

In southern Germany the Interim was introduced and enforced by armed might. In northern Germany it was often ignored and, in some cases, especially at Magdeburg, it was vigorously protested. The Lutherans were ordered to comply. Maurice objected, as did nearly all the Lutheran states. Some 400 Lutheran ministers in Saxony were exiled. The churches stood empty; and in areas of Germany not occupied by Spanish troops, including the Lower Saxon Circle, the edict was ignored. In southern Germany the Lutherans were badly hurt and seriously divided. Fritschel points out that the emperor's policy failed in part because of the opposition of the pope, who felt that the Interim did not go far enough. Several of the Catholic rulers in Germany became estranged from the emperor.

Most serious of all, Maurice became disaffected primarily because of the treatment of Philip of Hesse and the hatred he encountered from his own people.

Leipzig Interim

Finally the happiest event in the whole sorry affair was Maurice of Saxony's dissatisfaction with the document—both on theological as well as political grounds—which led him to balk at implementing the Interim.[22] He felt that Charles had misled him. Maurice feared that he could never impose the Augsburg Interim on his people, particularly in his newly acquired portions of electoral Saxony. He also was beginning to have conscience pangs and considerable unhappiness over the treatment of Philip of Hesse and John Frederick. It was fine to steal the poor man's territory, but seeing him locked in prison and constantly humiliated was too much. He was even denied the comfort of a Bible in his imprisonment. On May 18, 1548, Maurice informed Charles that he could not carry out Charles' commands at the present time. Typically, he first took the route of compromise.

Maurice ordered the "Lutheran" faculties of Wittenberg and Leipzig to prepare a compromise document that would be more acceptable to the Lutherans. At this point Melanchthon, one of Maurice's theologians, became involved. Melanchthon at first had opposed the Augsburg Interim, largely in private and in letters to friends. He had also let Maurice know his feelings. But he concealed his feelings in public, and since he was the acknowledged leader of Lutheranism and the successor to Luther, many Lutherans were disheartened and confused by his constant refusal to speak out publicly. As mentioned, over 400 Lutheran pastors were deposed from office, and several were killed. But Melanchthon, instead of giving leadership, agreed to help in preparing a substitute document, the Leipzig Interim; and he allowed these atrocities against Lutheran pastors to go unlamented and unprotested. The revisions called for at Leipzig attempted to clarify the compromising position of the earlier document on justification, but the verdict of history is that this effort failed. The key word Melanchthon used with reference to many issues was that they were matters of indifference, adiaphora.

This word came into common usage to describe the attitude of Melanchthon and his professorial friends and also the serious controversy that emerged from the Interims. Matters that came under the heading of adiaphora were extreme unction, the mass, lights, vestments, vessels, images, fasts, and festivals including the Corpus Christi. Basically the obnoxious features of the Augsburg Interim were retained in the Leipzig document but toned down.

Maurice's theologians completed their work on Dec. 22, 1548 at which time Maurice inaugurated what is known as the Leipzig Interim. In a document prepared largely by Melanchthon himself, the Lutherans agreed to submit to the will of the emperor regarding popish ceremonies; they acknowledged the authority of the pope and the bishops if they would tolerate the true doctrine. Bente sums up his discussion of the matter by saying, "The Leipzig Interim, too, was in every respect a truce over the corpse of true Lutheranism."[23] Melanchthon frankly admitted that they signed it to preserve peace and avoid persecution. Even the *sola fide* was removed from the doctrine of justification. Infused righteousness was taught. Good works were declared necessary for salvation. The Roman Catholic concept of combining justification and renewal was retained. Papal supremacy was restored, and room was given for the Erasmian view of free will. It was unquestionably Melanchthon's greatest error, and proud as he was, he ultimately confessed his "sin" in the matter in a letter to Flacius in 1556.[24] He also said he should have stayed away from the whole thing. However, the Wittenberg and Leipzig theologians continued, even after the danger passed, to defend the Leipzig Interim and their part in it even up to 1560. Melanchthon blamed the politicians who got him into the mess.

Within three days of its adoption the Leipzig document was under protest, particularly among the north Germans. It spelled 35 years of controversy for Lutheranism. And the entire career of Chemnitz hinged upon it. Melanchthon never again regained his position as the one and acknowledged leader, nor did anyone else hold a leadership position until years of controversy had passed. It was at this point that the terms Gnesio-Lutherans and Philippists began to be used. Out of this conflict came other efforts, usually involving Melanchthon, to make common cause with the Reformed against the Romanists and even with Romanists themselves. Even after a political settlement was achieved by the Religious Peace of Augsburg in 1555, the acrimony and controversy continued. Wittenberg never regained the confidence of the church until Duke August drove out the Crypto-Calvinists in 1574. Even Calvin was critical of Melanchthon for his pusillanimous stand.[25]

Consequences of the Interims

Ultimately Maurice was able to cast himself in the role of the deliverer of Germany and thus redeem himself in the eyes of his Lutheran subjects and friends. Recall that Maurice was the most apt student of Charles in the art of duplicity. Beginning in 1549, he undertook secret plans to rebel against his mentor by making secret treaties with some of the Lutheran rulers and with France. Maurice almost captured Charles, who was forced to flee over the Alps carried in a litter because of his terrible gout. On April 5, 1552, Maurice entered Augsburg as the savior of Lutheranism and abolished the Interim. The whole episode resulted in the Treaty of Passau of 1552, the forerunner of the Religious Peace of Augsburg of 1555, which settled things for nearly the next century. Maurice died the next year in the famous Battle of Sievershausen. Charles, in the meantime, having completely failed in his policies, abdicated in 1555 and retired to Spain where he died in 1558.

Maurice's treachery toward Charles resulted in the abolition of the Interims and made the whole previous conflict unnecessary. True, Lutheranism was saved and given free but unequal status in the empire. It must be pointed out that the Catholics gained the point that territories ruled by bishops would remain Catholic even if the ruler changed religions. This later played a role in the fact that the Palatinate turned Reformed and that the ruler of Brandenburg, but not his people, became Reformed. The only exception was that the duchy of Braunschweig in 1568 became Lutheran after the death of its Catholic ruler, Henry the Younger, but this was because his son, Julius, working with Chemnitz, had such control that the papal party could not prevail.

While Maurice redeemed his reputation, the same cannot be claimed for Melanchthon and his Wittenberg co-workers.

Melanchthon's reputation was badly tarnished, and to this day we see the Reformed Manschreck trying to claim him as a Reformed theologian and the Lutheran Rogness trying to rescue him for Lutheranism. His position rendered him incapable of a clear identification. We have already referred to Calvin's unhappiness with him. And since he did not clarify his position adequately, he was unjustly accused of making such points as justification by faith alone and the Lord's Supper also matters of adiaphora with the result that the adiaphoristic controversy was far-reaching, extending beyond matters only of ceremonies. Neve, as quoted earlier, says much the same:

> We have to keep in mind that Melanchthon had no doctrine of the Eucharist of his own. It was in his nature to evade the controversy rather than to solve the problem. He preferred to leave conflicting principles untouched. There is something eclectic about him.[26]

Fritschel is a little kinder. He suggests that Melanchthon had "a double soul—a public one and a private one."[27]

Schmauk quoting Philip Schaff tersely says, "It was the greatest mistake of his life. . . ."[28] Robert Kolb adds another dimension of the case. He says,

> Civil power structures played a vital role in the Reformation, of course, and both Philippists and Gnesio-Lutherans welcomed governmental support for their ecclesiastical programs. However, the Philippists tended to be ready to compromise with their princes and to try not to irritate them while the Gnesio-Lutherans, though willing to use the prince's aid in executing their own reform plans, resisted encroachment into the affairs of the church from friendly princes as well as inimical ones. Melanchthon and his colleagues at Wittenberg had supported resistance against the emperor by their own elector, John Frederick, and his Smalcaldic League allies before and during the Smalcald War of 1546–47, but they quickly submitted to the new political arrangements imposed on them in Charles V's and Moritz's [Maurice] victory over the Evangelical armies. In early1548 Melanchthon, Major, and the colleagues were initially opposed to compromising with the Roman party, but they finally went along with Moritz and his secular counsellors in working out the concessions of the Leipzig Interim.[29]

Kolb continues by pointing out that 15 years later the Wittenberg theologians were still afraid to disagree publicly with their elector regarding the Lord's Supper and thus went underground with their disagreement and ultimately suffered exposure and rejection by him. Kolb also provides much documentation to show how the Gnesios often disagreed with their rulers and paid the price for it.[30] Such would also happen to Chemnitz in his dealings with Duke Julius. Fritschel summarizes, "The doctrinal history between 1546–1576 is in reality a history of Melanchthonian concessions and the necessary reaction against his twofold endeavors to reach a union by compromising the Church of the Reformation."[31]

MOST IMPORTANT THEOLOGICAL WORKS

Melanchthon was extremely popular as a teacher. In an ordinary year he would have about 800 students compared to Luther's 400. In his long career, he delivered over 180 learned papers on many different subjects.[32] Heading the list of Melanchthon's work in theology certainly must go his efforts on the translation of the Bible. From the very beginning he was an important member of the team both in checking out Luther's solo work on the New Testament as well as the work done primarily by his committee on the Old Testament. Luther worked on his translation of the Bible all the rest of his life, and Melanchthon was always involved.[33]

In addition to Melanchthon's important contributions to Luther's translation of the Bible, his theology is best known from three works, two of them of a confessional nature and one which he used for teaching purposes. The first two, his best known and most widely used, were the Augsburg Confession and its Apology, and the third was his *Loci Communes*. Each of these works is a classic and each has been received and honored in Lutheran circles and more widely for over four centuries.

Melanchthon's greatest work beyond the Augsburg Confession and its Apology, the *Loci Communes* (*LC*), was first published in 1521, when he was 24 years old. In 1521 two editions appeared, and during the first period of the *Loci,* 1521–25, no less than 18 Latin and several German editions appeared. In the second period of the *Loci,* 1525–35, Melanchthon greatly enlarged and edited it. The greatest changes occurred in the third period, from 1535 to 1559, but not much revision was made after 1555. In this period the document was altered to four times its original size and fundamentally changed. The 1555 Latin edition of the *LC* was done by Melanchthon—although Rogness doubts that the 1555 German edition was by Melanchthon himself. The German and Latin editions are quite different, though they bear the same date.[34] Chemnitz in his *Loci Theologici*[35] uses the 1543 Latin edition, which has also been published in English.[36]

To some degree, Melanchthon advanced beyond Luther in areas such as the doctrine of Law and Gospel, which is already evident in the 1521 *LC*. Melanchthon and Luther correctly understood that Agricola was undermining the entire ethical concept of Christianity. Luther's quarrel with Agricola left its mark on what is considered one of Luther's greatest works, namely, his *Lectures on Galatians,* delivered in 1531–32 and published in 1535, and which he referred to as "my Katie von Bora." Here the old Luther and Melanchthon stood together. In fact, Kittelson tells us that "these lectures which required three years to complete, were quickly reworked by Melanchthon and his students and then published as Luther's Great Commentary on Galatians,"[37] indicating how closely Luther and Melanchthon were working at that time. Melanchthon's emphasis on Law and Gospel, while having its roots in the teaching of the early Luther, in some ways refined and certainly helped and guided Luther. Note the fine material on this point in Melanchthon's *LC* of 1521.[38] It is hard to speculate on how much influence Melanchthon had on Luther in the 1530s when the latter was actually working on his *Lectures on Galatians,* but it is a certainty that Luther's position on Law and Gospel became clearer and that he and Melanchthon were very close together at this time on this point. We also have the famous disputations of Luther against Agricola, delivered during this same period. Chemnitz shows great appreciation for both the Galatians lectures and the disputations against the antinomians and cites them constantly in his *LT*. Thus the three great theologians stand together.

Melanchthon's treatment of the doctrine of forensic justification and the imputation of Christ's righteousness (rather than relying on the inherent righteousness of man, as did Osiander) is a definite plus. Although some criticize Melanchthon's doctrine of justification,[39] this aspect of the doctrine of justification and his opposition to Osiander put him on the side of Luther and the Gnesio-Lutherans, as well as Mörlin and his young assistant Chemnitz—who had already tangled with Osiander. The case also demonstrated that even though Luther was dead and parties within Lutheranism were forming, yet the theologians were able to debate issues and not personalities (which was all to the good and which has not always been the case in theological conflicts). Although Pelikan describes Melanchthon's doctrine of justification as "suspect," he concludes by saying, "But Osiander's objection to the Melanchthonian formulation could not succeed because of the foreign and even Roman elements which he introduced into it."[40] Seeberg summarizes the Osiandrian controversy by saying, "But it must, after all, be accounted a blessing, that the Melanchthonian and not the Osiandrian scheme met the approval of the church."[41]

It would be interesting to know exactly how young Chemnitz and Isinder dealt with Osiander, when they "pressed him so tightly." We get a hint of Chemnitz' line of argumentation with Osiander in Chemnitz' *Iudicium* of 1561 where he certainly berates Osiander and accuses him of Crypto-Romanism. We get a fuller view of Chemnitz' overall view on justification in his later *LT* in a chapter entitled "The Vocabulary of Justification,"[42] where he deals with this important subject—not only in the narrow way that Pelikan lays at Melanchthon's door (although a reading of the entire Article IV in the Apology shows great breadth). Melanchthon's treatment of justification in the many pages of the Apology deals with synonyms and other motifs of justification beyond and in addition to the forensic approach. In other words, Melanchthon believes that justification by faith alone is not a peculiarly Pauline dogma but is taught throughout Scripture.[43]

MELANCHTHON AND THE AUGSBURG CONFESSION

At this point a few remarks about the Augsburg Confession (AC) might be in order because we are here dealing both with Melanchthon's theology as well as his influence on later generations.[44] The AC played a pivotal role in the subsequent political and theological history of Lutheranism, particularly in the period of the

Formula of Concord. Therefore to deal with this matter at this point will be helpful.

The Importance of the Augsburg Confession

The AC, even more than its Apology, was basic to Lutheranism and of paramount interest to all committed to maintaining Lutheran theology, particularly in the generations immediately after the death of Luther and Melanchthon, and this for several reasons.

First, the document had the distinction of having been presented to none less than Emperor Charles V himself at an important official diet of the Holy Roman Empire. It was born in a scene of great courage, a scene recognized by all as a significant moment in history. It was signed by seven princes of the empire and the representatives of two great Free Cities, and before the diet was over four additional cities signed. All of these cities and territories were feudal underlings of the emperor and sought to safeguard their feudal control over the churches in their territories. The princes represented nearly all of northern and eastern Germany. This meant that the document had great prestige even with Charles who rejected its theology. But because he needed the financial, military, and moral support of these princes and cities, he was willing to give it a status politically that his conscience told him it did not deserve theologically. Charles always put his empire ahead of the pope and probably his conscience also. The heroic action of the Lutheran princes and cities gave to the AC an aura that no subsequent confessional document achieved. It was especially precious, for it represented Lutheranism at a moment of great glory and courage.

Second, the AC held a unique position in the ecclesiastico-political situation. Both Charles and the Lutherans were willing and anxious to honor the AC as holding a unique position in the ecclesiastico-political world of that moment. Even as early as 1530 the Lutherans were troubled not only by the papists, but also by the Anabaptists, various other enthusiasts, and the Zwinglians who were also troubling the Romanists. In a sense, the Lutherans, represented by their princes—one of whom was an elector of the empire and all of whom represented rich and powerful German states—were cutting a deal with the emperor who needed them badly, to the exclusion of the other dissenting groups in the empire. The Anabaptist refusal to bear arms and take oaths made it easier for both Charles and the Lutheran princes to stand together opposing them. Furthermore, several of the articles in the Confession were so orthodox as to receive no criticism from the papists, including Article X on the Lord's Supper, which in the 1530–31 edition was entirely satisfactory to the papists. These facts gave to the Lutherans the opportunity on the one hand to demonstrate their orthodoxy to the papists and on the other hand to exclude the sectarians and Zwinglians, whom they despised just as much as the papists did. Thus the AC, while never accepted by the Roman church or the emperor, at least made the Lutherans more acceptable to Rome. While no one probably ever seriously expected the AC to be accepted by Rome,[45] it gave the Lutherans their first sense of identity and individuality. It was conciliatory without being compromising, firm without being caustic, a true symbol around which its adherents could confidently rally and that adversaries had difficulty in attacking.

Third, the document was brief and incisive, capable of being understood by all who read it, encapsulating the basic concerns of Luther and his by now countless followers. It dealt with the basic matters Christian people were concerned about: God; our sin; Christ; justification by grace through faith; the ministry; the new obedience; the church; the sacraments, together with confession and repentance; order in the church; church practices; civil government; the return of Christ; freedom of the will; the cause of sin; the relationship between faith and good works; the saints. It also contained a series of articles dealing with other matters clearly under controversy in the church, such as the use of both elements in the Lord's Supper, the marriage of priests, the mass, confession, distinction of foods, and the power of bishops—all topics under discussion not only in Germany or among Lutherans but in many parts of Europe. The AC was the right document for the right time.

Fourth, the AC was adopted in a most appropriate manner. It was never regarded by any, with the exception of Melanchthon, as the personal possession of Melanchthon or anyone else. It held the position of being an official document more than any other of the age. It was from the very beginning the property of the Lutheran church, speaking generically, and the Lutheran churches specifically. This is exactly the position of Chemnitz.[46] Chemnitz and his co-workers of his generation assert that the AC of Luther is the 1530–31 edition, for he most strongly influenced this edition. They also affirm that the Formula of Concord is the correct interpretation of Luther and the AC. From Chemnitz' standpoint we should point out that in his long efforts to get a solid confessional base that was acceptable for all of Lutheranism, he constantly referred to the AC and its Apology as being basic confessional documents for those who called themselves Lutherans and who already had adopted the AC of Luther. There is no question that Chemnitz and his contemporaries, in their desire to secure peace and tranquillity among the warring adherents of the AC always began with the basic fact that a Lutheran church, by whatever name it might be called, was a church that adhered to the Unaltered Augsburg Confession (UAC), the AC of Luther.

This was particularly the case with reference to disputed points. Thus it was Article X of the UAC that always set the standard for the doctrine of the Lord's Supper. This viewpoint was strengthened when Melanchthon in one of his many revisions of the AC made such sweeping changes in this basic article that it could not fail to arouse public indignation. Seeberg points out that at the Imperial Diet at Naumburg in 1561 the conflict between the UAC and the Variata surfaced particularly because of Melanchthon's deviations regarding the Lord's Supper.[47] The difference between Luther and Melanchthon had become painfully obvious, for ever since the adoption of the Interim by Melanchthon in 1547, the year after Luther's death, he had been under increasing suspicion. In other words, although Melanchthon wrote the AC and the Apology, writings of Luther himself—the Catechisms, the Smalcald Articles—were added to the Corpora Doctrinae, at least in part to make certain that Luther's interpretation of the Lord's Supper, justification, grace, free will, etc. was always paramount in the church's understanding of the AC and its Apology. The capstone was the Book of Concord of 1580 which was designed to become and did become the *corpus doctrinae* for all of Lutheranism, replacing all such previous regional and territorial documents.

Conversely, Melanchthon's Variata editions of the AC were never given the weight that their author wanted them to have—as correct and official interpretations of Lutheran confessional theology. Note, for example, the Solid Declaration of the Formula of Concord VII 41, "The true meaning and intention of the Augsburg Confession cannot be derived more correctly or better from any other source than from Dr. Luther's doctrinal and polemical writings." Again, in FC SD VII 34, the author—Chemnitz—says, "From these statements and especially from the exposition of Dr. Luther, as the chief teacher of the Augsburg Confession, every intelligent person who loves truth and peace can understand beyond all doubt what the Augsburg Confession's real meaning and intention in this article have always been." In other words, in the opinion of Chemnitz and the other signers of the Solid Declaration Luther is the real author of the AC and its only interpreter.

Chemnitz and his associates therefore had the difficult task of rejecting all of Melanchthon's errors and doing it in such a way as not to anger Melanchthon's many disciples in the churches of the AC. In addition, they had to protect the AC and the Apology from misinterpretations, which included rejecting the various Variata editions of the AC that Melanchthon had produced down through the years as he attempted to make the AC his own property rather than the confessional property of the church. Melanchthon tried to make the AC reflect the endless permutations of his own theological pilgrimage—the kind of permutations that took place with his great teaching tool *Loci Communes*.

Melanchthon's Alterations of the Augsburg Confession

Melanchthon, rather than treating the Augsburg Confession as an official document, regarded it more as his own personal writing, which gave him the right to alter it as he saw fit. It is interesting, in connection with the history of the AC, to recall the many slight changes that Melanchthon made in the document even while the discussions were going on at Augsburg. Melanchthon was trying to water down Luther's theology and make it more palatable to the papal party, and Luther, sitting out at the Coburg, wanted his own strong thrust to be maintained. At this point we shall cite some examples of Melanchthon's distortions of the AC and its Apology, as well as of his own *Loci Communes*. His two basic theological errors and deviations from Luther dealt with conversion or free will and the Lord's Supper, but there are several subordinate points on which he came near to error, which are reflected in the Formula of Concord.

Free Will

First, in Article II of the AC, "Original Sin," the version submitted to Charles V in 1530 and published in 1531 has a second paragraph that reads, "Rejected in this connection are the Pelagians and others who deny that original sin is sin, for they hold that natural man is made righteous by his own powers, thus disparaging the sufferings and merit of Christ." Melanchthon in the Variata editions of the AC omitted this paragraph, and while he never went so far as to adopt Pelagianism, by this omission he changed the article in such a way as to leave an opening for a positive action of a person's will before conversion, thus paving the way for his own idea of the three causes of conversion, as set forth openly in his 1543 version of his *Loci Communes*.[48] In this version, Melanchthon, despite shifting back and forth between man in the unregenerate state and the regenerate, is obviously speaking of the three causes not only of good action (*bona actio*) but also of conversion, and he uses the truly damning expression in the same connection that "Free choice in man is the ability to apply oneself toward grace" (*liberum arbitrium in homine facultatem esse applicandi se ad gratiam*). Manschreck observes,

> In his Commentary on Romans, 1532, Melanchthon asserted that in justification "there is some cause in the recipient in that he does not reject the promise extended." Melanchthon the humanist was trying to assess the individuality and responsibility of man; he was not claiming that man is the author of justification. The fact that man preaches the word and calls upon man to repent implies that the hearer does something.[49]

Melanchthon also felt that predestination or election was contrary to religious experience and ignored the ethical personality of man. This led Melanchthon to his famous *causa concurrens*: the Holy Spirit and the word are first active in conversion, but the will of man is not wholly inactive; God draws but draws him who is willing, for man is not a statue. Man has a genuine freedom and responsibility that God does not abolish.

Actually we encounter the term *three causes* at least as early as the 1535 edition of the *LC* which Melanchthon dedicated to King Henry VIII of England,[50] but Melanchthon's language here is so guarded that the reader cannot be certain whether he is speaking of man before or after conversion. Still, he uses language that history has always labelled synergistic when in the 1543 edition he says,

> Know that God wills that in this very manner we are to be converted, when we pray and contend against our rebelliousness and other sinful activities. Therefore, some of the ancients put it this way: The free choice of man is in the ability to apply oneself toward grace [*Liberum arbitrium in homine facultatem esse applicandi se ad gratiam*], that is, our free choice hears that promise, tries to assent to it and rejects the sins which are contrary to his conscience. . . . This will cast light upon the connection of the causes which are the Word of God, the Holy Spirit and the will of man.[51]

Chemnitz, commenting on Melanchthon's *LC,* upholds the use of the three causes of "good action," but he does not use the term in connection with conversion. He very carefully says,

> The Spirit goes before, moves and directs the will in conversion, not in the way He works in a general action by merely changing or overthrowing the counsels of the ungodly . . . but through the voice of the Gospel. . . . Because faith comes by hearing, Rom. 10:17, therefore the Spirit is efficacious through the voice of the Gospel which is heard and considered; and the grace which precedes is directed and ordered by the Word. And it is correct to say that there are three causes for a good action: 1) the Word of God, 2) the Holy Spirit, and 3) the will of man, if this is rightly and properly understood.[52]

But in a set of 19 theses prepared by Chemnitz in connection with his work on the Formula of Concord and the third and fourth books of his *Examination of the Council of Trent,* which theses Leyser adds to his edition of the *LT* as a way of briefly covering some of the items not handled in the *LT*, Chemnitz has several theses on free will and conversion.[53] For example note thesis VI on free will:

> But in actions and activities which are spiritual which pertain both to the knowledge and worship of God and to the conversion of man, Scripture does not grant to the natural man or to the unregenerate, and even takes away from him, any power or faculty with which he might be able to be pleasing to God, as if from himself he either possesses the ability or can think, desire, begin or do anything, so that of himself man neither has nor can do anything.

He goes on in thesis XV,

> From this it is easy to judge the arguments as to whether it is correct to say that there are three causes for conversion, the Spirit, the Word and the Will of man which assents and rejects. Some become sophistic about this and picture that there are three concurring causes in conversion. But it is a different matter when it is said that in the regenerate there are three causes of good action.

Obviously Chemnitz is taking the safe ground. There are many more statements of this kind, which sound remarkably like the Formula of Concord where the three causes are ultimately and totally rejected as being synergistic in Epitome II 19 and Solid Declaration II 90. Just to complete this point, we should understand that Chemnitz never attacks Melanchthon, but he carefully steers around his errors. Instead of synergistically and rationalistically trying to find a place for man's will and sense of responsibility in the process of conversion, Chemnitz comes out clearly and unequivocally for divine monergism. Pelikan asserts,

> The debate which ensued over Melanchthon's synergism issued in Article II of the Formula of Concord, in which Melanchthon's stand is repudiated. Under the leadership of Martin Chemnitz, the Lutheran Church in the Formula rejected synergism and with it one of the basic planks in Melanchthon's theological position. Thus the traditional interpretation is correct when it sees the Formula as the defeat of Melanchthon in the Lutheran Church.[54]

ELECTION

Melanchthon's views on predestination is another area in which he shifted. He did not touch the issue in the original Augsburg Confession and his views on this subject never really become a matter of general discussion among either the Philippists or the Gnesio-Lutherans—despite the inclusion of the subject in at least some editions of the *Loci*. But the problem did exist, particularly over against Calvin but also to a degree among Lutherans as Chemnitz' dealing with the church at Göttingen indicates and as indicated by his famous sermon on Matthew 22, delivered in 1573 at Wolfenbüttel.[55] And yet it is interesting (as Manschreck shows) that although there is certainly a close relationship between the doctrines of conversion and of election, it would seem that since Melanchthon's views on conversion are well known, his views on election might well be considered as affected thereby.[56] Yet Melanchthon avoids the thorny problems of the relationship between foreknowledge and predestination. Instead he quite properly focuses on the fact that we must consider election or predestination not from the standpoint of the Law or reason but from the standpoint of the Gospel. For election is concerned only about those who are saved, which is echoed in FC XI. In summary, while Melanchthon avoided predestination and gave it rather short shrift, in what he did say he was correct and gave a direction that the FC picked up in its fuller discussion of the matter. Thus Manschreck's statement that Melanchthon's development of the three causes came from his views on predestination does not appear entirely correct.

LAW AND GOSPEL

Melanchthon made a statement in Apology XII 45 on the basis of Mark 1:15, which says, "Repent, and believe in the Gospel," that can be (and was) interpreted as failing to distinguish between the so-called narrow and broad senses of both the word *repentance* and the word *Gospel*. This, in turn, had caused confusion regarding the proper distinction between Law and Gospel, which was exacerbated by the antinomian controversy and by Melanchthon's developing synergism. Thus Chemnitz and his co-workers felt the need for including Article V 2–9 in the Formula of Concord in which this point is corrected. In a footnote on page 559 Tappert suggests that this problem arose out of Melanchthon's ill-considered assertion that the "Gospel is also *doctrina poenitentiae* (doctrine of penitence)." This statement appears, for example, in Melanchthon's *Loci Communes,* 1543 edition, which reads, "The Gospel is the preaching of repentance and the promise."[57] Tappert's footnote is certainly correct in attributing this notion to Melanchthon, but it ignores the great influence of Agricola and his antinomian followers. Chemnitz' *LT* in dealing with this topic in his locus on justification, under the chapter heading "The Common Definition that the Gospel Is the Preaching of Repentance and the Forgiveness of Sins," immediately in the second paragraph of the article asserts: "the papists on the basis of definitions of this kind spread their traps for the truth, so that we should walk with careful steps. For Islebius [Agricola] with devious intentions tries to build his antinomian error on the basis of this definition."[58] Chemnitz also criticizes those who pervert Melanchthon's definition, although Chemnitz' own Formula of Concord demonstrates that Melanchthon had not spoken felicitously. But most of this chapter in Chemnitz is directed against the antinomians. Perhaps one of the reasons that Chemnitz speaks so softly regarding Melanchthon is that Melanchthon, to his great credit, had, with Luther, taken and maintained a strong position against Agricola, a position that Chemnitz and his co-workers likewise maintained. Another reason may be Melanchthon's generally correct position regarding the distinction of Law and Gospel, which, of course, is the issue in Article V.

In other words, this article is in the Formula of Concord more because of the vagaries of Agricola than of Melanchthon, whose definition, after all, is a direct quote from Scripture (Acts 20:21). Actually the entire chapter in Chemnitz' *LT* is directed against Agricola, with magnificent quotations from Luther's various *Distputationes contra Antinomos* as well as his great *Lectures on Galatians.*

Although Melanchthon is not really guilty of error specifically in the area of Law and Gospel, his constant confusing of the term *Gospel* in the broad and narrow senses—in the face of both the antinomians and the papists, who were always looking for careless language—was detrimental to a Lutheranism that was very concerned about the proper distinction between Law and Gospel and with maintaining the true doctrine of justification (as well as a hermeneutical tool). In a sense Articles IV, V, and VI of the Formula of Concord all pertain to the matter of this inadequate definition of the Gospel and the distinction between Law and Gospel.

Melanchthon already in 1549 had suggested to Chemnitz that distinguishing between Law and Gospel was the "chief light and best method" in the study of theology. It is interesting that Chemnitz in the Solid Declaration begins this locus with the words, "The distinction between law and Gospel is an especially brilliant light" (V 1). Perhaps Melanchthon's words took deep root in Chemnitz' soul.

LORD'S SUPPER

Finally, the difficulties that Melanchthon stirred up regarding the Lord's Supper and the related controversy on the person of Christ are reflected in Articles VII and VIII of the Formula of Concord. Note, for example, Melanchthon's altering of Augsburg Confession Article X, the first stages of which are seemingly reflected even in Apology X 1 and 4, a point that Lutherans appear to have overlooked, but the Reformed Manschreck has caught. In speaking of the Variata of 1540, Article X which reads, "the body and blood of Christ are truly tendered to those who eat in the Lord's Supper," Manschreck notes that "'tendered' [*exhibeo*] replaced 'distributed' [*distribuo*]," and the words "and they disapprove of those who teach otherwise." Manschreck contends that this "reflects a desire to allow a Calvinistic interpretation of the Lord's Supper . . . rationalistic humanism figured in the change."[59] This change also made possible the elimination of the idea of the unworthy communing and thereby weakening "Luther's concept of the real, true, and substantial presence of Christ's body and blood." That is to say, while the Unaltered Augsburg Confession of 1530 uses the expression "the body and blood of Christ are truly present and are distributed [*vere adsint . . . distribuantur*]," Melanchthon in the Apology, while still asserting that "the body and blood of Christ are truly and substantially present [*vere et substantialiter adsint*]," even at this early date of 1531, substitutes the more general "tendered" or "offered" (*exhibeantur*). This might lead one to believe that as early as 1531 Melanchthon was trying to leave the gate open for a Calvinistic interpretation of the Supper. Yet at this time it seems to have been a perfectly suitable word, used and approved by Luther himself. In fact, Article X of the Apology also could be interpreted by Romanists as suggesting transubstantiation. Seeberg indicates that this is exactly the way the Romanists did interpret the article.[60]

Exhibeantur came to be understood, apparently as Melanchthon understood it, as a cover term for suggesting that the body and blood are present and offered but received only by believers while the unbelievers do not receive the true body and blood. Of course, as the years went by, as Manschreck tells us, "Melanchthon himself had come to believe in a real, spiritual presence, which was a drift from the physical 'distributable,' 'this-is-my-body' presence held by Luther."[61] Melanchthon's Variata edition of 1540 does indeed permit a completely Calvinistic understanding of the Augsburg Confession, though it might be more accurate to speak of Melanchthon's understanding not as Calvinistic, but as Melanchthonian. The word *distribuo* has also disappeared from the various editions of Melanchthon's *LC* at least as early as the 1535 version, and if any word is used it is the less definitive *exhibeo,* which seems to be entirely absent from the 1542–55 Latin editions. However, these versions assert that "Christ is truly present giving [*dans;* present tense] through this ministry his own body and blood to him who eats"[62] and uses expressions that would certainly convince the unwary that he was still in the Lutheran camp. But it is language that Calvinists apparently could also accept.

The Formula of Concord at its very opening, in Andreae's Epitome VII 2, 6, immediately and forthrightly picks up on this situation and summarizes the points at issue. The question is, "Whether in the Holy Supper the true body and blood of our Lord Jesus Christ are truly and essentially [*vere et substantialiter*] present, are distributed [*distribuantur*] with the bread and wine, and received with the mouth [*ore sumantur*] by all those who use this Sacrament, whether they be worthy or unworthy, . . . believing or unbelieving; by the believing for consolation and life, by the unbelieving for judgment? The Sacramentarians say, No; we say, Yes" (Triglotta, 809).

The same points are taken up more fully in the Solid Declaration which is primarily the work of Chemnitz. It is interesting, however, to note the point he brings up which Manschreck seemingly has missed, namely, that while the word *distribute* (*distribuo*) is clearer and came to be the dominant word, yet in the Latin edition of the Large Catechism of Luther of 1529 and in the Smalcald Articles of 1537 and also in Chemnitz' own *The Two Natures of Christ* of 1570 the word *exhibeo,* which is translated by Manschreck and Bente as "tendered" and by Tappert as "offered," is used as a synonym for *distribuo,* referring to the fact that the body and blood are "offered and received" by the communicants in the Lord's Supper. For example, note Luther's words quoted in SD VII 14, where "offered" (*exhiberi*) and "received" (*sumi*) are joined together, or in SD VII 24, where Chemnitz cites Luther's Large Catechism in which in one short paragraph the two words *exhibeo* and *distribuo* are certainly used synonymously as meaning "distribute." But this is not to deny Manschreck his point. It would seem quite logical to conclude that the wily Melanchthon in his Apology much preferred a somewhat ambiguous word like *exhibeo* rather than a quite concrete and definitive term such as *distribuo.*

Development of Melanchthon

Much is made of the distinction between the young and the old Luther, but in a sense every confessional Lutheran has also been compelled to choose between the young and the old Melanchthon. The strife in Germany was in a sense between the older disciples of Melanchthon, who had also studied under Luther himself and thus interpreted Melanchthon through Luther's eyes, and the younger students of Melanchthon who had not studied under Luther and had come, wittingly or unwittingly, to regard Melanchthon as the true and sole arbiter of what was truly Lutheran in theology.[63] Or to put it another way, the Melanchthonians came to interpret Luther through Melanchthon's eyes. This created an immense amount of difficulty, which few if any of the theologians of the period seemed willing to admit or discuss, even though it is obvious that Chemnitz and the framers of the Formula of Concord were insisting that their age read Melanchthon through Luther's eyes and that Luther was the correct interpreter and the sole arbiter of what was truly Lutheran. Melanchthon changed—at first gradually and guardedly and then much more rapidly after Luther's death—and thus he is extremely difficult to evaluate unless one always knows the date of his writings. Manschreck and Stupperich, for example, show that he was changing very early. His habit of constantly revising his own works also contributes to the confusion, a confusion that began in his own day and has not entirely disappeared down to our own time. Thus some of his writings, especially his early ones, clearly mark him as a solid Lutheran, and others have been used by Calvinists to demonstrate that he made almost a complete switch. Both viewpoints have considerable weight on their side.[64]

The charge was made in later generations that the notorious syncretist Georg Calixtus was a new Melanchthon, and that is probably a correct analysis. The difference between the two was that Calixtus was out in the open, while Melanchthon kept everyone guessing. Pelikan has an excellent description of Melanchthon's unionism, from which Chemnitz rescued Lutheranism and which was defeated in the adoption of the Formula of Concord

> Melanchthon's somewhat squeamish nature was alarmed at the fact that Luther's Reformation had split visible Christendom, and repeatedly he compromised his position in an attempt to heal that breach. More than once in his life he was drawn near to reunion with Roman Catholicism. His desire for a reunited Christendom at almost any price also lay at the basis of his watering down of the Lutheran doctrine of the real presence in an effort to conciliate Calvinism. The strengthening of the Lutheran stand against Calvinism and consequently against Melanchthon's appeasement of Calvinism, came with Articles VII and VIII of the FC. Largely through the work of Chemnitz, Lutheranism developed a formulation for the doctrine of the person of Christ that made its differences from Calvinism very clear. . . . Thus Melanchthon's attempted harmonization of Calvinism and Lutheranism on the doctrine of the Lord's Supper and the person of Christ came to naught through the theological scholarship of Chemnitz and the adoption of the FC.[65]

Endless Theological Controversies and the Need for Harmony

The situation just described characterized the years of Melanchthon's ascendancy. As long as Luther lived there was some semblance of order in the Lutheran ranks, but with the signing of the Interim by Melanchthon in 1548, everything fell apart. Many theologians quite properly felt the need to attack the Interim and with it Melanchthon. Obviously he was also defended, and from this point on he was successful in turning his Wittenberg colleagues against the more conservative elements in Lutheranism, although this only gradually became evident. But the divisions were appearing and individual theologians were voicing their concerns. Probably all of them, with the exception of Melanchthon who had already in his mind defected from Luther on the Lord's Supper, felt they were expressing the mind of Luther, or at least that they could find something in his writings to justify their position. This was certainly the case with Agricola himself and with Osiander and Flacius. In fact, a very good case could be made with each of these men that they were actually trying to be faithful to Luther and his teachings and were trying to keep Lutheranism from departing from Luther. It is almost a truism to assert that the Late Reformation period was preoccupied with the matter of determining what Luther actually taught and in keeping Lutheranism faithful to Luther rather than to any other leader, Lutheran or otherwise.

But regardless of their reasons or their apparent kinship with Luther, the fact is that many theologians, including Melanchthon himself and the others mentioned above, were going off on their own, bursting into print with little or no consultation with their respective faculties or fellow pastors or theologians, writing letters, conspiring against one another, and in some cases influencing the rulers to exile their opponents. Chaos reigned, and Melanchthon was incapable of stemming it and in some cases encouraged it. Melanchthon set an unhealthy example for his followers with his dissimulation, which included public support of Luther and private disapproval. The very name *Crypto-Calvinist* is a memorial to his perfidiousness and cowardice. A forthright and ethical person like Chemnitz must have chaffed under such hypocrisy, and it is very likely that during his short stay in Wittenberg in 1553–54 when the controversies were raging, he was greatly offended and determined to get out. Recall that he had had the same feelings at Königsberg when the Osiandrian controversy arose, and ultimately he left because of it. Subsequent history showed that Chemnitz did not like or want controversy but also that he would not back away from it forever. Throughout his entire life he was anxious to settle conflicts but always in a scriptural way and with as little acrimony as possible. By the mercy of God Chemnitz was able to help in settling all of these problems that had raged for over 30 years.

PART 2

THE MAN

There are two basic sources for the actual biography of Chemnitz. One is a brief autobiography written for his own family, which he began, as he informs us, in 1570. The actual story closes about 1555, the year he married and the year in which his real work at Braunschweig began, but he does append a list of his children which mentions that his daughter Hedwig died on Oct. 15, 1577. There is no substantive biographical material in this document after 1555, but it was obviously updated in later years presumably by Chemnitz himself. The entire autobiography appears in Rehtmeyer. It has also been translated into English from the Latin and German by August L. Graebner and appears in the *Theological Quarterly* III, 4 October (1899) 472–87 under the title "An Autobiography of Martin Kemnitz." This translation will be followed throughout with a few emendations.

The second basic biographical piece is the famous *Oratio* produced in connection with Chemnitz' funeral in April 1586 and published in 1588 by his understudy John Gasmer. This is an excellent work and is basic to all the biographies produced since that time. It contains a great deal of information, some of it found no place else. It is also evident that Chemnitz' autobiography was known and used by Gasmer, but Gasmer adds much material not included in the autobiography. Gasmer probably got his material directly from Chemnitz during their many years of close association. Their churches were a short walk apart. Gasmer was the secretary of the ministerium and the translator of many of Chemnitz' writings.

Several early brief biographies of Chemnitz were produced. For example, see the biographical series by Melchior Adam (d. 1622), who has a short chapter in his *Lives of the Theologians,* mainly Protestant (1615–20). The most important source of biographical information is Philip Julius Rehtmeyer's *The Church History of the Famous City of Bruns (Antiqvitates Ecclesiasticae Inclyte Urbis Brunsvigae, oder, der Berühmten Stadt Braunschweig Kirchen-Historie),* 1707–20, and following, in five volumes, which draws on the many official records of the time. It is an excellent work and the source for every person who undertakes to study Chemnitz and the history of the church of Braunschweig. It also has a great deal of information regarding Mörlin and his administration. Rehtmeyer is very accurate. He quotes his sources properly, many of which are included in his own *Beylagen* (appendices). Many of these are official records that were available to Rehtmeyer, and amazingly, are still available today in the Stadtarchiv in Braunschweig, in the Herzog August Bibliothek at Wolfenbüttel, and in the Niedersächsischen Staatsarchiv also at Wolfenbüttel.

For reasons not clear to me, in the 19th century within one decade four excellent biographies of Chemnitz appeared. In 1861 Edward Preuss wrote a short biography of Chemnitz in Latin as part of his edition of the same year of Chemnitz' *Examen Concilii Tridentini.* Theodor Pressel produced a *Leben und ausgewählte Schriften der Väter und Begründer der lutherischen Kirche,* 1862, which included a short biography of Chemnitz. In 1866 C. G. H. Lentz wrote *Dr. Martin Kemnitz Stadtsuperintendentin Braunschweig . . . ,* and in 1867 Hermann Hachfeld produced *Martin Chemnitz nach seinem Leben und Wirken . . .* emphasizing Chemnitz' relationship to the Council of Trent.

Also very helpful has been the Festschrift, *The Second Martin of the Lutheran Church (Der zweite Martin der Lutherischen Kirche),* published at Braunschweig on the occasion of the 400th anniversary of the death of Chemnitz in 1986 by Pastor Wolfgang Jünke—pastor, most appropriately, of the Martin Chemnitz Church in Braunschweig. In this volume are several essays dealing with biographical data pertaining to Chemnitz. There are also several modern items in recently published periodicals, particularly the writings of Inge Mager and Theodore Mahlmann, that are very helpful and give viewpoints different from the older writers.

3

From Treuenbrietzen
to Braunschweig

CHEMNITZ' ANCESTRY

The name *Chemnitz* is the shortened form of the Latinized
Chemnitius or *Chemnizius*—each of which spellings were first used
by Chemnitz himself for the original *Kemnitz* (also Latinized occasionally as *Kemnitzius*). This in turn was the original spelling for a
name applied to a family of the lower nobility of the Pomeranian
Wends.[1] The name was derived from a stone called Kamien in the
Polish or Wendish language. The family had been forced to flee
Pomerania because of feuds among the Knights Templar and had
lost all of its property in the process. The family spent some time
in Danzig (Gdansk) and ultimately came to Pritzwalck in Brandenburg, where they settled and again became quite prominent.

Martin's great-grandfather married a woman of Brandenburg
and settled in the city of Brandenburg in the electorate of the same
name. By this time the family, largely because of poverty, had lost
all interest in its ancient connections with the nobility and had in
actuality joined the burgher class. They were, however, a very thrifty
and enterprising family. Rehtmeyer puts it this way, "It is now evident that from the nobility of the Kemnitz family many commoners
had derived, but since all, as mentioned, had to leave Pomerania,
they had not only settled down in Pritzwalck, but they had continued to be very upstanding people . . . and among the most important developers of the city."[2]

Great-grandfather Chemnitz produced one son, Nicholas
(Klaus), and died early. His widow remarried. She married a man
named Schüler who had close connections with the elector of Brandenburg. One of their sons, Balthasar Schüler, became Burgomas-

ter of the city of Brandenburg. He also became Martin's guardian when his father died. One of Balthasar's sons was George Schüler (1508–67) who called himself Sabinus. He became the educational mentor of Martin Chemnitz and also married a daughter of Philip Melanchthon. He was probably the most outstanding poet in Germany in that era.[3]

Martin's grandfather, Klaus Kemnitz, also married a woman of Brandenburg. They moved to a town called Britzen, about 35 miles west-southwest of Berlin, on the road from Berlin to Magdeburg, in an area called the Mark, near the border between Brandenburg and the electorate of Saxony. Britzen at an earlier point in its history, at the time of the Crusades, had remained loyal to the Duke of Brandenburg when all others deserted him, and in recognition of this he had changed the name to Treuenbrietzen (Faithful Britzen).

TREUENBRIETZEN YEARS

Klaus Kemnitz became a flax and fish merchant and handed the business down to his son Paul who added cloth-making to the enterprise. Paul was the father of Martin. He married Euphemia Koldeborn,[4] the daughter of a pious man from the city of Jüterbog, also in Brandenburg. They had three children, a daughter Ursala who died unmarried, a son Matthew who carried on the family business, and little Martin. Matthew at first did well with the business, but when his mother refused to allow him to marry a girl he loved, he married another and drifted into a "wild and wayward life and squandered nearly all he had," as Chemnitz tells us in his autobiography. This probably accounted for Martin's difficult financial problems during the years he was seeking an education. Martin's father also died early, in 1533.

In his autobiography Chemnitz tells us that he had figured out by his "mathematical studies" that he was born "A.D. 1522, on the 9th day of November, at 47 minutes after 12 p.m." and "named Martin on account of the feast." Actually the Feast of St. Martin is on Nov. 11, but that is probably the date of Martin Chemnitz' Baptism. It is unlikely that he was named after Martin Luther who was actually born on Nov. 10 and baptized on Nov. 11.

Chemnitz' childhood was comparatively uneventful, except that as a small boy he fell into a little brook from which he was quickly rescued, but the accident so frightened him that for three or four years afterward he stammered badly and walked in his sleep. These ailments gradually left him, but they may have contributed to the fact that he was not very active in playing with the neighborhood boys but spent a good deal of time alone, reading or talking to himself. During these years he was also blessed in that one of his teachers, Laurentius Barthold, who later became pastor in the town, recognized "a certain ingenium" in him and encouraged Chemnitz' mother to get him an education.

EDUCATION

Wittenberg, 1536–38

When Chemnitz was 14, in 1536, he was given the opportunity to go to Wittenberg to live with relatives of his mother in that city and attend what he calls "the elementary school." This lasted for about a year and a half, and when his hosts, the Kelners, concluded that the arrangement was "without any particular profit" and that "the expenses of keeping me at Wittenberg so early were without any avail" they "advised my mother to take me back home." He does say, however, that "it gave me great pleasure to see excellent people and hear Luther when he preached." During this stay he also developed an interest in Latin, although he had not done particularly well with it while at school.

In 1538 he had to leave school entirely, even the none-too-good one at Treuenbrietzen, and at the insistence of his brother he entered the cloth-maker's trade, for which he had "no liking" and did "poor work," meanwhile studying "the elegancies of Latin speech."

Magdeburg, 1539–42

Finally, in 1539, the opportunity came. Two notable citizens of Magdeburg, one of them related to Chemnitz, visited Treuenbrietzen, which gave Chemnitz the opportunity to show them some of his Latin work. They persuaded Mother Chemnitz to send her gifted son to Magdeburg, where they would get him free board. Here he did very well in his studies and remained till 1542. In addition to Latin he studied poetry, dialectics and rhetoric, astronomy and Greek. Gasmer describes him as inexperienced in his work, but humble and not arrogant and compares him to David, who started out with only a sling but became a great king. His relative George Sabinus, professor in the ducal academy at Frankfurt, recognized Chemnitz' gifts and wanted to promote his fortunes.

Calbe, 1542

But again the laments about money began, and in 1542 he was compelled to leave Magdeburg, but not before the authorities there procured for him a tutorship at Calbe on the Saale. There he began his independent studies, this time working in Greek with the *Dialogues* (*Sophista*) of Lucian. He showed great interest in the rules of grammar, giving evidence of his later insistence on correct language, proper definitions, and the rest.

Frankfurt on the Oder, 1543–44

In April 1543, he left Calbe for Frankfurt on the Oder where he was helped again by Sabinus, who was a member of the Frankfurt faculty. Chemnitz devoted himself to improving his Latin style and added work in mathematics, astronomy, and what we today would probably call physical science. He remained there about a year during which time he obtained his bachelor's degree. Again the money ran out, and this time he worked at Wrietzen on the Oder for 18 months. During this period he served both as a teacher and as a clerk in an office collecting revenues from the fish trade. Naturally his brother wanted him to make the position permanent. But academia called.

Wittenberg, 1545–47

Chemnitz returned to Wittenberg in 1545, and Sabinus through another relative, the burgomaster von Brück, arranged an introduction to Melanchthon and asked that he show special friendship to the young man. Chemnitz discussed his academic plans with

Melanchthon and gave to Melanchthon some of the work he had translated from the Greek into Latin, including one of Demosthenes' *Epistles* against King Philip of Macedon (presumably one of his *Philippics*). Melanchthon approved his work, gave some suggestions, and urged him to work in mathematics, which Chemnitz did. This led him next into astrology, which Luther had opposed but Melanchthon favored. Chemnitz apparently was very good at astrology and became known to several famous men who rewarded him generously for his efforts. Actually Chemnitz at this time wanted to go into theology but was diverted. For example, Wilhelm, the landgrave of Hesse, asked his opinion on the new Gregorian calendar, of which he approved but hesitated to implement lest it give the impression that the pope was dictating to the Lutherans which calendar they should use. It was not approved until the 1580s.

Also while at Wittenberg, in the words of Gasmer, "He at that time, heard Dr. Martin Luther teaching and preaching, a revered man and worthy of eternal memory, who was without doubt divinely raised up to rescue the doctrine of the Gospel from the corruptions of the papacy, the brightest sun, the Helias of our age, and he also heard his last disputation."[5] But Chemnitz in his own autobiography says it was "not with due attention."

Melanchthon in the meantime came to admire more and more the genius of Chemnitz and decided that he was to take his master's degree. He also had written to Prince George of Anhalt asking for money for this purpose, but the Smalcald War dispersed the students at Wittenberg and the plans went awry.

Königsberg, 1547–53

Chemnitz decided to join Sabinus who had recently moved to the newly opened (Aug. 17, 1544) University of Königsberg, in Prussia. At this point, however, Chemnitz comments that most of what he learned he did not get at universities but by private study because of his nagging poverty and forced migrations from one place to another. He arrived in Königsberg on May 18, 1547. The ever-helpful Sabinus got a position for Chemnitz as tutor for some young Polish noblemen. Chemnitz also took up astrology in earnest and supported himself quite well at this endeavor. Among his clients were Duke August of Prussia and Margrave Hans of Brandenburg-Küstrin. In 1548 he also took over a school close to Königsberg at Kniephof, with which Sabinus also had a connection. In the same year, on Sept. 27, in addition to his other activities, and again with the help of Sabinus, he received his master of arts degree, the first of the first three to be awarded this degree by the university—and all at the expense of the duke. Gasmer adds that at this time the adiaphoristic controversy began, in which Chemnitz later became involved.

In 1549 Sabinus took a trip to Wittenberg to pick up his family and take them back to Königsberg. Chemnitz accompanied him, met with Melanchthon, and asked him about taking up theology. Melanchthon came with his memorable and significant reply that "the chief light and best method in theological study was to observe the difference between the Law and Gospel." They had barely returned to Königsberg when a pestilence broke out, and Sabinus and Chemnitz moved to Salfeld where the latter spent the time reading Luther's sermons and Lombard's *Sentences,* along with other ancient books, beginning to prepare himself for the study of theology.

Although he returned to Königsberg in 1550, Chemnitz had determined to leave the city, but the duke who had come to rely on his astrological works prevailed on him to stay by offering him the position of librarian at a good salary in the ducal library of the duchy. This took place on April 5, 1550. It is possible that the rector, Sabinus, also had a hand in this. Chemnitz said, "I look upon this as the greatest fortune God bestowed upon me during the time of my studies." This marked the turning point in his life, and he then determined definitely to take up theology. He disliked superficial studies, but now that he had all the books he wanted and could study things in depth, he turned all his attention toward theology. At that time the university had a professor named Staphylus who shortly thereafter relapsed into Catholicism. Of him Chemnitz says, in a prophetic manner describing his own attitude, "Having heard Staphylus, who subsequently apostatized, for about two years, I had never known him to advance anything that was sure and solid. Yet, to nourish godliness, my mind was always inclined [*inclinabat*][6] toward this study."

Chemnitz tells us a few things about his method of study. First he read through the biblical books, comparing the various versions, making notes on anything he thought memorable. He then read the fathers, taking notes in the same way. He then proceeded to read modern authors or contemporaries, especially polemical writings, of which there were many—all the time making notes. For three years he continued this independent study of theology, which he described in his autobiography as "living in clover." He lived in the home of a burgrave whose children he tutored, ate well, had all his bills paid, mixed with "chancellors, marshals and counselors of high standing, with whom I was in great favor, received presents, was bothered with nothing, and studied with delight."

Osiandrian Controversy

Chemnitz became embroiled in his first public theological controversy in the year 1550. On October 24, 1550, Andrew Osiander held his first disputation promoting his view on justification, "that man is made righteous (*gerecht gemacht*) through an essential righteousness of the indwelling of God." Rehtmeyer tells us that Osiander "in this disputation gathered some different and strong opponents, among whom were M. Martin Chemnitz, presently the librarian at Königsberg, and Melchior Isinder,"[7] a member of the faculty of the university. Osiander also had some synergistic and Christological twists to his position. Osiander had made a record for himself as a confessor of Lutheranism. He had been exiled because of his strong opposition to the Interims and had fled to Königsberg, where because of the duke's great friendship for him he was given in 1549 the position of professor primarius at the newly established university. In the same year he had incurred the opposition of the entire faculty because of erring views on justification and for having been placed above many of them in rank. Osiander was a signer of the Smalcald Articles in 1537. He had come from southern Germany where he had brought the Reformation to Nuremberg in 1520 and was a close personal friend and co-worker of Brenz, who never publicly attacked him.

Chemnitz, in studying the issues, which we will discuss later, concluded that Osiander was wrong in regard to certain aspects of the doctrines of justification and Christology. Together with the other budding theologian Isinder, Chemnitz pressed Osiander so strongly that the man was speechless. Yet the duke—who had been converted to Lutheranism by Osiander—stood by him, and when Superintendent Mörlin, who at first had been placed in the role of reconciler between Osiander and his opponents, including Staphylus, finally gave up on Osiander and joined the opposition, Mörlin himself was sent into exile by the irate duke. But Chemnitz was not similarly dealt with because of his abilities with the horoscope and perhaps because of Sabinus' support. There is no evidence that Melanchthon gave Chemnitz any instruction on the matter of Osiander's doctrinal deviation, and yet it is noteworthy that this young man, just turned 30, with little or no formal training in theology, took a position on Osiander that became the one of all of Lutheranism, including both Gnesio-Lutherans and Melanchthon.[8]

Modern scholarship has taken a different view of the Osiandrian controversy than was taken at the time, when the entire Lutheran church of all different persuasions lined up against Osiander. Rogness, who is very supportive of Melanchthon in most respects, cites Karl Holl, for example, who suggests that Melanchthon was the one in error, not Osiander.[9] Rogness, in a very useful summary, faults both Melanchthon and Osiander for speaking past each other and being in error.[10] He goes on to point out that Melanchthon's great fear was that Osiander, whose theology in some respects resembled Rome's, was trying to lead the Lutherans back to Rome and works-righteousness, and thus he reemphasized Luther's well-known doctrine of the objective imputation of Christ's righteousness, which some interpret as making this doctrine abstract and too greatly separating justification from sanctification.

Martin Stupperich suggests that the debate over Osiander's 81 theses was limited entirely to the matter of the imputation of the righteousness of Christ and that Chemnitz and Isinder pressed Osiander strongly in their public debate with him for his explanation of the relationship between faith and this righteousness and the indwelling of Christ.[11] In his LT, however, Chemnitz criticizes Osiander for making "our righteousness before God something inherent in us";[12] for maintaining that "we have countless kinds of justifications, such as the grace of God, the blood of Christ, the remission of sins, all of which he says are our justification before God";[13] for confusing the two natures of Christ in the image of God;[14] for saying that "our obedience is the essential righteousness of God, so that our renewal stands in the face of the judgment of God beyond and outside of Christ";[15] for suggesting that "in baptism the guilt is not taken away from our concupiscence";[16] and for being confused in his use of Hebrew.[17] Thus the debate between Osiander and the rest of Lutheranism was wide-ranging and impinged on many points besides the matter of imputation.

Pelikan, after describing the Osiandrian controversy, also asserts that "Melanchthon's view of justification was a caricature of that of Paul and Luther" and was "suspect."[18] This may or may not be the case, but it is important to note that when he has demolished Melanchthon and his views on justification, Pelikan concludes by saying, "But Osiander's objection to the Melanchthonian formulation could not succeed because of the foreign and even Roman elements which he introduced into it."[19] To those who seem to be faulting Melanchthon for deemphasizing the Christ-in-us, one can find in Luther, Melanchthon himself, and certainly Chemnitz, ample Scripture-based evidence that they held and maintained this doctrine but never in the area of justification. Justification was God's act, and in no way should be attributed to people. That was one of the main pillars of the Reformation. As has been noted, Seeberg says, "But it must, after all, be accounted a blessing, that the Melanchthonian and not the Osiandrian scheme met the approval of the church."[20] Melanchthon had his faults, even when he and the Gnesios land on the same side, but by common consent, most agree that Osiander was worse. Osiander was heavily influenced by cabalistic Platonism. Chemnitz rightly saw that this philosophical conceptual framework was antithetical to Luther's biblical base.

The Osiandrian controversy soured Chemnitz on Königsberg, and toward the end of 1552 he asked permission to leave to continue his studies, and finally the duke granted permission upon his promise to prepare a few horoscopes for him each year.

Wittenberg, 1553–54

On April 3, 1553, Chemnitz left Königsberg and stopped off on the way to prepare a horoscope for Hans of Küstrin, the margrave of Brandenburg-Küstrin. Hans was known as "the wise man of Küstrin." He was married to an older sister of Duke Julius, and while the young Julius was in flight from his father, Duke Henry the Younger, because he (Julius) had espoused the Reformation, he had stayed at Hans' home. While there he fell in love with Hedwig, the daughter of the elector of Brandenburg. It is possible both Chemnitz and Duke Julius were at Küstrin at about the same time.

Chemnitz arrived at Wittenberg on April 29, 1553, again armed with letters from Dr. Sabinus. This time he became a boarder, a commensal, at the home of Melanchthon. We still are not told that he actually sat at the feet of Melanchthon as his teacher, but at any rate as a boarder, he tells us that he was "an attentive hearer, because I now understood more correctly what he taught."

In October of that year Chemnitz was sick for four weeks with a high fever which the doctors asserted might lead to permanent bodily damage, but apparently this did not occur, for he lived for over 30 years after this bout and experienced unusually good health.

This really completes the account of Chemnitz' formal education, except for the fact that in 1568, the year after he became superintendent at Braunschweig, he received his earned doctor's degree at the University of Rostock. Since each of the three previous superintendents had had the doctorate, the city council at Braunschweig released him and paid his expenses to enable him to obtain his degree. His disputation dealt with "The Benefits of the Son of God, Our Lord and Savior Jesus Christ." It was received with great praise and rejoicing.

In describing Chemnitz' educational experiences up to this point, we have actually also covered about all there is to say concerning his life in general. Aside from the work in the woolen mill and the fish house, all he had done was to study and to travel between places of study. We shall take up his professional career shortly. We shall include a brief report on Chemnitz' marriage at this point. It gives a good picture of the times and the relationship between a superintendent and a coadjutor.

MARRIAGE

In 1555 Mörlin concluded that his coadjutor needed a wife, so he arranged a marriage for his 33-year-old assistant to "a daughter of Hermann Jaeger, Licentiate of Laws, who was a native of Arnstadt and had married Peter Hahn's daughter at Cöhten," as Chemnitz tells us in his autobiography. He also goes on to say, without mentioning the Christian name of either his bride or her mother, that Jaeger was then a resident of Braunschweig, "the espousals were on March 19, and the dower, 200 [Florin] coin." The wedding took place on Aug. 19 at the home of the burgomaster. Chemnitz notes that as "wedding presents [he] received 1 gold plated goblet from the Duke in Prussia; 2 silver cups from the Supervisors; 1 silver cup from the preachers; 1 from the school-teachers; 1 from Nicholas Gallus of Ratisbon . . . [and] other presents." The bride's name was Anna, and she is described in Gasmer's work as "a model of piety and most excellent morals. . . . During her entire marriage she was zealous in piety toward God and in love toward her husband and in raising her family, industrious and frugal in governing her household." Again he describes the marriage as "pious, peaceful, and fertile." Ten children were born to this union, of whom six reached maturity.

ECCLESIASTICAL CAREER

Chemnitz spent his entire career, unlike many of his contemporaries, in only two places: at Wittenberg in the year 1554 and at Braunschweig from 1554 to his death in 1586.

Wittenberg, 1554

In January of 1554, after Chemnitz had spent only a few months at Wittenberg as a student, upon the recommendation of Melanchthon, he was made a member of the faculty of the university and given the task of examining students preparing for their M.A. degrees. In May of that year Melanchthon and Chemnitz journeyed together to a theological conference at Naumburg, and on the journey Melanchthon suggested that Chemnitz on the basis of all the reading he had done at Königsberg "should make an attempt at lecturing in Theology." No sooner said than done! "On our return home, M. Philip wrote an announcement of a course of lectures on the *Loci communes,* under my name, which was affixed on the 6th of June. I opened the lecture on June 9. . . ." The crowd was so great that the class was moved to the largest hall at the university. Melanchthon was present for the first lecture. The size of the audience continued, but by the end of that year Chemnitz' teaching career at Wittenberg had ended. Chemnitz was not the first aspiring theologian to be given such an assignment. Apparently the practice was developed as a way of looking over likely candidates for teaching positions.

Chemnitz was not comfortable at Wittenberg and would leave soon for Braunschweig—almost in haste, as his autobiography clearly indicates.[21] Mörlin by this date, 1554, was a clear leader among the Gnesio-Lutherans in whose number Chemnitz may be counted.[22] This is not to suggest that Chemnitz was a radical, a Flacian, or an extremist. He was never an extremist or a radical, as all his subsequent history testifies, but clearly his sentiments lay in the direction of a very orthodox interpretation of Lutheranism rather than with the Philippists, and the evidence certainly indicates that Chemnitz was in no way sorry to leave Wittenberg. The descriptions of his relationship with Mörlin for the rest of their lives indicate genuine friendship and theological concurrence.[23] Seeberg says that Chemnitz, along with some other original Melanchthonians, who had previously broken with him, ultimately broke with Melanchthon.[24] But he supplies us with no evidence to show that theologically Chemnitz had ever been a devotee of Melanchthon or on the other hand that he ever publicly broke with him. In his *Iudicium* of 1561 Chemnitz shows the same theology he showed until the end of his life, which points to a far greater devotion to Luther and a far closer relationship with Mörlin than ever existed with Melanchthon. And yet, Chemnitz did retain the methodology of Melanchthon.

It would appear that Chemnitz was by nature a careful and scrupulous man. Because of his familial and educational relationship with Melanchthon, he was not going to criticize him publicly or join the vociferous clamor of many of the Gnesio-Lutherans, but he never yielded a point to Melanchthon or any others who deviated from the path of sound Lutheran doctrine. This is evident in every public writing and every posthumously published private writing we possess today, and there is no record of any private correspondence or conversation that indicates anything else. Certainly the will of Chemnitz, written shortly before his death, in which he selects the books he particularly wants to be remembered, points to the unchanging character of his theological position. His contemporaries never call him a Melanchthonian, a Philippist, or a former Melanchthonian, as was certainly the case with Selnecker.

Braunschweig, 1554–86

Later in the same year that he became a faculty member at Wittenberg, Chemnitz received an invitation from his old friend of Königsberg days, Joachim Mörlin, informing him that the office of coadjutor was vacant, along with the pastorate at Martin Church, and he wanted Chemnitz to fill both positions. Chemnitz took a little "stroll" to Braunschweig, arriving on Aug. 6, 1554. He preached the prescribed trial sermon on Aug. 12 and was shortly thereafter called to the position. The Wittenberg faculty tried to dissuade him, and Melanchthon offered him additional preaching work, but, says Chemnitz, "God inclined my heart [again using that peculiar Latin-German word] toward Braunschweig," and on Sept. 28 he accepted the call. He finished his lectures on Oct. 20 and bade farewell to his students. On Nov. 25 he was ordained by Bugenhagen, the reformer of the city of Braunschweig. On Nov. 30 Chemnitz left Wittenberg, and on Dec. 15 he was installed in his new office. The next day he preached his first sermon in St. Egidius' Church.[25]

On April 22, 1555, he resumed his lectures on Melanchthon's *Loci Communes* with the great encouragement of the superintendent and continued these almost to the day of his death. It is significant that the last paragraph in his autobiography, which ends with the year 1555 (although, as indicated, the treatise must have been revised in later years), deals with the subject of his *Loci Theologici*. He says in his autobiography,

In the year of our Lord 1555, on the 22nd of April, I commenced, at Brunswick, my exposition of the *Loci Communes* of Philippus. I was unwilling to burden my hearers with extensive dictations, but gave them by recital what I deemed useful and necessary by way of explanation. But these lectures were taken down by many, and particularly Johannes Zanger, pastor of St. Peter's, diligent herein. After the lectures he endeavored to put into proper shape what he had taken down, and this he submitted to me for correction. But as the work of correcting was difficult and burdensome, and I began myself to put into order and, as it were, cast into form, what I had brought together in the exposition of each *Locus* and delivered by recital. This was how I came to put down in writing my meditations and collections on the several *Loci,* as far as I got in my expository lectures. These annotations are frequently of great use to me now and in a way serve as aids to my memory. But not everywhere have they been sufficiently filed, nor have matters been set forth and explained with sufficient exactness. But I intend, if God grant me life, leisure and opportunity, to find, correct, and amend those annotations. For many things have I meanwhile learned as I taught.[26]

Appparently his *Loci Theologici* was very dear to his heart and constituted one of the primary concerns of his ministry. In his old age, when physical weakness compelled him to lay down certain aspects of his work, the lectures on the *Loci Theologici* were the last to go.

Chemnitz gives no reason for his sudden decision to change not only dwelling places but also professions. But it is well known that he and Mörlin were fast friends and certainly saw eye to eye on theological matters and ecclesiastical problems, and from the standpoint of hindsight, it is apparent that Chemnitz made a wise decision in going to Braunschweig. He seemed ideally suited for the kind of position he took, served well and honorably, and was able to accomplish a great amount of good for his beloved Lutheranism. He shows throughout his life a pastoral heart and an appreciation for being on the cutting edge of the church's life.

Also as part of his preparation for his life's work and his desire always to have a full understanding of things, Chemnitz took up the study of Hebrew in 1556. He became very proficient at it, as his *Loci Theologici* particularly demonstrates.

4

The City of Braunschweig

THE CITY AND THE DUCHY

A few words about the city of Braunschweig and its relationship with the duchy of Braunschweig will be helpful. We must always distinguish between the two places because Chemnitz was called to the city and always retained his relationship with the city as its coadjutor and superintendent, but after the accession of Duke Julius he had a special and almost unique relationship with both the duke and the duchy over which he ruled.

The city of Braunschweig, or Brunswick, was a large and flourishing place, and during the Chemnitz years it became the theological and religious center for northern Germany, actually replacing Hamburg as the center of religious activity for the entire Lower Saxon area. The city of Braunschweig is situated on the Oker River, about 40 miles southeast of Hamburg and some 57 miles northwest of Magdeburg. The city dates back to the ninth century and gets its name from its founder, Bruno, the son of Duke Ludolph of Saxony. Later under the famous Henry the Lion (1129–95) who in 1181 became Duke of Braunschweig-Lüneburg and who is still regarded with great admiration in the city, the place was fortified and became an important military, commercial, and religious center. About 1173 Henry also began the building of the St. Blasius Cathedral, in which his remains still lie. The beautiful building was completed by him in 1194. He also was involved in the building of several other churches that still stand and are still in use, including the Martin Church that Chemnitz served as pastor.

In 1181 Henry the Lion was put under the imperial ban, and some of his lands were taken from him, but the territories of Braunschweig and Lüneburg remained in his possession, and from these two adjoining areas the ruler took his title. By the time of Chemnitz, as a result of further division of the duchy to take care of the various families and princes, the duke was sometimes called the duke of Braunschweig-Wolfenbüttel. The latter city, though much smaller, was the southern administrative capital and the home of the duke. It is about seven or eight miles south of Braunschweig.

THE HANSEATIC LEAGUE

Of great importance for subsequent history was the entrance of the city of Braunschweig into the Hanseatic League, an association of German traders, located in various cities, mainly along the Baltic and North seas. The cites in which these traders lived and from which they conducted their business became members of the league. They gained great wealth and influence. They had increasing independence from territorial rulers and the pope, and they often adopted the Reformation. These cities were both the cause and result of a great German migration, particularly to the east, reminiscent in some ways of the Germanic expansions to the south at the time of the fall of Rome. This migration also gave encouragement and example to the later mercantile expansion of England, Holland, and other countries into Asia, North America, Africa, and elsewhere. This migration of Germans reached as far east as Krakow in Poland (a virtual invasion of Slavic territories) and Tallinn (Revel) in Estonia. In the north it extended in the 14th century into Bergen in Norway, and it involved active trade with England and Holland and Bruges in the west. Cities in Germany as far south as Cologne and even Breslau were members of the league. At one point it had over 70, perhaps as many as 80 member cities, some of them obviously quite small. Trade was even carried on with Novgorod in Russia for a long time. Such a phenomenon was permitted to develop because of the weakness of the Holy Roman Empire, which had even previously permitted the development of Free Cities all over Germany. This very weakness, however, also meant that the member cities had little military strength or protection, except that of their own devising. Ultimately, even at the time of Chemnitz, the organization along with the empire was fading. But the ruling councils of these cities had learned something about governing, about resisting the pope and the territorial prince, and about determining their own destiny. The centuries of relative freedom had imparted a tradition of independence in the city of Braunschweig over against the duchy. This was particularly so in the case of Braunschweig because it was one of the four most important Hansa cities in Germany.

RELATIONS BETWEEN THE CITY AND DUCHY

The city and duchy of Braunschweig had long had poor relations, which were exacerbated by both the religion and the personality of Duke Henry the Younger. The details of this story are beyond the confines of this book,[1] but it suffices to say that when the Reformation was introduced into the Free Cities, the Hansa cities, and the territories of Germany, this bad relationship came to involve everyone—the city and the duchy, the empire, the neighboring princes, Luther, Duke Henry and his son Julius, Mörlin, Chemnitz, the Smalcald League, the Catholic League, and others.

Duke Henry the Younger was a complete autocrat, totally loyal to the emperor and the pope, cruel and hard-headed. He was the last Catholic ruler of his territory, which was the last territory in northern Germany to accept the Reformation. Even though his lands were overrun by the Smalcald League and turned nominally Lutheran, the minute he regained his holdings, he tried, not completely successfully, to turn back the clock in matters of religion. All of this was known and discussed far and wide. Hence, he was extremely unpopular and unrest was everywhere in his duchy.

THE REFORMATION COMES TO THE CITY

The comparatively independent Hansa city of Braunschweig, as might be expected, had embraced the Reformation early. The triumphal advance of the Reformation toward the city began as early as 1521 under the leadership of a monk, Gottschalk Kruse, who had studied at the feet of Luther, Melanchthon, and Carlstadt at Wittenberg. He carried the message to the religious and political leaders of the city. The conversion of neighboring Lüneburg to the Lutheran faith also contributed to the progress of reform in Braunschweig, despite the strenuous opposition of Henry. Finally in 1528 the Reformation was formally introduced into the city under the leadership of

John Bugenhagen of Wittenberg. In a visit that extended from May 20, Ascension Day, to Oct. 10, Bugenhagen carried on an almost round-the-clock preaching and instruction program, selected and installed officers, and most important of all, drew up the first *Kirchenordnung* for the city, written in Low German.[2] Thus by the time of Chemnitz' arrival in 1554, religious affairs were quite well organized and functioning, especially under the dynamic leadership of Joachim Mörlin. A complete reorganization took place after Chemnitz' assumption of the superintendency in 1567 and Duke Julius' accession shortly thereafter.

CHEMNITZ' MENTORS AT BRAUNSCHWEIG

There were two men who would shape Chemnitz' career at Braunschweig and with whom he would work for many years: Dr. Joachim Mörlin, who until his departure for Königsberg was the superintendent in Braunschweig and Chemnitz' predecessor, and Duke Julius of Braunschweig-Lüneburg, with whom Chemnitz worked closely almost to the time of his (Chemnitz') death in the reformation of the duchy of Braunschweig and the preparation of the Formula of Concord. Chemnitz' career at Braunschweig is rather nicely divided into two parts, each involving one of these mentors: 1554–67 as coadjutor when he worked closely and constantly with Superintendent Mörlin, and 1567–86 as superintendent when he worked with Duke Julius. So close were these relationships that we can quite properly describe Chemnitz' life and career in terms of his relationship with these two men, and it is impossible to do so without some acquaintance with them. We start with Superintendent Mörlin, who was such a major factor in Chemnitz' decision to move to Braunschweig.

Joachim Mörlin was born April 6, 1514, at Wittenberg, the son of Jodocus Mörlin, professor of metaphysics at the university.[3] His mother was a daughter of the vinedresser for the elector of Saxony. At the encouragement of Luther, Jodocus gave up his teaching career and became a pastor near Coburg. At 18 Joachim entered Wittenberg and became an avid reader of Luther. At 22 he received his M.A. degree. In 1539 he became Luther's chaplain and thus advanced rapidly in his career, aided also by the support of Bugenhagen who helped him in his work for the doctorate, which he received in 1540. He began his ministry in the town of Arnstadt. He started on the wrong foot with the council there, and finally in 1543, when the duke had wrongly permitted a man to be hanged for stealing some fish, Mörlin boldly objected from the pulpit. This in turn resulted in his being given a leave of absence and not permitted to preach. His concern for humanity and justice cost him dearly. He complained about this to Luther, who replied, "Give room for the thorn, and it will be more tender, and shake the dust off your feet."

After some more months of wrangling, Mörlin was called and moved to Göttingen in 1544 as inspector and preacher with the blessing of the Wittenberg faculty. Things went well there until 1548 when the Interim was forced on the church of that city. Mörlin publicly and courageously preached against the Interim, stating that he would not obey it and would not keep silence. In December of 1549 the ruling Duke Erich, after seizing and imprisoning some of the Göttingen pastors, ordered the instant dismissal of Mörlin. After several delays, the Göttingen fathers felt they had to obey. Finally with the help of Duke Erich's Lutheran mother, Mörlin managed to escape, followed quickly by his family. In March 1550, they arrived in a safe haven in Schleusingen, near Braunschweig, after traveling through almost impenetrable wilderness. By August of that year Mörlin was called, again through the help of one of the princely ladies, to Halland in Prussia. But when Margrave Albrecht heard him preach, he arranged to have him remain in Königsberg, and Mörlin quickly received a call to one of the churches of that city. In September of that year he received an appointment to the cathedral church in Knipffhof near Königsberg.

When Mörlin had been in Königsberg less than a month, Osiander held his first disputation promoting his peculiar views on justification. This was apparently the occasion when Mörlin and Chemnitz first met, for this was the day when Chemnitz and Melchior Isinder tangled with Osiander. Mörlin was given the assignment to bring about reconciliation, but by April 18 of 1551 he wrote to Osiander refuting him; and Osiander in turn began publicly attacking Mörlin and preaching against him. Osiander was a rather crude and coarse man with a brilliant mind, poor manners, and a large ego. The margrave, who owed to Osiander his conversion to Lutheranism, did not take kindly to Mörlin's attacks on his favorite, and finally on Feb. 4, 1552, the council of Knipffhof was compelled to give Mörlin a leave of absence, and he departed for Danzig (Gdansk). A peaceful protest of some 400 people, led by some godly women, tried by means of a petition to get the margrave to reconsider. They knelt before him as he passed. But he refused. There was something very modern about this episode, for when he refused their petition, the people, mostly young boys and women, processed to the castle plaza and there sang "Ach Gott vom Himmel, Sieh," ("O Lord, Look Down from Heaven"); then "Es Woll Uns Gott Gnedig Seyn" ("May God Bestow on Us His Grace"), both by Luther, naturally; and finally "Erbarm Dich Mein, O Herr Gott" ("O Lord, Have Mercy on My Loved Ones"). This episode, however, was never forgotten, and it was people involved in this effort who finally got Mörlin back to Königsberg to almost a hero's welcome. He had a powerful personality, and he inspired confidence and respect wherever he went. In further defense of Mörlin it must be stated that Osiander was very outspoken. Despite his espousal of the Reformation and his leading the people of Nuremberg to accept it, he had been unpopular there, and he proceeded to develop the same situation at Königsberg. He died in the midst of the uproar on Oct. 17, 1552, but the conflict raged on.

While Mörlin sat in Danzig, in early April 1553, he received a letter from the city of Braunschweig, offering him the superintendency. Just a few days later, on April 17, the city council of Lübeck offered him their superintendency, and in June Count Poppo of Henneberg came all the way to Danzig to importune him to become the superintendent at Smalcald. But the affirmative answer had been given to Braunschweig, and he arrived there in July 1553. Mörlin seems to have had a talent for being at the storm center of activities, though his polemics and controversies in no way lessened his popularity or the demands for his services. But when he arrived in the city of Braunschweig, the situation in the duchy and city had passed beyond the merely controversial stage. There was a full-scale war in progress. The year was 1553, one year after Maurice of Saxony's victory over Emperor Charles. This had given the Lutherans much leverage, but the times were still so turbulent that Duke Henry the

Younger of the duchy—who had always resented the fact that the city of Braunschweig, the main city in the duchy, had asserted its independence toward the territorial duke and joined the Reformation—saw in the situation a chance to get his city back and on Sept. 18 laid siege to it. On Oct. 11 Mörlin had a close call with a 12-pound cannon ball.

However, in the Battle of Sievershausen, which had taken place in July of 1553 near Braunschweig, not only was the brilliant if treasonous Maurice of Saxony killed, but Henry the Younger lost his two older sons, young men who had been steeped in Catholicism in order to continue their father's political and religious struggles. This was momentous for the later history of both city and duchy. Despite all of his troubles, Henry managed to prevent the reformation of his duchy until his death in 1568, the year after Chemnitz became superintendent in the city.

The Battle of Sievershausen is important not only because of the illustrious casualties suffered in it but because it involved one of the most erratic and warlike men of the age, Prince Albert Alcibiades of Bayreuth (1522–57). Brought up in a Lutheran home, he seemed to have only one religion—war. Though nominally Protestant, he was popular with Emperor Charles because of his talent for war and lack of political or religious convictions. He reveled in war for war's sake. He fought as an ally of Charles against France in 1543 and again as his ally against the Smalcald League in the Smalcald War, but he was captured in 1547 by the elector of Saxony. However, he was released after the Lutheran defeat at Mühlberg. He then threw in his lot with his hero Maurice, the new elector of Saxony, deserted the emperor, and took part in Maurice's war against Charles. But when that was over, instead of retiring in 1552 under the Treaty of Passau, he went on a wild rampage of looting and pillaging and again offered his services to the emperor who sanctioned all his thievery. Finally a league of German princes was organized to stop him, and it was these forces who defeated him at Sievershausen on July 9, 1553. Ironically, the traitorous Lutheran Maurice and the contentious Catholic Henry were on the same side; and, although their casualties were tragic, they won the battle and defeated Albert, who then, almost as a mercenary soldier, hired out to the French and died in battle in 1557. The times were turbulent.

Thus Mörlin arrived in the city at a historic moment. The city of Braunschweig lost this particular battle with the duke and had to pay him a large fine. The city was soon returned to Lutheran control, however, under terms of the Treaty of Passau. Mörlin immediately set to work writing a history of the Osiandrian controversy and included other documents related to the matter. He also began to produce some wonderful and highly appreciated sermons on the psalms. By 1556, the city council of Braunschweig forbade all popish masses, processions, and festivals. In that same period Mörlin was involved in a successful exorcism involving a young girl.

Within a year he arranged for the calling of an assistant, a coadjutor, and he named Martin Chemnitz for this position in 1554. As coadjutor, Chemnitz was given a variety of duties and areas of responsibility. He preached regularly, conducted his lectures on Melanchthon's *Loci Communes* for the pastors and theological students, handed down theological opinions for other churches and faculties, and was active in the daily life of the church of Braunschweig. And thus the years passed.

The Reformation period opened the era of the married pastor. Orders began to go out from princes and city councils that parsonages should be built. Chemnitz' parsonage was directly across the street from the Martini Church. The parsonage has long since disappeared, but recent archeological excavations have uncovered the basement of the old building where archaeologists found the old German tile furnace that Chemnitz used. One of the tiles contained a picture of Martin Luther.

Chemnitz spent time taking care of the physical needs of his pastors, getting them pensions and arranging for their retirement and the care of their widows and orphans. Hospitals had long been in existence, and their general supervision was also a part of the superintendent's area of concern, as was the care of the poor and the mentally ill. Many pastors seemingly were well paid, but some were treated shabbily. Chemnitz was also involved with securing and examining pastors for vacant churches.

Since preaching had been largely a lost art under the popes, the Reformation also had to train and develop preachers. By and large they apparently were not outstanding. What they lacked in preaching skill they made up for in length. At first Chemnitz himself had not been an outstanding preacher. Mörlin was more dynamic, but as time went on Chemnitz greatly improved. Soon he was imitated by most of the preachers, more so than Mörlin because he was better organized and more logical.[4]

CHURCH LIFE AND ACTIVITIES

To illustrate church life and discipline in those times, we want to mention a particular case. A certain layman named Klod fell into error regarding the Lord's Supper. He also wanted to be married to a certain widow (presumably rich), but the pastor involved was forbidden by Mörlin to join the unhappy couple until Herr Klod got straightened out on the doctrine of the Lord's Supper. Herr Klod tried to go over Mörlin's head by going to the city council and citing Melanchthon as the authority for his doctrinal position. The council met with the man, asked him several questions, and refused to uphold him. He then sent his son to Melanchthon for what he hoped would be a statement of support. But Melanchthon replied, "The University of Wittenberg is absolutely not disposed to disturb the unity of the Christian Church in the beloved and Christian city of Braunschweig, and advises that the Council and the pastors give counsel to this man in order to bring about reconciliation." After some more skirmishing the council unanimously condemned Klod as a sacramentarian and exiled him. As expected, he went to Wittenberg, and several years later, in 1559, Melanchthon criticized Mörlin, saying that "certain good, learned and wealthy citizens had been driven out of Braunschweig for the sole reason that they would not believe that the body of Christ was present in every place." The city council then attacked Melanchthon for his impropriety. Finally after five years, in 1561, Herr Klod made his peace and subscribed in a general way to the position of the council. He was also willing to stand in the chancel of the church to pray for the forgiveness of God and of the congregation, and then he was restored to full fellowship.[5] Rehtmeyer never tells us if the poor man was ever permitted to marry.

CONFESSIONAL ACTIVITIES

A great deal more can and should be said about Mörlin and his confessional activities, in which Chemnitz was nearly always involved. As early as 1556 Mörlin, together with von Eitzen of Hamburg and Dr. Beckern of Bremen, had met with Albert Hardenberg of Bremen trying to dissuade him from his Calvinism, which was constantly being secretly encouraged by Melanchthon. But to no avail. This episode, together with the appearance in Lower Saxony of other Calvinistic factions regarding the Lord's Supper, caused Mörlin on Jan. 14, 1557, at a meeting of the Hansa cities attended both by lay rulers and clergy, to ask that a delegation be sent to Melanchthon to discuss the matter of the Lord's Supper. The delegates included the superintendent at Lübeck, Mörlin himself, Dr. Paul von Eitzen, superintendent at Hamburg, and the superintendent at Lüneburg. Their directive was "to exhort Philip Melanchthon that he would show from the heart whether he held that John Calvin was an enemy of the Lord's Supper, as he [Melanchthon] had so often called attention to his own hostility toward Joachim Westphal." "But," says Rehtmeyer, "they received poor thanks for their efforts, for Philip Melanchthon cried out with a loud voice that they had come to 'destroy' him," and Dr. Crell, also of Wittenberg "took pleasure in viciously lampooning them." But Mörlin was undaunted. On Feb. 1, he went to Wittenberg again, this time taking Chemnitz, and finally "in order to avert distrust," Melanchthon in a letter to the superintendents of Lower Saxony assented in a general way to the articles that had been drawn up by them.[6]

Rehtmeyer tells us a great deal about the administration of Superintendent Mörlin and church life in Braunschweig, all of which casts light on the career of Chemnitz and the history of the development of Lutheranism, together with the problems attendant upon it in northern Germany in those turbulent years. There are stories of a plague that killed about 6000 citizens of Braunschweig and all but three of the pastors, but Mörlin steadfastly remained at his post to the gratitude of the people. The histories are filled with stories of women dying in childbirth, of dedicated pastors and incompetent ones, and of moral laxity and heroism. In 1567, when Mörlin and Chemnitz returned from Prussia they found that during their absence a man had beaten his father to death and had been acquitted and freed by the city council. The two ecclesiastical leaders were stunned. They called together the ministerium and asked that each pastor denounce this travesty from the pulpit the next Sunday. This was done. The city council called in the two and begged them to cease "making a public issue" about the matter. This episode may have played some part in Mörlin's decision to leave Braunschweig, and it also may have had something to do with the carefully spelled out conditions that Chemnitz laid down before accepting the superintendency.

Mörlin spent much time in maintaining the doctrinal position of Lutheranism. He also struggled to maintain moral standards. He spent many hours in securing good pastors. He was involved as part of his office in every major doctrinal controversy of the time, and there were many. Most difficult were the conflicts that grew out of Melanchthon's weakness and defection on the Lord's Supper. Not only was there the major case of Hardenberg, but there were little Crypto-Calvinists among both clergy and laity everywhere, such as Klod, mentioned above. Mörlin and Chemnitz took part in the colloquium at Regensburg in 1557 and the ill-starred colloquium at Worms later in the same year. Mörlin was one of 12 theologians chosen to represent the Lutheran side, and Chemnitz went along as his understudy and as a witness to the proceedings. Mörlin, along with the ducal Saxons Schneff, Sacerius, Strigel, and Stöffel walked out of the Worms meeting. We are not told what Chemnitz did, but as Mörlin's assistant he probably did what Mörlin did. Brenz was angry at the treatment they received but apparently did not walk out. Mörlin in a letter to his friend Marschus explains the reason for this walkout, which historically has usually been treated as a mere case of bullheadedness on the part of the five. But there was good reason for their action.[7]

From the standpoint of the development of Chemnitz' career and importance to the church, the year 1561 was crucial. In 1560 Mörlin had been instrumental in asking the faculty at Jena (which after the division of electoral Saxony had become the headquarters for the Gnesio-Lutherans) to call a meeting to try to resolve the Calvinistic controversy among Lutherans. Originally the proposal had involved the idea of a general synod or council of the Lutherans, but this was rejected by Melanchthon and his followers.

When the idea of a synod failed, Duke Christoph of Württemberg (1515–68), the cousin of Duke Julius and the mentor of Andreae, called for this meeting of princes and political leaders to be held at Naumburg from Jan. 20 to Feb. 8, 1561. While Andreae was not present, one can scarcely doubt his influence on Duke Christoph. Perhaps the recent death of Melanchthon and the weakening position of Flacius also played a part. The meeting ultimately involved two electors, from Saxony and the Palatinate, and nearly all the rulers of Lutheran territories. Some 50 princes, counselors, and delegates attended; and all the great Protestant territories of the empire were represented, except for Prussia, which, however, watched with great interest.[8] Neither Mörlin nor Chemnitz attended the meeting. In fact, theologians were kept out as much as possible.

The purpose was to unite all the adherents of the Augsburg Confession in a common front against the Council of Trent and also to establish a common position in the face of rising Calvinism, as exemplified in the Hardenberg case. Perhaps some of the planners of the conference felt that the recent death of Melanchthon and the forthcoming dismissal of Flacius boded well for such a meeting. Adherence to the Augsburg Confession had become sort of a certificate of loyalty on the part of the German Lutherans toward the Holy Roman Empire. But the question had arisen as to which edition of the Augustana was official. At first the princes could not even agree on this point. Was it the original German edition of 1530–31, which in Article X stipulates the real presence most clearly but is less clear on transubstantiation, or the 1540 Variata in which transubstantiation is clearly rejected in Article X, but the real presence not so clearly enunciated. Both points are important. We have already seen how the papists interpreted the 1530–31 edition to favor transubstantiation but also how the Calvinists interpreted the 1540 edition to permit a Calvinistic understanding of the presence. This is why Chemnitz, Chytraeus, and their co-workers always insisted on the use of the Smalcald Articles, which cleared up both points. The final result of the meeting regarding this point was the acceptance of the 1530–31 German edition, but also of the 1540 Variata, a compromise. The action is important because it marks the first effort to get rid of the 1540 Variata edition of the Augustana, something that was not completely accomplished until the adoption of the Book of Concord in 1580, when the Variata was quietly set aside and the edition of 1530–31 adopted as the only correct interpretation of the 1540 edition.[9] Tappert notes that Chytraeus attempted to get the princes at Naumburg to give formal adoption to the Apology, which had never been done previously. This was done, but his efforts to gain their adoption of the Smalcald Articles failed.[10]

The Naumburg meeting also decided unanimously that since the pope had invited them to the council calling them "my beloved sons," that none would attend. There was also a communication from the Huguenots asking the convention to request the French and Spanish monarchs to show mercy toward them. This was done, but without result, of course. Queen Elizabeth of England sent an ambassador to the convention asking for closer cooperation between England and the German Evangelical princes over against Trent. The convention agreed.

A study of the preface to the Book of Concord[11] will clearly show the great importance of the Naumburg meeting for the future direction of Lutheran confessional theology. By patient, continual, and conscientious work, the Lower Saxon theologians under Chemnitz' leadership came to be the dominant voices and gradually acknowledged leaders—and this even before the departure of Mörlin.

It is also significant that at the very time the princes were meeting at Naumburg, the theologians and other princes were meeting at Braunschweig. The purpose was in part, at least, the settlement of the Hardenberg conflict at Bremen. All the important theologians of the Lower Saxon circle were present, including Mörlin and Chemnitz. Great efforts were made to bring Hardenberg around to a solidly Lutheran position, but they failed. The net result of the meeting was that the entire convention ruled that Hardenberg should resign. He agreed to this decision. One might have hoped that the controversy was over, at least in that city. But one of his partisans, a burgher, continued the quarrel and was ultimately successful in getting the city to reject Lutheranism and adopt Calvinism.

Later, in July of that important year of 1561, a meeting of Lower Saxon princes and theologians at Lüneburg upheld the action of

Naumburg regarding the 1530–31 edition of the Augustana, as well as that regarding the Apology. This group went one step further and gave formal confessional status to the Smalcald Articles and Luther's catechisms. But the meeting refused to recognize and uphold the preface to the Naumburg Agreement because they regarded it as ambiguous and vague. The Württemberg leaders shared in this opinion.

5

Chemnitz Comes
to the Fore

INTRA-LUTHERAN ACTIVITY

At this point, in 1561, while still the coadjutor, Chemnitz begins to come to the fore. He produced three of his major writings that year, which affected not only his own future but that of the Lutheran churches that ultimately allied themselves with the Formula of Concord. The three works were (1) *Repetitio sanae doctrinae de vera praesentia corporis et sanguinis in Coena* . . . (A repetition of the sound teaching regarding the true presence of the body and blood in the supper . . .); (2) *Anatome propositionum Alberti Hardenbergii de Coena Domini, quas exhibuit ordinibus Saxoniae inferioris in conventu Brunsvigensi* . . . (An analysis of the propositions of Albert Hardenberg regarding the Lord's Supper which he set forth before the clergy of lower Saxony in the colloquium at Braunschweig . . .); (3) *Iudicium,* called *De Controversiis quibusdam, quae superiori tempore circa quosdam Augustanae Confessionis articulos motae et agitatae sunt, Iudicium d. Martini Chemnitii* (The judgment of Dr. Martin Chemnitz regarding certain controversies which in an earlier time were stirred up and agitated concerning certain articles of the Augsburg Confession).

The *Repetitio,* which Chemnitz began in 1557, is in part a defense of Mörlin, who had been attacked by Melanchthon.[1] It is one of Chemnitz' major works on the Lord's Supper, only replaced in 1570 by his even more famous *Fundamenta sanae doctrinae de vera et substantiali praesentia, exhibitione et sumptione corporis et sanguinis Domini in Coena* (The fundamental points of the correct doctrine of the true and substantial presence, offering and reception of the body and blood of the Lord in the Supper). Mörlin wrote the

115

introduction for the *Repetitio*, undoubtedly in gratitude for Chemnitz' support. Both the *Anatome* and the *Repetitio* dealt with the Supper, again reverting to Melanchthon's departure from Luther. Perhaps as a result of the Naumburg convention special stress was laid on correctly interpreting Article X of the Augustana.

The *Iudicium* was written in 1561, but only as a private paper for Chemnitz' own study. It is not surprising that a careful and analytical student like Chemnitz would want, after all the meetings that had been held, to sit down and collect his thoughts and put them in written form. Much had been going on in the months just previous, and the *Iudicium* is useful in giving us a picture of exactly how Chemnitz and probably many of his co-workers were thinking at the time. It was not published until after his death. Polycarp Leyser put it out in 1594, in his introduction calling Chemnitz "the most outstanding theologian of our age." It certainly expresses Chemnitz' thinking in that crucial year of 1561, and this thinking was clearly expressed to the churches. However, Ebel, writing in 1980, has much more to say about the *Iudicium*. He suggests that even at this early date Chemnitz was quietly proposing the *Iudicium* as a document to counter the *Corpus Philippicum*. He also raises the question as to whether the document may have been prepared for the meeting at Nürnberg of the princes, who might try "to reconcile conflicting opinions by painting them over and pretending to settle them," (cf. *Iudicium*, p. 1). Ebel also suggests that the document may have been prepared for the forthcoming Lüneburg meeting.[2] In view of Chemnitz' close involvement in all of these matters, his great interest, and his keen theological mind, a positive answer to both might well be expected, but we will never know for sure.

The *Iudicium* shows how far Chemnitz had already come in his thinking about peace and concord among the Lutherans on many different subjects. This treatise does not touch on the Lord's Supper, for Chemnitz apparently felt that this point was sufficiently covered in his other two documents. It is manifest, however, that Chemnitz and his superintendent were in complete agreement on all points, and it also became evident that the same situation pertained in the case of all the Lower Saxon theologians. This is clear from the Lüneburg Articles, or the *Erklerung . . . und kurzer Bericht,* which were drafted by Mörlin and adopted by all the Lower Saxon cities in the same year.

Thus by 1561 the work of peace and concord was quite well established in Lower Saxony, and it was on this solid basis that the work of concord proceeded in an ever-widening circle throughout much of Germany, a testimony not only to the leadership of Mörlin but perhaps even more substantively to his bright young coadjutor. Both Mörlin and Chemnitz had also been involved in the July 1561 meeting at Lüneburg in the subscription and acceptance by the Lower Saxon cities of the *Erklerung . . . und kurzer Bericht*, or the Lüneburg Articles.[3] The document bore the name of Mörlin, but it is hard to believe that Chemnitz did not have a hand in it, though he signed it only as *Martinus Kemnitz Prediger zu Braunschweig*. This document was subscribed to by the Lower Saxon cities (Lübeck, Bremen, Hamburg, Rostock, Magdeburg, Braunschweig, Lüneburg, and Wismar). The full title is *Erklerung aus Gottes Wort und kurzer Bericht der Herren Theologen welchen sie der Erbarn Sechsischen Stedte Gesanten auff dem Tag zu Lüneburg in Julio des 61 Jars gehalten fürnemlich auff drei Artikel gethan haben* (An explanation from God's Word and short analysis of the theologians which they have drawn up and sent to the honorable Saxon cities, for the Lüneburg day or meeting in July of the year '61 dealing particularly with three important articles).[4]

The 1569 *Kurzer Bericht* of Chemnitz, prepared during his superintendency for the church order of the duchy of Braunschweig was also contained in the *Corpora Doctrinae Julium* of Braunschweig of both 1569 and 1576. The latter corpus also contained Urbanus Rhegius' *Formulae Caute Loquendi* (Formula for speaking carefully), including Chemnitz' unsigned appendix to it called in German *Wohlgegründeter Bericht* ("The fully established report") dated 1575 and in Latin "Formulae recte sentiendi, pie, circumspecte et citra scandalum loquendi de praecipuis horum temporum controversiis" ("The formula for believing correctly, piously, and circumspectly and for speaking without offense regarding the most important controversies of these times"), dated 1576. Chemnitz' *Kurzer Bericht* of 1569 was also contained in the *Corpus Doctrinae Wilhelminum* for Braunschweig-Celle, whose duke, Wilhelm, had especially requested Chemnitz to include it.

In 1569, Chemnitz began the preparation of his *Enchiridion*, a document in which, by a series of questions and answers, pastors could prepare for their semi-annual examinations or their first examination upon entrance into the ministry. It was published after Mörlin had left Braunschweig and was an outgrowth of Chemnitz' work in visitation and in preparing the various *corpora doctrinae*. It is also a result of the discovery of the ignorance and incompetence of large numbers of the clergy. This document and others prepared at this time are of great value in showing both the theology of Chemnitz and the religious priorities of the times. We shall touch on these later.

In light of the above it might be worthwhile to add a few statements from Chemnitz' *Iudicium,* which he wrote in late March 1561, just after the Naumburg meeting, and retained for his own private use.[5] It reflects his thinking not only of recent past events but sets a course that he followed for the rest of his life. The opening chapter deals with the subject of "A Definite *Corpus Doctrinae*." On the opening page he asserts that there are two improper approaches to controversies: some try to paper everything over, and others try little by little to overturn even moderately helpful *corpora doctrinae* by starting new and unnecessary arguments.

> Neither side should be approved. Both for the sake of teachers as well as learners and also for the sake of our adversaries, there must be a correct form and systematic summary [*methodica summa*] of the divine teaching which through the ministry of Luther has been by God's work [*divinitus*], purified on the basis of the prophetic and apostolic writings, in that true sense which is expressed in the approved symbols of our church, by the blessing of God, and still confessed. And if any statements fail to measure up to this norm, they should not require some clever interpretation or some whitewashed reconciliation, but they should be clearly disapproved and rejected. For otherwise the purity of doctrine cannot be retained. For just as in the Council of Ratisbon in the year 1541, where skillfully worked-out compromises of disputed dogmas were set forth with great and plausible moderation, our people very wisely and correctly replied, with this intention and in these very words, "In controversies involving religion, certain ideas are proposed with too great a desire for compromise, but it is more important in the church to have boundaries which serve as limits to our compromises. Often in the church

not only the princes and the political leaders but also the theologians by their human judgment seek compromises that draw men away from the purity of the Gospel. Therefore, it is necessary in the church that the Word of God be the rule for our compromises, so that controversies may indeed be settled and that they be kept on the correct course and approved according to the norm of the Word of God and the apostolic church." In the same way we have to express our disapproval of those who quietly gnaw away without serious and necessary reasons at the things that have been taught, that can be explained very well, so that even in the case of a *corpus doctrinae* they little by little undermine and overturn the whole system [*totum systema*] by speaking first of the intention and then of the mode of expression. . . . For our people always, when they wanted to demonstrate what kind of doctrine should be universally taught in our churches, testified that they adhered to the Augsburg Confession which had been delivered to the emperor and to the Apology which had been added to it. Then in the year '37 there were written by Luther in the public name of our churches the Smalcald Articles which were signed and received. And the reasons why they were written and received by our churches after the Confession Luther himself tells us in the preface, namely that both at Augsburg and afterwards attempts were often made for reconciliation with many people thinking that in the articles of the Augsburg Confession certain points could be yielded and concession made to the papists. Further, because many fanatics and sectarians, under the pretext of following Luther, were spreading their ravings among the unwary, as if Luther understood the doctrine of the Augsburg Confession differently, therefore the Smalcald Articles were written to be both a confirmation and a true, certain, and permanent explanation or interpretation of the Augsburg Confession, as to how its meaning, while Luther was still alive, was to be handed down and understood among all of our churches. . . . Therefore, just as the ancients had their symbols in which in opposition to the corruptions of heretics there was the form and pattern of sound words for the sake both of those who teach and those who learn, so for us is the *corpus doctrinae* of our churches, which we judge to be the true and unchangeable teaching of the prophetic and apostolic writings in that sense that is expressed in our approved symbols, that is, the Augsburg Confession and its Apology and the Smalcald Articles. And there are serious and weighty reasons that we want the Smalcald Articles to be added. For certain points are more fully explained there, such as, concerning the pope, the power of bishops, Zwinglianism, transubstantiation, and the sins which drive out the Holy Spirit.

Chemnitz then takes up the difficult problem of the two editions of the Augustana, pointing out that Calvin and his followers eagerly espoused the 1540–42 edition particularly in Article X, "because he [Calvin] sees there a cothornum [a kind of shoe that could fit both feet] that can easily fit the feet of Zwingli, but he rejects the article as it was presented to the emperor and as it stands in the edition of the year '31 because this affirms that the body is truly present in the Supper and it disapproves of those who 'teach otherwise.'" But at this point in his career, at least, Chemnitz supports the Variata edition of 1540–42 as a "clarification." He goes on to say that the Lutherans cannot reject the 1530–31 edition for this is what was delivered to the emperor and to this edition, all the churches subscribed. He also does not see how they can "reject or condemn" the 1542 edition that was used at the colloquies at Hagenau and Ratisbon, and "this was done as a result of the advice of Luther with his approval and consent." The Variata was used in many of the meetings to the point that the 1530–31 edition was almost forgotten. So great was the influence of Melanchthon and his Crypto-Calvinist supporters! Chemnitz concludes,

> It seemed most prudent that the edition of '31 be restored to the churches and commended to them as the fullest and first authority. And the edition of the year '40 should also be retained as an explanation which must not be in conflict with but in all respects be in agreement with the first edition. And Article 10 must be restored, so that the mention of the elements be retained.

On the same page he speaks of the reading of the 1542 edition in Article X as a *mutilatio*. On pages 8–9 he also calls for the revision or omission in Article X, 2 of the Apology of the statement that speaks of the "mutation" of the bread into the body of Christ, because it leaves the door open to transubstantiation, as we have already seen in Manschreck's comments.[6] The Formula of Concord in Article VII, 1 clearly rejects transubstantiation and gives a correct interpretation to the ambiguity of Article X, 2 in the Apology. There is a direct line from the 1530–31 Augsburg Confession, Article X, through the Apology, to Chemnitz in 1561 and finally to Formula of Concord Article VII in 1577. Chemnitz was the chief player. The same can be said for other points raised in this interesting, private, and virtually unknown *Iudicium*. Chemnitz was moving foreword.

We can only speculate as to whether he ever shared his remarkable document with his superintendent, but it has to be asserted that he shared his thinking with him and that Mörlin urged him to publish his writings.

Inge Mager, professor of church history at Göttingen, in a very interesting article published in connection with the 450th anniversary of the introduction of the Reformation in the city of Braunschweig adds a further dimension of the work of Chemnitz as coadjutor. She quotes him, "Such a *corpus doctrinae* dare not consist of private documents. But rather it must consist of documents issued in the name of the people, approved and accepted by them; they must be documents like the Augsburg Confession, its Apology, and the Smalcald Articles, among which must also be considered the Small and Large Catechisms of Luther."[7] Chemnitz in chapter 1 of his *Iudicium* makes it very clear that he considers *corpora doctrinae* to be the official statements adopted by the church in contradistinction to the work of individuals who often fly off in different directions. This is understandable in light of his debate with Osiander and the problems caused by the Interim. Mahlmann is certainly correct in asserting that Chemnitz was putting official *corpora doctrinae* in opposition to and above the "personal productions of the theologians of the late Reformation period" which he saw as only "additional complications."[8]

While the Gnesio-Lutherans had favored a synod to achieve theological concord, the credit for the development of the concept of *corpora doctrinae* really goes to Melanchthon who, however, never achieved the point of having his own writings, except for those in the Book of Concord, given confessional status. It is not clear for what reason the Gnesio-Lutherans favored a synod, while Melanchthon favored the *corpora doctrinae*. It was seemingly for the exercise of secondary authority in the church. Melanchthon, although he opposed a synod and felt that *corpora doctrinae* should be more general rather than detailed, in his old age did begin to prepare one that was to include only his own writings. He died in 1560 and never lived to see the publication of his work, but it did appear under the title *Corpus Doctrinae Christianae,* more commonly *Philippicum* or *Misnicum,* in late 1561, published by his son-in-law Peucer. In 1561, when Chemnitz wrote his *Iudicium,* Melanchthon's *corpus* had no confessional status at all, and only in 1566 did it receive some degree of official position in Saxony and a few other areas. But it created trouble for Chemnitz as late as 1570. Melanchthon's hope, as suggested in the title, *Corpus Doctrinae Christianae,* was that his document might become a *corpus doctrinae* for all of Protestantism. But despite Melanchthon's failure, the idea of a *corpus doctrinae* for all of Lutheranism caught hold among the Gnesio-Lutherans, and the ball began to roll. Actually, the idea had surfaced as early as the 1540s in Hamburg, so Chemnitz in 1561 is speaking of a subject that was under great discussion and that in the previous year, right after Melanchthon's death, had received a new impetus.

Perhaps one of the first negative reactions to the *Corpus Doctrinae Philippicum* as well as to the Naumburg Agreement was expressed at the Lüneburg Convention in July 1561, where the theologians of Lower Saxony accepted Mörlin's *Erklerung . . . und kurzer Bericht* as binding and also condemned the errors of Osiander, Major, the sacramentarians, and the adiaphorists (all of which are mentioned in Chemnitz' writings of 1561 and most of which involve Melanchthon), along with the papal pretensions shown at Naumburg. Mager states,

> Now Chemnitz makes crystal clear his antithesis to Melanchthon's *Corpus Doctrinae Philippicum* when he says, "Such a *corpus doctrinae* dare not consist of private documents. But rather it must consist of documents issued in the name of the people, approved and accepted by them; they must be documents like the Augsburg Confession, its Apology, and the Smalcald Articles, among which must also be considered the Small and Large Catechisms of Luther." . . . Of great significance in this connection are Chemnitz' comments about the authority of the two reformers. As a former pupil and interpreter of Melanchthon, Chemnitz did not simply disown his great mentor but respected the professional value of his writings. Nevertheless, he considered Luther's works as more important and set up this principle for the Lower Saxon churches: "Therefore the writings of Philip must not be cited

against Luther but rather understood and interpreted according to Luther's writings."[9]

This principle prevailed during all of Chemnitz' career and is manifest in the Formula of Concord. Such was the theological state of affairs in the city of Braunschweig during the superintendency of Mörlin and the coadjutorship of Chemnitz.

In 1563 Mörlin as superintendent and Chemnitz as coadjutor undertook the first of three revisions of the *corpus doctrinae* of the city of Braunschweig. This document contained Mörlin's *Erklerung . . . und kurzer Bericht* which had been adopted as the Lüneburg Articles at the meeting of the Lower Saxon cities in 1561. It also included the high German revision of the original Bugenhagen *Kirchenordnung* of 1528–31, the Augsburg Confession, its Apology, the Smalcald Articles, and Melanchthon's Treatise on the Power and Primacy of the Pope. By rather common consent the catechisms of Luther were also understood as included. Mahlmann states,

> In 1563 the Bugenhagen Church Order of 1528, which Chemnitz had described as "a proven and tested confession," with the addition of the Lüneburg Articles was further expanded to be a conscious opposition to the *Corpus Doctrinae Philippicum,* a document to which the name *corpus doctrinae* should never have been applied in the first place. According to his contemporaries, Chemnitz had found this document to be in conflict with the understanding of the Lord's Supper and lacking in the clarity and formal understanding which had up to this time been attained.[10]

Thus, through the work of Mörlin and his coadjutor the spread of the confessional Lutheran spirit was advancing in Lower Saxony. All of this in turn effected the ultimate spread of confessionalism that resulted in the Formula of Concord.

COUNCIL OF TRENT AND CHEMNITZ' *EXAMEN*

Chemnitz did not spend all of his time on intra-Lutheran problems, though many of his co-workers did. Andreae, for example, devoted almost his entire career to the intra-Lutheran situation, including the problems with Calvinism, as did Selnecker, and Mörlin. In 1562, the year following the momentous events of 1561, Chemnitz was about his theologizing again, this time on a broader scale. He produced his *Main Points of the Theology of the Jesuits* (*Theologiae Iesuitarum praecipua capita. Ex quadam ipsorum censura, quae Coloniae anno 60 edita est . . .*), which was reproduced under a somewhat different title in 1563 and continued to be printed in German until 1730. Since the work, though important, was overshadowed by its successor document, the *Examination of the Council of Trent,* we shall at this point give a few pertinent historical facts about it.

John Monheim was a rather evangelically inclined Roman Catholic living at the time at Düsseldorf. He was an educator and head of a very successful school. He had produced a catechism based on Erasmus, which while essentially Roman Catholic, had advocated Communion in both kinds. In 1560 he produced a new catechism, in which he shows borrowings from Calvin's *Institutes* and Luther's catechism, and he even tried to draw a middle course between Luther and Calvin on the Supper.

The Jesuits had been established in 1534 and had already established for themselves a reputation for total commitment to the papacy which included, if possible, the extirpation of Protestantism. Thus in 1560 the Jesuits at Cologne attacked this evangelically inclined Monheim in a treatise entitled *A Censure and Learned Explanation of the Errors of the Catechism of John Monheim* (*Censura*). Other attacks came, as well as defenses from Lutherans, for example, from Herman Hamelmann of Gandersheim. In 1562 Chemnitz entered the fray, not so much to defend Monheim, whose name he did not mention, but to attack the Jesuits. He was apparently one of the earliest to recognize the extreme danger that this group, the spearhead of the Counter-Reformation, posed for Protestantism. He dedicated his treatise to Duke Joachim of Brandenburg, reminding him of his own Brandenburg origins and his relationship with George Sabinus.

Chemnitz begins this treatise with a rather sarcastic attack on the Jesuit order, commenting on the Roman preoccupation with the saints rather than Christ and then reporting on various understandings that were circulating regarding the etymology of the word *Jesuit.* He suggests that the term was derived from the Hebrew word *Esau* or *Jebusite.* He rather inclines to a German origin, the word *Jesuwiter* from *Jesu wider,* meaning "against Jesus." From there he proceeds to 2 Thess. 2:3–4, where Paul speaks of the man of sin who opposes himself to God, concluding with the suggestion that their *Censura* clearly shows them as the agents of the pope, the Antichrist. He then cites each of the points in the *Censura* and refutes it briefly. The topics covered are Scripture, sin, free choice, the Law, the Gospel, justification, faith, good works, the Lord's Supper, the invocation of saints, penance, confirmation, extreme unction, images, and celibacy. He closes with a discussion of certain axioms that the Jesuits have propounded concerning traditions, the papacy, the superiority of priests over civil magistrates, and the use of force to maintain religious conformity.

Chemnitz' book produced great commotion and was widely acclaimed. Naturally it also produced a reply, in 1564, by the Portuguese scholar Diogo Paiva de Andrada of the University at Coimbra, a man who had personally attended the Council of Trent, which he brought into the discussion. This gave Chemnitz an opportunity to undertake what came to be the largest and most carefully prepared theological work of his career, the *Examination of the Council of Trent.* Thus the discussion moved from the Jesuits to the council itself, which had begun in 1545 and concluded in 1563, only three years before Chemnitz' rebuttal began.

The examination of Trent was undertaken by Chemnitz as the coadjutor of Braunschweig. The first two parts, of four, appeared in 1566, while he was still the coadjutor. The other two parts appeared in 1573, after he had become superintendent. The work went through more editions, had greater impact, had a greater readership, and brought him greater fame than anything else he produced in his life. The full title is *Examen decretorum Concilii Tridentini, in quo ex sacrae scripturae norma, collatis etiam orthodoxis verae et purioris antiquitatis testimoniis ostenditur, qualia sint illa decreta et quo artificio sint composita . . .* (An examination of the decrees of the Council of Trent in which on the basis of the norm of Holy Scripture and after comparison with orthodox testimonies of the true and purer ancient church are shown what kind of decrees these are and with what trickery they have been prepared). The work has been republished in every century since the time of its appearance, in 25 editions, and has been translated into German, French, and English. We shall not at this point discuss the work further, except to say that it is one of the greatest theological masterpieces ever produced in Lutheranism.

CORPUS DOCTRINAE PRUTHENICUM

Back on the intra-Lutheran scene, in 1567 Chemnitz and Mörlin were invited to return to Prussia to help clean up the mess left by the Osiandrian controversy. Among the things they did was to produce a *corpus doctrinae* for the duchy, the *Corpus Doctrinae Pruthenicum*. They arrived in the duchy on April 9 and had completed their assignment and written their report in both German and Latin by May 6. Rehtmeyer tells us that they told the people that "they did not really need a new confession but rather should strongly declare their adherence to the Augsburg Confession and its Apology and the Smalcald Articles as documents that were based on God's Word and had already been accepted, including the clarifications contained in the writings of Luther."[11] They followed the pattern of the *corpus doctrinae* for the city of Braunschweig of 1563 and also of Mörlin's *Erklerung . . . und kurzer Bericht*. In the final analysis they again called for subscription to the Augustana, its Apology, and the Smalcald Articles.

They also included in the corpus a document written by Chemnitz entitled *Repetitio Corporis Doctrinae Ecclesiasticae oder Widerholung der summa un inhalt der rechten allgemeynen Christlichen Kirchen Lehre . . . von Fürstlicher Durchleuchtigkeit zu Preussen . . . angenommen* (A repetition of the body of ecclesiastical doctrine, or a repetition of the sum or content of the correct universal Christian church . . . adopted by his ducal eminence of Prussia). In his *Repetitio* Chemnitz included a section on the principles of pure teaching and Christian unity, together with eight new controversies within Protestantism, dealing with the Trinity, Christology, Law and Gospel, original sin, justification, good works, Baptism, and the Lord's Supper. His opening section on the subject of a *corpus doctrinae* asserts that the church must be based on sound doctrine for the sake of its own peace and unity. He speaks of the clarity of Scripture in all points necessary for salvation and then shows how a summary, or *summa,* of the faith is contained in the ancient creeds, the Augustana, the Apology, and the Smalcald Articles. In this treatise there are hints of the rise of Polish antitrinitarianism, which was beginning to affect the church in Prussia, and a strong support for forensic justification, which Osiander had denied. Since Osiander's errors also impinged on the doctrine of Christology, Chemnitz' in his *Repetitio* also dealt with this locus. He constantly stresses Scripture, saying, for example, "We poor, incompetent, poverty-stricken people must hold captive our shameful reason in subjection and submit our wisdom to the Word of God."[12]

The *Corpus Doctrinae Pruthenicum,* as far as it concerned the new doctrinal or theological portions, was actually the work of Chemnitz, as Mager indicates, but as was normally the case in such documents it was treated as the work of the committee or the church that adopted it.[13] Personal authorship was unimportant. This document was especially important because it provided a significant step toward the Formula of Concord in that it clarified the most important controversies that had arisen regarding the Augsburg Confession and among those adhering to it, and it established the concept of a binding doctrinal standard (*Lehrurteil*).[14]

In addition to the important works cited above, Chemnitz also produced several minor opinions, or *Gutachen,* relating to various subjects, but time does not permit a study of them here. In the last year of Mörlin's superintendency, he and Chemnitz met with Melanchthon and some of his followers on Jan. 9 in the hope of settling the controversy regarding the Lord's Supper, but says Gasmer, "The mission was not accomplished because their [the Wittenbergers'] minds were poisoned by certain followers of Melanchthon who inflamed and instigated problems."[15] Finally in December of that year at the infamous colloquy at Worms, where Catholics and Lutherans met for the last time in a vain attempt to iron out their differences, Mörlin and Chemnitz attended, representing the city of Braunschweig. From Chemnitz' standpoint the meeting was not a total loss, since he met several prominent Lutheran leaders with whom he kept in contact in the years ahead, such as Brenz, Marbach, Schnepf, and others.

The net result of the Prussian endeavor, in addition to the preparation of the *corpus doctrinae,* was that the Prussians were so impressed with both of the Braunschweigers that they extended calls to both of them. Lengthy and complicated negotiations followed. The final solution was that Mörlin went to Prussia as Bishop of Samland, and Chemnitz remained in Braunschweig but was promoted to the office of superintendent on terms that he set forth carefully. This was not surprising in view of both his tremendous services to the city and the large number of calls he had received to other places to serve as their superintendent, never as a coadjutor.

Thus Mörlin left Braunschweig early in 1568 to return in triumph and vindication to his beloved Prussia. But his joy was short lived. Before two years had elapsed, he was struck down with gall stones and spent the last year of his life in dreadful misery, most of the time bedridden. He also lost his beloved wife during this period. On May 23, 1571, he departed this life, at age 57. He had great influence on his times and particularly on his Chemnitz. Rehtmeyer says of him,

> He was a splendid and energetic theologian who through his eloquence, intelligence, fidelity, and oversight brought the churches of Braunschweig to a very good condition. Under his guidance both secular and domestic matters also prospered. With regard to the refugees and the poor he constantly showed himself as more open handed than necessary, and at his door every poor man received either bread or money. He was a loving example, and though he often preached strong sermons, he was regarded as a good and kind man by the city council, as well as by his colleagues, because of his fear of God and his uprightness. He loved his church and his congregations very much and held his ministers in high esteem. His predecessor, Dr. Medler, said that Mörlin "only wanted to run everybody by himself" [but predecessors are known to talk that way]. He held firmly to Luther's doctrine in the face of Majorism, Osiandrianism, synergism, Calvinism, etc. . . . and he strongly supported Luther's doctrine of the Lord's Supper.[16]

It is difficult to find a kinder summary of any official's ministry. Chemnitz added to his praise by expressing great appreciation for Mörlin's work with the catechetical training of the young and for the way in which he guided his young pastors.

Gasmer describes the relationship between Mörlin and Chemnitz:

> There was between these two men genuine and mutual love, whereby both having the same love were one in thinking and

speaking. They sought nothing through strife or vainglory, but each out of modesty considered the other better than himself and had consideration for the public benefit of the church rather than his own. What shall I say about the smooth and pleasant combination of the gifts of these two men? For although in Mörlin there was no vulgar zeal, if at times it appeared that he might become a little too excited, the moderation of Chemnitz would little by little calm him down. And on the other hand, the forcefulness of Mörlin could in turn dispel the inclinations of Chemnitz to become depressed, so that they protected the splendor and the very useful moderation of the church of Christ. Many good men who knew them testified that there had been the same kind of agreement between the two brightest lights of all Germany, Luther and Melanchthon. I have mentioned above that immediately after the death of the blessed and great Luther most dangerous controversies arose . . . between the Wittenbergers, Flacius the Illyrian, and the Saxon churches.[17]

This brings us to the close of the first portion of Chemnitz' career. Almost at once he began his own superintendency and in the following year Duke Julius ascended the throne of the duchy of Braunschweig, opening a new era in the history of the duchy itself and of Chemnitz as Julius' special and most trusted theologian.

6

Chemnitz' Superintendency

INITIAL PHASES

Before taking up the interesting and extremely productive relationship that developed between Chemnitz and Duke Julius, we should spend a few moments discussing the initial phases of Chemnitz' superintendency, points that came up in the short period before the accession of Julius.

We must remember that the Roman Catholic city of Braunschweig had been reformed only in 1528 in a whirlwind visit by John Bugenhagen. The bishops had been largely deposed in German Lutheranism, although a few remained and some were reemerging; but in general the Reformation brought to Germany the problems that come from developing a form of church government.[1]

To get a picture of the office of superintendent, we need to go back to Luther's *Instructions for the Visitors of Parish Pastors in Electoral Saxony* of 1528, where the office was really established. Luther says,

> This pastor (*Pfarrherr*) shall be superintendent of all the other priests who have their parish or benefice in the region, whether they live in monasteries or foundations of nobles or of others. He shall make sure that in these parishes there is correct Christian teaching, that the Word of God and the holy gospel are truly and purely proclaimed, and that the holy sacraments according to the institution of Christ are provided to the blessing of the people. The preachers are to exemplify a good life so that the people take no offense but better their own lives. They are not to teach or preach anything that is contrary to the Word of God or that contributes to rebellion against the government.

130

If one or more of the pastors or preachers is guilty of error in this or that respect, the superintendent shall call to himself those concerned and have them abstain from it, but also carefully instruct them wherein they are guilty and have erred either in commission or omission, either in doctrine or in life.

But if such a one will not then leave off or desist, especially if it leads to false teaching and sedition, then the superintendent shall report this immediately to the proper official who will then bring it to the knowledge of our gracious lord, the Elector. . . .

We have also considered it wise to ordain that in the future when a pastor or preacher either by death or otherwise leaves his benefice and some one is accepted in his place by the patron, such a one shall be presented to the superintendent before he is given the benefice or received as a preacher. The superintendent shall question and examine him as to his life and teaching and whether he will satisfactorily serve the people, so that by God's help we may carefully prevent any ignorant or incompetent person from being accepted and unlearned folk being misled. For time and again and especially in recent years experience has shown how much good or evil may be expected from competent or incompetent preachers.[2]

Virtually every line of this statement of Luther, which was later buttressed by Melanchthon, is imbedded in the job description of Chemnitz and the men of his era. Luther lies at the root of both pastoral theology and pastoral supervision within the Lutheran church.

Reform was in the air. Even in Catholic countries the Lutheran revolution produced strenuous efforts to reform the moribund Roman Church. Witness the efforts of St. Teresa of Avila to reform the spiritual life of the nunneries of her country.[3] The Council of Trent, however hidebound it may appear to Protestant eyes, was a sincere attempt within Catholicism to bring about internal reform in the Roman church. Of course, reform was moving forward with lightning speed in countries where the secular leaders had been able to shake off the papal yoke.

Braunschweig, along with the majority of German cities, had chosen the route of establishing the superintendency. Chemnitz was the fourth to hold this position since 1528. The first, Görlitz, did not seem to have been particularly forceful or innovative. The second, Medler, contended vigorously against the Interim, and we already have seen the story of Mörlin. But apparently Chemnitz felt that a review of the duties and work of the superintendent was in order, and quite logically he felt that the time to undertake this review was at the beginning. Just before his election to the position there had been that tragic episode when the ministerium had all joined in public criticism of the city council regarding the murdered man. Ever since the beginning of the Reformation there had been problems over the relationship between the state and the church and also between pastors/theologians and lay people often of the burgher class, the worst being those involved with the Hardenberg case in Bremen. Such struggles are merely the continuation of medieval tensions between Christian rulers and the church and between the anticlericalism of prominent laity (and probably not-so-prominent laity) and the clergy.

In the proposals that Chemnitz made to the city council of Braunschweig he wanted a clear area for the church to determine its teaching and carry out its discipline, unmolested by the state, yet supported by it. He does not call upon the state to punish the sins of Christian church members but rather to let the church set its own ecclesiastical penalties. But in Chemnitz' scheme there is no place for inquisitors, as suggested in Brenz' proposals. In Chemnitz the state has a role more closely approximating that of maintaining public morals and order rather than acting as the punitive agent of the church. The difficulty was that public morals were almost entirely based on biblical standards, and thus the separation of church and state was almost obliterated, as it still is today in certain areas. It is interesting that Chemnitz comes much closer to Luther than Brenz does,[4] in that both had an inherent uneasiness with the concept of the princes serving as secular bishops over the church. Chemnitz wanted greater freedom for the church in matters of theology and discipline, and, unlike Brenz, he does not ask or even want the state directly to carry out church discipline, but only to allow the church to do so. In the episode in 1567 he had seen the failure of the state to handle the murder case properly, and thus he wanted the church discipline aspect of such matters put back under the church. Chemnitz perhaps also saw the forceful but benevolent personality of Julius coming on the scene; he saw any mistakes Mörlin may have made; he had seen certain problems arise among the clergy; he knew his own strengths and weaknesses; he knew the great number of calls he had received to other places and the great popularity he enjoyed throughout Germany; and thus he seemingly felt, despite the fact that the salary as superintendent was as great as that of a Wittenberg professor, that now was the time to get a few things straightened out while he was in a strong position.

Thus, before accepting the position the council had offered him, Chemnitz made his counterproposal, with sections dealing with the clergy, with the city council, and with the financial officers, giving the terms under which he intended to carry out his duties.

To the clergy he said the following:

1. Since in this praiseworthy church there has been up to the present, through God's special grace, a blessed and godly unity, it will be my total concern that this church, through the grace of God, may retain and increase this unity against all sects and errorists. But since a truly blessed and continuing unity must be created by the bonds of the Spirit, so that we may be one in the faith, Ephesians 4, and all speak with one voice, Romans 15, there is great need that we remain together solidly in the accepted *corpus doctrinae*. And just as we preach and teach the positive points in the one Spirit, so we will all fight on the same side in necessary controversies and stand together against errors, and when new conflicts arise, we will not each follow his own judgment and personal opinion but rather will deliberate together in conference over the points under controversy. Likewise the young brethren must not each follow and trust in his own notions and seek out things that are new and bring them into the pulpit or spring them on the people.

2. Likewise, we must all stick together, as we have in the past, and retain the practice that each does not build up himself or act as lord in his congregation and do what he pleases in preaching, administration of the sacraments, liturgical practices, discipline and the other aspects of his office, acting only according to his own ideas, but rather all these things shall be and remain the business of the entire ministerium. And because the conference meets regularly every two weeks, matters of this kind should be brought there and discussed, matters that are problems of the whole church and require our mutual concern or consideration.

3. There must be among the members of the ministerium brotherly unity and friendship not only in matters pertaining to the ministry but also in their common life and conversation. Therefore, there must be no belittling or speaking evil of one another, but rather when some complaint arises, the matter must be put before the conference and settled while the meeting is still in session, so that a person does not leave the meeting without reconciliation.

4. If I notice something pertaining to the office or life in a brother, I must speak about it either privately or before the whole conference, gently and with brotherly seriousness, and the brethren must not treat this with disdain or anger but accept it in humility. Likewise, if a brother finds some fault or failure in my person or the conduct of my office or my life, he shall treat me in the same way. In this way we will by God's grace properly guide the church when in our conferences we say nothing about other people's problems but talk only among ourselves about how we can improve things.

Chemnitz also made the point that though he sought no personal honor, the brethren should give the superintendent due reverence and obedience for the sake of the proper conduct of his office, even though he did not care to be honored for his own sake.

To the city council he proposed the following:

1. The honorable council will abide by the accepted *corpus doctrinae*, and I have no doubt it is your intention to do so. But it is very important to me that before we finalize these arrangements, this matter be clear that I am undertaking the superintendency with the understanding that the council will allow us to remain undisturbed in the *corpus doctrinae* that has been adopted and that the council will permit us to follow sound doctrine and attack all erring contradictions of this on the basis of God's Word and that the person who puts himself in opposition to this *corpus doctrinae* will not be permitted or allowed to remain under our jurisdiction. And if some new result of the Council of Trent or some other error arises, the city council will not depart from the accepted *corpus doctrinae* or remain silent or temporize in opposing such corruptions, as did happen at the time of the Interim, but rather that at the time of such an occurrence the council shall permit the ministerium to establish an appropriate confession against the error, freely and without hinderance. To this end we in

134

the ministerial office shall conduct our office faithfully and diligently in accord with the approved *corpus doctrinae.*

2. The council will allow us to carry out our total ministry, not only what pertains to teaching but also what belongs to the area of discipline, be it for false doctrine or ungodly and offensive life. And if for a short time there are misunderstandings and disputes, the council will continue our salaries so that we have the opportunity to clear up our problems with each other.

In no way do I mean that the council must let us do whatever we wish in the conduct of our ministry, as if it has not Christian authority of its own to call us to account in a legitimate manner, for that would truly be papistic tyranny. But rather, if it seems to the council that we are not conducting our work properly, then the council has the authority, the right, and the power to speak to us and to demand an accounting. Only this must be done in a loving and not in an acrimonious way, and the council must listen to our account of the matter. And if we can demonstrate that we are acting in keeping with good reasons on the basis of God's Word, then we must not be hindered in our work.

3. What pertains to the disciplinary aspect of the ministry, particularly the use of the authority of the ministry, must be based on the Word of God and must always be conducted, if action is to be taken, in such a way that it is not a matter of public knowledge and it must be discussed with you gentlemen personally and confidentially. But the things that are open sins, these must, in keeping with Paul's teaching, be openly rebuked, whether it concerns a little person or an important one, a person in authority, or an underling. And should the council not understand this or accept it, this detracts from their personal conduct of their office. For since the power to govern brings with it a great responsibility, wherein something can easily be carried out or neglected, our God has always sent prophets to the kings so that they may be reminded from God's Word about their duties, instructed, and disciplined. Thus Christian government can use the sword with more joy and authority if God through His Word has given them the sword Himself. It would also produce more willingness and obedience in the subjects toward the discipline of their rulers, if they heard that God through His Word was directing and governing the ruler also. Thus there would be no uproar when the ruler punishes in a Christian way, in keeping with God's command, that which is

worthy of punishment. Luther says of the uproars in his time that if the common man is punished all the time by hanging by the neck and the great lords are not even slapped on the fingers, then there is trouble. But if discipline is carried out in this way, if my lords burden flesh and blood and command such actions [as hanging], then as a result we have a stinking government and the preaching of rebellion.

4. The honorable council will not hinder church discipline but rather help support it, since the binding key is a necessary part of the ministry. I beg rather that the council will understand us correctly as to what we are intending by discipline, for the pope has so confused things with his ungodly ban, that when a person thinks of church discipline, he immediately jumps up and screams that this is the old [Roman] ban and that nothing good will come of it. But this discipline takes place when a person does not attend the preaching of the Word, does not partake of the Sacrament, or lives in open sin, so that the pastor admonishes him to take hold of himself, and he speaks and warns him earnestly on the basis of God's Word to live a better life. Likewise, such a person must not be allowed to stand at a Baptism or help serve at Communion, and if such a person has not attended Communion in the last two years, it must be solemnly stated that there be no singing or music at his grave side.

These things are nothing new or dangerous, and I do not doubt that the honorable council will declare such things to be Christian, since if there were no church discipline, I know that the office of the ministry could not be carried out, since the crude mass of the congregation would only laugh at the preacher's efforts at discipline.

5. As far as the ministerium is concerned, it is necessary that the honorable council will hold to the concept that unity must be preserved within the ministerium, and thus no preacher can be received or called into the conference without the consent of the conference or ministerium, who has not met with and been examined by the conference, and no person may be installed in office without the consent of the superintendent and the ministerium. And if my lords notice a problem with a preacher, they will not immediately cover it up but will tell it to the superintendent and try to improve the situation.

6. Since we must have Christian schools and churches, the inspection of the schools must be part of the responsibility of the superintendent and the conference. The school teachers must be requested and accepted through the superintendent, so that we do not engage people with fanatical notions or offensive lives for our school teachers or people who are permissive of such things. Understand me, my worthy brethren, that in the past I have spent an entire half year to help the schools and support the pastors as they had need.

7. Since the arrangement has been made in the church order that there shall be a coadjutor for the superintendent, and since in many respects the work is the same for both individuals, I want to have for myself the privilege of prior approval, so that the council and the consensus of the church workers do not take action in this area without my knowledge and approval and so that the person who shall be brought into this office shall have the same kind of compatibility with me that I had with Mörlin.

To the financial officers and deacons he proposed this:

The treasurers shall be fathers to the pastors as they carry out their work. They shall also provide for the physical welfare of the pastors, so that they are not in want. And when the plight of the poor is brought to the attention of the pastors, Galatians 2, then the deacons shall follow the testimony of the pastors when alms are distributed, and the preacher shall not refuse to intercede for the poor. Finally the prayers of the congregation should also be called for before the election of the treasurers and the deacons, and the people who are elected to the office of treasurer should be willing to serve. They should have the prior approval of the pastor as to their faith and life.[5]

In the minutes of the ministerium we can still read the statement of Chemnitz that on Sept. 20, 1567, he was unanimously called to the position of superintendent of the city of Braunschweig, and on Sept. 24 his proposals were unanimously accepted by the city council, the ministerium, and the lay officers and deacons. He was installed in office on Oct. 15. At the same meeting the members resolved to send him to Rostock, at their expense, to receive his doctorate. He spent the better part of the year 1568 there and received his degree on June 30, 1568. His disputation dealt with "The Benefits of the Son of God, Our Lord and Savior Jesus Christ."

He was enthusiastically praised by the Rostock faculty not only for his disputation, but also for his great work on the Council of Trent. Rostock was important later also for the significant contributions of David Chytraeus to the peace effort and the Formula of Concord.

Chemnitz was in the midst of publication of several other important treatises, and almost from the day he began his work, other churches were seeking his advice on theological matters. In December of 1568 the council designated Chemnitz and his family as members of the burgher class and obtained from him a promise that he would remain among them for the rest of his life.

From the very beginning Chemnitz was involved in raising the spiritual level of the people, calling for repentance. The pastors should not only preach but also have private admonition about such things as poor church and Communion attendance, an unchristian life, and even gross sins. As a result of this kind of instruction even a convicted murderer was brought to reconciliation with the church and received public absolution. The pastors were to deal with the ordinary run of such things, with the superintendent involved in the more difficult matters. Even the gross sinners did not appear before the entire congregation but before the church council in the presence of lay officers. The refusal of one convicted adulterer of the burgher class to take part in this procedure almost resulted in a rebellion, for he asserted that the pastors were bringing back the papacy, but Chemnitz cooled things by preaching on the subject of Christian church discipline. Ultimately the man complied, and the city council came out strongly in support of the practice of church discipline.[6]

Chemnitz was even successful in getting the women to give up wearing jewelry and other finery to Communion and to wear either white or black clothing as a sign of their humility and Christian piety. No problems developed. 1 Peter 3:3 plus a long quotation from Luther apparently took care of things. The practice of announcing weddings in advance was also adopted, because the city was filled with strangers and refugees, and thus innocent people were protected against fraud and bigamy. He also instituted reforms in the school curriculum and issued directives regarding beggary.

DUKE JULIUS

The second most influential person in Chemnitz' career at Braunschweig was Duke Julius of Braunschweig-Lüneburg (1528–89, reigned 1568–89).[7] Duke Julius' career helps to give us a clearer picture of Chemnitz' life and theology.

Chemnitz' superintendency over the ecclesiastical affairs of the city of Braunschweig was administratively separate and distinct from his close association with Julius, the duke of the duchy of Braunschweig. In addition, unlike the first position, which Chemnitz kept until the time of his retirement in 1584, the second position was always a matter of personal arrangement on the part of Julius. Nevertheless, the two are so intertwined that at some points they are indistinguishable. Fortunately the goals of both the city and the duchy, the superintendent and the duke, were so similar that a pleasant and amiable relationship existed not only between the two men but also between the two political jurisdictions for the next 20 years.

Julius was the son of Henry the Younger, Duke of Braunschweig-Lüneburg, and his wife Mary, the daughter of Duke Henry of Württemberg. Julius was born on June 26, 1528. Injured in infancy by the carelessness of a nurse, he was compelled to wear leg braces and to be carried in a sedan chair for the rest of his life. This caused his father to plan an ecclesiastical career for him, and he had him made a canon at Cologne. As a result, Julius received a superior education and was an expert in Latin. In his later wanderings he also spent some time in Paris and became well acquainted with the French language. He was intellectually, academically, and temperamentally well prepared for the position he finally came to occupy.

A few words are necessary regarding Julius' father, Henry the Younger. Rehtmeyer describes him as "a warlike Duke," and indeed he was, politically, militarily, ecclesiastically, and personally.[8] The Hansa city of Braunschweig and the Free Imperial City of Goslar, about 30 miles southeast of Braunschweig, had become Lutheran at about the same time. They were the two largest and most important cities within Henry's purview, and both had joined the Smalcald League in the 1530s. Henry, on the other hand, had steadfastly supported the emperor and the pope and naturally had joined the

Catholic League. He also was at odds with Philip of Hesse and Elector John Frederick of Saxony who had overrun his territory on July 13, 1542, forced him to flee, and undertook to turn his duchy Lutheran. This was easily done because the people favored it. The duchy was finally converted to Lutheranism in 1545. Henry was released in September of 1545, recaptured by his Lutheran enemies in October of the same year, but eventually restored after Charles' victory at Mülhausen on April 24, 1547. He reigned until his death in 1568. The Reformation was suppressed in the duchy but not in the city of Braunschweig. Henry tried to bring the territory back into the Catholic fold by means of the good Lutheran device of a visitation. Despite his determination and stubbornness he was only partially successful.

The acrimony created by all this uproar involving Henry the Younger was so sharp that by 1546 nearly 100 treatises had been written on this matter, as well as rhymes, songs, and satires—the most famous being Luther's *Against Hanswurst*,[9] which appeared in 1541 along with more than 30 treatises during that single year.[10] Luther's work did not particularly concern itself with the political issues and the personal invective that had arisen but rather with Henry's bad theology because of his continuance with Rome. Thus Luther's work, while intemperate, did concern itself with substantive theological matters and is thus of value to this day. Portions of it dealing with the doctrine of the church were even included in an edition of the Smalcald Articles.[11]

Thus in the mind of Duke Henry not much good could be said about Luther or Lutheranism or the princes of Lutheranism. The pamphleteering had resulted in the military action mentioned above. Finally, in the Battle of Sievershausen of July 9, 1553, the two oldest and most Catholic sons of Henry were killed ("by divine providence" says Rehtmeyer[12]), leaving the poor, neglected, crippled Julius in direct line to the throne.

To top off everything else, Julius had become an avid Lutheran. Reller indicates that the precise reasons for this or the exact time are not known, but a great deal of subsequent history hinges on this decisive action.[13] Naturally Henry was determined to keep Julius from the throne. His first idea was to have his son walled up for the rest of his life as an apostate, and the vault was duly prepared.

But Julius was warned by a servant who used a fire tong to write in the ashes of the fireplace, "Flee, flee." Julius fled with only the clothes on his back. He took refuge with his sister Catharine, who was married to Margrave Hans of Brandenburg-Küstrin. Julius spent several years there and was married there.

Henry had been told by his legal experts that Julius was the lawful heir, a ruling he would not accept. First he tried to make an heir of the unborn child that he hoped would be born to Princess Sophia of Poland whom he had married in 1556, but she remained childless. Then he tried to get his illegitimate son by his mistress Eva von Trott legitimized by the pope, but this failed. This idea was utterly unacceptable to the members of his family and especially to his princely and Lutheran sons-in-law, so after some difficult negotiations Julius returned to his father's court at Wolfenbüttel and lived there quietly. Henry finally recognized the impossibility of converting his son or even of keeping the duchy out of the Lutheran church, and father and son were reconciled. Rehtmeyer relates this little vignette: "Some of the people at the court began singing Luther's hymn 'May God Bestow on Us His Grace.' They were accused by one of the priests of having become heretical Lutherans, and when the duke asked what kind of song they were singing, the reply was, 'May God Bestow on Us His Grace.' The duke responded, 'Shall the devil bestow grace on us? Who shall be gracious to us but God alone?' Thus the priest was regarded as an evil man, and the songs of Luther were publicly sung."[14] Finally, when Henry realized that no council would be held, he came out publicly in support of the Augsburg Confession and departed this life on July 11, 1568, at the age of 79. Not all believe in the genuineness of his virtual death-bed conversion. He was buried according to the Lutheran rite, however, in the Marienkirche in Wolfenbüttel; an epitaph still marks the place where he together with his three sons and their families are memorialized.

On Feb. 25, 1560, Julius married Hedwig, the daughter of Elector Joachim of Brandenburg. To this union were born 11 children, of whom nine survived. Rehtmeyer tells this rather touching and revealing story about a mellower Henry:

> On Oct. 14, 1564, in Hesse was born a highly respected young
> man, whom they had named Henry Julius and whom his noble

grandfather loved very dearly. On one occasion, when the little boy was standing on a table before his grandfather, he grabbed the old man's beard with both hands and pulled hard. The grandfather said to his son Julius, "See, see, my dear son, you are doing very well, and there will still be another little Hanswurst for me."

We shall hear more about this second little Hanswurst, for in 1566, when the boy was two years old, and shortly before the old duke publicly espoused Lutheranism through arrangements made by the old duke, the boy was elected Bishop of Halberstadt, a city a few miles to the east of Braunschweig, with the condition that the administration of the office should for the next 12 years be allowed to remain with the chapter, which was still Roman Catholic.[15]

Julius is described as being the

exact opposite of his father, peace-loving and moderate, thrifty and diligent; always concerned with the welfare of his subjects; united with his wife in an unwavering faithfulness; and dedicated to the evangelical faith. In only one respect was he like his father, Henry: he was an autocrat, who wanted to make all decisions on his own, who refused to be deterred once he had made up his mind to do something . . . and who was sensitive to criticism. Ecclesiastical advisors and councils who refused to obey him and dared to express their own opinions were summarily dismissed.[16]

This treatment ultimately touched Selnecker and Chemnitz along with many others.

Upon Henry's death in 1568 Julius immediately ascended the throne, and his first task was the reformation of the duchy. Kronenberg dates the beginning of the reformation in the duchy from the very day of Henry's death, with Julius' first order being the abolition of the mass.[17] To accomplish this goal he called upon "the indisputable and uncommon learning of the famous superintendent Dr. Martin Chemnitz,"[18] who had only in the previous year become superintendent of the city of Braunschweig. Julius was particularly fond of Chemnitz because he had read some of his writings, and thus on July 28 of that year, 17 days after the death of his father, he invited Chemnitz to come to Wolfenbüttel, a distance of about eight miles, to discuss plans with him. Since Chemnitz had been formally and lawfully called to the city of Braunschweig, a position that he held until his retirement, he first took up Julius' request with the city council of Braunschweig, which he always considered his primary employer and which for generations had had poor relations with the successive dukes. The council advised Chemnitz to proceed. Julius also felt he should consult other Evangelical princes. Thus he asked assistance from his "chosen father," Elector August of Saxony, and also his cousin Duke Christoph of Württemberg. August sent him Nicholas Selnecker, who arrived in 1570, and Christoph sent Dr. Jacob Andreae, the chancellor of the University of Tübingen in Württemberg, who had arrived in 1568. Thus these three important and pivotal figures were brought together. This period of cooperation between the three is of utmost significance for the wooing of Selnecker and Andreae to Chemnitz' points of view. Their cooperation proved to be a dress rehearsal for work on the Formula of Concord. Other theologians and government officials also took part in the discussions.

The plans for the reformation of the duchy on the part of Julius basically embraced four points, all of which he accomplished within the first year of his reign, with the supportive and positive help of Chemnitz. First, as happened in all areas undergoing a reformation, there was to be a visitation of the churches. Second, this was to be accompanied by the drawing up of a church order (*Kirchenordnung*). Third, this in turn would include as its centerpiece the *corpus doctrinae*. Fourth and finally, unique to Braunschweig because of the long and unhappy relationship between duchy and city, Julius with Chemnitz' help developed an oath of allegiance between the people of the city, including their churches, and the duke.[19]

THE VISITATION

The visitation proceeded with amazing speed. The entire concept goes back to Luther, who as early as 1527 worked with the Elector of Saxony to visit and bring order to the churches of Saxony. Several revisions were made in the following years, and the concept of the visitation took hold in all parts of Germany. For example, James Estes has documented a similar project in Württemberg under Brenz, beginning about 1535.[20] In fact, there is a remarkable similarity between Luther's work of 1527 and that of the Braunschweig Church Order of 40 years later; and since Braunschweig was almost the last territorial church to be reformed, there was ample precedent for what Chemnitz and Andreae prepared in the way of instruction for the visitation, which in turn accounts for the speed with which they accomplished the task both of carrying out the visitation and preparing the church order.

> Written instructions were inadequate and thus on-the-spot examinations were also used to determine how the pastors were discharging their duties, how the members were being cared for spiritually, how the financial and business affairs of churches were being conducted, and how the pastors' physical needs were being met. Directions, admonitions, and instructions are more clearly and more effectively given in personal visits.[21]

Luther had insisted on the participation of laypeople, particularly finance people, so that the physical needs of the pastors would not be neglected.[22] Lawyers were usually also included in the visitation, since they together with the pastors were governmental employees.

The visitation in the duchy of Braunschweig under Chemnitz and Andreae was carried out on the basis of the church order that Chemnitz had prepared before the arrival of Andreae and that was revised after the visitation and appeared in revised form as the Church Order of Braunschweig-Lüneburg of 1569.[23] The visitation included not only congregations, but also cloisters, monasteries, the schools at all levels, and the pastors themselves. Even the courses of instruction at the lower grades were stipulated in the church orders. Julius had a list prepared giving the names and locations of all the churches and the names of the pastors, and he included such matters as the patrons, the finances, the inheritances, and rents due the congregations. Both Chemnitz and Andreae were among the visitors who carried out this work, along with other clergy and laypeople. Schedules were set up, and the entire task was accomplished between Oct. 8 and Nov. 15, 1568. As examples of the time involved, 24 pastors were examined at Alfeld on Oct. 28, and on Nov. 10, 14 were examined at Bockenem. Kronenberg, citing records in the church archives, informs us that the visitation produced "a list of pastors who were to be retained (26); pastors who were to be retained on condition that they show significant improvement (90); pastors who should be transferred (13); those who should be retired from office (78); pastoral vacancies (60); those who were questionable because of age (11). There were 278 pastoral positions in all, excluding the city of Braunschweig."[24] They also examined the superintendents, and some of them were questionable. An examination was to be administered every six months thereafter. This was conducted by a man who found time to produce the *Examination of the Council of Trent* in the midst of these duties! Chemnitz held the title under Julius of ecclesiastical advisor and as such also was in charge of the content of both the church order and the *corpus doctrinae.*

Julius also called for an examination of the cloisters and monasteries, which he did not expropriate but kept for the religious use of the Lutheran church, for such things as schools and meeting places. There were actually some celibate women still in some of these cloisters at the time of Chemnitz. Some of these places are still in use as churches and administrative centers.

A number of horror stories emerge from the visitations. For example, Rehtmeyer has the rather raunchy story of a certain presbyter in Wolfenbüttel at the Marienkirche, who remained a papist, and "when the congregation sang 'Lord Keep Us Steadfast in Thy Word,' [perhaps in reference to the 'murderous pope and Turk' in the first stanza] he said openly in the chancel, 'These words come from the hind end of the devil, and smell like their place of origin.' But his mouth was soon stopped, and he was sent packing to Halberstadt."[25] Kronenberg has other stories. One pastor was described as "totally uneducated and useless for the office of the ministry." Another: "This pastor is old, uneducated, responded negatively, has fallen from faith three times, leads a wicked life, and should be dismissed from office." Another: "This pastor answered more like a papist than a Christian, has no understanding of religious matters, leads a wicked life, and must therefore be gotten rid of as quickly as possible." Again: "This pastor is a young, impertinent person, knows neither papistic nor evangelical doctrine, needs to be dressed down." Another was simply called a "numbskull" (*idiota*).[26]

However, the visitation revealed not only weaknesses. It also revealed suffering and hardship. There were heroes among these pastors: They had suffered a great deal for the sake of the Gospel. One had been jailed because he distributed Holy Communion in both kinds. Many others had been driven out by Duke Henry.

Wilhelm Pauck in *The Heritage of the Reformation* has some interesting points regarding the development of the Protestant ministry of the later Reformation period. Because of the centrality of preaching in the thinking of the reformers, this function became paramount, with the result that the term *preacher* [*prediger; predikant*] was the most commonly used title. Pastoral care was also important, and books on pastoral theology appeared as early as the time of Martin Bucer (1491–1551). The terms *pastor* and *minister* came into use later. The term *pfarherr* or parson, was in early use, often to designate the head pastor of a congregation. In Scandinavia the term *priest* (*prest*) continues to this day.[27] Church workers were nearly always designated by the title of the primary purpose for which they were called, and when they held an advanced degree this was used. For example, Luther and Chemnitz and the others who held the doctorate were almost always designated as doctor. Melanchthon was always called Master Philip because this is the highest degree he attained. Luther, Chemnitz, and Melanchthon were not called *pastor* or *preacher,* titles reserved for those actually in the preaching or pastoral office.

Apparently no one actually sat down and planned a strategy for the education or procurement of pastors. Things developed as needs and conditions demanded. There were a few constants, such as the divine institution of the office of the holy ministry (but not fully developed or defined), the concept of the divine call, the centrality of preaching and soul care, the supervision of doctrine and life, the attempt to bring uniformity and order out of the chaos and ignorance that were everywhere. The princes were brought in to help almost from the very beginning. Luther had called them emergency bishops, and no one knew quite how to function with them or without them. No well-formulated doctrine of church government or of the relationship between church and state was ever developed in Lutheranism purely on the basis of Scripture, the early Confessions, or the history and tradition of the church. Perhaps it was impossible to do so. There was a great shortage of pastors, yet caution had to be observed to keep out charlatans and fortune-seekers.

Pauck tells us that the visitations "showed that many preachers were rough and uncouth fellows, careless and sloppy in their way of life and manner of dress and inattentive to their duties. The most common complaint about them was that they drank too much. . . . Mathesius . . . tells of a preacher who took a jug of beer with him into the pulpit." In Hesse they even called for the jail to be reopened for such preachers.[28] The pay was poor and many pastors were living in poverty. But the presence of wives helped to improve morals and behavior, and gradually the lot and the position of the clergy improved.

Great efforts were made to prepare competent pastors, and much of Chemnitz' time was devoted to the education of clergy. Universities, including Helmstedt in the duchy of Braunschweig, sprang up in nearly all Lutheran territories that had as one of their primary purposes the education of clergymen. The actual situation in the late Reformation period was that there were two levels of clergy, the educated and university trained men and those with minimal or inferior training. The courts, the cities, the universities, and the administrative posts got the better educated men, and the rural areas and villages the less educated and less competent. In fact, in some areas if a rural man wanted to aspire to a city church, he would have to undergo another series of examinations, often involving further education. Ultimately, the goal was reached that all pastors were to be university trained, but this took many years.

The visitation continued to be the most popular and effective method of determining the condition of the churches in both the cities and the territorial areas, and they were of some help in identifying not only problems but also potential leadership and in developing some form of organization. As we see in the case of Chemnitz himself, the various cities and territorial churches were free in borrowing manpower from one another. Another result was that by this cross-pollenization, the organizational structures, the liturgies, and the theology of the various churches came to be quite similar. But one of the constant problems was leadership. This void came to be filled more and more by the princes serving as "bishops" who exercised the function of "nursing fathers" or "the chief members of the church." As might be expected, this chaotic organizational condition produced an ever-expanding list of doctrinal problems and deviations. We saw this in the case of Luther and Carlstadt as early as the 1520s, and it never ends. The eternal question always is this: Who is in charge?

The visitation in the duchy of Braunschweig involved an examination of both the superintendents and the entire clergy. Chemnitz, under his title of ecclesiastical advisor, directed the preparation and content of the church order and the *corpus doctrinae,* which were completed in 1569 and which served as the basis for the theological examination in connection with the visitation, and thus the standard for membership in the ministerium of both duchy and city. In his office under the duke, Chemnitz also served as chairman of the consistory, which was the governing ecclesiastical body, making him the chief ecclesiastical and theological leader of the principality, without, however, giving up his position as superintendent of the city.[29]

The work load for a preacher was onerous. Luther in *The German Mass* tells us that in Wittenberg there were three Sunday sermons on the Epistle and Gospel for the day, followed by a vesper with a sermon on the Old Testament lesson, in all cases following the pericopal series for the church year. Then on Monday and Tuesday mornings there was a German sermon on the Ten Commandments, the creeds, the Lord's Prayer, Baptism, or the Lord's Supper. On Wednesday there was a sermon on a text from Matthew, on Saturday vespers on John. On Thursdays and Fridays there was a sermon on an epistle.[30] At least one church service was held every day, but in the rural areas there were less. The Wittenberg schedule probably obtained in most cities. Most large parishes had several pastors. The use of sermons prepared by others, particularly by Luther, in the early period, was common and quite understandable. Better a good sermon copied than a poor one delivered. The art of preaching also had to be developed, because it had become almost an unknown art under Rome. A part of the work of the superintendent was to teach men to preach. Melanchthon was also occupied with this work in Saxony. The sermons were long, and most of them not very interesting. Bugenhagen is reported on one occasion to have preached a seven-hour sermon. The churches were unheated.

CHEMNITZ' *ENCHIRIDION*

Another outgrowth of Chemnitz' work in the visitation as well as the *corpora doctrinae* (see next section) was the publication in 1569 and in several succeeding years of his *Enchiridion,* dedicated to the spiritual leaders of the duchy of Braunschweig. First published under the title *Die fürnemsten Heuptstück der christlichen lehre, wie darin die pastores der kirchen im fürstenthumb Braunschweig etc. in den jerlichen visitationibus also examiniret.* . . . (The main points of the Christian doctrine on which the pastors of the churches in the duchy of Braunschweig, etc. shall be examined in the annual visitations. . . .) (This work was translated into English under the title *Ministry, Word, and Sacraments: An Enchiridion* by Luther Poellot, [St. Louis: Concordia, 1981].) It received the name *Enchiridion* in its 1593 edition, published by Polycarp Leyser. It was of great importance in establishing the theological direction of the church of Braunschweig and neighboring churches, since it was used in the initial examination and then in the annual or semiannual examinations administered to each pastor in the territory. The work appeared in both German and Latin. Thus all the pastors in the duchy had basically the same theological training, reaffirmed every six months, as first set forth by Chemnitz in his questions and answers.

By 1593 Leyser as Chemnitz' successor at Braunschweig republished the 1579 version of the work, dedicated to the clergy of the duchies both of Braunschweig and Lüneburg, and also reinforced it by the addition of Urbanus Rhegius' work. Leyser's work came to fill more than 600 pages and included besides the basic *Enchiridion* also Rhegius' *De Caute Loquendi* and Chemnitz' *Wolgegründter Bericht,* or *De Caute Sentiendi.* By the 1603 edition of this work, Chemnitz' treatise on the Jesuits had also been added. Leyser liked Chemnitz very much. Chemnitz (even back in 1569) shows his love for the use of theses and antitheses, and this practice is followed in the Formula of Concord in part at his insistence. The entire preface of Leyser is worth reading in the Poellot edition, *Ministry, Word, and Sacraments.*

THE CHURCH ORDER

The church order for the duchy of Braunschweig was completed by Chemnitz and Andreae between Oct. 17 and 29, 1568, used in connection with the visitation, published in revised form on Jan. 1, 1569, and sent out to each church and monastery shortly thereafter. Chemnitz had the unique position of being directly tied to a city council for his work in the city of Braunschweig, including the preparation of its church order, and yet being the chief theological and ecclesiastical advisor to Duke Julius, the ruler of the duchy, thus giving him a hand in both areas of church administration. The superintendent in a city usually had more freedom than his counterpart in a territorial church, and the city clergy were thus more powerful and independent, but not entirely so, as the city councils had prerogatives also. Actually Chemnitz had produced the *corpus doctrinae,* which was the centerpiece of the church order, before Andreae came; but the two men together prepared the church order in only 12 days time, basing their work on the church orders of their respective areas, the Württemberg Order of 1559, in which Andreae had had a part, and the Lüneburg Order of 1564, in which Mörlin and Chemnitz had had a role. The resulting document covered church law, directions for worship and church ceremonies, liturgies for special days, the agenda for all official acts, directives for the conduct of the office of all church servants, and directions regarding the schools. Also included were directives for the work of caring for the poor, the hospitals, the orphanages, the beggars, and even the monasteries. There were also regulations regarding the lawful calling (*rite vocatus*) of pastors; their placement, installation, ordination, salaries, and housing; and nearly every aspect of their work. Likewise there was a section under church law regarding marriage, divorce, the forbidden degrees of matrimony, parents, and children.[31] Divorce was permitted for adultery, desertion, and certain other causes, such as brutality. The forbidden degrees of matrimony were rigorously maintained.[32]

There was already the feeling that these church orders should be as much alike as possible. Kronenberg states,

> What the duke wanted was a church order that was, first of all, faithful in every detail to the Word of God and the Christian Augsburg Confession. In regard to ceremonies, however, he also

150

wanted the neighboring churches of this principality to have as much similarity as possible, so that the disparity in rites would not result in offense being taken by the undiscerning and by those Christians who are not adequately trained in God's Word.[33]

The church orders attempted to lay down regulations that were in keeping with Scripture; and when dealing with matters not specifically touched on in Scripture; then the injunction of the apostle that "everything should be done in a fitting and orderly way" (1 Cor. 14:40) was utilized. For example, in the area of church festivals, all from the Catholic times were kept that pertained to Christ, except the Corpus Christi, and those dealing with Mary were kept except for the festival of her assumption. The Braunschweig Church Order included rites for Baptisms, churching of mothers, confirmation, confession, weddings, visitations of the sick, private Communion, and burials.[34]

It became almost universal that when a congregation desired the services of a pastor, the man went through one or more oral examinations and a trial sermon before the ministerium and the church council, sometimes also before the duke. Thus both clergy and laity were involved in the calling process. If a man measured up, he was ordained (in the case of his first call) and then installed into office. The ordination was regarded as a public confirmation of the fact that the man had been called. Ordination was normally performed by the superintendent or bishop, but in some cases, as in Chemnitz' own, the ordination was performed by a faculty member. As time went on, the role of the faculties gained in importance in normal church administration; but, as Pauck points out, this was a two-edged sword because sometimes the professors involved their ministerial students in their own theological quarrels, and thus new controversies were introduced into the congregations.[35] The ordination vow was increasingly used to secure the subscription of the candidate both to Scripture and the general Lutheran Confessions but also to the church order and *corpus doctrinae* of the particular city or territory. Chemnitz in his *Loci Theologici* gives a good picture of the way in which the call and ordination were regarded in his day, which was much like our own.[36] But in no case within Lutheranism do we find any reference to special spiritual gifts or an indelible character attached to the office of bishop, superintendent, faculty member, pastor, or to the rite of ordination itself. The authority came from the Word and not from anything inherent in any ecclesiastical office beyond the terms of the call extended by the church.

The superintendents, while in many cases not holding the title of bishop until after World War II, certainly carried out the function of this office, although usually on a more limited geographical scale.[37]

The chief function of the superintendent was the supervision of the doctrine and life of the pastors, their education and examination, and the overall care of the congregations. The call was understood to be both inner and outer, but the outward call was the one that received the attention of the church and placed a man in the so-called public ministry. This is the ministry to which the term *rite vocatus,* or *legitime vocatus,* was applied. The terms under which this call was extended have been mentioned above. Implicit in the concept of *rite vocatus* was also the pastor's right to leave the place of his call or to resign and the right of the calling agency, state, congregation, or ecclesiastical official to remove him from office. Pastoral conferences were regularly held, with those in Braunschweig being examples for many others. These conferences were designed to uphold sound doctrine, to create and maintain unity, to inform the pastors of current activities, and to bring moral and doctrinal miscreants into line. Bible study and doctrinal discussion were major features.

The Reformation created a new social and vocational class of clergy, but it was no longer the clerical caste system that had existed under the papacy. The preacher was basically a middle-class, or burgher-class, person. The nobility no longer went into the clergy as they had done under Rome, and in some cases the nobility were barred from the Protestant ministry, although the upper classes and nobility had supplied most of the ruling clergy under the pope.[38] The middle-class status of the Lutheran clergy kept young men of the nobility out, which was probably for the ultimate good of all, yet very early in the late Reformation period we begin to see the emergence of clergy dynasties, wherein the sons and later genealogical heirs of certain prominent clergymen carried on generation after generation sometimes for over a century. This was noteworthy in

Chemnitz' own family and also in such other families as the Carp-zovius family. There was also a considerable amount of intermar-riage among the children of clergymen, just as today. On the other hand, few clergy came from the peasant class.

Aside from the members of the burgher class and the nobility, the laity had few special rights. In nearly all cases the closest the laity ever got to the calling of their pastors was at the level of the church or city council. But serious attempts were made to work with the laity in a meaningful manner. The doctrine of the universal priesthood of all believers had not been entirely forgotten,[39] although it was not at the center of the ecclesiastical stage at this period. Great care was taken that pastors had the ability to teach and to preach and to work with their people. Church discipline was instituted for the spiritual welfare of the people. Great con-cern was shown for the faith, the morals, and the general welfare of the parishioners. The work of caring for the poor, the aged, the orphans, the sick, and the education of the young was placed in the hands of the clergy. Strenuous efforts were made to keep chil-dren and young people safe from worldliness and temptation. The church orders give careful instructions for the founding and opera-tions of schools, the qualifications of teachers, and the course of instruction, especially in the area of religion. Catechisms, especially Luther's Small Catechism, were produced en masse, especially after the general and widespread ignorance of the people became known. Various kinds of sermonic material quickly came into use to aid pastors in their ministrations. Nearly all preaching was highly doctrinal, but it had practical purposes for the edification of the flock. Great stress was laid on proper instruction preceding the proper and regular use of the Lord's Supper. A form of private con-fession and absolution was retained for this purpose. Pastors were generally held in high esteem, and it was almost blasphemous to speak evil of a pastor.

Nor were women omitted from the concerns of the church. The educated women, such as Mrs. Urbanus Rhegius, were held in great honor, and their opinions sought and respected. Duke Julius' wife, Duchess Hedwig, shared in many of his theological discussions and decisions. The history of the period is filled with examples of noble and dedicated women who contended for the Lutheran faith, who carried their protests to the rulers, who exercised strong influence on the religious and moral atmosphere of the parsonage, the community, and the court. The *programma* on the occasion of Chemnitz' reception of his doctorate at Rostock signed by Simon Pauli, D.Th. and dean and Lukas Backmeiester D.Th. was dated "on the day of the meeting [*congressus*] of the holy matrons Mary and Elizabeth, which was the first church council [*synodus*] of the New Testament."[40] Pauck tells of one woman, Wilbrandis Rosenblatt, who was married in succession to John Oecolampadius, Wolfgang Capito, and finally to Martin Bucer.[41] Several times a year Chemnitz conducted Bible or catechism classes to which all members, including women and children, were invited.

THE *CORPUS DOCTRINAE*

The duchy of Braunschweig was almost the last state in Germany to draw up a church order and the *corpus doctrinae* which was included as part of the church order. For purposes of definition we might begin by pointing out that a *corpus doctrinae* is the doctrinal, theological, or confessional portion of the church order, representing the formally and lawfully adopted doctrinal position of a city or territorial church. In the case of cities, this was done by the city council, and in the case of territories by the ruling prince. The *corpus doctrinae* normally consisted of the public doctrinal statements to which the church subscribed. Thus, included in the *corpora doctrinae* of all Lutheran churches was first Scripture and then the ancient creeds, following the example of the Augsburg Confession, then the Augsburg Confession itself, the basic doctrinal platform of Lutheranism. The *corpus doctrinae* was included in the church order, but the church order was much broader and dealt with many more items than the simple theological or confessional basis of the church. In a sense the ancient creeds were the *corpus doctrinae* for the church of that era, and the practice revived at the time of the Reformation when the Lutherans were compelled at Augsburg to make a public confession of their faith.

The ancient creeds were always included in the Lutheran *corpora doctrinae,* as well as the so-called Lutheran Confessions, or Symbols, but as the years went on, some churches adopted more confessions or additions to their *corpus doctrinae*, and others less, depending often on the caprice of a ruler or the political situation. For example, the King of Denmark wanted nothing to do with the Formula of Concord and banned it in his territories, while many of the German princes insisted on its adoption and use in theirs. Likewise Julius of Braunschweig after lavish support of the Formula of Concord, at the end refused to have his duchy subscribe to it because he became angry at Martin Chemnitz. It was their common adherence to the Augsburg Confession and the almost universal use of Luther's Small Catechism that caused these cities and territorial churches to recognize one another as Lutheran churches. Julius introduced his church order thus: "We, Julius, by the grace of God, Duke of Braunschweig and Lüneburg, wholeheartedly pledge ourselves without any reservations whatsoever to this *corpus doctrinae*, which is set forth in this our church order, . . . and we are resolved, by the grace of God, to abide by it steadfastly, firmly, and without deviation until we die."[42] It was signed by Julius himself, his wife the duchess, along with Chemnitz, Selnecker, and Kirchner, the professors at the Gandersheim school (which was the closest thing to a university that Braunschweig had at that time), and all the pastors of the duchy.

Inge Mager tells us that actually the practice of drawing up *corpora doctrinae* goes back to the Augsburg Confession itself, and that this practice was widely carried on in Lower Saxony as early as the 1540s in the Hansa cities of Hamburg, Lübeck, and Lüneburg, where the noted Hamburg superintendent and theologian John Äpin began writing treatises on various subjects which were adopted by the area territorial churches. Covered were such matters as the Interim, adiaphora, Osiandrianism, and Majorism (all of which Chemnitz touches upon in his *Iudicium*). Äpin's successor, Paul von Eitzen, wrote a treatise on the Lord's Supper that achieved the same status in Hamburg. By 1560 every pastor in these churches was required to subscribe to these documents. This action in 1560 by the Hamburg city council represented the first action by any Lutheran group toward the formal adoption of an area *corpus doctrinae*, but the idea caught on and was actually supported by Melanchthon himself, who at first had opposed it.[43] By 1560 the same pastors were also required to make formal subscription to the Augsburg Confession, its Apology, the Smalcald Articles, and Luther's Small Catechism. In other words, there were generic Lutheran Confessions to which all subscribed, and then there were specific local doctrinal statements (*doctrinalia*) to which only those in particular areas had to subscribe. Interestingly, while the efforts were being made for the adoption of the Formula of Concord in all Lutheran areas, at the same time local churches were also adopting their particular local doctrinal statements. Both were important and were not contradictory to one another.

Finally, shortly before his death Melanchthon on his own and without the request of any church began to prepare his own *corpus doctrinae*, which appeared in 1560, shortly after his death, as the *Corpus Doctrinae Christianae,* or *Philippicum,* or *Misnicum.* It contained only material written by Melanchthon himself and apparently was intended to be broad enough to include all Protestants. As was the case with most things prepared by Melanchthon in those years, this received vigorous opposition. The Lüneburg Convention of July 1561, with representatives of the three lead cities of Lower Saxony (Lübeck, Hamburg, Lünburg) plus Bremen, Rostock, Magdeburg, Wismar, and Braunschweig, formally adopted Mörlin's *Erklerung . . . und kurtzer Bericht* (the Lüneburg Articles), which was much more pointed in its confession of sound Lutheranism. The convention also specifically condemned Osiandrianism, Majorism, enthusiastic Sacramentarianism, and Adiaphorism, all of which Chemnitz had condemned in his writings of the same year, his *Iudicium* and his attack on Hardenberg. The convention also reacted against the Council of Trent, against which Chemnitz was writing at the very time. At the same meeting, the delegates of the Lower Saxon cities also were critical of the new preface to the Augsburg Confession prepared by Melanchthon and stated:

> However, so that all men might know how we understand and defend the Augsburg Confession in our churches and that we are not introducing anything new or foreign or any contradictory opinions and corruptions into the Augustana, we are retaining the same sense that was expressed in its Apology, as well as in the Smalcald Articles, and finally also in the catechisms and other writings of the sainted Luther, all on the basis of God's Word.[44]

In addition to authorizing the church order for the reorganization of the church in the duchy of Braunschweig, Duke Julius placed the greatest emphasis of all on what he considered the heart of the church order, namely, the *corpus doctrinae*, the doctrinal basis for his newly reformed church. The main human instrument used by Julius for the preparation and writing of this document was Martin Chemnitz. However, there were many forerunners for this work. In 1557 Mörlin, in cooperation with the superintendents of Hamburg, Lübeck, and Lüneburg, had written the Eight Articles, which were designed to bring peace between Flacius and Wittenberg on the question of adiaphora. Consensus was to be achieved on the basis of the Augsburg Confession, its Apology, and the Smalcald Articles. This document was really the beginning of the Braunschweig *corpus doctrinae*.

Also in 1557 Mörlin prepared Six Rules for Normative Doctrines, again based on the same three early Lutheran Confessions, plus "other writings of Luther." This also had to be subscribed to by the pastors of the city.

All of the above set the stage for the ultimate adoption of the *corpora doctrinae* of both the city and the duchy of Braunschweig. Mörlin's *Erklerung* was included in the Braunschweig city *corpus* in 1563, a document that Mager informs us was prepared largely by Mörlin together with Chemnitz.[45] The same *corpus doctrinae* also contained a high German translation of Bugenhagen's original church order of 1528–31, together with the Augsburg Confession, its Apology, the Smalcald Articles of Luther, and Melanchthon's Treatise on the Power and Primacy of the Pope.

As indicated above, the *corpus doctrinae* of the city of Braunschweig also played a significant role in the installation of Chemnitz as superintendent in 1567. In the conditions he laid down for both the clergy and the city council he refers to the *corpus doctrinae*.

In connection with his installation he refers to the Lüneburg meeting of 1561 and writes:

> In 1561, because of the need and opportunity of their churches, the honorable cities of [Lower] Saxony sent their political delegates and their leading theologians to Lüneburg, where they prepared a number of articles. And in order to preserve Christian tranquillity

and continuing unity in the churches, the honorable council of the noble city of Braunschweig gave orders to print along with their church order a *corpus* [*doctrinae*] which included the Augsburg Confession and its Apology, which was first sent to Charles V in 1530 and again in 1531 after its first printing. It also included the articles that Luther wrote for Smalcald and finally also the Lüneburg Articles . . . which were binding for all its pastors, teachers, and congregations.[46]

Note that the Augsburg Confession now is specifically identified as the 1530–31 edition, and a little later Chemnitz refers to both of Luther's catechisms.

The 1568 church order for the duchy of Braunschweig-Lüneburg was produced almost entirely by Chemnitz before Andreae arrived on the scene.[47] Sehling tells us, "Martin Chemnitz is the sole author of the *Kurzer Bericht.* As early as Sept. 16, 1568, shortly after the arrival of Andreae in Wolfenbüttel, he presented this document for the attention of the duke, and Andreae had declared himself to be in agreement with it."[48] It calls for subscription to the three ancient creeds, the Augsburg Confession of 1530, its Apology, the Smalcald Articles, the [Small] Catechism, and "other writings of Luther."

It is also manifest in the *corpus doctrinae* of 1568–69 that Chemnitz is reacting vigorously against the *Corpus Doctrinae Philippicum,* which while never widely accepted had been accepted in 1566 in Saxony. Thus he specifies that a *corpus doctrinae* must not be a privately produced document but "must consist of documents issued in the name of the people, approved and accepted by them; they must be documents like the Augsburg Confession, its Apology, and the Smalcald Articles, among which must also be considered the Small and Large Catechisms of Luther."[49] At this point Mager quite correctly refers to the *corpus doctrinae* as *Das Braunschweiger Bekenntnisbuch* (The Braunschweig confessional book).[50]

THE OATH OF ALLEGIANCE

Duke Julius was not only a devoted Lutheran and a strong promoter of the Reformation. He was also a clever man. He was fully aware of the bad relationship between his father and the largest city in the duchy, a relationship created largely by the religious quarrel. This had now been cleared up, and Julius saw in this situ-

CHEMNITZ' SUPERINTENDENCY

ation an opportunity to improve his political relationships with the city, as well as to achieve confessional solidarity with the city he and his father had so much coveted. But he faced a city filled with grievances and suspicion, so he proceeded cautiously. It was customary at the beginning of a reign to call for an oath of allegiance.[51] This Julius also did, and in 1569 he secured from the nobles of his realm such an oath. He also asked for such an oath from the city of Braunschweig, but since all of the grievances had not yet been handled, the city council submissively congratulated him but refused to give the oath until Julius was willing to give them a letter of peace regarding all the disputed points. Finally on Aug. 10 the duke yielded and a treaty was signed. Thereupon the duke, his royal mother, his wife, and the crown prince, together with other notables entered the city with great pomp, and on Oct. 3 he received the oath of homage and allegiance from the council and burgers of the city, including the leaders of the five townlets, or subdivisions, into which the city in a peculiar manner was divided. The oath reads as follows: "That we will hold to the gracious master Duke Julius of Braunschweig-Lüneburg and the royal family and will be true and faithful to them as the rightful trustees of our money and [we grant them the right] to hold the treasure of the city of Braunschweig and our properties, so God and His Word help us."[52] The act of submission was accompanied by a congratulatory speech to the family, a panegyric poem on the history of the duke of Braunschweig. The duke passed out a great deal of money for the occasion. And a new beginning was made that lasted for many generations.

But no oath of allegiance was of much value without the cooperation and participation of the church, and there was one thing the duke particularly wanted from the city and its churches, namely, the services and support of their famous and highly respected superintendent. He also wanted peace and harmony with the city, especially the church. As indicated previously, the duke in his desire to speed the reformation of his duchy had engaged the services of Andreae from Württemberg and Selnecker from Saxony. Chemnitz and company had expressed great dissatisfaction with Andreae's earlier efforts to come to a painted-over peace with the Wittenbergers, and when Selnecker arrived in Braunschweig the first thing that met him was a protest against his support for the *Corpus Doc-*

trinae Philippicum and a letter from Chemnitz vigorously objecting to his position. Since peace and homage were the order of the day, Chemnitz as superintendent of the city, on behalf of the ministerium, presented to the duke the church order of the city. He pointed out both that it was older than that of the duchy and was officially recognized by all the pastors and churches of the city and would continue to receive this recognition. As an outgrowth of their *corpus doctrinae,* they had prepared a document called *Erklerung aus Gottes Wort und kurzer Bericht, der Hearen Theologen. . .* (A simple Christian explanation and brief report of the ministerium [of the Churches of the City of Braunschweig]). This document, called the *Erklerung,* or *Declaration,* had been written by Mörlin as superintendent.

There were five important churches in the city, one in each of the townlets, that in the Catholic days had been endowed and maintained by the duke. They were the Martin Church where Chemnitz had his pastoral call, the Catharine Church, the Andrew, the Magnus, and the Ulric, the latter of which had been merged with the ancient monastic church of the Brothers and called the Ulrici-Brüdern Kirche. All of these churches still stand and are in regular use today. In Chemnitz' day the term *saint* was not applied to the name of a church, though obviously in Catholic times the name had been St. Martin's, etc. In previous times these churches had been endowed by the dukes, but when the city became Lutheran and the quarrel with Duke Henry warmed up, he had ceased subsidizing them. As a result they had to limp along on half of their normal income, plus income from vacant parishes that was allocated to them. This situation called for examination. Duke Julius restored the subsidy, but with money goes control. He wanted an oath of allegiance from the people involved, plus a say in filling the pulpits. Thus the duke insisted on nominating the head pastors for these five churches along with a lay representative from each church. These people, usually mature and seasoned men, then automatically became members of the consistory. The duke then restored to the churches their incomes, rents, interest, and other income due them, including provision for the care of the pastors when they became old. Each pastor was given a letter of call from the duke, and the congregation and was made a member of the consistory. On the other hand, each pastor had to pass the examinations imposed by the city and subscribe to the city church order as well as that of the duchy, which was not difficult since the two were much alike and certainly in agreement theologically. When this was done, the duke installed and invested them. He also gave a certain amount of freedom to the pastors to speak out against current evils and in extreme cases to name names, something that the pastors were anxious to do and the rulers frowned upon.

The point of Chemnitz' strong opposition to Selnecker's suggestion that the *Corpus Doctrinae Philippicum* be imported into Braunschweig came not only from his theological disagreement with Melanchthon's work, but also from his belief that it would disrupt the sensitive relations between the city and the duchy, which had been so carefully worked out in connection with the oath of allegiance.[53] This oath of allegiance was important because it was a public recognition by all parties that after the decades of poor relationship between duke and city, peace had come at last. This meant that the city clergy subscribed both to their own church order, including the *corpus doctrinae,* but also to the ducal church order of 1569. Chemnitz saw to it that in agreeing to sign the ducal church order, they were saying that it was in total accord with the city church order, although there were some differences in wording and also in external ceremonies. Obviously he felt that both were in accord with Scripture and the Augsburg Confession, but when push came to shove the city *corpus* took precedence.

This oath of allegiance proved beneficial also because it prevented people who wanted to escape certain doctrinal responsibility from pitting one *corpus* against the other, as happened in the case of Chemnitz' successor, John Heidenreich, who tried to evade signing the city *corpus doctrinae* because the duchy had not done so. Heidenreich had a quarrel with Polycarp Leyser, who ultimately replaced him as superintendent of the city. Chemnitz' hand was further strengthened by the fact that Westphal of Hamburg committed his churches to the Braunschweig ducal *corpus doctrinae,* and so did Rostock and Mecklenburg.

Then in August of 1570 Julius attended an important meeting of Lower Saxon delegates at Paul's Church in his own Wolfenbüttel, to which he brought along his two favorite theologians, Andreae and Selnecker, to see and be seen and to bear witness to their sub-scription to the ducal *corpus doctrinae* and to give assurance that they would introduce no other. Julius also asserted his own sub-scription for the rest of his life. This acceptance by these three men also included the *Declaration,* or *Erklerung,* of Chemnitz. The meet-ing also afforded an opportunity for Chemnitz to explain to the pastors of both city and duchy the precise terms of the oath of alle-giance and the investiture of the five men, including the financial arrangements. Again the *Erklerung* was reaffirmed, as were the Augsburg Confession of 1530, the Apology, the Smalcald Articles, the two catechisms of Luther, and the Lüneburg Articles of Mörlin. Everyone had his chance for questions, and when the meeting ended the problems were in the past, the difficulties between city and duchy settled, and all was well. They refused to consider Andreae's *Conciliations,* a document they considered too weak. After a few more explanations and apologies, the problems with Selnecker were resolved, at least as far as Chemnitz was concerned. However, Selnecker was always unhappy at Braunschweig, and he finally left for the happier climate of the University of Leipzig.

FURTHER WORK ON THE *CORPORA DOCTRINAE*

Chemnitz' work with *corpora doctrinae* did not end with the adoption of the Braunschweig Ducal Church Order of 1569. The Göttingen Church Order of 1568 certainly reflects the Braunschweig City Order with which Chemnitz had been actively involved. He was also directly involved with the last two *corpora doctrinae* to be adopted in Lower Saxony, both in 1575–76: the one for the duchy of Lüneburg-Celle called the *Corpus Doctrinae Wilhelminum* for Duke Wilhelm, and the other a revision of the 1569 Duchy of Braunschweig *corpus* called the *Corpus Doctrinae Julium,* dated 1576. Note that these two documents were adopted only a year before the beginning of the adoption of the Formula of Concord. But both of these later *corpora doctrinae* are important because of the excellent content, the close involvement of Chemnitz, and their relationship with the Formula of Concord.

The *Corpus Doctrinae Wilhelminum* arose out of two develop-ments. One was a minor skirmish over a new document for examining candidates for the ministry that seemed to call for an authoritative settlement, and the other was the appearance of a new treatise that was so good that it deserved confessional status, namely, Chemnitz' appendix to the earlier writing of Urbanus Rhegius, his *Formulae quaedam caute et citra scandalum loquendi.* . . . (Certain formulas for speaking carefully and without offense) of 1535. Rhegius as a refugee from Augsburg had been called to Celle as its superintendent. His *Formulae caute loquendi* was known and appreciated in that area. Chemnitz personally had a high appreciation for the work. He cites it repeatedly in his *Loci Theologici.* Apparently, without any fanfare or perhaps even a request, Chemnitz produced an appendix, or update, to Rhegius' work. It was brief, to the point, in thetical form, easy to read and comprehend, and written in both Latin and German. At some point Chemnitz produced and published this appendix but did not claim any credit for it. It was simply regarded by most people as an additional work by Rhegius. The ministerium at Braunschweig knew of its true origin, and in 1592 in a treatise called *Rettung der Ehren . . . Martin Chemnitz* (Preserving the reputation . . . of Martin Chemnitz), they mentioned the treatise. In Chemnitz' own will, which he wrote in 1580, he asserts that he wrote the appendix and considered it one of his best works.[54] The German title of 1576 is "Wolgegründter Bericht" . . . ("A Solidly Grounded Report"), and the Latin of 1575 is "Appendix de Formulis recte sentiendi, pie, circumspecte et citra scandalum loquendi de praecipuis horum temporum controversiis" . . . ("An appendix concerning formulas for believing correctly and speaking piously, carefully, and without scandal regarding the major controversies of these times"). There is a great likelihood that Duke Wilhelm, knowing of Rhegius' important connection with the city of Celle and learning of Chemnitz' high regard for the document, asked Chemnitz to help in republishing the original along with his own appendix as part of the revised church order for his duchy.[55] Krumwiede makes the following remarks regarding the Rhegius work: "In Bugenhagen we see the lineal descent from the reformer's breakthrough of Luther to the faith of the Evangelical congregation in the form of the development of an Evangelical book of instruction, and thus Urbanus Rhegius' *Formulae caute loquendi* connects with still the next level of this work."[56]

Rhegius had good credentials for the important position he occupied. He was a good friend and supporter of Luther from the very beginning (despite a brief flirtation with Zwinglianism on the Lord's Supper, which he rapidly repudiated). In 1530, though a south German, he was under call from Duke Ernest of Lüneburg, who himself was one of the original seven signers of the Augsburg Confession. Rhegius was forced to flee from the south and went north with his mentor to carry on the work of educating pastors for his duchy. His *Formula caute loquendi* of 1535 was produced in fulfillment of this assignment. In 1537 he signed both the Smalcald Articles and Melanchthon's Treatise on the Power and Primacy of the Pope. Chemnitz was acquainted with Rhegius' work from early on, and it is significant that in his own work of preparing pastors and the *corpora doctrinae* for various churches he made use of it and even amplified it, just as he used and amplified Melanchthon's *Loci Communes* for the same purpose in his *Loci Theologici.*

We might add at this point that it is not quite fair to lay all the banes of orthodoxy, real and imagined, at the feet of Melanchthon and his methodology. Chemnitz, who much more than Melanchthon can be called the father of orthodox Lutheranism, would not include any of the late works of Melanchthon in his various *corpora doctrinae*, not even Melanchthon's *Loci Communes,* with which he was intimately acquainted and on which he had lectured for so many years; but he did include Rhegius' work and even anonymously added to it. Even a brief examination of Rhegius' writing shows that this man who had never attended Wittenberg University and thus, presumably, was not directly influenced or corrupted by Melanchthon also used the thetical method of instruction and handed it down to still a third "level." Thus the so-called thetical method was not a monopoly of Melanchthon nor a sign of a Scholasticism or of Aristotelianism, which were to be avoided by all true Lutherans. The problem with Melanchthon was not with his method but with his ecumenism and his theological deviations.

The new church order of Wilhelm, dated May 5, 1576, contained in its *corpus doctrinae* the Augsburg Confession, its Apology, the Smalcald Articles, Melanchthon's Treatise on the Power and Primacy of the Pope, Luther's catechisms, and the German edition of the Rhegius document which Chemnitz had produced. Mager concludes by saying, "Therefore the *Corpus Doctrinae Wilhelminum,* for the development of which Chemnitz as the theological advisor to the duke was largely responsible, is a document of great importance and responsibility for territorial church politics."[57] Its third publication in 1621 was included with the Formula of Concord.[58]

Finally, the *Corpus Doctrinae Julium* of 1576 was again the work of Chemnitz, presumably planned at the same time as the *Corpus Wilhelminum* of Lüneburg of 1575 to which it is similar. Duke Julius introduced it with the words written by Chemnitz for him:

> By the grace of God all men know very well . . . that in assuming our princely role, in view of our divinely established office, we are charged not only with the observance of the first table of God's commandments but also of the second, including all political matters and actions of this world. Therefore, we have made it our first and foremost responsibility to reform the churches and schools of our duchy.[59]

The *corpus doctrinae* contains the three ecumenical creeds, the Augsburg Confession of 1530–31, its Apology, the Smalcald Articles, and Luther's catechisms. At the suggestion of Dr. Timotheus Kirchner, it also contains Chemnitz' *Kurzer Bericht,* which had been in the earlier church order of 1569, and also, as was the case in the *Wilhelminum,* the Rhegius document along with Chemnitz' appendix, making it the longest and most complete *corpus doctrinae* yet produced. The 1576 Braunschweig Ducal Church Order reflects the argument between Selnecker on the one hand and Chemnitz and Kirchner on the other regarding the *Corpus Philippicum,* of which we shall speak at a later point, but this quarrel does argue for the production of a new *corpus doctrinae* and for a complete rejection of Melanchthon's *Corpus Philippicum.* The new corpus was completed just in time for the opening of the new university at Helmstedt and received the subscription of the faculty. This church order has remained in force until this day in the territorial church of Braunschweig, and while the city subscribed to the Formula of Concord, the duchy did so only much later.

To summarize, it would not be an exaggeration to say that Chemnitz was the author of more confessional statements than anyone of his age. He played a material role in the production of four church orders and *corpora doctrinae* for three territorial churches: ducal Prussia in 1567, Celle-Lüneburg in 1575, and two for Braunschweig-Wolfenbüttel, 1569 and 1576. It was helpful that Andreae had also endorsed Mörlin's Lüneburg Articles, and this may have played a role in his dedication of his Six Christian Sermons to Julius in 1573. Chemnitz also was in the background of Mörlin's work in the city of Braunschweig and on his Lüneburg Articles. The church order for the city had great influence on the church order of the duchy, and Chemnitz was involved in both. The work on the church orders for city and duchy, plus Julius' investing of the city clergy, also helped to unite the clergy of the two jurisdictions. But in a special sense Chemnitz' work had only begun.

The Formula of Concord

Chemnitz' real claim to fame was his work on the Formula of Concord. While the various territorial churches were busy revising and perfecting their own church orders and *corpora doctrinae* and while they were trying to bring these closer together, on the broader scale even more dramatic efforts were being made by many of the same people to bring all of the Lutheran states of Germany together in one common statement of faith, one *corpus doctrinae,* which would settle the burdensome controversies and enable them to present a united front to both the Roman Catholics and the Reformed. The very proliferation of these documents gave great impetus to the creation of the Book of Concord. In this endeavor Chemnitz and Duke Julius were also in the forefront. Ebel points out that Chemnitz "must be considered the primary author of the Formula of Concord so far as its overall concept and its contents are concerned."[1] The subject of the Formula of Concord and the Book of Concord is so vast and occupies so great a place in Chemnitz' life that we shall devote special space to it.

THE DEVELOPING CONFESSIONAL CHURCH ORGANIZATION

To understand the rest of Chemnitz' professional career and his work on the Formula of Concord we need to speak a few words about the development of the church organization in Braunschweig.

As the years went by, various forms of church government emerged in Lutheran Germany. Württemberg was the most bureaucratic, while Hesse and Braunschweig gave at least some power to the laity and local congregations. All systems, however, were under the rulers, and such notions as the autonomy of local congregations were centuries away. Consistories, or ducal or city church councils, were developed, based on the older concept of the visitations in which both clergy leaders and laymen who were usually lawyers and business managers played an important role. In Braunschweig the ministerium, in some ways almost like a modern pastoral conference, was very important in doctrinal and church discipline matters. Chemnitz tried to enhance the power of the clergy over against the government. The record mentions several instances in which Chemnitz as superintendent would direct his pastors to attack certain aberrations of the city council or even of the duke personally, and the pastors would obey their superintendent, even at considerable personal risk. One instance was that of Timothy Kirchner, who lost his job at Helmstedt because he supported Chemnitz against the duke.

On the other hand, Julius spent a great deal of time and money on the church. He helped congregations to obtain pastors; to get their buildings repaired; to maintain schools; to build churches, schools, and parsonages; to uphold public morals; to care for old pastors and their widows; and to care for the poor and the sick. Above all Julius worked to secure and maintain unity of faith among the warring Lutherans by his great support for the church orders and the *corpora doctrinae*—especially the Formula of Concord. Julius also respected the rights of pastors to carry out their duties unmolested, including their right to engage in some degree of church discipline. But he was at all times in charge. No detail was too small for him, and the records of the time show how great his interest was in every feature of church life. And he carried out nearly all of his work through Martin Chemnitz, his ecclesiastical advisor.

Although Chemnitz was safely and permanently ensconced in his office of superintendent of the city, his new position as advisor to the duke meant that in a sense he was working for two masters. Normally these masters got along very well, but there were difficulties. In his original conditions for accepting the position of superintendent, Chemnitz had insisted that the superintendent be consulted on all the pastors called to the city and in the selection of his helpers, especially the coadjutor. In the case of the men employed by the duke for completing the reformation of the duchy, Chemnitz may have been consulted (we do not know), but the duke had the final decision. The decisions were probably not what Chemnitz would have favored. But the fact is that Andreae and Selnecker arrived, and the work of reforming the duchy and developing a means of uniting the Lutherans of Germany received an impetus that never stopped until the goal was achieved in a remarkable way. Whether he liked these men or not, Chemnitz was associated with Andreae from almost the beginning of his superintendency until the completion of the Book of Concord, and with Selnecker almost that long. Chemnitz had a good influence on both of them, and the association proved miraculously beneficial for Lutheranism. For evidence of some of the infighting and disagreements among them see the extract from Selnecker's diary in Jungkuntz.[2]

THE ARRIVAL OF ANDREAE AND SELNECKER

Julius' goal was wider than only the duchy and city of Braunschweig. He wanted to settle the controversies that had torn Lutheranism all over Germany ever since the Interims by drawing up a *corpus doctrinae,* or doctrinal statement, that would express the faith of Lutheranism, particularly Luther himself, and give all of the churches a symbol around which to rally in the face of the Roman Counter Reformation and the constant inroads of Calvinism. The hope also was that in this way peace might be achieved, political unity enhanced, the rulers freed to devote their attention to other aspects of their work, and the fruits of the Reformation enjoyed in tranquillity. Basically the chief forces behind this laudable goal were the princes themselves, who were acting both out of their Christian convictions as well as political considerations. In a nutshell, we might say that the rulers had more vision for the overall church situation than the theologians generally had and the theologians more religious considerations than the princes. We have already noted, for example, the desire of princes both in England and in Germany to expand the Protestant relationships to the point where these Protestant lands could work more closely together in mutual defense against pope and emperor, while the theologians including Chemnitz were extremely cautious on these endeavors. Perhaps the most politically oriented theologian of the era was Melanchthon, and of course this got him into difficulties. But the theological orientation of such men as Duke Julius, Duke Christoph of Württemberg, and Elector August of Saxony served as a good counterbalance.

Beginning with Andreae's arrival in Braunschweig in 1568 and Selnecker's in 1570, not only was the reformation of the duchy advanced, but also the groundwork was laid for the later Formula. It is not our intention the go over in minute detail the well-trodden path of the development of the Formula of Concord, the part of our story which is best known. But rather we shall deal primarily with those aspects of the matter in which Chemnitz was heavily involved. From the outset we need to stress that the strongest impetus toward peace among the Lutherans and the Formula of Concord came from the princes. The distrust and rivalries among the theologians were so great that had it not been for the constant push of the secular rulers, it is doubtful if there would ever have been a Formula of Concord. Chemnitz did not trust either Andreae or Selnecker. Andreae and Chemnitz seemed constitutionally opposed to one another in almost every point of procedure. Selnecker could not stand Andreae, and while Chytraeus was a great admirer of Chemnitz, he became disillusioned with the entire process of producing the Formula of Concord and in many ways simply backed out of it. Most of the time Andreae seemed oblivious to his lack of popularity. At least it did not change his conduct much. It even seems that dislike for Andreae actually prevented Prussia and Schleswig from subscribing to the Formula.

It is almost a matter of certainty that (at least at the beginning) Chemnitz would not have welcomed or requested these men if he had had his way. Andreae had already been on the scene, at the direction of his prince, attempting to unite the divided Lutherans, and one of his chief opponents had been people in the Lower Saxon cities, including Martin Chemnitz who found Andreae's efforts not sufficiently clear and firm. Selnecker in 1570 had been a strong supporter of the *Corpus Doctrinae Philippicum*. In fact, his prince, Elector August of Saxony, who at this point had not yet caught on to the machinations of the Crypto-Calvinists, urged him to try to inject the *Corpus Doctrinae Philippicum* into the Lower Saxon cities. It is a testimony to the desires of all three theologians for Lutheran unity that they were able to overcome their previous differences and come to the high degree of agreement that they did in the Formula of Concord in 1577. This is not to say that Julius was trying to scuttle Chemnitz or undermine his position, but Julius perhaps did not understand the problems fully. And Chemnitz was not able fully to voice his opinions partly because of his relationship with Julius and partly because of his long-standing resolve not to attack Melanchthon publicly. Somehow he managed to prevail almost to the completion of the Formula without disrupting his connections with the duke or becoming a strident critic of the Preceptor.

A few remarks about Andreae might be helpful in clarifying the situation. Jacob Andreae (1528–90) was a south German from Württemberg, a courageous opponent of the Interim, and a disciple of the great John Brenz, the most noted Lutheran in southern Germany, from whom he learned and held to the doctrine of the so-called ubiquity, or omnipresence, of the body and blood of Christ. From Brenz he seemingly also learned to favor a centralized and bureaucratic form of church government, whereby decisions were made at the top and the orders given from the top. Temperamentally Andreae was ideally suited for his role in history. He had tremendous determination and energy, was unswerving in achieving his goals, cared little for the opinions of others, and was not nearly so interested in theological niceties as he was in accomplishing his purpose of getting the Lutherans together and carrying out the orders of his dukes. In the progress of his career, he made countless people unhappy and angry. Coming from the artisan class (his father was a blacksmith), he moved among the princely class with little finesse and had little personal concern for the feelings of his co-workers, most of whom also came from the middle class. Piepkorn describes him as follows:

> Andreae emerges as self-assured and self-willed, frequently tactless and overbearing, all too often imprudent in his choice of words; at the same time he was deeply pious [a point which Selnecker questions], conscious of his own faults, endlessly diligent and industrious, a powerful preacher, an eminently practical theologian, and a tenaciously and honestly devoted proponent of Lutheran unity.[3]

In sum, if Andreae alone had prepared the Formula, it would never have been accepted and probably would not have been much good. He had to have a Chemnitz and a Chytraeus. On the other hand, it is doubtful there ever would have been a Formula if only Chemnitz and Chytraeus had been in charge. They needed an Andreae who, unpleasant and rough as he was, could push things through, keep up the determination of the princes, and keep the program moving. Chemnitz and Andreae had had several associations before 1568 when Andreae came to Braunschweig to help reform the duchy. It is a tribute to both of them that they were able to work together so well and ultimately produce such a great theological document as the Formula. Chemnitz supplied the theological integrity and expertise, and Andreae did the selling job. They needed each other, and the church benefited greatly from this combination of talents. Andreae had never attended Wittenberg, and thus had no theological or emotional attachments to Melanchthon. The other authors of the Formula were all graduates of Wittenberg.

Nicholas Selnecker (1530–92) arrived in Braunschweig in 1570 on a kind of loan from Duke August of Saxony to Duke Julius to serve as superintendent in the newly reformed duchy. The son of upper middle-class parents, small of stature, and often sickly, he was known as a great musician and hymn writer, as well as a sensitive soul who disliked criticism. He had studied under Melanchthon and admired him greatly. Until late in life he was not a fighter and was greatly irritated by Andreae and certainly to some extent by Chemnitz, who immediately proceeded to make certain that Selnecker abandoned his support for and use of Melanchthon's *Corpus Philippicum*. Rehtmeyer cites a speech made by Chemnitz to the ministerium:

> When Selnecker was called to the superintendency of the duchy, all kinds of efforts were made to throw the *Erklerung* [of Mörlin] entirely out of the church order or to alter it. But because there was fear of some looseness [in doctrine], since in the agreement, or treaty, between the duke and the city the doctrinal points were clearly set forth in the ducal church order and Selnecker had endeavored to inject the Wittenberg *corpus doctrinae* into the church of this duchy, he came under suspicion. And when he permitted himself to speak a few words against the *Declaration* [Erklerung] of our ducal church order, I strongly persuaded him against this in writing and cancelled my appointment [perhaps

his approval of Selnecker's appointment]. Then some angry letters came.[4]

Chemnitz also discussed this matter with Julius, and some
sparks flew for a time, but Chemnitz kept going back to the treaty
regarding the oath of allegiance that all the churches in city and
duchy had accepted. Finally he prevailed. It appears that Duke
August had urged Selnecker, when he came to Braunschweig, to
push for the *Corpus Doctrinae Philippicum*.

The happy result of this altercation, however, was that Selnecker
came completely around to the position of Chemnitz on the mode
of Christ's presence in the Supper, especially after the Crypto-Calvinists at Wittenberg published their Wittenberg Catechism and were
finally exposed and driven out by Duke August in 1574. But poor
Selnecker was under attack from the Gnesio-Lutherans all the time
he was at Braunschweig, tried to resign in 1571, was unable to
administer well, and had the territory over which he served as
superintendent divided. Finally in 1573 he returned to Saxony and
became a professor at Leipzig, a role for which he was much better suited temperamentally. But when the Crypto-Calvinists were
exposed the following year, Selnecker, apparently using the knowledge acquired in Lower Saxony, was one of the first and the most
vehement to reply to their errors. Thus he was drawn back into the
inter-Lutheran dialogs and served with distinction and courage in
the period leading up to the adoption of the Formula in 1577. In
1576 he had added to his reputation for orthodoxy by his opposition to the Crypto-Calvinistic Wittenberg Catechism and by his
public opposition to the *Corpus Philippicum*. He was even instrumental in urging Duke August to call Andreae to Saxony to help him
in his efforts for Lutheran unity. The result of the meeting between
August and Andreae was that Chemnitz, Chytraeus, Musculus, and
Körner were invited to Torgau in May of 1576, and the result of
this meeting was the so-called Torgau Book, which became one of
the constituent documents of the Formula of Concord. Selnecker
became a very helpful person, and he and Chemnitz patched up
their differences and became close friends and co-workers. In fact,
in the production of the Formula itself, Selnecker and Chytraeus
supported Chemnitz in differences that arose between him and

Andreae on theological points, the method of presenting the material, and getting acceptance.

THE EXPOSURE OF THE CRYPTO-CALVINISTS AT WITTENBERG

We have mentioned previously how little by little Saxony had fallen into the grip of the Crypto-Calvinists, or sacramentarians, who had even advanced beyond Melanchthon (at least his public statements) in moving the Lutheranism of Saxony into the orbit of Calvinism regarding the Lord's Supper. The opponents of Melanchthon after the Flacian fiasco were demoralized and divided. The Calvinists were publicly claiming Melanchthon as having espoused their position. The victory of Crypto-Calvinism appeared complete. Andreae in his first unity efforts had thought it possible to win over the Wittenberg sacramentarians, but especially after the publication of the *Corpus Doctrinae Philippicum* they dug in even more deeply, as witnessed by Selnecker's strong support of it even in 1570, 10 years after Melanchthon's death. Andreae had finally concluded that his unity efforts really would have to be developed without the inclusion of the Wittenbergers and thus really of all of Electoral Saxony. Chemnitz certainly was of the same mind, as is seen by his opposition to Andreae for even trying to bring them in in the first place, at the expense of Lutheran doctrine and Augustana X in the unaltered form. It is obvious from what has already been said in many different ways that Chemnitz was reconciled to the concept of losing Saxony, Wittenberg, Leipzig, and other areas that were heavily influenced by Melanchthon and his followers. The borders of Lutheranism were shrinking.

Then a remarkable and providential thing happened. Duke August, the elector of Saxony, was a pious Lutheran who believed in the teachings of Luther and the Augustana of 1530–31. While he had been warned by various Gnesio-Lutherans of the defection of Melanchthon, he refused to believe these warnings and even, at the urging of some of his close advisors, exiled hundreds of orthodox Lutheran pastors. As early as 1535 Melanchthon in writing to Brenz had spoken of Luther's doctrine of the Supper as a "new dogma" which was not found in the early church fathers.[5] But finally, nearly 40 years later, August's eyes were opened.

Melanchthon's strategy had always been one of silent waiting, keeping his mouth shut and avoiding conflict and cautioning such people as Hardenberg also to avoid conflict. But Melanchthon's followers were not so constituted. They got too bold and they got caught. In 1573 there appeared a document known as *Exegesis perspicua et ferme integra controversiae de sacra coena* . . . (A clear and complete explanation of the controversy regarding the holy Supper), the authorship of which was first claimed by a printer at Leipzig named Vögelin. After some investigation the conclusion was reached that the actual author was a Wittenberg professor named Christoph Pezel (1539–1604), a philosopher and theologian, who had help from Melanchthon's son-in-law Caspar Peucer (1525–1602), a physician and mathematician. Some credit for this was also laid at the door of Rüdinger, a professor of physics at Wittenberg and the son-in-law of Melanchthon's good friend Camerarius. All of these men had sworn to uphold the Augsburg Confession. The obvious intent was to finish off Luther's doctrine of the Lord's Supper. A medical doctor named Curaeus also claimed authorship. This may account for the reference to medical doctors, mathematicians, scientists, and philosophers in Selnecker's impassioned polemic which he used in the introduction to Chemnitz' *The Two Natures in Christ* in the 1578 and final edition[6] and which was directed against the Philippists at Wittenberg. It is interesting to see the complete about-face of Selnecker by this date.

The *Exegesis perspicua* marked the end of the hidden and underhanded efforts of those within Saxony who had espoused Calvinism. Everything was out in the open. These men repudiated the sacramental union, the oral eating of the body of Christ, and the eating of the body by the wicked. They held that Christ's body is enclosed in heaven and Christ is present in the Supper only in His power. There is no union of the body of Christ with the bread. The ubiquity doctrine of Brenz is repudiated as Eutychianism, an ancient heresy that asserted that after the union of the divine and human natures in Christ only one nature remained. Believers who participate in the Supper, the Wittenbergers asserted, become members of Christ who is present and efficacious through the symbols of bread and wine. They lavished praise on the Reformed and urged immediate union with them in opposition to the papacy. The doctrine of the Supper should not be an obstacle to full fellowship, and the peculiar points of Luther, his "new dogma,"[7] should be set aside in favor of Melanchthon's view.

The war was on. The elector's eyes were opened. Intrigue was rampant. A letter was misdirected in which plans were revealed for involving the elector's wife, Mother Anna, in the plot. Letters were impounded. Charges and accusations flew. Lies and denials were uncovered. Finally many people lost their sinecures, a few were exiled, and a few went to prison. August struck a medal. But the document designed to calm things down, another *Kurz Bekenntnis* subscribed at the Diet of Torgau in 1574, did not indulge in much condemnation, to the disappointment of Selnecker who was one of the first to raise the cry at the publication of the *Exegesis perspicua*. Melanchthon was treated as being in agreement with Luther, and all the blame was laid on a few Crypto-Calvinistic fanatics. But sound Lutheranism was again confessed. It is interesting to note that Calvin, Beza, Bullinger, and the Heidelberg theologians are condemned by name, but so is the ubiquity doctrine.

Lucas Osiander and Balthasar Bidembach, both of Württemberg, were commissioned to write a document that would put the whole matter in clearer perspective, which they did by the preparation of the Maulbronn Formula of 1575, a document used by Andreae in preparation for the later Formula of Concord. He may have had a hand in its writing, and he supported it vigorously.

Elector August called a meeting at Lichtenberg in 1576 at the urging of Selnecker, who was instrumental in getting the Wittenberg Catechism, the Dresden Consensus, and the *Corpus Philippicum* rejected. This resulted in the arrival of Andreae in Saxony in 1576 at the behest of Selnecker, who then convinced the elector to call a meeting of theologians known to be hostile to Philippism but not extreme supporters of the radical Gnesio-Lutheran position. Chemnitz, Andreae, Selnecker, Chytraeus, Körner, and Musculus, gathered at Torgau, also in 1576. There, to everyone's surprise and joy, they produced the so-called Torgau Book, which is one of the basic documents of the Formula of Concord. Thus the triumvirate of Chemnitz, Andreae, and Selnecker came into being. These men had known each other and worked together for years. At last they were on the same track and going for the same goal. In 1577 the Bergic Book resulted. The triumvirate became the trusted advisers to Elector August. With his participation, along with that of Julius and Ludwig of Württemberg, who had succeeded his father Christoph, the path toward the Formula became smoother and much more inviting to other territories in Germany.

OVERVIEW OF CHEMNITZ' WORK ON THE FORMULA OF CONCORD

Throughout this book we have made reference to Chemnitz' work with the writing and adoption of the Formula of Concord. This is the work for which he is best known in the history of the church, which had the greatest significance for Lutheranism, and in which the average reader will ultimately come to understand his theology, even though he was not the total author of the document and even though we can get a fuller picture of his theology from other writings. But the Formula is of paramount importance in any study of the life and theology of this great man. On the other hand, more has been written on this subject than on any other aspect of Chemnitz' work, and much additional material has been added to this body of literature by the recent celebration of the 400th anniversary of the Book of Concord in 1980. It is not our purpose in this book to give a detailed description of the development of the Formula or the Book of Concord. For a brief summary of the centuries-old concept of seeking doctrinal consensus and unity, see, for example, *Bekenntnis und Einheit der Kirche,* particularly the article by Klaus Schreiner, "Die Lehrverpflichtung und ihre Auflösung . . . zur eidlichen Verpflichtung von Staats- und Kirchendienern auf die 'Formula Concordiae' und das 'Konkordienbuch.'"[8] The framers of the Formula were doing nothing new in seeking doctrinal unity.

However, a brief review is in order. The real push for union among the divided and warring Lutherans began in Württemberg in the councils of Duke Christoph, with the active participation and encouragement of the chancellor of the University of Tübingen, Jacob Andreae. It is difficult to determine which of the two was the leader in this. Perhaps both were of the same mind at about the same time. It is also a certainty that Duke Julius, who was a close friend and relative of Christoph, came to the same point of view upon early discussions with Andreae. The goal was a common statement of faith to which all loyal adherents of the Augsburg Confession would agree, obviously reflecting the concurrent development of church orders in all parts of Lutheran Germany. The basic point at issue, of course, was the question of whether Lutheranism would follow the lead of Melanchthon, which was taking them into the waiting arms of Calvin, or the older and more conservative position of Luther himself, thus remaining separate from the Calvinistic siren songs. In other words, was the theology of these Lutheran churches to become Philippistic or remain Lutheran?

Basic to the discussion was the common belief of all that the Scriptures were normative for all theology. Immediately, however, arguments arose over which edition of the Augustana should be used, the version of 1530–31 or the Variata of 1540 and following. The Gnesio-Lutherans made much more of the Apology and the Smalcald Articles than did the Philippists, and even the catechisms of Luther were unsatisfactory for the Philippists later on. The above-named confessions, however, for Chemnitz and his associates were regarded as normative confessions because they were in accord with the Scriptures and they asserted a continuum of orthodox theology beginning with Scripture and continuing through the three great ecumenical creeds, the orthodox fathers of the ancient church, the writings of Luther, the Unaltered Augsburg Confession, the Apology, the Smalcald Articles, and the catechisms of Luther. There were many documents, but one theology. This attitude had already manifested itself in the appearance of the many *corpora doctrinae* of the various churches and had became the standard way of dealing with the post-Luther conflicts that had arisen and that were ultimately settled by the Formula. The sacramentarians disagreed, obviously, but the Lutherans prevailed both in the Formula and as the years went by within almost all of Lutheranism.

Underlying the entire endeavor was the constant quarreling among Lutherans which began while Luther and Melanchthon were both alive, but which gained in momentum after the death of Luther in 1546 and especially after the adoption of the two Interim documents of 1548. Even before the death of Luther, the antinomian controversy had begun; and Melanchthon, who held with Luther in this controversy, had been busily engaged in undermining the position of Luther regarding the Lord's Supper (this going back to the time of the adoption of the Augustana itself) and the matter of free will and synergism. But with the adoption and imposition of the Interims the situation got much worse. An entire new group of controversies arose. Finally now, about 25 years after the death of Luther and 10 after the death of Melanchthon, the leading secular princes and at least some of the theologians recognized that if they wanted to save Lutheran theology and even the organization of Lutheran churches, something would have to be done. It is important that the secular princes who led in this endeavor were the three highest among the German rulers, the three Lutheran electors of the Holy Roman Empire. They were followed by scores of lesser dignitaries.

It may be helpful to give a brief description of the controversies that by 1570 had arisen within Lutheranism, the most serious of which related to Melanchthon and his indecisive and confusing leadership, which together with his involvement with and support of the Leipzig Interim brought nothing but grief to his church. Spitz observes, "It is impossible to comprehend the asymmetrical thrusts of the Formula of Concord without a knowledge of the controversial developments between 1537 and 1577 within Lutheranism, a reason for paying special attention to the Formula of Concord."[9] It must be said for Melanchthon, however, that he was not personally responsible for all the conflict.

In every controversy these questions were at issue: What did Luther teach and what did the Augsburg Confession teach? And each side always attempted to have Luther and the Augustana on its team. Obviously this did not always work, because Luther had written a great deal and said things that appeared at least to support conflicting views. We shall discuss the actual details of some of these conflicts and the theological issues actually involved when we come to the consideration of Chemnitz' theology.

The Formula of Concord was an attempt to settle controversies on certain subjects. Basically, of the 12 articles in the Formula of Concord, 11 pertain to intra-Lutheran controversies, seven of which were public, of which two dealt with two different subjects, and two others were brewing but not yet a matter of public concern. Of the seven public controversies, three, namely, the Osiandrian on justification, Article III and to a degree Article VIII (cf. AC IV); the antinomian on Law and Gospel and the third use of the Law, Articles V and VI; and the Flacian on original sin, Article I, arose from individual theologians within Lutheranism, namely, Osiander, Agricola, and Flacius. In opposition to these three men, Melanchthon was correct and supported by the Formula of Concord. The two not-yet public conflicts, Christ's descent in hell, Article IX and predestination, Article XI, arose also from two separate quarters within Lutheranism, but Melanchthon was not directly involved. But the remaining five controversies related in one way or another to Melanchthon and the Leipzig Interim, namely, FC II on free will and the synergistic controversy (cf. AC II); FC IV on good works and the Majoristic controversy (cf. AC VI and XX); FC VII on the Lord's Supper and the sacramentarian controversy (cf. AC X); FC VIII on the person of Christ, which also grew out of the sacramentarian controversy; and particularly FC X on the matter of adiaphora, which was the first and most obvious fruit of the Leipzig Interim.[10]

The Formula of Concord was not a complete summary of Lutheran theology. It was an attempt to settle existing controversies on the basis of Scripture, the ancient creeds, the Augsburg Confession, and the other earlier Lutheran Confessions.[11]

The matter of predestination had been under discussion since the early 1550s when Calvin and Beza began to publish their views denying universal grace. In 1573 Chemnitz preached a sermon entitled "On the Providence [Versehung] or Election of God unto Salvation, Based on the Gospel in Matthew 22." It was preached in the ducal chapel at Wolfenbüttel on the Twentieth Sunday after Trinity. This sermon was well received and became kind of a normative statement among Lutherans. It is reflected in Article XI of the Formula. Thus we can see that also in this respect Chemnitz from early on was calling for a document such as the Formula and indicating almost the entire table of contents.

However, Chemnitz did far more than merely publish theological articles and list the problems. He was fully involved in the unity process. It is almost impossible to list all the meetings, letters, preliminary papers, and discussions in which he was involved and which went into the production of what ultimately was the Formula of Concord. The document certainly did not "burst full-blown from the head of Zeus." It was the result of tremendous labor.

Usually historians suggest that the actual substantive effort for the Formula began with the famous Six Christian Sermons (formally, Six Sermons on the Controversies within the Lutheran Church from 1548 to 1573, "How a Simple Pastor and Common Christian Layman Should Deal with Them on the Basis of His Catechism, So That They Do Not Become a Scandal for Them") of Andreae of 1573. Recall that as early as 1557 at the colloquy at Worms with the Roman Catholics, a meeting which both Chemnitz and Andreae had attended, Andreae had become convinced of the need to unite the embattled Lutherans and settle their controversies. In 1561 at the meeting of the princes at Naumburg, Andreae's Duke Christoph had already outlined a plan for bringing about theological concord.

The invitation to come to Braunschweig, at least as interpreted and carried out by Andreae, did not have as its only purpose to reform this latecomer to the Lutheran scene, but also to bring about concord on a pan-Lutheran scale, although Jobst Ebel asserts that Duke Christoph had not made this a part of Andreae's agenda. According to Ebel, this was his own idea. He cites Christoph's instructions, "And since disputes about articles [of faith] are taking place at the present time among several of the adherents of the Augsburg Confession, he [Andreae] is not to engage in any public debates with anyone nor to condemn any by name but is to conform in every detail to the clear sense of the aforementioned Augsburg Confession."[12] On the other hand, Fritschel affirms that Julius gave Andreae a double assignment: "(1) of organizing the Lutheran Church of his possessions and (2) of bringing about an agreement between the churches."[13]

Perhaps Christoph was protecting his flanks against the accusation of interference in another church, while letting Julius make the second assignment. This may also account entirely for Andreae's presence in Braunschweig, for Chemnitz was certainly capable of reforming the duchy and producing the necessary documents all by himself. But perhaps Julius felt that Andreae, and Selnecker for that matter, would put greater stress on the peace effort, which we know Julius favored and supported with generous financial gifts.

But this is mere speculation. In renewing his acquaintance with Chemnitz and working with him, Andreae was with another man who felt the same need for concord, and Duke Julius was easily won over to an interest in this project. However, from the beginning Chemnitz showed far greater concern for and integrity about coming to true agreement on controverted points and not merely papering things over. He was not for a minute taken in by Andreae's peace efforts. Chemnitz was making unity efforts.

At first Andreae tried in his peace efforts, which bear a strange resemblance to some of Melanchthon's endeavors, to include the Philippists at Wittenberg, but this idea was opposed by Chemnitz and the Lower Saxons. During this period Andreae did some things that he was never quite able to live down, especially in places such as Prussia. He tried in his so-called Five Articles of 1569 and following to use two or perhaps more versions, one with theses and antitheses for the Lower Saxons and a different document with only the positive theses for the Wittenberg Saxons. (Ebel asserts that this idea can be traced to the 19th-century historian Johannsen, but actually this is not historically correct.[14]) At any rate Andreae's activities at this point lost him credibility that he never entirely regained. Chytraeus objected. In a letter to Marbach of Strassburg, dated Nov. 21, 1569, he says,

> At this time I am concerned about the peace efforts of Dr. Jacob Andreae. . . . In Wolfenbüttel last year, I received from him a Latin document in which he had explained his ideas about establishing peace among our churches. In it the article on free will and some other points were very clearly and fully explained and the errors which were in conflict with the correct understanding were clearly rejected by the addition of canons or theses. I understand that he is circulating a German document that is much briefer, with the omission not only of the references to persons and individual controversies but of almost all the errors in the individual articles under discussion and a clear-cut rejection of them.

(Ebel points out that there were almost countless variations of Andreae's Five Articles, so perhaps both Ebel and Johannsen are correct.[15]) Apparently at this period Andreae was trying to reconcile not only the Wittenbergers and the rest of the Lutherans on the Lord's Supper, but also the Osiandrians and the Flacians.

THE FORMULA OF CONCORD

The Wittenbergers wanted Melanchthon's *Corpus Philippicum* and actually secured Andreae's verbal acceptance of it. At this point even his fellow Swabians in Württemberg lost confidence in him. Chemnitz was entirely turned off and succeeded in cooling Julius' ardor after a lengthy argument. At a conference at Zerbst in 1570, which Andreae had supported but which almost totally failed to achieve unity, Andreae began to change his tune and quit working to gain support for his Five Articles. But Zerbst had succeeded in getting the Wittenbergers at least to acknowledge as their confessions the Augsburg Confession, its Apology, Luther's catechisms, and the Smalcald Articles, but the hidden agenda was that they insisted on interpreting all of these in the light of the *Corpus Philippicum* and of course maintaining the Variata edition of the Augustana. So Zerbst failed too.

But Andreae was undaunted. He gave up on the Wittenbergers and concentrated his attention on the Lower Saxons, who had not been as vociferous in their criticisms of Melanchthon as some of the Gnesio-Lutherans, but yet basically agreed with them in doctrine and in their desire to move away from Philippism. This also meant that public criticism of opponents, which the Gnesio-Lutherans had insisted upon, could take place, at least to a degree. Chemnitz was always cautious about this, as we have indicated. In the opinion of this author, Robert Kolb is correct in labelling Chemnitz as a Gnesio-Lutheran theologically.[16] The difference between the Lower Saxons and those commonly designated as Gnesio-Lutherans lay not in any theological disagreement (except for the theological errors of Flacius and Amsdorf and a few others as stipulated in the Formula of Concord), but in the matter of how best to achieve unity, whether by direct personal attacks or by simply convincing the opponents of the superiority of one's own arguments, the method that Chemnitz used successfully during his entire career.

What really gave Andreae a break and promoted his unity endeavors was the exposure of the Crypto-Calvinists in Wittenberg in 1574. Thus all three groups of true Lutherans were for the first time in many years able to sit down at the table and devote their efforts to their internal problems. Just about this time Andreae providentially published his Six Christian Sermons. At this point and on these sermons Chemnitz was willing to talk. The year was 1573, 12

183

years after Chemnitz' *Iudicium,* yet note the contents of the sermons: justification, good works, original sin, Law and Gospel, the person of Christ, and the ever-present adiaphora. The list had not changed. It is not surprising that Chemnitz was impressed. The sermons named names. The sermons were most appropriately dedicated to Duke Julius. Chemnitz and Chytraeus both approved of the content but proposed that the sermonic form be set aside in favor of a thetical and antithetical method and that the document not be issued in Andreae's name but in that of the Tübingen faculty. Andreae agreed, went home, rewrote the document, got the approval of his faculty after he had personally rewritten it, and in 1574 produced out of his Six Christian Sermons the Swabian Concord, which had the same content but a different form than the sermons. It followed the Braunschweig *corpus doctrinae* closely. He added an article on predestination.

Andreae sent his Swabian Concord to Duke Julius, who in turn asked Chemnitz to check it over and get approval for it. Chemnitz got the suggestions and approval of two conferences of Lower Saxon theologians and sent it to the faculty at Rostock for further revision, thus securing input from the highly respected Dr. Chytraeus, who had studied under Melanchthon and like Chemnitz was drawing away from him. Chemnitz incorporated into the revision many statements from official documents previously adopted by the Lower Saxons, thus giving to the Formula of Concord a historic tie with previous doctrinal endeavors. A meeting of leading Lower Saxons was held at Mölln in July of 1575, after the exposure of the Crypto-Calvinists, and the revised document was approved. It was sent back to Andreae after Chemnitz had secured the approval of still other Lower Saxon cities. The document they produced came to be called the Saxon-Swabian Formula. This document was officially sent to Elector August of Saxony by Duke Julius.

To revert briefly to the exposure of the Crypto-Calvinists, we should point out that after Elector August recognized that he had been duped, he did not warm up to the Gnesio-Lutherans whom he had persecuted during the ascendancy of the Philippists. However, he apparently felt that he owed something to his true Lutheran brethren and thus began to assert a leadership position among the princes in seeking Lutheran unity among the Lutheran states. In his own realm he worked for the restoration of orthodox Lutheranism.

Accordingly, in 1575 he proposed to his fellow princes that peace-minded theologians be appointed to "meet in order to deliberate how, by the grace of God, all [the existing various *corpora doctrinae*] might be reduced to one *corpus,* which we all could adopt . . . and the ministers in the lands of each ruler be required to be guided thereby."[17] Two Württemberg theologians, Lucas Osiander and Balthasar Bidembach, were appointed to the task. Their work followed the order of the Augsburg Confession. It was discussed by other south Germans and adopted at a meeting at the cloister at Maulbronn in January of 1576. The document was thus called the Maulbronn Formula. It contained articles on original sin, the person of Christ, justification, Law and Gospel, good works, the Lord's Supper, adiaphora, free will, and the third use of the Law. It was submitted first to several south German princes, then in February of the same year to Elector August of Saxony, who had already received the Saxon-Swabian Formula. He then discussed both documents with Andreae, who favored the Maulbronn Formula because it was briefer and avoided technical language, and it was a document in which he may have had a part in the writing. Even more important, Andreae suggested that August call a meeting of select theologians to give leadership in this matter and that among them be Chemnitz and Chytraeus. Actually he had been rather reluctant to invite them, but after the appearance of the Maulbronn Formula he felt that for the sake of getting the support of the Lower Saxons he had to do so.[18] About the same time the elector held a meeting at Lichtenberg on Feb. 15, 1576, with 12 Saxon theologians headed by Selnecker who considered and gave approval to Andreae's ideas for developing unity. They also recommended that the basis for the hoped-for unity be the Scriptures, the ancient ecumenical creeds, the Unaltered Augsburg Confession and its Apology, the catechisms of Luther, and the Smalcald Articles.

The Saxon theologians also suggested that Andreae be invited to Saxony. Andreae and August conferred, and the result was an important meeting of theologians from several parts of Germany, held at Torgau from May 28 to June 7, 1576, attended by Selnecker and the Lichtenberg Saxons, together with Chemnitz, Andreae,

Andrew Musculus, Christopher Körner, and Chytraeus. This meeting produced the so-called Torgau Book, which represented a kind of conflation of the Saxon-Swabian Formula and the Maulbronn Formula. This book contained the 12 articles of the later Formula of Concord. It is primarily the work of Chemnitz and primarily drawn from the Saxon-Swabian Formula which, as Ebel points out, makes up about 85 percent of the final product. Ebel summarizes by saying that "hardly a single statement formulated by the authors of the Maulbronn Formula appears in the Formula of Concord."[19] The Torgau Book was signed by the six men who ultimately produced the Formula. Upon the completion of the meeting Chemnitz felt that he had witnessed a miracle. Services of thanksgiving were held in several Lower Saxon cities and in Mecklenburg. The Torgau Book was sent to the Lutheran princes for the reactions of their theologians, and the great majority of them approved of it. Suggestions for minor changes were made, and many were accepted. Chemnitz did most of this work after consulting with many other theologians and getting their input.

A few words about the other framers of the Formula must be spoken here. We have already given considerable information about Chemnitz, Andreae, and Selnecker, the triumvirate.

Next in importance to the above three framers was David Chytraeus (1530–1600). A south German, educated at Wittenberg under Melanchthon, he spent most of his professional life, 49 years, as professor at Rostock in Mecklenburg in north Germany. Like Melanchthon he was never ordained.[20] Next to Chemnitz he was the brightest and best theologian of the group. Despite his irritation at having much of his material disregarded in the final product, he had been and remained a devoted friend and supporter of Chemnitz and a supporter of the position of the Lower Saxons, as well as the Formula itself. Like many others he had become disenchanted with Melanchthon and turned against him on the Lord's Supper. He also in the process of the negotiations became disenchanted with Andreae over the fact that nothing he (Chytraeus) had written had actually gotten into the Formula, and thus he felt he was not an author but only a subscriber. Thus he was never an ardent supporter of the document. Ebel, on the other hand, asserts that Chytraeus' hand can be found in many places in the Formula and that he was not nearly as neglected as he felt he had been.[21] He felt that he and Musculus and Körner were brought in more for political purposes than for anything else. Perhaps this was true, but this aspect of the work was also necessary. He was not radical, however, and he disliked quarrelsomeness. Because of his important work with the Torgau Book he should be considered a genuine author of the Formula.[22] Chytraeus supported Chemnitz' philosophy regarding the content and style of the Formula and the method of its adoption over against Andreae's more high-handed methods. Chytraeus played an important role in bringing the Reformation to Austria.

Dr. Andrew Musculus (Meusel, 1514–81), Wittenberg graduate under Luther, professor and general superintendent at Frankfurt on Oder, was probably the most outspoken and the closest to a Gnesio-Lutheran of the six. He was also the oldest of the participants. He is mentioned by name and negatively in Andreae's Six Christian Sermons. In a long forgotten passage in Chemnitz' *Loci Theologici,* inserted by Polycarp Leyser as an instance of Chemnitz' theological acuity, is a paper that was never part of the *Loci* but which Chemnitz had written for his own private study. In it, he attacked Musculus for a position that verged on antinomianism, a position he had adopted out of a correct concern over the error of George Major. Musculus was a brother-in-law of Agricola, and some of Agricola's antinomian concerns had rubbed off on him. Chemnitz never published the material because Musculus soon gave up his erroneous views, and the entire matter quieted down.[23] Musculus was expected to make a more practical contribution to the project. He had been a vigorous opponent of the Interims, the Philippists, and the Osiandrians. In fact he was embroiled in controversies both at home and in the intra-Lutheran circuit all of his career. Naturally he was accused of error himself. He was really what we would call a fire-and-brimstone preacher, who talked a great deal about the last times, death, and the devil.[24] He had expressed a sincere interest in the peace and unity efforts that were going on and in bringing the Brandenburg churches more directly into the endeavors. Apparently the elector of Saxony on the basis of these facts wanted Musculus to be appointed to the committee to draw up the Formula because he, and also Körner, represented the elector of Brandenburg with whom August of Saxony was very close. Thus the two electorates, plus Braunschweig and Mecklenburg and south Germany, were represented on the final committee. Musculus actually had little or no visible effect on the outcome of the work. Koch says, "It was perhaps chiefly due to the personal intervention and diplomatic skill of Jacob Andreae that there was no rupture at Torgau because of the resistance of Musculus."[25]

Christopher Körner (1518–94) had been a professorial colleague of Musculus at Frankfurt on Oder since 1564. He played an even less important role than Musculus in the final outcome of the work toward the Formula. He produced an analysis of the undertaking of the Bergic Book and thus had some knowledge of the work that was going on and was supportive of it, but he was really not substantively involved.

In March of 1577 a meeting of the triumvirate, Andreae, Chemnitz, and Selnecker was held at Bergen Abbey near Magdeburg to consider all of the suggestions that had been submitted concerning the Torgau Book. Because there was almost universal criticism that the document was too long, Andreae had prepared an epitome that avoided all technical language, quotations from church fathers, and complicated arguments. This document was adopted by the group and became what today we call the Epitome. It is actually the only part of the Formula written by Andreae. It contained a brief summary of each controversy, a positive statement of the correct doctrine, and the false doctrines rejected. Ebel may be rather hard on Andreae when he says, "The truth is that the Solid Declaration is the more precise, official text, while the Epitome is valid only to the degree that it is a correct summary of the facts."[26]

A second meeting of the triumvirate was also held at Bergen and was attended also by Chytraeus, Körner, and Musculus. Chytraeus felt that his contributions, which generally were lengthy, had been disregarded, but he went along with the changes proposed. Plans were made for the preparation of an introduction, and basically the document, now called the Bergic Book, was complete and was presented to the elector on May 28, 1577. This is the document that today we call the Solid Declaration of the Formula of Concord. The enormous task had been completed.

Ultimately the vast majority of Lutheran states in Germany accepted it. A few places rejected it because it made no mention of the contributions of Melanchthon, and Prussia rejected it because it did not condemn him. Sadly, the duchy of Braunschweig did not accept it officially because of Julius' pique against Chemnitz, although nearly the entire clergy held to it. However, the duchy did finally adopt it 90 years later. Strange to say, both Julius himself and Heshusius of Helmstedt University who, largely at the behest of Julius quibbled about the document and stalled against receiving it, had both previously accepted it enthusiastically. Nearly all of the controversies dealt with in the Formula remained settled, and while new controversies constantly arose, and while the Lutheran churches never again had either the secular or theological leadership or the general unity to deal with them as had been the case with the Formula, yet a great deal of good was accomplished, and Lutheranism as a theological entity was saved for the next four centuries.

A few words might be said about the declining influence of Andreae and the total and final ascendancy of Chemnitz. Ebel points out that the true ultimate author of the Formula was Chemnitz. While Chytraeus was upset about his lengthy additions being deleted, it was Andreae who was finally pushed out of the front and center role he had played for so many years. Apparently the other authors of the document favored this action. Ebel at the end of his article asserts,

> In conclusion, we can say that Andreae is not primarily responsible for the nature of the text that was intended to demonstrate the agreement of the Lutheran theologians. His primary contributions are instead his persistent efforts to produce a unifying formula and his all-out organizational and rhetorical efforts in behalf of the Formula of Concord during its nascent period. In addition to that, his influence extends to the formulation of individual articles. In general, however, his contributions have been overestimated. Andreae refused to cooperate in the writing of an apology to the Formula of Concord [something in which Chemnitz and Selnecker were very much involved]. He clearly was afraid of again losing control in such an effort, because the reason he gives for not participating is not the futility of such an effort, but rather his concern that renewed strife among the apologists would break

out. He himself was anxious to publish written defenses against attacks on the Formula of Concord. These contain primarily an interpretation of the Formula of Concord as a support for the Württemberg doctrines on Christology and the Supper. Therefore, it is not surprising that, aside from his stated goal, the Formula of Concord plays a relatively minor role in his later publications. . . . To my knowledge there is not a single statement by Andreae which mentions the role of the Formula in this context.[27]

On the other hand, Selnecker and Chemnitz supported and upheld the document the rest of their lives and also remained close friends and co-workers. Ebel in another article concludes,

> In general the Saxon-Swabian Concord, therefore, bears the stamp of Chemnitz' earlier efforts on behalf of unity. And since the Saxon-Swabian Concord became the basis of the Torgau Book and since the Formula of Concord was based on the Torgau Book, he [Chemnitz] must be considered the primary author of the Formula of Concord so far as its general concept and its contents are concerned.[28]

Chemnitz is the real author of the Formula, and it expresses his theology in nearly every point. His document received greater and more universal personal support than any other theological statement ever adopted within Lutheranism, with the exception of the Small Catechism of Luther and the Augsburg Confession. Perhaps nothing better illustrates the importance and general acceptance of the Formula than the number of its signers: three electors of the Holy Roman Empire, 20 dukes and princes, 24 counts, four barons, 35 Free Imperial Cities, and 8000 pastors, embracing two-thirds of German Lutheranism.

Though it has been said previously, it bears repetition at this point: The basic document of Lutheranism was always the Augsburg Confession, and now after several years of debate, the Unaltered Augsburg Confession. Gerhard Müller puts it succinctly,

> It is important for us that the authors of the Formula of Concord did not presume to collate the total confession of Lutheranism. In their opinion the Augsburg Confession was sufficient for that purpose. They wanted to take up only those points about which there had been arguments during the last decades. Hence the Formula must be read as a supplement to the confession of 1530.[29]

Indeed the Formula is the most important and most lasting of all commentaries on the Augustana. Then, as the capstone of the entire effort, on June 25, 1580, the Book of Concord saw the light of day on the 50th anniversary of the Augsburg Confession. A German translation by Selnecker appeared in 1582, and in 1584 the official Latin text, prepared under the direction of Chemnitz, appeared.

THE FORMULA OF CONCORD AND LUTHER

One of the most important, yet overlooked contributions of the Formula of Concord is its role in determining the place of Luther and Luther's writings and how to interpret Luther. In fact, this was one of the most important tasks of Chemnitz' life. A gradual shake-down was taking place in the 30 years following Luther's death, with the best of Luther coming to the top and becoming normative for Lutheran theology, while other material was being put back into the closet. This is notable in Chemnitz' *Loci Theologici,* which in many ways lies behind the Formula of Concord.[30] Chemnitz in his *Loci Theologici* follows the practice, also used in *The Two Natures in Christ* and elsewhere, of establishing his position first by citing Scripture, then the ancient creeds and councils, then the fathers, and finally concluding the fathers with quotations from Luther, whom he treats as the last church father.[31] It is interesting to note briefly the works of Luther that Chemnitz used. Chemnitz in his *Loci Theologici,* the portion of which has been translated, cites Luther's *Lectures on Galatians* of 1531–35 at least 29 times, more than any other work of Luther, and his *Lectures on Genesis* delivered from 1535 to 1545 at least 25 times. He cites the *Last Words of David* of 1543 at least eight times. He refers to the catechisms of 1529 eight times; to his *Disputationes contra Antinomos,* delivered in the last years of Luther's life, at least nine times; to the Augsburg Confession of 1530 (which Chemnitz regarded as entirely the work of Luther) six times; to the Apology of 1531 six times; and to the Smalcald Articles of 1537 also six times. *The Judgment of Martin Luther on Monastic Vows* of 1521 is cited seven times and *The Freedom of a Christian* of 1520 only five times.

We hasten to add that there are some features of Luther's life and theology that are not duplicated in Chemnitz, and there are

191

many works of Luther that Chemnitz does not allude to. They did not have quite the same agenda. Time had brought about changes, changes in Rome, changes within Protestantism, and changes within Lutheranism. For instance, there are many points that Luther felt it necessary to prove that by Chemnitz' time were taken for granted. The anti-Roman arguments of Chemnitz' *Examination of the Council of Trent* are more sophisticated than those of Luther, particularly with regard to grace, justification, and good works. The Romanists were granting a great deal to Luther, without mentioning the fact, and were trying to cover their basic errors, which they had never given up by using much more careful language. The error remained, but its defense by Rome was more cautious, and this is reflected also in Chemnitz who kept abreast of developments within both the Roman and the Reformed communions. The same can be said about *The Lord's Supper,* where Chemnitz draws heavily on Luther, yet the arguments are not quite the same.

Much the same pattern obtains in the Formula of Concord in which the longest portion, the Solid Declaration, was written basically by Chemnitz. The Formula of Concord quite naturally quotes from those writings of Luther that by 1577 had become confessional writings of Lutheranism. (This would include the Augsburg Confession, which again was regarded entirely as Luther's.) The Formula of Concord quotes the Augsburg Confession at least six times, the Apology at least 30 times, the Smalcald Articles 11 times, and the catechisms five times. Although they had been treated as such in many circles for many years it was not until the publication of the Book of Concord in 1580 that some of the writings of Luther achieved confessional status. The confessional action of 1580 settled once and for all that the Smalcald Articles and Catechisms of Luther achieved permanent and almost universal confessional status. The only document not written by Luther to be included among these last confessional writings is Melanchthon's "Treatise on the Power and Primacy of the Pope," which had been officially adopted at Smalcald in 1537 and came to be attached to the Smalcald Articles of Luther (the latter for peculiar reasons not having been adopted at Smalcald).[32] It is significant that virtually the same people were instrumental in the publication and adoption of the Book of Concord as had been active with the Formula of Concord.

192

The Formula constantly quotes Luther and treats him as the last and greatest of the church fathers, but it totally omits reference to his most scurrilous works and concentrates on the great ones. The Solid Declaration cites Luther's *Confession concerning Christ's Supper* (1528) at least seven times, his *Lectures on Galatians* seven times, and his *On the Councils and the Church* (1539) four times. In the Solid Declaration, primarily the work of Chemnitz, Luther is cited in all but one article. The sources are again from among his best and most mature writings, the Smalcald Articles, the Large and Small Catechisms, the *Confession concerning Christ's Supper,* the *Bondage of the Will,* his *Lectures on Galatians,* his preface to Romans, his *Against the Sacramentarians,* and various sermons.[33] But also in the Epitome of the Formula of Concord, which is the work of Andreae, Luther is cited in six of the 12 articles, with the references being the Smalcald Articles, the *Bondage of the Will,* the Large Catechism, his *On the Councils and the Church,* and his great Torgau sermon on the descent into hell.

In their use of Luther the authors of the Formula of Concord (including Chemnitz) utilized the entire range of Luther's writings, picking the most outstanding works which to this day are his most highly regarded. They did not determine the merit or worth of a writing by Luther by the date when it was written but by the theological content.[34] The men of 1580 were Luther-promoters, not just because they agreed with him but also because all Lutheranism could unite around him. He was the true symbol of Lutheranism. Melanchthon was being put into eclipse, and the great Luther, his career now under scrutiny and review by his own followers, was reemerging as the undisputed and unchallenged leader of the confessional movement that bears his name. The situation has not changed for the past 400 years, sometimes to the neglect of the contributions of Melanchthon and many other leaders in Lutheranism in the period between the death of Luther and the adoption of the Book of Concord.

In the same way, a glance at the articles under consideration in the Formula of Concord shows that the very basics of Lutheran theology were under discussion. Here are no frivolous and insignificant points, no arguments about church government, liturgical niceties, or matters of personal dignity and prestige. Luther, even from the grave, is still writing the agenda. We are right back at the cold stone floor of the monastery struggling through the basic Christian issues—issues Luther brought to the fore even prior to his Ninety-five Theses (see, for example, Luther's *Lectures on Romans* of 1515–16 and note especially chapter 6 dealing with sin and its power over us)[35] and that continued to the end of his life—namely, how the sinner finds peace with God. That is why the theology of Luther and the Lutheran Confessions have stood the test of time so well. The Confessions, including the Formula of Concord, deal with things eternal—the nature of people as sinners, the role of the human will in salvation, the role of faith in justification before God, the righteousness of faith versus the righteousness of Law, good works, Law and Gospel, the role of the Law in the Christian life, the Lord's Supper, the related matter of the person of Christ, and the descent of Christ into hell. Only then do we get to matters that might not seem of the essence of the Christian faith—church usages, the doctrine of election, and finally factions and sects in the church at the time.

Make no mistake about it, the authors of the Formula of Concord were determined to keep Luther in the position of highest leadership among the churches of the Augsburg Confession. The Formula of Concord had certainly as one of its purposes to insure this, and thus we see in almost every article the idea of going back to him, whether we talk about sin, justification, the Lord's Supper or any other points. Therefore, when a new conflict arose in Lutheranism on Christ's descent into hell, the Formula of Concord cites a sermon of Luther in Article IX. Predestination had not been a major issue in Luther's time, but when the matter arose the Formula of Concord dealt with it in Article XI, where in the Solid Declaration Chemnitz again cites Luther. When Chemnitz finds it necessary to go more deeply into the doctrine of Scripture in the *Examination of the Council of Trent,* he is pitting Luther's doctrine of *sola Scriptura* and the Lutheran dogma of testing all teachings by the standard of Scripture against Rome, with its canonization of the Vulgate, its doctrine of tradition, and its concept of a magisterial church.[36]

Theologically Luther was almost a god to all parties in the intra-Lutheran controversies. As he advanced in age, his polemics were more often directed against secular rulers, who were men of power and—in many cases—of intellectual strength as well. But his example of courage and strength gave heart and direction to his followers. There is no question that the personality and bravery of Luther during his entire public career had much to do with the success of his reforming efforts.

8

Chemnitz' Break with Duke Julius

After all the work had been completed, after such enormous labors had almost come to a glorious completion, a terrible thing happened. We have referred earlier to the fact that in 1566 Julius' father, Duke Henry the Younger, had procured the bishopric of Halberstadt as a possession of his grandson, Henry Julius, Julius' oldest son, then two years old. Henry Julius was to come into possession of the office at the expiration of 12 years. Late in 1578 the time had arrived. To make sure that death would not complicate matters further, the two younger brothers of Henry Julius were also to receive the tonsure. It had been the request (*Wunsch*) of the old duke, with the consent of his Lutheran son, that the grandson be chosen as bishop of Halberstadt, primarily for political and presumably financial reasons and that the consecration take place according to the Roman rite. Duke Julius, in keeping with his original promise, complied, although the boy had been brought up to be neither a Catholic nor a clergyman. A particularly vehement Roman abbot was used to perform the ceremony that took place on Nov. 27, 1578, in the Abbey of Huesburg [Huysburg] and involved the especially offensive use of the first tonsure, a haircut used in connection with ordination and installation into the priesthood and involving the complete or partial shaving of the head. Furthermore, the entire ritual was according to the Roman rite at the request of the local cathedral chapter that had requested a ceremonial mass as part of the induction and enthronement. Consent had been received from the emperor, but of course, not from the pope.

The entire proceeding took place with the greatest possible secrecy. No one seems to be able to state why it was that Julius felt it was necessary to carry out this aspect of the proceeding except to keep a promise given in his naive youth, or why he thought he could do this without criticism and without consulting his best theological advisor, or how he thought he could keep such a thing secret. Perhaps he felt that out of respect for the wishes and sentiments of his dead father that things should be done according to his religion and desires. Or perhaps Julius felt bound by legal technicalities involved with the transfer to his son. When the news reached Chemnitz from sources outside his official position, he "mounted the walls."[1]

The city of Halberstadt, a few miles east of Braunschweig and about 25 miles southwest of Magdeburg in the duchy of Brandenburg, an ancient Hansa city, had already become Lutheran. Monasteries and cloisters were closing all over Germany, and while some were still functioning, largely because no one quite knew what to do with the inhabitants, these people were systematically becoming Lutherans. There was no objection from the Lutheran side that a 14-year-old boy become a bishop. Everyone realized that he would be bishop in name only and that it was perhaps for the income that the whole episode took place. Nor was there any Lutheran objection to the office of bishop. The only objection lay in the fact that the duke and his sons took part in a Roman mass. There was no talk about the young prince becoming Roman Catholic, and in fact shortly after Henry Julius took over, the entire operation became Lutheran. Nor was there any pressure on Julius from any of his courtiers or fellow princes. It was quite the opposite. It seems to have been an entirely independent action of Julius, who must have felt some qualms about it, because he did not consult Chemnitz and kept the matter so secret.

Theodore Jungkuntz, has described the event as Julius' "taking advantage of a good business deal."[2] But there is no solid evidence for this. Julius already had the diocese, and no one was about to take it away from him. The business deal was already completed, and the title was in Julius' pocket. At another point he took over the territory of Kalemberg, which still had many Catholics at high levels, made a considerable show of force to solidify his position, and turned the territory Lutheran, including the introduction of a church order, without any fuss. He could be very decisive. It appears that the best explanation for his Halberstadt action lies in the fact that he felt bound to the promise he had made to his father, and Julius was a man who once having made up his mind could not be moved, even if he made a mistake in the process.

Andreae tried to smooth things over. But Chemnitz was just as intransigent as Julius. And in reacting to Julius the way he did he made enormous sacrifices. He had been brought into the duchy at the very beginning of Julius' reign, had directed the writing of the church orders, conducted the original visitation and the subsequent annual visitations, received from Julius a ducal office as advisor on church matters (*Kirchen Rath*) and the highest superintendency of the entire duchy with a handsome annual stipend, and served as chairman of the general ducal consistory. He lost it all. Further, he lost the support of Julius in promoting the Formula of Concord.

He had written a letter to Julius on Dec. 1—after the event unbeknown to Chemnitz had occurred—warning against such an action, but Julius said nothing. Then, on Dec. 19, 1578, after he had heard about the matter, Chemnitz in a seven-page letter bared his soul as few people ever do.[3]

Inge Mager has written a convincing article in which she suggests that as part of Chemnitz' concept of his duties as superintendent and theological advisor was his role of a watchman, under such Scripture passages as Ezekiel 3 and 33. She points out that this same concept appears in his reaction to the attempt to introduce the *Corpus Doctrinae Philippicum* into Braunschweig, as well as the edict permitting Jews to live in the city, both of which were entirely theological and religious matters. It was his scriptural duty to warn the duke, his good friend and a Christian man. She compares Chemnitz' letter to Luther's commentary on Psalm 110, where he says, "The common man is always grabbed by the neck when punishment for public sin is given, but the high and mighty fellow will not have so much as a finger slapped for the same wrong-doing."[4]

We shall not quote Chemnitz' letter to the duke in its entirety, however. He says that he is speaking out of his heart and out of love for the duke, under his call as a theologian. He says,

> A painful and terrible and shameful offense has recently taken place, which has been reported so widely that under my call and office as a theologian I cannot and will not withhold from your majesty my opinion on the matter. Your majesty will receive this in no other way than as coming from my heart and in love toward you. It pertains to the fact that your majesty has permitted your

three royal sons to receive papal orders or the first popish tonsure from the Abbot of Huysburg, a strong and pernicious papist, in the presence of some from the cathedral chapter at Halberstadt, and in the induction of the illustrious princes to the episcopate there was a full liturgical service belonging to this religion along with the crosses, the banners, and the monk carrying the zipfel and placing it upon the altar.

Chemnitz then cites from two letters that had been sent to him. Apparently the question was being raised whether Chemnitz had given his approval or advice on this matter. Thus Chemnitz' own reputation was involved, and he felt he was being accused of doctrinal indifference. For example, Pouchenius, superintendent at Lübeck, wrote to Chemnitz,

> There is no place, no dinner, no gathering, be it ever so insignificant, where this is not spoken about and discussed how unchristian and unevangelical it was on the part of your prince who has forgotten all fear of God and the honor of His name by handing his three sons over to the Roman Antichrist, just as in the Old Testament the godly kings offered their children to the idol Molech. . . . Old Duke Wilhelm of Celle . . . cried, "Before I would let my children be shorn and smeared, I would follow them to the grave in the churchyard."[5]

Chemnitz also felt that the episode might subject Julius to scorn and ridicule and jeopardize the emerging Formula of Concord—which it did to an extent, inasmuch as Julius kept the duchy from accepting the Formula. However, toward the end of the process of adopting the Formula of Concord he did interest himself in it again to some degree. But Julius' reputation never recovered. Pressel tells us, "The papists immediately rejoiced that the ducal house through God's enlightenment was returning to the womb of the one saving church, while the Philippists boasted that in this action they had found concrete proof for their contention that the Formula of Concord was leading right back to the papacy."[6]

On the issue of being held personally responsible for Julius' action, Chemnitz continues,

> Therefore I cannot in good conscience approve or support your highness, as the writings about this public action testify, or conceal my feelings by my silence, since we poor preachers have

from our Chief Shepherd, who has placed us in our office and guided us in our performance of it, a stern command in Ezek. 3:[17–18] and repeated in Ezek 33:[7–20], "You shall take the Word from My mouth and warn them from Me, and where you do not warn them that man shall die, and his blood will I require at your hand." Now I know full well that if this matter is publicly reported that you have not been willing to receive this warning and admonition from the Word of God, at least it has been given faithfully from the heart. The prophet has spoken directly to this situation in Is. 30:10, "Speak pleasant things to us," and in Hos. 4:4, "Let no man contend or reprove another, for your people are like those who contend with the priest." Nor am I so foolish as not to know that a person who acts in this way in dealing with people and particularly with courts often receives a reward which is unfavorable to him. But the stern command of God still stands there in Ezekiel 3 and 33, and Paul in Gal. 1:10 says, "If I carried out my duties so as to please men, I would not be a servant of Christ my Lord." And likewise your highness would not be properly advised or served, if in such cases preachers would remain silent or dissimulate on matters that pertain to your highness' good name and conscience. . . . This would not be faithful to your highness. I pray that your highness will read for yourself how strongly our faithful God warns us that one should not endure such preachers but get rid of them, for they are blind watchmen and dumb dogs who will not bark, Isaiah 56. In Ezekiel 13 the old dilapidated wall is touched up with chalk or whitewash, pillows are put under the arms of people and cushions under their heads, the value of a life is a handful of barley and a morsel of bread, as it says in Isaiah 3, "My people who call You blessed are lying to You."

Chemnitz continues, probably with a veiled criticism of someone close to the duke,

Your highness' thinking about church matters and religious concerns is not always entirely solid, and many of your advisors talk with their mouths, so that your highness can make mistakes and fail in these areas by doing too much or too little, especially since your highness from time to time in such matters does not use the advice of your theologians in order to understand matters better. But your highness does know that it is required that you hear and follow our faithful God. To this end I want to bring to your highness the Word of God and hold it before you, and in this way your highness may see and judge what should have been done in regard to this matter on the basis of God's Word, and your highness will then be able from this to take counsel as to how to rectify the situation, find a way out for your conscience, turn away the offense, and regain a good and Christian reputation in the matter.

Chemnitz could also have quoted from the preface of the church order that he prepared and that Julius issued in his own name in which the duke had said, "It is our desire that when political matters affecting the church need our consideration, the theologians shall be consulted by our political councils prior to final decisions."[7] Or he could have quoted a letter written by Julius to Chemnitz as recently as April 23, 1578, "Whether it bends or breaks or falters, falls or grows cold at the hands of the electors and the princes, or whatever happens regarding the Formula of Concord, I will not permit myself to be turned away from it."[8]

Chemnitz continues with the citing of several more Scripture passages and then says,

It is God's command written in Rev. 18:4, "Come out of her, My people, lest you share in her sins and receive her plagues," that your highness repudiate the papacy with Christian zeal and everlasting honor. But now we find popish ordinances and tonsures and the understanding that these ordinances convey, namely, that whoever receives such ordinances from the pope, thereby and through the participation and involvement in the popish rite, becomes a partner in the popish church, and it can be accepted by no honest evangelical teacher that a person should accept such orders from the pope whereby he becomes a participant or a partner in the popish church, gives entree to their religion, and thus grants fellowship [Gemeinschafft] or place to the popish church. . . . And just as the same kind of thing was attacked by the prophets when the people were offering up their children to Molech, as a frightful and inexcusable sin, so through the papal order and tonsure to bring children to the papacy is likewise to practice the same thing and to make them participants in a damnable religion and worship, and it will make their prebends, dignities, and emoluments to be of the same character. . . . I know that your highness would never have understood this in the sense that there would be a return to the papacy or to lend support to this godlessness, but you only considered it an outward thing without giving any support to popish unbelief or that through this action an occasion might be given to the pope to do damage. . . .

Chemnitz then brings up probably the sorest point of all,

Likewise this action conflicts with the Formula of Concord, because in the article on adiaphora we are taught from the Word of God that a person should not be involved with openly stubborn papists in such matters, even in outwardly neutral things, and we cannot comply in good conscience or give willing consent or indication by our ceremonies that we accept the religion of the papists.

In a sense this was the first public test of the not-quite-finally-adopted Formula of Concord. It is a little difficult to understand why, with all the measures Julius took to express his displeasure with Chemnitz, he also felt he had to withdraw support from the Formula. First, Julius had spent a great deal of his own time and money on the endeavor for the Formula of Concord. Second, all the people who criticized him had been in the concord effort and stayed with it despite his defection. Third, both Andreae and Selnecker, with whom Julius had worked closely, continued to support the Formula, even though Andreae was openly critical of Chemnitz for his altercation with Julius. Perhaps a better explanation for Julius' action regarding the Formula lay in the fact that some of his professors at Helmstedt, such as Hoffmann and particularly Heshusius, were against the Formula on entirely different grounds, and this episode with Chemnitz gave them a chance to withhold and even to withdraw their former support for the Formula, though they accepted much of it. They and Julius were definitely in collusion on this matter, Julius for reasons of personal pique and the professors for presumed theological reasons, but actually their reasoning was pretty thin. But the tragic loser in the encounter was the only person who had shown genuine integrity through the entire episode, namely Martin Chemnitz.

Chemnitz was not finished. He proceeded to list seven offenses that would result from Julius' action: (1) The stubborn papists would become even more hardened and are already boasting that the evangelicals are on their way back to Rome. (2) It would encourage other evangelicals to make deals with Rome in order to obtain fat benefices. (3) Doubt is cast on the sincerity of those producing the Book of Concord. (4) The sacramentarians will raise a cry and demand equal rights for their erring position. (5) The sons of Julius themselves might become enmeshed in papal abuses. (6) The newly established University of Helmstedt will suffer. (7) Pious people will be greatly offended, the reputation of Julius damaged, and Rome will rejoice. But the greatest wrong of all lay in the fact that the Word of God was being despised. Chemnitz continues to cite Scripture, such as Ps. 1:1, "Blessed is the man who does not walk in the counsel of the wicked . . . or sit in the seat of mockers." He closes with a plea to the prince to repent and make amends.

Perhaps at no point in his career does the integrity and total commitment of Chemnitz shine forth more clearly. Mager in her article on Chemnitz' concept of the theologian as watchman has clearly caught his spirit. There was no court theologian here, no catering to higher powers, no playing games. Theology comes from God as He reveals Himself and His will in His Word; and this is no game, no bagatelle. While Chemnitz was obviously unhappy over the treatment he received from Julius, there is never any indication that he would have done things differently had he had the opportunity. He was disappointed at the compromising and politically inspired position of Andreae and could hardly work with him at what later meetings they had. Chemnitz was dismissed as a member of the duke's consistory and replaced by the disloyal and troublesome Dr. Daniel Hoffmann, who had ridiculed Chemnitz for his letter to the duke. Hoffmann also was probably responsible for the duke's new coolness toward the Formula.

Pressel makes this statement:

Thus Chemnitz came in a very irritable mood in February 1580 to Bergen Cloister for the final revision of the preface [to the Book of Concord]. . . . The meeting of the two men [Chemnitz and Andreae] was cool, yet Andreae did achieve his goal and Chemnitz signed the preface to the Book of Concord. But the strained relations between the two men continued during the conference at Bergen, and on April 8 Chemnitz wrote a very critical letter in which he reproached him [Andreae] for his dishonorable conduct over against Duke Julius and said to him flatly that he had "acted like a cat which licks with its tongue and scratches with its rear paws. Chemnitz' irritation continued with the other man till the conclusion of the work on the Concord."[9]

Pressel opines that this may have played a role in Chemnitz' decision to become involved in the so-called Apology to the Formula of Concord, which he published in 1582 together with Selnecker and Kirchner.[10] It also tells us that Chemnitz, despite his personal hurts from both Julius and Andreae, never allowed his own feelings to interfere with his much greater goal of a united Lutheranism, which the Formula of Concord did achieve. Pressel concludes, "Chemnitz had given the whole strength of his life to the work of concord, and he earned rich rewards for this work. . . . The most lovely reward was the many sighs of relief at the fully completed work. He had sown, others were to reap what he had sown for the truth."[11] This episode also reveals a great deal about Chemnitz' fundamental views on the relationship of church and state.

OTHER ACTIVITIES OF CHEMNITZ DURING THESE YEARS

During his years as superintendent, Chemnitz was busy with many activities beyond working in the area of developing doctrinal statements and carrying out the preparations for the Formula of Concord; and even Andreae and Selnecker were not devoted, at least in the early years, to the preparation of the Formula. They were there in the interest of reforming the duchy. But Chemnitz, particularly as superintendent of the city, had a host of duties, which are recounted primarily by Rehtmeyer. We shall briefly discuss some of these.

In 1569 Chemnitz was invited to visit Austria, where under the rather benign administration of Emperor Maximilian II (1527–76, emperor 1564–76), the nephew of Charles V, a degree of freedom of religion had been granted. This resulted in the immediate rise of Lutheranism. Several territories were in need of help to complete the work of reformation. They first wanted help from Chemnitz in getting things organized and then called him as their superintendent, but Chemnitz graciously declined the call.

In 1570 Chemnitz, along with some other Lower Saxon theologians, was invited to visit Göttingen to settle a controversy regarding the free will of man. They met with both parties separately, and concluded that the problem lay in confusion over the use of words. They stated that if the parties were agreed on the theological substance of the matter they should not each insist on precisely the same terminology. In this day of rigid orthodoxy they asserted,

> Now because both parties have clarified their positions so that everything that has been brought forward concerning the form of doctrine and sound words shows what their thinking and intention has been, and through God's grace, is and remains the same, therefore, the visiting theologians report to the city council of the city of Göttingen that in their churches among the people in the ministerium they found no irregular, erring, heretical, or schwarmerish teaching, but rather that the preachers stood as one on the basis of the pure doctrine and the understanding of it and that thus in their handling of the proper position there is the basis for establishing a true, firm, and Christian unity through God's grace.[12]

The city council was to deal with what was basically a personality conflict and see that pastoral conferences were regularly held, because under the present conditions "each man was bishop and pope in his own church."[13] Matters of this kind should be discussed and settled at the local level. All pastors must attend and vote. The council should appoint an older man to help the superintendent and assert its own authority over the ministerium and should provide for a *corpus doctrinae* for the city. There was also a problem regarding absolution, and Chemnitz and his companions advised that this be covered in their *corpus doctrinae*. Case closed!

In the same year, 1570, Chemnitz published his famous *The Two Natures in Christ*, dedicated to Duke Julius. It is one of his most outstanding works. It was revised in 1578, and in 1580 Selnecker republished it with a beautiful dedication to two of Chemnitz' closest friends and co-workers, Gregory Stammichius and Andreas Pouchenius. Nothing testified more fully to Selnecker's complete change of heart. The book deals with the doctrine of Christology, particularly the communication of attributes, and grew out of the Wittenberg Crypto-Calvinistic controversy. It is still a classic today. It received lavish praise from Chytraeus.

Also in 1570 Duke Julius opened a school (*paedagogium*) at Gandersheim, which ultimately became the University of Helmstedt.

He used an old Franciscan monastery. The school was opened to poor people as well as wealthy, and financial support was given to the needy. Chemnitz preached the dedicatory sermon and Selnecker delivered a Latin oration.

In the meantime the Wittenbergers were hard at it, with many documents flying back and forth regarding their doctrinal deviations. Until caught by Elector August, they were arrogant and aggressive in their contentions for their position. One piece of literature to emerge from this interchange was Chemnitz' *Trewhertzige Warnung . . . Martini Kemnitzii zur antwortan einen erbarm rath der stadt Hall in Saxen . . . von dem newen calwinischen Catechismo der theologen zu Wittenberg* (A frank caution of Martin Chemnitz in reply to the honorable council of the city of Halle regarding the new Calvinistic catechism of the theologians at Wittenberg), written in 1571.[14] This was followed in the same and the following year by opinions of the entire Braunschweig ministerium on the same subject, and the church in Prussia also issued a similar edict. Similar statements were issued at the same time regarding the Heidelberg Catechism.

When the elector of the Palatinate complained to Julius about the action of the Braunschweig city ministerium, Julius replied that that ministerium was not under his control and that both city and duchy held to the same *corpus doctrinae*. Further problems arose with the Wittenberg faculty until Elector August turned on them in 1573. Other actions were taken and documents written to assert the complete adherence of the Lower Saxons with Luther and the Unaltered Augsburg Confession.

During the year 1571 Chemnitz also drew up material on the proper form for private confession, the churching of mothers, the practical matter of the costs of midwives, usury, whether a brother had the same rights as a father in giving away a bride, in this case one who had been previously married. He preached in various places; he dedicated a new church; he continued counseling with the Austrian Lutherans in their distress. In 1573 Duke Julius asked Chemnitz to prepare a refutation of Flacianism, which was making some headway in Regensburg.

Chemnitz prepared on behalf of the Braunschweig ministers "An Opinion Regarding the Controversy on the Question Whether Sin

Is a Subject or an Accident." The Regensburg leaders quickly adopted this as their own position, and other areas began to move against the Flacians more vigorously.[15]

In 1571 he was called to be Mörlin's co-adjutor in Prussia but felt he must decline because at that time he had many problems over the impoverished state of some of his clergy and their widows. There was also the situation in which the council felt it necessary to cancel a call they had issued to a man who turned out to be inadequate for the position. The result was a set of new regulations regarding the calling of pastors and teachers and regarding the relationship of a pastor to the superintendent and the ministerium. Chemnitz was also called urgently and at the personal request of Emperor Maximilian II to Austria, if not on a permanent basis at least for a year or so; but Braunschweig would not let him go. He was also again called to Prussia, this time as the bishop of Samland. He declined but obtained the position for his friend Tilleman Heshusius, a Gnesio-Lutheran, who later became professor at Helmstedt, also due to Chemnitz' help. When Chemnitz was in great need, Heshusius watched from the sideline.

In 1573 Chemnitz undertook to edit his *Harmonia Evangelii,* (Harmony of the gospels), which he wished to dedicate to Duke Albrecht of Prussia. But Chemnitz, under the pressure of so many other duties, never finished the job. Finally the work was continued by Leyser and finally completed by John Gerhard, in three large folio volumes. Chemnitz' original work was quite short.

In that same year he lost the services of his valued co-adjutor Andreas Pouchenius, who accepted the superintendency at Lübeck. He and Chemnitz always remained close friends, and Pouchenius was among those who ministered to Chemnitz at the time of his death.

Pouchenius was succeeded in 1577 by John Zanger, a lifelong friend and a man who translated many of Chemnitz' Latin writings into German. He is often called Oenipontanus, a Greek-Latin combination to describe the town in Hungary where he was born, Weinbruck. He had a marvelous singing voice and as a child had been attached to the court of King Ludwig of Hungary. He was educated at Vienna and Prague, continued in Holland and Cologne, and finally took up theology at Wittenberg under Melanchthon. He was called to Braunschweig first as a teacher and then as a pastor. He worked closely with Chemnitz on the *Examination of the Council of Trent* and on his *Loci Theologici* and was the secretary of the ministerium. As a preacher he had the habit of calling everything "dear" and occasionally even spoke of "the dear little devils" (*die lieben Teufelchen*), a term some prankster even put into the printed edition of his sermons.

In 1574 Chemnitz was invited to Lübeck to settle a quarrel over whether it was proper to mix unconsecrated with consecrated wine, on the grounds that the power of the consecrated wine rendered all of the wine consecrated. Chemnitz ruled to the contrary and said all wine should be specifically consecrated. All were satisfied. He constantly received requests on matters of this kind. He ruled against a duchess who wanted her own personal preacher and stated that such a man must come under the jurisdiction of the territorial church also. He also bailed out a superintendent who was accused of false doctrine by his pastors, concluding after seeing the evidence that the man was not guilty.

One of the most historic involvements of Chemnitz as theological advisor to Duke Julius pertained to his help in establishing the University of Helmstedt. Julius, like most princes of his age, had the ambition to establish a university. Nearly every territory had one, and it was a prestige item. As noted earlier, in 1570 Julius had taken an old monastery at Gandersheim and made it into a kind of preparatory school, a *paedagogium*. The city of Gandersheim had never shown much interest in the school, and in 1574 the school was transferred to another monastery, this time in Helmstedt. Three professors were called and duly examined by Chemnitz himself. School opened, students came crowding in, and Julius sought the official endorsement of Emperor Maximilian. This was rapidly and happily granted. More professors were called and installed by Chemnitz, although some were not entirely to his satisfaction. Chemnitz, in consultation with Chytraeus, had prepared at Julius' request a kind of rationale, or set of objectives and regulations for the school, which was called the Julius University. This document was included with Chemnitz' inaugural address at the formal opening of the university. Julius had also sought the help of other appropriate people. The duke was impressed with Chemnitz' work and rewarded him generously.

The great day was Oct. 14, 1576. Chemnitz preached, the elector of Cologne was present, and many royal personages attended. Five hundred horsemen were there, 14 trumpeters, and four kettledrummers. The parade lasted three hours under a lovely sun on a beautiful day. Timothy Kirchner, Doctor of Sacred Theology, gave the Latin oration, and Chemnitz the inaugural address. Young Prince Henry Julius was made the rector, dressed in his black bishop's garb. He was followed into the church by six handsome young men carrying the paraphernalia of such an occasion, including a Bible, the church order, and the regulations of the school. It was a gala day. The main hymn was "Lord, Keep Us Steadfast in Thy Word." Chemnitz' sermon dealt with the appointment of the 12 apostles and with the history of education. Following the church service the faculty and others went to a meeting room where the rules and regulations were read to them. This was followed by a great banquet. The whole affair lasted for three days. It was certainly one of the high spots of Julius' career, and a great day for Chemnitz also. While Prince Henry Julius was officially the rector, Timothy Kirchner was the de facto head of the school. Before the first year was completed, Duke Julius had provided financial support for several impoverished students, and he asked Chemnitz to make proper arrangements for the handling of the funds.

The school continued to prosper for many years. Out of this school grew the famous Herzog August Bibliothek in Wolfenbüttel, which to this day is the glory of the city and which became the recipient of the great Helmstedt library. The Herzog August Bibliothek grew out of the collection of Julius' distant relative and successor, Duke August. In the 1810s, after Helmstedt was closed, its library was moved to the Herzog August Bibliothek.

Chemnitz experienced many events, both pleasant and unpleasant, in the years following the work on the Formula. But relations with Duke Julius were strained from late 1578 through the rest of their lives. In August of 1578, Julius issued an edict permitting the return of Jews to the territory, including apparently also the city. When the city council demurred, he pointed out to them some small print in the peace treaty they had signed at the time of the oath of allegiance. The ministerium, however, was so disturbed by this that each pastor mounted the pulpit and objected publicly. Julius did not take kindly to this action. His reason for permitting the Jews to return was that, perhaps especially after the financial problems caused in Spain by the expulsion of the Jews under Ferdinand and Isabella in the previous century, many rulers had come to look upon the presence of Jews in their territories as being a financial benefit to them, perhaps almost a good-luck charm. It did not represent any theological change in their thinking. But the preachers, sadly in this instance following in Luther's train and probably for the same indefensible reasons, objected. Obviously they lost, and a strain between Chemnitz and Julius began. This strain became permanent after the matter of the tonsure.

We have already noted the punishment that was meted out to Chemnitz following the tonsure matter, but we must not from this conclude that all was lost for Chemnitz. He continued on as the superintendent of the city and enjoyed the same high reputation in all parts of Germany except at the court of Duke Julius. In the tonsure episode, no less than three electors, of Saxony, Brandenburg, and the Palatinate, and several other princes, including his old ally the Duke of Württemberg, had written Julius expressing their dismay at his action. It took Julius nearly a year to reply to them. In the meantime Chemnitz continued his good relations with the city and with the general public. He was invited to come to Halle and straighten out a problem. The city council of Braunschweig was engaged in drawing up a series of regulations involving punishment for various crimes, the dress of women for weddings, and other such matters. Chemnitz was constantly consulted. Ludwig, the elector of the Palatinate, one of the signers of the Formula of Concord and the last Lutheran prince over that territory, begged Chemnitz to come, even if for only two years to help stop the intrusions of Calvinism into Heidelberg University and the territory of the Palatinate. Chemnitz did not accept but recommended his friend Timothy Kirchner, temporarily out of work after being fired from Helmstedt in the tonsure matter. Kirchner accepted but still could not stop the Calvinistic takeover. In 1584 Chemnitz was asked to help with problems in the territory of Duke Wolfgang of Braunschweig-Lüneburg and also again in Austria.

Rehtmeyer, in his overview history of the church of the city of Braunschweig, cites case after case of Chemnitz' pastoral work and describes the lives and joys and sorrows of the pastors during this era and the life of the congregations. It would be a benefit to the church of today if this entire work could be translated, so that we of modern times could compare our own church life with that of the 16th century. There are many similarities and some deep differences. For example, Rehtmeyer has one paragraph that we shall quote in full, so that the modern reader can get a little glimpse of life in the days of Chemnitz:

> Along with so many highly educated men, our Braunschweig now and then had also produced an educated woman, such as the one who at that time and in the following years lived here in Braunschweig, Justitia Sengers, who had been born blind. She had written an interpretation of Psalm 69 with reference to Christ's passion and had had it printed and dedicated to the King of Denmark, Frederick II, under the title *A Writing of the Holy Spirit regarding the Suffering and Death of Our Lord Jesus Christ, Written by a Woman Born Blind, Justitia Sengers of Braunschweig, as a True and Final Admonition for This Impenitent World,* published in 1593 at Hamburg. In regard to this book Michael Sachs in his *Kayser-Chronic* wrote that he had scarcely been able to read through her explanation of the passage with dry eyes and without shedding tears of joy.[16]

Orthodoxy had a little heart too!

Another story is told—this one sad and poignant. Readers who possess or have looked at the 1876 edition of Chemnitz' *Examination of the Council of Trent* (edited by Preuss) has probably noticed a four-page, small-print poem at the very beginning of the book, which was also in the original. The poem deals with the history of the Nicene Creed. It was written by Mathias Berg, rector of the St. Catharine's School in Braunschweig. One can imagine the pleasure Berg received from having his poem published as part of the great work of Chemnitz and certainly also the pleasure Chemnitz received from including it. The same Berg had written the panegyric poem at the time of Duke Julius' grand reception in the city. As an educator he had also written books for young people, a book on Latin etymology, two books of hymns for the Gospel lessons of the church year, and a commentary on the book of Sirach, edited in both Greek and Latin. Thus he was an important person, with a prominent position in the city.

In 1578 Berg had signed the Formula of Concord but from the beginning had had some mental reservations. He got in touch with Beza and Marcus Meningus, the prominent Calvinist at Bremen, both of whom flattered him and made him promises and congratulated him on his intention to renounce the Formula. Finally Berg in 1580 wrote to the colloquium of the ministerium, voicing his objections to the Formula in regard to predestination, free will, the ascension and session at the right hand, and the Lord's Supper. But when Berg appeared before the colloquium, Rehtmeyer tells us, "He was no match for Dr. Chemnitz and was convicted of Calvinism" and changed his mind. Apparently no one had ever explained the matter to him so clearly before. The council and the ministerium "ordered him to make a public confession in church, which he promised to do."[17] He was ordered to kneel at the altar during Chemnitz' sermon and after the sermon to make his public recantation and reject the document he had delivered to the colloquium. He also wrote to Meningus telling him of this, which resulted in nasty letters from both Meningus and Beza. But again in 1582 he changed his mind, taught Calvinism, and stood firmly in this position. He was then exiled.

Another disappointment at this time was the unwillingness of Hieronymus Mörlin, son of Joachim, who had died in 1571, to sign the Formula. Hieronymus, a superintendent in Prussia, had the orthodoxy of his father but neither the wisdom nor the kindness. He had criticized Chemnitz' *The Two Natures in Christ* and had referred to the Formula as the *excrementum Satanae.* Chemnitz replied and chastened him, to which the young man replied that he had only been speaking in jest. Chemnitz did not think it was a laughing matter and on Feb. 27, 1577, wrote a scorching letter to him, saying, "I see that you wish to clear yourself regarding certain shameful words by reason of which you may have no doubt that all the churches have taken grave offense." The normally mild Chemnitz goes on:

> I confess that I was upset that the son of such a good father could be so different from him. Paul [in 2 Tim. 2:22] uses the term *youthful lusts,* under which I see that you are seriously laboring, with your insolence, your brashness, your precipitousness, your impu-

dence, and your love of being disagreeable, criticizing, and speaking evilly. . . . That you as a young man should speak such nonsense so rashly and self-confidently makes me grieve at the memory of your father, and I am amazed at what kind of interpretation you have for the Eighth Commandment in your catechism. . . . Who is there to whom your insolence attributes anything good? . . . Your letter contained so many points that are neither grammatical nor scholarly nor even spelled correctly that I could hardly keep from laughing. I grieve for the church that is upset by your criticisms.

He concludes with a real zinger:

I have written you a longer letter than I usually do, for I see that your impudence has ranged very widely and is seeking to stir up disturbances even in other churches, so that you need to be held in check. And thus I have acted in such a way that you will not constantly condemn my moderation. Farewell and learn to act more temperately.[18]

But the professors and some of the leaders of Prussia did not sign the Formula, although the pastors did.[19]

Also in 1578, after the completion of the Formula of Concord, attempts were still made to win over some of those who had refused to sign. On Oct. 13 of that year, a conference was held at Herzberg involving five of the six drafters of the Formula (all but Chytraeus) and representatives of the principality of Anhalt, led by a rather arrogant but articulate young man named Wolfgang Amelung. Not much was accomplished at this meeting, and Anhalt, through the efforts of Amelung, was ultimately lost to Lutheranism; but the transcript of this meeting shows the ability of Chemnitz to function on his feet and under stress. Amelung not only attacked Andreae and Brenz and the concept of general ubiquity, but he also went after Chemnitz' ubivult presence. He asserted that there can be no extension of the body of Christ, despite the clear and explicit words of Scripture. The body of Christ has to be confined in heaven.[20]

In 1583 the Protestant King Henry of Navarre, later the Catholic King Henry IV of France, in an attempt to get German Protestant help for the Huguenots in France, approached the electors of Saxony and Brandenburg, Wilhelm of Hesse and Julius of Braunschweig, together with other German princes, asking that a meeting be held to discuss these matters. The elector of Brandenburg approached Chemnitz for his theological opinion, although the princes felt they could handle the matter better politically than the generally strong-headed theologians could. The elector's question pertained to the matter of how best to bring the French churches over to the Lutheran position. Chemnitz was generally supportive of the concept but was anxious that the French be won over to the Augsburg Confession. The elector upon Chemnitz' advice replied to the king, telling of the great success among the Lutherans in achieving unity in the Book of Concord and urging that the French and Germans together engage in such a process. The other Lutheran estates supported the elector in this approach. So, despite Duke Julius, Chemnitz right up to the end remained the greatest authority on theological matters in Germany.

PART 3

THE THEOLOGIAN

We now come to a consideration of Chemnitz as a theologian. We have looked at his life, his ecclesiastical career, his leadership of the church of Braunschweig, his constant involvements in the controversies and confessional efforts of the time involving all of German Lutheranism, and now in this third part we wish to give an orderly description of his actual theology. The material that follows will be based primarily on his *Loci Theologici* (*LT*), which is the closest thing he ever produced to what we today would call a general dogmatics. As mentioned previously, the *LT* follows the order and general content of Melanchthon's *Loci Communes* (1543), but it is much longer than Melanchthon's work and at points diverges from him and disagrees with him. Chemnitz' *LT* was one of the most widely used books on Christian dogmatics within Lutheranism and remained in this premier position until 1700. Leonard Hutter in his *Compendium Locorum Theologicorum* (1609), which was the most widely used book in theological instruction in the period of Lutheran orthodoxy, cites Chemnitz more than any other theologian except for Luther and Melanchthon, particularly because of his teaching regarding the Bible as the Word of God.[1] John Gerhard, in his *LT*, refers to Chemnitz as the "incomparable theologian."[2]

Although Chemnitz wrote on nearly every topic of theology, he made his greatest and most distinctive contributions to Lutheran theology on those topics that deal with Scripture, Christology, Jus-

215

tification, and the Lord's Supper. It is also noteworthy that Chemnitz' greatest works correspond to these topics. It is in his *Examination of the Council of Trent* (*ECT*) that he deals most extensively with the doctrine of Scripture, devoting nearly one entire volume (out of four) to the subject. In the area of Christology Chemnitz has given us his magisterial *Two Natures in Christ* (*TNC*). Similarly, on the doctrine of the Lord's Supper we have his masterful treatment of *The Lord's Supper* (*LS*). Finally, in Chemnitz' *LT*, we find his most thorough treatment of justification. To be sure, all of these are summarized in the one confessional document, the FC, in which Chemnitz played so pivotal a role. His Enchiridion provides a handy summary of these topics as well. In the sections that follow it is our intention to quote extensively from Chemnitz' own writings. For the sake of the English-speaking reader for whom this volume is primarily intended, we shall cite from the English translations of Chemnitz' works. Rather than use countless endnotes, we shall simply refer to the work and the page in the existing English translations.[3]

9

Scripture and the Theological Task

Following Luther and Melanchthon, Chemnitz does not have a formal locus on Scripture, nor does he engage in any formal discussion of the topic even in his *LT*. When Chemnitz does address the issue as in his *ECT*, he does not do so in an abstract way. His *ECT* is basically an attack on the errors of Rome, not a book on systematic theology. Hence, while this work contains more from Chemnitz' pen on the subject of Scripture and is the one work that beyond all others gives him the reputation as the first Lutheran to develop the doctrine of Scripture, yet it still is not a treatise on the doctrine of Scripture in a formalized manner. In his *ECT* he is reacting to what Trent has to say about the Bible. Actually Trent said very little, but what was said gave Chemnitz an opening to say a great deal on this subject. Thus Chemnitz, against the backdrop of Trent, devotes a great deal of space to the canon of the Bible, to tradition, to versions of Scripture and to its interpretation, emphasizing the authority of Scripture throughout. Much of what Chemnitz said seems to have influenced Gerhard, who covers almost the same material, sometimes even using Chemnitz' own words, but in a more formal and systematic manner.

SCRIPTURE AND THEOLOGY

Even before taking up Chemnitz' doctrine of Scripture per se, we must take a brief look at his view of the nature and purpose of theology. The doctrine of Scripture is not an abstraction. It is an integral part of his theology. Chemnitz in his *LT* (p. 41) says that the "total sum of all Scripture is the understanding of God and knowledge of ourselves. In other words, the subject of all theology is God and man, because theology is the knowledge of God, and

217

this consists of two aspects, the essence of God and the will of God." Thus the doctrine of Scripture is important only as it serves the purpose of discussing God, His essence, His will, and His relationship to man.

Chemnitz regards theology as a spiritual gift given by revelation of God in His Word, in which He reveals Himself most completely to His church through the Word. "To this revelation God has bound His church, which alone knows, worships, and adores Him, as He has manifested Himself in His Word, so that also in this way the true and only church of God may be distinguished from all the religions of the gentiles" (*LT*, I, 54). Hence theology is an activity of the church, to whom God has entrusted His will and word. Theology is church doctrine at work in the church. There is no theology or confession apart from the overall work and mission of the church. For Chemnitz there is only one church.[1] Thus theology in general, together with the entire work of the church and its ministry, such as proclaiming the Law and the Gospel; edifying the flock; comforting the troubled, the sick, and the poor; bringing the Gospel to the unchurched; carrying on the general work of a pastor in the church; confessing and defending the faith, including polemics against all error—all are part and parcel of the same entity.

Chemnitz was not a professional, withdrawn, or scientific theologian; nor an irascible polemicist; nor even a confessor except in the context of the living church of his day as it confesses its faith in its struggles under the cross against many evils, especially against false doctrine. He followed Luther, who in his attacks on the abuses of Rome removed from consideration as genuine church work such expressions of Christianity as pilgrimages, monasticism, and separation from the world. They were simply aberrations. The church is to be the custodian and proclaimer of "the pure doctrine" and "the pure Gospel" in all the world.

SCRIPTURE AND THE WORD OF GOD

Chemnitz' doctrine of Scripture begins with the premise that Scripture is the Word of God and the norm for all teaching. He merely stresses throughout all his writings that Scripture is God's Word and the supreme authority in the church. That is taken for granted, a given, a presupposition, an *a priori*. This makes for a view very much in opposition to today's scientific theology. The Scripture in the Reformation era is regarded as God's message to humanity, centering in the relationship between God and human beings. It is unique among all religions and all books. But there is no need for Chemnitz to prove this point. Hence Chemnitz' doctrine of Scripture begins with the premise that Scripture is the Word of God and the norm for all teaching and teachers.

That Scripture is the Word of God is taught on nearly every page of Chemnitz' writings, including the Formula of Concord. The concept occurs at least five times in the three-page introduction to the Solid Declaration (Tappert, 501–3). The FC describes the AC as "Christian and thoroughly scriptural. . . next to the Word of God" (ibid., 502). It speaks of the princes who presented the AC as having "accepted the pure doctrine of the Holy Gospel and had allowed their churches to be reformed according to the Word of God" (ibid., 501). The title page of the FC SD, in which Chemnitz played a major role, describes the document as

> A general, sure, correct and definitive statement and exposition of a number of articles of the Augsburg Confession concerning which there has been a controversy among some theologians for a time, resolved and settled according to the Word of God and the summary formulation of our Christian doctrine (ibid., 501).

The SD continues,

> We pledge ourselves to the prophetic and apostolic writings of the Old and New Testaments as the pure and clear fountain of Israel, which is the only true norm according to which all teachers and teachings are to be judged and evaluated" (ibid., 503–4).

We could go on at great length, but no clearer expression of Chemnitz' doctrine of the authority of Scripture can be found anywhere. It is significant that these statements are from his last and greatest confessional writing, and the last confessional writing of Lutheranism.

This basic conviction is repeated many times throughout the entire corpus of Chemnitz' writings. For example, in his *ECT*, Chemnitz says,

It is the opinion of the men on our side that in religious controversies the Word of God itself is the judge. . . . For some pious
men always follow the Word as the judge. . . . That teaching,
therefore, has standing in the church which agrees with the Word
of God. . . . The judge was the Word of God, that is, the testimonies from the Gospel. . . . The judge is the Word of God. . . .
For God wants to have the ministry of the Word in the church
. . . faith and worship rest on the Word of God . . . (*ECT* 1.256–7).

Similarly, in his *TNC* Chemnitz writes, "God has revealed to us
in His Word, through His Spirit. . . ." (*TNC*, 17). He continues, "the
true teaching was again drawn from the Word of God. . . . demonstrating on the basis of Scripture the pious and learned 'form of
sound words,' . . . the thinking of the ancient orthodox church, in
accord with the Scripture. . . . the fear of God and on the basis of
His Word. . . . on the basis of God's Word" (ibid., 19). The same concept is re-echoed in his *LT* (p. 320).

Chemnitz draws a line of distinction between "Word of God"
and "Scripture" in the sense that while the Scripture is certainly the
Word of God, yet the Word is something prior to, above, and
beyond the Scripture (*Enchiridion* pp. 39–41). God spoke His Word
to mankind before the Scripture came into being, but in order to
preserve that revelation He willed that the things spoken and
revealed to the patriarchs be put down in written form. To that
Word, "comprehended in the prophetic and apostolic writings, He
bound His church, so that whenever we want to know or show
that a teaching is God's Word, this should be our axiom: Thus it is
written; thus Scripture speaks and testifies." (ibid., 40–41) He continues with the question: "Are all things that are sufficient for people
as the Word of God for faith and conduct of life contained in the
sacred writings?" (ibid., 41) To which he replies: "Jn 15:15; Acts
20:27. The Holy Spirit therefore will not, through prelates of the
church or [through] councils teach other, new, and different things
than those that have been revealed through Christ and proclaimed
through the apostles." (ibid.)

SCRIPTURE AND REVELATION

Chemnitz divides the question of how God brought His Word to
men into different categories, involving inspiration and revelation.

In his *ECT* (I, 49–63), he devotes considerable space to this matter. He begins by saying, "God has from the beginning of the world, both before and after the Fall, come forth from His hidden dwelling place, which is an unapproachable light, and revealed Himself and His will to the human race by giving His sure Word and adding manifest miracles. (*ECT*, 49)" This Word was given to Adam and his family, but shortly after this revelation was given, Cain fell into sin and the rest of humanity corrupted the heavenly doctrine and adulterated the Word. The first step was the purification of the human race by means of the Flood, but again the sons of Noah fell away.

> From the confusion of the languages until Terah became the father of Abraham. [Not even 200 years had passed] Yet Terah . . . served strange gods. . . . and corrupted and adulterated it [the true doctrine]. . . . God restored the purity of His doctrine through special revelations made to Abraham. . . . He spoke directly with Isaac and Jacob (ibid., 50–51).

Finally, Chemnitz says, that at the time of Moses,

> It does much to shed light on the dignity and authority of Holy Scripture that God Himself not only instituted and commanded the plan of comprehending the heavenly doctrine in writing but that He also initiated, dedicated, and consecrated it by writing the words of the Decalog with His own fingers. . . . God chose not to write the whole Law Himself, but, having written the words of the Decalog, He gave Moses the command that he should write the remainder from His dictation. . . . This is how the Scripture began (ibid., 53–54).

And thus the Scripture is called "the revealed heavenly doctrine," and "the divinely revealed heavenly doctrine" (ibid., 47). "God has . . . revealed Himself. . . [in] His sure Word" (ibid., 49). Again, through His Word God reveals doctrines (*TNC*, 447). In his Enchiridion he says,

> What is the Word of God? It is the wisdom of God hidden in a mystery (1 Cor. 2:6–7), by which [wisdom] God has made known and revealed to mankind, by a certain Word which has been given, His essence and will (at least so far as it is necessary for us in this life), so that we thereby recognize sin . . . and know how and through whom we are freed from these evils, so that we as a result rightly recognize and worship God and learn well

221

to arrange and conform our life according to the norm and rule of His commandments, and finally that we be taught what will be and what is to be expected for us after this life (*Enchiridion,* 39).

Note that the definition of the Word of God includes the knowledge of God Himself, the concept of Law and Gospel, correct worship, the sanctified life, and the life hereafter, in short this very complete passage sets forth the whole purpose of Scripture.

SCRIPTURE AND INSPIRATION

Inspiration has to do with the writing down of revelation into the Scriptures. Note Theses 1:6 (*LT,* I, 49–220), which encompasses everything said above.

> And from the many long speeches of the patriarchs, the prophets, Christ and the apostles, by the judgment of the Holy Spirit, certain things were put in writing and chosen which were judged by God Himself to be sufficient for repentance, faith, and pious living, since nothing else, nothing different or contrary to what was given by the living voice, but a brief and sufficient summary of those things was to be included in the Scripture with God Himself as the author.[2]

In the same theses he repeats this thought that "God Himself is the author of Scripture." In *ECT* he tells us that God "instituted and gave the Scripture" (I, 49, 62). Again, "The first beginning of the Holy Scripture must have God Himself as the author" (ibid., 52). Sometimes the Holy Spirit is credited with the authorship of Scripture (ibid., 100–101, 136), the Spirit guided and "dictated" to the human writers as to the content (ibid., 44), the Holy Spirit through His inspiration gives to the Scriptures their canonical authority (ibid., 176). The Holy Spirit also teaches us how to interpret the Scripture (*LS* 67–89).[3] *ECT* quotes from Jerome who says that "the teaching of the Holy Spirit . . . is set forth in the canonical writings" (39. cf. Theses V, VI, IX).

Again in his *ECT* Chemnitz defines inspiration:

> The canonical Scripture has its eminent authority chiefly from this that it is divinely inspired, 2 Tim. 3:16, that is, that it was not brought forth by the will of men but that the men of God, moved

by the Holy Spirit, both spoke and wrote, 2 Peter 1:21. But in order that this whole necessary matter might be firmly established against all impostures, God chose certain definite persons that they should write and adorned them with many miracles and divine testimonies that there should be no doubt that what they wrote was divinely inspired. . . . Thus in John 21:24 the testimony of the apostle and the witness of the church are combined: "This is the disciple . . . who has written these things; and we know that his testimony is true." (*ECT*, I, 176).

Thus Chemnitz also asserts that Scripture is the prophetic and apostolic Word. The prophets and apostles were people of special authority in the church, and God's use of them in giving His Word to men is a further sign of both the inspiration of Scripture and its authority. "Men of God spoke as they were moved by the Holy Spirit" (2 Peter 1:21). All of this is part of the concept of Scripture as inspired.

SCRIPTURE IS COMMITTED TO THE CHURCH

Having had his revelation committed to writing in the Holy Scriptures, God committed the Scriptures as the record of his revelation to the church. "The church is the pillar and bulwark of truth because of the possession and preservation of the apostolic doctrine" (*ECT*, 112). Following in the same vein is a statement in *ECT*,

> The church of the children of Israel was a pillar and ground of the truth, because to them had been committed the oracles of God (Rom. 3:2). . . . They were commanded to be the guardians of the Scripture, in which God by His divine inspiration had caused to be committed to writing the heavenly doctrine, which had been committed to the patriarchs from the beginning of the world and which had been revealed to Moses (*ECT*, I, 55).

"To the same [church] He entrusted His Word and the Sacraments"(*LT*, 101) together with "the ministry" of the same Word and Sacraments (cf. Rom. 3:2; Eph. 4:12; *LT*, 701). "To this revelation God has bound His church, which alone knows, worships, and adores Him, as He has manifested Himself in His Word, so that also in this way the true and only church of God may be distinguished from all the religions of the gentiles" (*LT*, 54).

Related to this concept is Theses 1:4, "God wills that His church be bound to the Word which He has given and not to spiritual apparitions or the appearances of people from the dead (Is. 8:19), or to the hallucinations of our heart (Deut. 12:8), or to the traditions of men (Is. 29:13)."[4]

Having been committed to the church, Scripture is also the minister's primary tool. A further development of this concept is that to the ministry of the church has been committed the preservation of the true doctrine. "He [Paul] had entrusted to him [Timothy] the ministry in the church at Ephesus that he should deliver and confirm the sound doctrine, refute 'those who taught another doctrine,' rebuke whatever conflicts with sound doctrine in morals . . . " (*ECT*, I, 112). "The question now is, whether a man of God, that is a minister of the Gospel, when he possesses and rightly uses the divinely inspired Scriptures, needs anything more outside of the Scripture to discharge the duties of the ministry, or whether the divinely inspired Scripture sufficiently contains everything that belongs to and is required for the ministry of the Gospel?" (*ECT*, I, 138) According to Chemnitz, "the papalists uphold the former opinion; we hold the latter concerning the perfection and sufficiency of the Scriptures, because, when it is asked with pious zeal to which of these meanings Paul agrees and adds his vote, the matter is clear beyond all argument, for he says that the Scripture is profitable for this, that a man of God may be 'complete,' 'equipped' for every good work" (*ECT*, I, 138). This does not mean that the ministerium of the church has a God-given monopoly to be the sole interpreter of the Scripture. This is aimed at the magisterial role of the church which Rome claimed (cf. *ECT*, I, 207). ". . . out of the gift of interpretation they [the Romanists] make a kind of dictatorial authority" (*ECT*, I, 209). He expands on this point at great length, including the notion that the gift of interpreting the Scripture has been committed to a succession of bishops.

SCRIPTURE IS SUPREME AUTHORITY IN THE CHURCH

The FC is a good place to start for a view of Chemnitz' own mature thinking on the authority of Scripture in the church. The FC

SD, written largely by Chemnitz himself, describes itself in its title as "a general, pure, correct, and definitive restatement and exposition of a number of articles of the Augsburg Confession concerning which there has been a controversy among some theologians for a time, resolved and settled according to the Word of God . . . " (Tappert, 501). The SD continues by speaking of the princes who presented the AC as having "accepted the pure doctrine of the Holy Gospel and had allowed their churches to be reformed according to the Word of God" (ibid.). The AC is described as "Christian and thoroughly scriptural. . . next to the Word of God (ibid., 502). The SD continues, "We pledge ourselves to the prophetic and apostolic writings of the Old and New Testaments as the pure and clear fountain of Israel, which is the only true norm according to which all teachers and teachings are to be judged and evaluated" (ibid., 503–4).

However, important as the FC is as an expression of Chemnitz' mature thinking, by no means is it correct to assume that his study or discussion of the subject of Scripture began only at that point. We observe the same theological stance in his earliest writings, "On the Reading of the Church Fathers" and in his *Iudicium* in an excellent discussion of Law and Gospel. In his *TNC* he makes a remarkable summary statement,

> Moreover, let us not show a lust for controversy, nor an inclination for disputing, an impudence to argue, a desire to win, nor a foolish longing to show off one's wisdom, but rather a mind desirous of the truth, a humble spirit, and a heart which fears God, so that in God's sight and with His Word leading us, we may depend on the word of His mouth alone and not pervert the things which He has revealed to us in Scripture according to the norm and measure of our own reason, but humbly and firmly embrace them in the simple obedience of faith (p. 258).

In all of his works Scripture is the basis for every dogmatic assertion. Chemnitz' doctrine of Scripture is particularly evident in his *ECT*, where the longest chapter is devoted to the authority of Scripture. As noted earlier, it was really this treatise in the *ECT* that gave him the reputation in his day as the father of the Lutheran doctrine of Scripture.

SCRIPTURE IS THE *SOLE* AUTHORITY IN THE CHURCH

Scripture is not the only supreme authority in the church. In a unique sense it is the sole and only authority, the only norm, rule, canon, foundation, pillar or support of the whole faith (*ECT*, I, 39–45, 53–56, 60–62, 101, 256–57; *TNC* 445–46; *LT*, II, 687). Chemnitz' *ECT* is replete with statements asserting the authority of the canonical books as over against the Apocrypha (*ECT*, 169–71, 187–89); over against the Vulgate, the Latin translation of Jerome (*ECT*, I, 39); and over against the authority of the church (*ECT*, 178–81 and 259–61). He also has an entire chapter in his *ECT* on tradition as opposed to Scripture (*ECT*, I, 38–41). The church with all its hierarchy and magisterial authority is secondary (*ECT*, I, 175–77).

SCRIPTURE IS TRUTHFUL AND INERRANT

While in the Reformation and late-reformation period the question of Scriptural inerrancy did not occupy the center stage that the Enlightenment and the use of the historical-critical method have given to it in the last two centuries, yet throughout the writings of Chemnitz the truthfulness and inerrancy of Scripture are commonly asserted. It comes through in such statements as "Let us heed Scripture as it explains itself. For this Word can neither deceive nor be deceived" (*TNC*, 319). Despite the Tridentine doctrine of doubt and modern subjectivism, Chemnitz and his colleagues believed both in the possibility of pure doctrine and also our ability to know and to express it.

> We showed above when we were dealing with the writings of Luke, namely, that we should be certain and safe with respect to the truth of the apostolic doctrine, and that we should be able to preserve its purity in a more certain, firm, and sure manner against the inroads of corruptions . . . (*ECT*, 131).

The Formula of Concord quotes Luther, "The third ground is that God's Word is not false nor does it lie" (Tappert, 483). Similarly, the SD Rule and Norm claims that "we base our position on the Word of God as the eternal truth . . . " (ibid., 506). Actually the truthfulness and inerrancy of Scripture are found constantly in Chemnitz in his handling of such matters as the normative authority of Scripture, the fact that God is its author, the inspiration of the Scripture, and virtually all that has been said above.

CANON OF SCRIPTURE

Virtually everything Chemnitz has to say about the canon of Scripture is found in his *ECT*, although he does allude to this point in his Enchiridion (pp. 43–46).[5] The Tridentine Council in reply to some of the arguments dealing with the subject of the Old Testament Apocryphal books and the distinction between the homolegouma and antilegomena in the New Testament had without further ado or discussion simply decreed in the First Decree of the Fourth Session that the Old Testament Apocrypha were of equal canonical authority with the rest of the Old Testament books and that there was no distinction between homolegoumena and antilegomena in the New Testament. They went on also to declare the canonicity of Jerome's Latin translation of the Bible, the Vulgate. The argument was important to Rome both because it gave her a chance to take a swipe at Luther and, more importantly, because many points attacked by the Protestants were found only in the Apocryphal books, they had themselves come under attack both because of the question of their canonicity and also because of their authority in the assertion of dogma. At the root of this discussion, of course, was the authority of the church as over against the Scripture in the assertion of authoritative dogma, with Tridentine and post-Tridentine Roman theologians stating that the church could even canonize the fables of Aesop if it chose.[6]

Without going into detail on these points, suffice it to say that Luther had been embroiled in a discussion of this matter, particularly in his attacks on the canonicity of James, a "straw epistle," which he had rejected for teaching salvation by works in opposition to Paul in Romans and Galatians. Luther had actually used only one criterion for asserting the non-canonicity of a book, namely, that it did not proclaim Christ. Chemnitz' treatment of this matter actually goes far beyond Luther in demonstrating further research on the matter and in greater restraint on his part (he does not attack James). But the conclusions of the two men are the same. Chemnitz demonstrates that the canonicity of a book is determined by its prophetic or apostolic authorship. This was corroborated by the testimony of the ancient church that heard and knew the apostles and thus could determine the divinely given content of the books (following Luther), and the divine authorship and thus the inspiration of the book in question (see *ECT*, I, 37–216).

However, after all that Chemnitz says on the subject of canon and the lesser authority of both the Old Testament apocrypha and the New Testament antilegomena, it is interesting to note that Chemnitz like Luther before him (despite his tirade on James) continued in the traditional usage of the entire 66 books of the Scripture. Both men made great use of the Old Testament Apocrypha, and both constantly used the antilegomena. It appears that both Luther and Chemnitz were in agreement with the later dogmaticians that the canon itself is not an article of faith, as it was for Trent and later for the Reformed. On the other hand the canonical books themselves are the Holy Scripture, and it is indeed an article of faith that the Scripture is the fount and source of all theology and dogma, the means used by the Spirit to bring us to faith and keep us in faith, and the bearer of the Gospel of Christ.

SCRIPTURE AND CONFESSIONS

Having spoken so fully on Chemnitz' doctrine of Scripture and its connection with tradition, we must also comment briefly on the connection between Scripture and the Confessions, which in a sense occupy a position within Lutheranism analogous to tradition. In addition, Chemnitz is better known in the history of the church as a confessionalist rather than a biblical scholar, although as the above material has indicated, that point might be debated. As the doctrine of Scripture has eroded over the past centuries, theologians have tended to divide between biblical scholars on one hand and systematicians and confessionalists on the other. But sometimes a good statement comes along in which a theologian cuts through both the systematics and the exegesis and tells it like it is. Such a statement occurs in Schlink, where the integral connection between the Bible and the confessions, the basic faith and the actual words of the confessors, shines forth. He makes a statement with which we may be certain that Chemnitz would be in complete agreement, for Chemnitz was not a theorist: he was a confessor of what he believed to be biblical truth as it stood written in Scripture and as it had been understood down through the history of the church. This is what the Lutheran Confessions were to those who wrote them, signed them, believed, taught, and confessed them. Schlink says,

> Confessions in their proper sense will never be taken seriously until they are taken seriously as exposition of the Scriptures, to be specific, as the church's exposition of the Scriptures. Confessions are not free-lancing theological opinions; they are statements of doctrine that must be understood even to their last detail in terms of that exposition of Scripture which is the church's responsibility, entrusted to it in and with the responsibility of proclamation. Confessions are primarily expositions of Scripture, more particularly summary presentation of the whole of Scripture, that is, a witness to the heart of Scripture, a witness to the saving Gospel. Resting on Scripture as a whole, the Confessions aim to summarize the multiplicity of statements from Scripture in doctrinal articles directed against the errors of their day and designed for the protection of the correct proclamation then and for all time to come.

Schlink follows with a statement that he could have taken directly out of Chemnitz' *Iudicium:*

> But exposition of Scripture in which a single member of the church takes his stand against false doctrines cannot yet be called a Confession. As long as Confessions are regarded merely as the writings of Melanchthon or of Luther, along with other writings of Melanchthon or of Luther, they are not yet taken to be Confessions. In the Confessions it is precisely not an individual, but the church which expounds Scripture. Even if the Confessions came from the pen of Melanchthon or of Luther, they no longer belong to these individual members of the church. On the contrary, the teaching church has assumed responsibility for them. They are now a sacrifice of praise offered by the whole congregation of believers, who therewith glorify the grace of God in common repentance and in common faith.[7]

Well spoken!

TRADITION

Likewise the *ECT* is our best source for information about Chemnitz' attitude toward tradition. Actually, this has already been covered by his stress on the sole authority of Scripture, but Chemnitz does not hold a fundamentalistic or simplistic view on this matter. He was an excellent student of church history, as were Luther and Melanchthon. Chemnitz, the conservative respecter of the "purer ancient church," was not about to throw out the baby with the bath water. He wanted to preserve that part of tradition which was edifying for the church of his day and for its posterity. His treatment of this subject in *ECT* is a classic which sets a standard for Lutheran thinking that still is followed today (*ECT* 217–307).[8] Unlike the Anabaptists, who had no appreciation for the history or tradition of the church, and who wanted to make a leap from the New Testament era to their own time (much like many of their fundamentalistic and biblicistic successors in the 20th century), Chemnitz had high respect for the ancient church and held with Luther that Lutheran theology was part of the great continuum of theology stretching from the New Testament down to the present. Chemnitz argues in the *ECT* that not the Lutherans but the Romanists have departed from the great tradition of the church, which had included justification by faith. Thus the inclusion of the three great creeds in the Book of Concord, and the reference to them in the FC were the Lutherans' way of stressing their commitment to the "tradition," the continuum of the faith, which had been "once delivered to the saints" (Jude 3).

Yet there was enough confusion about the matter of tradition within Lutheranism and enough attacks on Roman traditionalism, even by ecumenically minded people like Melanchthon, so that Trent was able to find a way to attack the Protestants on this point. In defense of their own position they had to counterattack. This gave Chemnitz an opportunity to frame the remarkable reply that appears in his *ECT*. In his usual cautious and objective manner he asserts that tradition, correctly understood, is a good thing. John F. Johnson writes,

> Chemnitz had high regard for tradition and frequently appealed to it. Indeed, characteristic of his approach is the contention that not only the Bible, but also tradition, can be used to substantiate

the Reformation point. The writers of antiquity do not know of any tradition which contradicts Scripture. For Chemnitz, then, the controversy between the Reformation and Trent is not over the question of acknowledging the importance and value of the dogmatic tradition. For him, the primary stumbling block was that other meaning that became attached to the notion of tradition; a meaning which claims that tradition includes practices and doctrines for which the Bible provides no explicit authority.[9]

Chemnitz makes clear that Lutheranism did not hold a fundamentalistic attitude toward tradition or the rejection of all things Roman Catholic; but all such beliefs and practices must be rooted in Scripture or at least in no way opposed to Scripture.

CHRIST IS THE HEART AND CENTER OF SCRIPTURE

This is another truism that is demonstrated on almost every page of Chemnitz' writings. For one thing, Chemnitz does not use the term Gospel in a loose sense or independent manner. Gospel is most commonly used in contradistinction to the Law on the one hand and in connection with the doctrine of justification by faith in Christ on the other. For example,

> [Paul] has undertaken the writing of this epistle [Galatians] with the object of explaining and confirming what he had delivered orally among the Galatians concerning the doctrine of the Gospel, namely, concerning Jesus Christ, the Crucified (in whom the whole story of Christ is summed up), and concerning the true application, explanation, and use of this story (*ECT*, 125–26).

But there is never a Gospel-reductionism in connection with the term Gospel or the doctrine of justification, whereby the only teaching of Scripture which must be believed by the Christian is the Gospel. All of Scripture must be believed by the Christian; but only faith in the Gospel, in Christ, saves him.

> Thus, when faith assents to the entire Word of God, it looks at the goal of all of Scripture and refers all the other articles of faith to the promise of grace for the sake of Christ the Mediator. . . . In vain does faith concern itself with the other objects of Scripture if

it does not hold firmly to the Head of Scripture, which is Christ, (Col. 2:19) (*LT*, I, 500).

He delimits this matter further: ". . . the object of justifying faith is not the Word of God in general, but the promise of the benefits of Christ the Mediator . . ." (*LT*, 501).

PURPOSE OF SCRIPTURE

The purpose of Scripture is reiterated by Chemnitz, namely, to make men "wise unto salvation through faith" in Christ Jesus and to teach them how to live godly lives (ibid., 41).

> Paul ascribes two things to Holy Scripture. First, that it can make the man of God, that is, a teacher of the church (for they are called people or men of God) perfect, sufficiently equipped for every good work (which is. . . necessarily required to perform the ministry of the church). 2 Tim. 3:16–17. Second, that a believer might be made wise unto salvation through faith. 2 Tim. 3:15. (*Enchiridion*, 41).

In his *ECT* he says,

> It is certainly clear as clear can be that the Scripture has been given for all ages, and for this use, that they should be certain that their sins are forgiven, that they know the Father who is from the beginning, that they overcome the wicked one, and that the Word of God remains in them. . . . When he [John] is about to conclude the epistle in chapter 5, he says, "I write this to you who believe in the name of the Son of God, that you may know that you have eternal life and that you may believe in the name of the Son of God." . . . John shows that he wrote both for the benefit of those who already believed, in order that, confirmed in the faith, they might know that they possessed eternal life . . . (*ECT*, I, 145–46).

POWER OF THE SCRIPTURE

The power of Scripture (its causative authority) comes from the Holy Spirit who works through the Word, as when Luther in his Small Catechism says, "The Holy Spirit has called me by the Gospel."

But the New Testament is the promise of grace on account of the Son and Mediator. With this is connected the promise and bestowal of the Holy Spirit, who by His power and operation writes into hearts the doctrine which is proclaimed through the ministry, whether it be orally or in writing; that is, He illumines the mind, regenerates the will and heart, so that we can embrace the promise concerning the Messiah in true faith from the heart. To those who believe in His name He gives power to become the children of God (John 1:12). And this is what Jeremiah says that the Holy Spirit writes the doctrine of the Gospel into the hearts of the believers, that it may be fulfilled what he says: "I will be their God, and they will be My people." After that the Holy Spirit also writes the doctrine of the Law into the hearts of the regenerate, that the heart may have its delight in the Law according to the inner man (Rom. 7:22) and that they may begin to obey from the heart (Rom. 6:17). (*ECT,* 76)

In the FC, SD, Chemnitz states, "God has His holy Gospel preached to us, through which the Holy Spirit wills to work such conversion and renewal in us, that through the preaching of His Word and our meditation upon it He can kindle faith and other God-pleasing virtues in us" (2.71, Tappert 535). Again, ". . . the Holy Spirit wills to work such repentance and faith in us through the Word and the Sacraments" (ibid., 627).

THE PRINCIPLES FOR THE INTERPRETATION OF THE SCRIPTURE

In the writings of Luther, Melanchthon, and Chemnitz, there are many rules for the interpretation of the Scriptures, but with all three men the rules or principles are simply enunciated in passing or in connection with some other point. Not until Gerhard (1610), one generation after Chemnitz, do we see a complete section of a *Loci Theologici* devoted to the principles of biblical interpretation.[10] Nevertheless, Chemnitz makes a number of important comments on the subject. C. G. H. Lentz quotes a summary statement from Chemnitz showing his principles of interpretation,

We must honor and hold in high esteem the grammatical study of the words. For the church by its interpretation is not producing new dogmas, but studies, learns and accepts the things which have been handed down and revealed by the divine voice. And just as the teachings themselves have been revealed by the divine voice in the Word, so also these same things cannot be correctly understood, except from the true and genuine meaning of the word which the Holy Spirit uses in teaching the heavenly doctrine. Therefore we are not dealing here with a war over grammar, as they call it, but to the degree that we err in regard to the words in the chief points of doctrine, to that degree we lose in the doctrines themselves; for if the true grammatical understanding is lost, immediately the light of the purer doctrine is lost. And when in our generation the true grammatical understanding of the words was restored, at once the purity of the doctrine was restored.[11]

The above contains a summary of almost all of Chemnitz' doctrinal and hermeneutical principles. The Scripture is made up of words, for which reason grammar and the understanding and interpretation of the words are imperative. He stipulates that the church can interpret but not create new dogmas, but rather must study, learn, and accept what Scripture teaches.

Scripture is a record of the divine voice or message; it is God's Word. The items presented us in Scripture are revealed by the Holy Spirit. This point is particularly important in the case of Melanchthon, because he was one of the world's greatest experts in his day regarding ancient secular literature, as indicated previously. He was dealing constantly with the translation and interpretation of the written word in both secular and sacred literature. Melanchthon treats the position and interpretation of Scripture exactly as Luther and Chemnitz do, that is, as something special and unique.[12] The point here is that all three of these men were schooled in humanism, all educated in philosophy and very well acquainted with ancient literature and textual criticism and the textual problems in both Scripture and other literature, yet all three stood on the same ground regarding the *doctrine* of Scripture, namely, that the Scripture is unique among all human literature because of its origin, its content, its authority, its purpose, its nature, and the methods of interpreting it.

We wish to emphasize this last point here, for it is a point which seems to have been lost in the abyss we today call modern theology. In our post-Enlightenment era, historical criticism has reduced the Bible to the level of all other ancient literature and obliterated the entire concept of Scripture as a unique book and a special kind of literature inspired by God. Luther, Melanchthon, and Chemnitz would all agree that it is impossible to speak of Scripture as God's Word and revelation, along with its authority, clarity, inerrancy, and its other characteristics including the principles laid down in Scripture for its own interpretation without at the same time emphasizing its total uniqueness. This is beyond debate among them. There is an aspect to Luther's central doctrine of justification and the three basic *solas* of Lutheran theology which derives from his virtually unique principle of understanding and interpreting the Scripture.

Thus, while we moderns frequently distinguish between doctrine and the principles of interpretation, it is important to be clear on the fact that this distinction was not quite so clearly delineated in the Reformation.[13] Thus it is incorrect in dealing with Chemnitz' theology to separate the doctrine of Scripture and make that something purely doctrinal, and to turn around and act as if the hermeneutical principles for interpreting the Scripture are purely matters of human judgment or opinion. The Scripture contains within itself the rules for its own interpretation. You will note in the following pages that Chemnitz never treats the question of how we are to interpret the Scripture as a matter of purely human judgment. For example (*Enchiridion*, p. 42), "Since Holy Scripture is a light shining in darkness and enlightening the eyes (Ps. 19:8, 2 Peter 1:19), it sets forth and interprets itself in clear words." Or to say it in a different way, the Scripture not only asserts its authority, it also shows how it is to be interpreted. For this reason, we must begin with comments on his doctrine of Scripture itself, for this underlies every locus in both Melanchthon's and Chemnitz' works. And both follow Luther.

In fact, as we shall attempt to show, when Chemnitz in a formal way and for the first time in Lutheranism, takes up the doctrine of Scripture per se in his *ECT*, it is manifest that the methods of interpretation of Scripture used by the Lutherans and those of the Romanists are very far apart, not only on the doctrine of justification but also on many other points. In short, to a degree not often demonstrated, the problem between Lutheranism and Rome dealt fundamentally with the principles for interpreting the Scripture. One

might even go on to assert that although in the early period of the
Protestant Reformation nearly all of the Protestants were in agreement on the interpretive principles which led Luther, Calvin, and
Zwingli, and many others to agreement on justification by faith; yet
the fact that very quickly the Reformed party diverged from the
Lutherans on the Lord's Supper indicated that a difference was
developing not only on the Lord's Supper but also on many other
points. Perhaps it is almost a miracle of history that for a few short
years there was that *kairos* when all of the Protestants agreed on
justification. But because of differences on how to interpret the
Bible, divergencies began to appear that have never been healed.

We could summarize by saying that Chemnitz' and Luther's
quarrel with Rome dealt with the basic problem of the authority of
Scripture and the principles for interpreting it as over against the
authority of the church; their quarrel with the Reformed ultimately
came down to the question of how to interpret Scripture, especially
in the use of figurative language and in the face of human rational-
izing, and despite all of the Reformed protestations in support of the
sole authority of Scripture. In other words, the principles of biblical interpretation (hermeneutics) are part of the doctrine of Scripture, not some general rules that apply to any kind of literature.

THE DISTINCTION BETWEEN LAW AND GOSPEL

Although it is a primary matter of doctrine and confession that
the Law and the Gospel be properly distinguished, yet this point
became so ingrained in the thinking of the Reformers that it takes
on the character of a normative principle of biblical interpretation as
well as a dogma for Luther, Melanchthon, and Chemnitz.[14] While
we could just as well discuss the matter under his doctrine of Scripture, or, as Melanchthon does, either under Law or Gospel, yet
because of the overarching involvement of this doctrine and its relationship to the interpretation of the entire Scripture, we shall deal
with it here as kind of a connecting link between Chemnitz' doctrine
of Scripture and his principles for interpreting the Scripture.

As early as 1515–16 in his "Lectures on Romans" Luther is beginning to see the light on this point. He says,

. . . the preaching of the Gospel is something lovable and desirable for those who are under the Law. For the Law shows nothing but our sin, makes us guilty, and thus produces an anguished conscience; but the Gospel supplies a longed-for remedy to people in anguish of this kind. Therefore the Law is evil, and the Gospel good; the Law announces wrath, but the Gospel peace . . . (*AE*, 25.416–18).[15]

By the time of his first "Lectures on Galatians" in 1519 Luther is in full swing,

The Law, I say, makes slaves, since it is from fear of threats and because of a craving for promised rewards, not without an ulterior motive, that the Law is fulfilled by them. And so it is not fulfilled. But since it is not fulfilled, it makes them guilty and the slaves of sin. Faith, however, brings it about that after receiving love we keep the Law, not under compulsion or because we are attracted to it for a time but freely and steadfastly.[16]

The greatest treatise of all on the subject of Law and Gospel is Luther's 1535 edition of his "Lectures on Galatians," where he really reaches his great theological height. The work is filled with references to this basic doctrine and interpretive principle. Compare these with Melanchthon's *Loci Communes* (1521),

. . . there are two parts to Scripture, law and gospel. The law shows sin, the gospel grace. The law indicates disease, the gospel points out the remedy. To use Paul's words, the law is the minister of death, the gospel is the minister of life and peace: "The power of sin is the law" (1 Cor. 15:56), but the gospel is "the power of salvation to every one who has faith" (Rom. 1:16). . . . the presentation of the gospel is scattered, and the promises are sprinkled throughout all the books of the Old and New Testaments. On the other hand, law is also scattered in all the books of the Old and New Testaments. . . . The whole of Scripture is in some parts law, in others gospel.[17]

These remarks are from the first edition of the LC, but the same teaching is found in the later editions of the work also.

When we come to Chemnitz, we find again the faithful follower of Luther and Melanchthon. Remember Melanchthon's famous words to him in 1549 that "learning to distinguish between Law and Gospel was the brightest light and the best method in the entire study of theology." Over and over again, in several different loci of his *LT*, we find various expressions in Chemnitz about the distinction of Law and Gospel. The Law comes in for some very close scrutiny in the writings of the Reformers, and the fact is that along with the rediscovery of the Gospel there was an enormous and sometimes radical rethinking and reinterpretation of the nature, purpose, and use of the moral law, and the concomitant careful shelving of the civil and ceremonial laws, in opposition both to Rome and to the Anabaptists. Whole books deal with this point, and it is manifest that Chemnitz was totally involved in this revolution. The endeavor was so massive that doctrine spilled over into the principles of interpretation, just as was the case with the Gospel itself, with Christ, and the doctrine of justification. For example, in his *LT* (449–50, 536, 589) under the loci on justification and good works Chemnitz has excellent sections on the distinction between Law and Gospel. If one reads the Lutheran Confessions with the understanding that the Reformation not only rediscovered the Gospel but also the Law of God, then several conclusions follow these revolutionary discoveries:

First, Lutheranism required a complete rethinking of the nature, purpose, use, and meaning of the Law of God. This one item was so revolutionary that even Luther could not absorb it all at once and Melanchthon himself backed away from his own assertions in the face of the Interims, the Romanists, and even the Anglicans. Rome has not yet faced this revolutionary understanding of the Law and the Gospel; and the modern Reformed church with its various forms of legalism, pietism, and social activisim, despite Calvin's original understanding and enunciation of the distinction of Law and Gospel, has at least to a large degree lost what understanding it once may have had. Second, many within Lutheranism itself never quite grasped the enormity of this point—witness Osiander, the Synergists, and later pietists on the one hand, and Amsdorf and Agricola on the other. Thus there was need in the FC for article II on Free Will, III on Justification or the Righteousness of Faith before God, IV on good works, V on Law and Gospel, and VI on the Third Use of the Law. The failure to understand completely the distinction of Law and Gospel produced those, such as Agricola and Amsdorf, who went too far, and Melanchthon and Major, whose synergism perverted their vision and did not go far enough. This is why confessional Lutheranism has always been and must remain on guard against pietism, legalism, the charismatic movement, and subjectivism of every kind which obscure the Gospel and prevent it from truly being the Gospel. Third, we see why the later Confessions and Chemnitz, following Luther and Melanchthon, so strongly stressed the distinction between Law and Gospel, that like justification and Christology it became more than a dogma; it also became a hermeneutical principle for interpreting all of Scripture.

As an indication of Chemnitz' involvement, note Article V of the FC. This article grew out of the antinomian controversy in which both Luther and Melanchthon had been involved on the right side, but the issue kept coming up and still needed attention at the time of the FC. Article VI on the Third Use of the Law also impinges on this aspect of the problem. Note how the matter has taken on hermeneutical aspects: in SD Article V, 1, the Formula reads,

> The distinction between Law and Gospel is an especially brilliant light which serves the purpose that the Word of God may be rightly divided and the writings of the holy prophets and apostles may be explained and understood correctly. We must therefore observe this distinction with particular diligence lest we confuse the two doctrines and change the Gospel into Law. This would darken the merit of Christ and rob disturbed consciences of the comfort which they would otherwise have in the Holy Gospel.

The article goes on to stress the importance of distinguishing between the broad and narrow meanings of the words *repentance* and *Gospel*. In other words, how one interprets the Scripture affects both doctrine and consciences. These two articles are excellent demonstrations of both the position of Lutheranism at the time but also the theology of the chief writer of the FC, Martin Chemnitz.[18]

One final point needs to be added, namely, that just as Law and Gospel form a principle for biblical interpretation, so does the doctrine of justification by grace, which is actually the same thing, except for a slight difference in emphasizing the forensic aspect of the Gospel. Robert Preus says this very well:

> Closely related to the hermeneutical function of the distinction between Law and Gospel is the emphasis upon the centrality of the gospel of justification and its function. Both Melanchthon and

Luther in the confessions had stressed the centrality of the article of justification and used this chief article hermeneutically. . . . The Solid Declaration agrees with the Apology and with Luther on the centrality of this doctrine [Tappert 540.6]. "In the words of the Apology, this article of justification by faith is the 'chief article of the entire Christian doctrine, without which no poor conscience can have any abiding comfort or rightly understand the riches of the grace of Christ.' "

He concludes by saying,

The chief article is used hermeneutically in the Formula exactly as in the Apology and the Smalcald Articles. It is used to counter false and unevangelical practices which undermine the Gospel, to combat rationalistic or legalistic exegeses which undermine the Gospel, and positively to offer a setting for the presentation of the articles of faith.[19]

SCRIPTURE INTERPRETS SCRIPTURE

While what has already been said about God as the author of Scripture, the infallibility of Scripture, the interpretation by the Holy Spirit, and other points demonstrate conclusively that Chemnitz believed that Scripture was its own best interpreter. In his *LS*, he comments on 2 Peter 1:20 ("No Scripture is of private interpretation"):

In order that our faith may be sure, the Holy Spirit has shown in Scripture itself that there is a definite method or analogy which must be followed in the interpretation of such passages. . . . But is there not such a thing as freedom in the interpretation of a particular passage of Scripture to the degree that seems good to each individual so that we may either retain the proper meanings of the words or through the use of a figure of speech depart from the simple, proper, and natural meaning of the words according to each person's own notions? . . . The answer is a categorical no! (pp. 67–68).

He continues,

For Scripture, especially when it treats of dogmas, because it is not of private interpretation, interprets itself either in the same passage or in other passages where the same dogma is touched on (p. 68).

THE ANALOGY OF SCRIPTURE: CLEAR PASSAGES INTERPRET THE LESS CLEAR

Chemnitz recognizes that not all statements of Scripture are equally clear and that the clearer passages help to determine the meaning of the less clear. For example,

> This observation is often useful and helpful, namely, that the testimonies which have been used from the very beginning of the church can be sought out, even if they often seem obscure, in order that we can become sure that at all times from the very beginning a particular statement of doctrine has been voiced in the church. For we are built not only on "the foundation of the apostles," but also "of the prophets," Eph. 2:20. Then to those rather obscure passages are added those which are clearer, so that a person may consider the manner in which the teaching in Scripture concerning the particular articles of faith has been handled in the passage of time and set forth more clearly. And in this series of testimonies we finally must come to those statements which are the clearest of all and which cannot be overturned in any way, so that our faith may have a firm and permanent foundation on which to rest (*LT*, I, 46).

In his *LS* he asserts,

> The true and natural meaning, however, can be gathered from other passages, where the dogmas are touched upon in simple, proper, and clear words. As Augustine says, *De Doctrina Christiana*, Bk. 2, ch. 6: "We must draw nothing from obscure passages which is not found written elsewhere in clear language." And in his *Contra epistolam Petiliani*, ch. 16, he says that the things which are spoken in an obscure, ambiguous, or figurative way cannot be rightly understood or interpreted unless we first hold with firm faith to the things which are spoken clearly (p. 78).

Note also Chemnitz' use of the three articles of the Creed in the Formula of Concord in order to refute the Flacian error. Chemnitz shows that Flacius' error would deny the article on creation, redemption, sanctification, and the resurrection of the body.

THE LITERAL SENSE VERSUS A FIGURATIVE INTERPRETATION

Chemnitz' basic hermeneutical principle is that the *sensus literalis*, the literal sense, is to be retained unless the context determines otherwise.[20] Chemnitz fully understands that certain portions of Scripture are figurative and that it was the intended sense of the writer that they should be such. In other words, the literal sense is to be preferred over a figurative of metaphorical interpretation unless the context demands otherwise. But for the establishment of a dogma a clear and literal statement is required. He says,

> There is a rule which is correct and of long standing which Jerome deals with, namely, that dogmas cannot be established or corroborated purely on the basis of figures of speech and allegories. For not just any kind of meaning ought to be derived from figures of speech, nor ought one develop any kind of dogma he wishes. But whatever is developed on the basis of improper words, figures of speech, obscure and ambiguous language—that, in order that the full assurance of faith might have a sure and solid foundation, must of necessity be taught and established on the basis of words used elsewhere in Scripture which are proper, clear, and commonly known and used. . . ." (*LS*, 79).

The concept of determining the literal sense and interpreting a passage literally instead of metaphorically or figuratively became a matter of primary concern among the Lutheran principles of biblical interpretation during the long and acrimonious controversies over the Lord's Supper. In fact, most of what Luther and Chemnitz have to say on this principle of interpretation is found in their writings on the Lord's Supper, on which both men wrote many treatises.

We cite here three statements from Chemnitz' *LS* (where the entire chapter 7 is entitled "The Arguments from the Clear and Continuous Analogy of Interpretation Which the Holy Spirit Has Taught Us to Observe in Those Passages Where Dogmas or Articles of Faith Are Treated and Established"). First, Chemnitz quotes Luther with approval,

> Therefore Luther is correct in saying that before the very judgment seat of the Son of God he would bring this defense: "Lord Jesus Christ, a controversy has arisen and an argument has come up regarding the words of Your last will and testament. Some are

contending that these words must be understood differently from the meaning indicated by their proper and natural sense. But because among these people there is no agreement as to what kind of figure it is or into what category it must be placed, they cannot with consistency or consensus demonstrate one sure interpretation of the words but rather drag the words of Your testament into many different and dissimilar interpretations. Thus I have not been able, nor have I wanted to commit my faith in this serious controversy to these uncertain, varied, and differing waves of interpretations and opinions. But on the contrary, I have seen that if Your words are taken as they stand in their simple, proper, and natural sense, then we can have one constant and certain understanding. Therefore, because I have determined that You have willed that there be one definite understanding of Your last will and testament, I rest on that interpretation which the words in their simple, proper, and natural meaning demonstrate and drive us to accept as the one, sure, and certain interpretation. For if You had willed that the words should be understood in a way other than in their literal sense, You would undoubtedly have given a clear and open declaration of this fact, just as You have done in those passages in which we may exercise our imaginations without any peril, as is not the case in the words of Your last will and testament." (Cf. "Confession concerning Christ's Supper" AE 37.305) (*LS* 87)[21]

Note that Luther here stresses, as does Chemnitz throughout, the simple, proper, and natural meaning of the words, the literal sense; but also the fact that the matter of interpretation is part of the doctrine of the Supper. The interpretation is something we take before the judgment seat of God. Chemnitz himself echoes this idea, when he says,

In order that our faith may be sure, the Holy Spirit has shown in the Scripture itself that there is a definite method or analogy which must be followed in the interpretation of such passages. As a result many clear, firm, and very weighty arguments have been developed which compel us not to depart from the proper, simple, and natural meaning of the words of the last will and testament of the Son of God (*LS*, 67).

He echoes Luther even more closely when he asserts,

Thus my conscience can safely rest on this foundation and resist all temptations with this assurance. This will be my constant defense before the Testator Himself, the Son of God: "I stand on the words of Your last will and testament with great care and solicitude, so that I might not discern Your Supper wrongly and thus incur judgment. But because Scripture is not of private interpretation, I see that You have done in the case of this dogma the same thing that You have established in other dogmas, namely, that what is repeated from time to time in the passages of Scripture contains within it the correct interpretation so that it is not necessary either to seek it elsewhere or to add something drawn in from somewhere else. Moreover, in these repetitions I have not found that You desire that the words of institution are to be understood in any way differently than their literal sense, but rather I have observed that the proper and natural meaning of the words is confirmed by these repetitions" (*LS* 70).

These ideas occur on almost every page of chapter 7 of his *LS*.

In the FC the same ideas are evident. In the SD VII, 48, written primarily by Chemnitz, we read, "All the circumstances of the institution of this Supper testify that these words of our Lord and Saviour Jesus Christ, which in themselves are simple, clear, manifest, certain, and indubitable, can and should be understood only in their usual, strict, and commonly accepted meaning" (p. 70). In VII, 50 we read, "In the institution of his last will and testament and of his abiding covenant and union, he uses no flowery language but the most appropriate (*propriis*), simple, indubitable and clear words, just as he does in all the articles of faith. . . ."

Closely related to the above is the desire of the student of Scripture or the theologian to determine the intended sense of the Scripture, that is, to determine what the biblical writer actually wanted or intended to say. This concept is commonly used in Chemnitz' writings. For example, see FC SD VII, 50, "There is, of course, no more faithful or trustworthy interpreter of the words of Jesus Christ than the Lord Jesus Christ Himself, who best understands His words and heart and intention and is best qualified from the standpoint of wisdom and intelligence to explain them." Similarly, *ECT* 128, "The intended sense will be learned if we consider. . . ." Chemnitz then proceeds to interpret several statements of Paul. Again, FC SD III, 36, "And this is St. Paul's intention when in this article he so earnestly and diligently stresses such exclusive terms as 'without works.' . . ."[22]

EQUALITY OF THE OT AND NT

In the theology of Luther, Melanchthon, and Chemnitz the Old Testament is regarded as one with the New Testament, not something separate or abstract from it.[23] Basically the two testaments are one and the same. The difference is that the OT looks forward to Christ, while the NT with greater clarity looks at Him. There is one God, one Savior, one Holy Spirit, one way of salvation, one theology, one church. For example, Luther in his *Lectures on Genesis*,[24] Melanchthon in Chemnitz' *LT* (274, 454, 461, and 721), and Chemnitz in his *LT* (55, 138, 456, 495, and 546) all use Genesis 3:15 as the *sedes doctrinae* for the fall of man, the doctrine of original sin and man's restoration through Christ, in short, as a summary of the Christian faith. This OT text is exactly as authoritative as John 3:16, and both proclaim the same Gospel and the same Savior and the same faith.[25]

CHEMNITZ' THEOLOGICAL METHOD AND STYLE

Although the following does not attempt to set forth an exhaustive account of Chemnitz' methodology, it will highlight a number of distinguishing characteristics about his theological method and style.

Chemnitz on Polemics

Chemnitz lived in a very polemical age in the history of the church. Almost all of Luther's writings at least to a degree had polemical elements. The same was the case with Chemnitz, except for his sermons and his lovely treatise on the Lord's Prayer. As might be expected, especially in view of Luther's sometimes outrageous attacks and his use of such foul language, many of his followers adopted the same attitude. It is also true that Luther's opponents were even more vicious in their attacks on him and on others.

To a remarkable degree, considering the times, Chemnitz is very restrained. Although his letters and personal documents reveal his ability to express himself in vehement language, as in his letters to Duke Julius and to Hieronymous Mörlin, still he is for the most part very mild. His public writings, while very direct, do not involve personal attacks or harsh language. In fact, he eschewed these practices. Over and over again in his writings we see attempts to heal breaches rather than enlarge them. His dealings with the pastors at Göttingen show this. His repetition of the expression that we must leave certain matters to settlement in "the heavenly academy" is noteworthy. This expression was often applied to the somewhat different emphasis concerning the matter of ubiquity between himself and Brenz. Andreae also held with Brenz, and the Formula of Concord shows this difference, without either man condemning the other. His long-standing aversion to attacking opponents by name, and his insistence on this policy in the FC, are well known. This was particularly true in the case of Melanchthon, whom he never seems to have attacked even in private correspondence, though some of his correspondents were vigorous in their attacks on Melanchthon, Andreae, and many others.

Chemnitz' irenic disposition is described very fully in Gasmer's *Oratio* delivered at the time of his mentor's death. It is evident that Gasmer himself was not enamoured of strident polemics. He cites Cyprian who says, "The truly poor man is not the man who is cursed, but the one who curses."[26] Gasmer tells us that Chemnitz often quoted Augustine, "He who tries to destroy my reputation unwillingly adds to my good name." Gasmer continues,

> I recall Chemnitz often reminiscing about Sabinus, and how he had on one occasion come into the Prussian Library and spying some polemical books there, although he found several praiseworthy statements in them by men who were contending loudly, he had become indignant and said that since in this unhappy age all desire to become famous, anyone can become an immortal in this way, but if a person were to gather from all these polemical writings the ways and words which are used to reproach others and bind them into one package, he would not be subject to criticism himself and he would easily have at hand both a supply of material and varieties of material if he should undertake to deal with this subject. The most brilliant man will surely take note of this cacophony of criticism and all good men must abhor it.[27]

He goes on to describe how Chemnitz ran his schools and trained them to study the catechism of Luther and other books of sound doctrine. Chemnitz also quoted Scipio Romanus who said that "a state is certainly in trouble, even while the walls still stand, if morals have disappeared."[28]

The Use of Definitions

An orderly mind like Chemnitz' required an orderly presentation of theology in order to edify the church and instruct the teachers as well as the students. Thus we find in his polemic and doctrinal writings constant references to definitions, categorizations, division of a discussion into separate parts. The influence of Melanchthon and also Luther is very evident in this respect. It would appear that the writing of Urbanus Rhegius, the *Formula Caute Loquendi*, to which Chemnitz added an appendix longer than the original, was also a great influence in the development of his theological methodology. While this method of presenting things is not as exciting as some forms of literature, it helps enormously in gaining exactness. We see this in his *Enchiridion*, which was designed for the doctrinal examinations of rank and file pastors. We see this in his *LS* and especially in his *TNC* where the very first chapter is devoted entirely to definitions, and in other chapters the various points are carefully defined. In almost every locus of his *LT* he provides definitions for the topic he is discussing. Supplying definitions and speaking according to them is one of the hallmarks of the good theologian, and Chemnitz is among the best in this area.

Word Studies and the Exegetical Method

As a scriptural theologian Chemnitz obviously was deeply committed to the Scripture as the source of his teaching and thus he was very involved in the use of the exegetical method. He did not engage in mere mouthing of Bible verses, but made in-depth lexicographical and exegetical studies employing the original Hebrew and Greek, the historical setting for the original account as to whether the Scripture reference was either literal or figurative. He was just as careful to avoid using figurative material literally as he was to use literal material figuratively. Both are errors, and he avoided both.

He was not as flamboyant as Melanchthon in his use of illustrations and mythological allusions, which are very interesting and make for good reading and easy memorization—although he does indulge in some of this. The real talent of Chemnitz was his use of the Scripture in its original languages, his ability to summarize and systematize this material, and to express his conclusions in simple and clear language. Even his *TNC*, which deals with some very abstruse subjects and requires a considerable knowledge of the original Greek, the ancient church fathers, Greek philosophy, and especially an accurate knowledge of the actual teaching of the Reformed in his own day, is written in such simple language and so carefully explained that even today a reasonably well educated pastor or layperson can read it with ease and benefit.

There are some excellent word studies in his *TNC*, for example chapter IX (pp. 115–41), under the title "Light Shed by Main Words Used by Scripture and Ancient Church," where he analyzes such terms as "was made flesh" in John 1:14.

Reference to Church History and History of Dogma

In his later years Luther, perhaps influenced by Melanchthon, began to make greater use of church history in his various controversies. A prime example of that is his Treatise on the Councils (1539).[29] Melanchthon also was well acquainted with the history of the church and used this knowledge in his theologizing. But Chemnitz, more than either of the former, was an astute student of church history, the history of the various controversies, and the councils that were called to settle them. He was acquainted with and used nearly every primary source available to scholars today. His chief sources were the same as our own, Eusebius, Socrates (not the Athenian philosopher), Sozomen, the proceedings of the councils, the *Historia tripartita*, and others. Together with his prodigious knowledge of the fathers, which enabled him to make all kinds of historical analyses of events in the church, his knowledge of church history was both extensive and greatly used by him.

Chemnitz' *TNC*, though having a very narrow purpose—the refutation of the Wittenberg Crypto-Calvinists—is a veritable history of the dogma of Christology. This work contains almost a complete account of every Christological heresy and controversy from the first century down to Chemnitz' own day, naming the names of the contestants, the point at issue and the outcome. Note chapter 18 (*TNC*, 233–40) on the Monothelete controversy and the Sixth Ecumenical Council, as only one example. One of the most interesting features of his *LT* is his ongoing discourse, almost a chronicle, on the Pelagian controversy, the roles of Pelagius, Augustine, Prosper of Acquataine, Julian of Eclanum, and Cassian, plus many of his own contemporaries, in a controversy which went on almost continuously from antiquity until Chemnitz' own time. The Lutheran doctrine of salvation by grace alone is constantly buttressed by the study of the history of this dogma down through the ages. The use of the history of the church is also manifest in his discussion of such other doctrines as God, the Trinity, original sin, and nearly all the rest.

Chemnitz' Use of the Church Fathers

Closely related to Chemnitz' knowledge of the history of the church and his use of this information in his theological work is also his colossal knowledge and use of the church fathers and their theology. It is significant that the very first document Chemnitz ever published, written on Nov. 25, 1554, while he was still at Wittenberg, was a Treatise on the Reading of the Fathers or Doctors of the Church (*Oratio de Lectione Patrum* . . .), which he used as a preliminary explanation to his lectures on Melanchthon's LC at Wittenberg.[30] His *Oratio* (1554), while brief and not particularly profound, bears marks which show up in all of his subsequent use of the fathers in much more weighty works such as his *ECT* , his *TNC*, and his *LT*. Chemnitz' treatise shows a pattern he regularly followed: he began with the earliest and closed the list with Luther, sometimes Melanchthon. At times he separated the Greek from the Latin fathers. His use of the fathers in the FC follows this pattern, except that Melanchthon is absent, and Luther is cited far more than any other father, except possibly Augustine. The Catalog of Testimonies attached to the FC, dealing with Christology, is a testimony to the entire Lutheran church of Chemnitz' interest in and mastery of this subject. Again, this use of the fathers demonstrates his concern that Lutheran theology was not something new but a part of the great historical continuum of orthodox theology which stretches from the first century to his own day. His prodigious scholarship is perhaps more evident in this area than in any other. For example, his *TNC* has one chapter that has over 300 citations or *testimonia* from church fathers, and others contain over 200 each.

This was the age of the Magdeburg Centuries, and it is a bit surprising that Chemnitz makes no reference to this work which was highly respected in his own age. It is impossible to think that Chemnitz did not know it. Perhaps the falling out of Mörlin and Chemnitz with Flacius, who had been their former friend, moved him to ignore this important work, which was produced in the years 1562–74, just when Chemnitz was at his literary height, and which demonstrated from the original sources how various heresies had diverted the church from the truth down through the ages until the restoration of sound doctrine by Luther. This was precisely what Chemnitz was doing in many of his books and treatises. But while Chemnitz does mention Flacius by name in certain articles, yet the same rule of refusing to mention the names of opponents was generally followed by Chemnitz in this case also. For instance, in Chemnitz' *LT* (pp. 316–20), Leyser (the editor), inserts into Chemnitz' locus on sin a treatise written in 1569 by Chemnitz, dealing specifically with the Flacian error. Leyser describes the proposals of Flacius as "ungodly and ridiculous," but Chemnitz in his 1569 essay only mentions Flacius' name twice and then in a totally neutral way. He attacks the ideas but not the author of them. Nowhere does Chemnitz refer to the Magdeburg Centuries by name.

Peter Fraenkel, the prominent Melanchthon scholar, begins his book on Melanchthon and the fathers by saying, "The Lutheran Schoolmen of the 17th century (and even of the 16th) wrote innumerable treatises on the fathers, they packed their systems of dogmatic theology with patristic quotations and argued the antiquity of their teaching. . . to show its truth and purity."[31] A study of Fraenkel reveals Chemnitz' great indebtedness to Melanchthon in this area, but also certain advances beyond him. Where Melanchthon seems to have some difficulty establishing the patristic origin for the specific Reformation doctrines, such as the will, original sin, justification by faith, the Lutheran doctrine of grace, the Gospel in the Lutheran sense, and other points, Chemnitz boldly wades in and is lavish in his use of patristic citations on these very Lutheran subjects, as witnessed particularly in his *ECT,* I. (e.g. pp. 439–46, 505–13; *LT,* I, 237–56; II, 490–99, 519–24).[32]

Fraenkel devotes his book to the question,"What were his [Melanchthon's] methods of employing their [the fathers'] teaching (or what he thought to be their teaching) in his own theological arguments; what were the ends he hoped to attain by alleging and criticizing them as he did[?]"[33] Fraenkel begins by showing that Luther, even before Melanchthon, had developed an interest in the fathers, particularly as their ideas might impinge on the Reformation teachings. As early as 1515 Luther's colleague, John Lang, had published a collection of Jerome's letters. By 1516 Melanchthon, while still at Tübingen, "saw in this return to theological sources the very marrow of the Wittenberg theology. . . ."[34] And even before the Leipzig Debate (1518) Melanchthon exchanged letters with Luther's opponent Eck "on what conditions, Luther was right in claiming for his views the support of the ancient church."[35] Fraenkel further points out that the final edition (*Tertia Aetas*) of Melanchthon's LC, which Chemnitz used as the basis for his own *LT,* makes far greater use of the fathers than do the two previous editions.[36] Nor does Melanchthon express any need to justify this practice. It goes without saying, and it was accepted by succeeding generations of Lutheran theologians.

We have pointed out that Melanchthon was a great student of the fathers, and quoted them assiduously to substantiate the doctrines of Luther and the Reformation. Fraenkel (pp. 266ff.), regards Chemnitz as a theological link between Melanchthon and Gerhard by reason of Chemnitz' *ECT* and also his *Oratio de Lectione Patrum*.[37] He applies this to their theology as well as their methodological use of the fathers. In fact, Fraenkel says something regarding Chemnitz which is absolutely correct, "Exactly as for Gerhard, the critical study and use of the Fathers is not restricted to the special field of Patrology as a distinct discipline within theology, but is part and parcel of the author's whole theological method."[38]

251

To return to the original point, Chemnitz is certainly one of the greatest, if not the greatest, student of the fathers in early Lutheranism, but this is not some bare-bones study of the fathers merely to become an expert in this exotic science known as patristics, as Fraenkel has indicated. Far from it! The Lutherans had a very great interest in being part of the continuum of theology which existed from the time of Christ and apostles down to Luther and their own time. It is also important to note that the reformers used the word *testimonium* to describe their patristic citations. The fathers were part of the "heavenly witnesses," men standing before the judgment seat of God and bearing witness to their faith. We are talking about a spiritual and godly action, not merely a linguistic study. The same spirit pervades the use of the term "Catalog of Testimonies" in the appendix to the FC prepared by Andreae and Chemnitz.

We may summarize the thinking of Chemnitz and the other reformers on the matter of the use of the fathers as follows: First, they were interested in using the very words, phrases and modes of speaking of the fathers to ward off the Roman charge of injecting new and strange notions into the church. Second, they believed strongly in the concept of the unbroken tradition or continuum of teaching. Chemnitz in his *ECT* (1.258), "We disagree with those who invent opinions which have no testimony from any period in the church, as Servetus, Campanus, the Anabaptists, and others have done in our time. We also hold that no dogma that is new in the churches and in conflict with all of antiquity should be accepted." Third, there was the spoken desire to identify with the ancient purer church:

> Andrada wrongs us. . . . For we can affirm with good conscience that we have, after reading the Holy Scripture, applied ourselves and yet daily apply ourselves to the extent that the grace of the Lord permits to inquiry into and investigation of the consensus of the true and purer antiquity. For we assign to the writings of the fathers their proper and, indeed, honorable place which is due them . . ." (*ECT* 1. 256).

Fourth, the reformers wanted to establish authority for their own teaching, and the use of the fathers aided this endeavor. Fifth, the fathers were used by the Lutherans to refute errors both in the

Roman camp, as the *ECT* so clearly shows, as well as in the Reformed, as his *TNC* and the FC demonstrate. Sixth, the Lutheran reformers used the fathers to show the great distinction between their human writings and God's holy Word. In his "Treatise on Reading the Fathers" Chemnitz is swift to point out that great as the fathers were, they erred. Scripture does not, and thus it is our ultimate authority. Seventh, the fathers were cited to help in establishing a normative interpretation for certain key doctrines and passages. This device is used throughout, especially in the *ECT* and the *TNC*. Finally, while it is never said, it is not beyond the realm of possibility that Melanchthon, Chemnitz and the others, most of whom were doctors of theology, were anxious to show that their viewpoints demonstrated not only zeal but knowledge, learning, and education. They were not a band of rustics, like the Anabaptists and other fanatics. They were cut from the same cloth as their Roman opponents!

The Use of Philosophy and Mythology

The desire to show that they were as learned as their opponents may also explain the use of philosophy in the writings of all the reformers. Luther, Melanchthon, Chemnitz and most of the other reformers were graduates of universities, and it was only natural in the age of Renaissance humanism that philosophy should make up an important part of their education. Luther had so strongly criticized Aristotle that he is normally absolved of all indebtedness to the great Stagirite and to philosophy in general; but Melanchthon, who genuinely loved philosophy, has been roundly condemned for his use of this science, as was also the case with most of the orthodox Lutheran theologians. In fairness to Melanchthon we should note that even in his 1542–59 version of the LC, which contains his watered-down treatment of the Lord's Supper and his three causes for conversion (in other words, Melanchthon at his worst), he says,

> For the teaching of the church is not derived from demonstrations, but from those statements which God has given to the human race in sure and clear testimonies through which in His great kindness He has revealed Himself and His will. In philosophy we seek

253

the things which are certain and distinguish them from the things which are uncertain. And the causes of certainty are universal experience, the principles, and demonstrations. But in the teaching of the church the cause of certainty is the revelation of God. . . . Even if philosophy teaches that there must be doubt about those things which are not perceptible to the senses . . . yet we know that the doctrine given to the church by God is certain and immovable even if it is not subject to the senses. . . . The cause of this certainty is the revelation of God, who is truthful. . . . We must make this point at the outset in order that from the very beginning we may understand that the things taught in the church are sure, certain and immovable, as the Son of God says, "Heaven and earth may pass away, but My words shall not pass away." . . . For these reasons God in His richness has preserved the ministry of the Gospel and restored learning in the churches and schools, so that we are the guardians of the prophetic and apostolic books and witnesses to the correct interpretation of them.[39]

The criticisms of Melanchthon for his use of philosophy, to the extent that they have any validity, pertain to his use of a philosophically-oriented methodology that he used for the sake of order and logical sequence of ideas—a practice that Chemnitz and other orthodox Lutheran theologians followed.

Chemnitz does not appear to be as interested as was Melanchthon in philosophic concepts, but he certainly accepts the idea of following proper order in presenting material, in the use of correct definitions, in summarizing, in the use of such devices as topics or loci. For example, in introducing his *LT*, under the title "On the Use and Value of Theological Topics [loci]" Chemnitz says,

Finally, in our own age, in the year 1517, God had mercy on His church and raised up Dr. Martin Luther, who undertook to purify the doctrine of the church, so that he might call it back to the fountains [*ad fontes*] of Scripture and to the rule of the prophetic and apostolic faith. And with the wonderful help of God the apostolic purity of the doctrine of the church was gloriously restored, but the explanations were spread out among the different books of Luther, so that it was not easy for the mind to grasp the complete body of doctrine [*corpus doctrinae*], since the individual parts of it were in a sense disconnected. As a result of this, at the very beginning there were often differences of opinion among those who confessed the same doctrine, and they did not always speak the same way. For no one had been given the assignment to gather together from the extensive literature a definite form of doctrine [*forma doctrinae*]. Therefore, by the singular wisdom of God, to the most praiseworthy explanations of Luther were added the labors of Dr. [sic] Philipp Melanchthon, who in the Augsburg Confession, on the basis of various writings of Luther, produced a complete body of doctrine [*corpus doctrinae*] which contained a summary of all the articles of faith explained in a proper and clear manner. . . . The *Loci Communes* were written so that by using the proper method the individual articles of doctrine were treated and explained (*LT,* I, 40).

It is obvious that if there is to be some definitive form of the doctrine [*forma doctrinae*], and if a modicum of consensus is to be preserved in teaching and learning, then the church cannot do without a writing of this kind. Luther himself recognized this and wanted his testimony on this treatise to be known. So in the preface to the first volume of his works he says, "By God's grace a great many systematic books now exist, among which the *Loci Communes* of Philip excel, with which a theologian and a bishop can be beautifully and abundantly prepared to be mighty in preaching the doctrine of piety. . . ."[40]

Chemnitz then continues by demonstrating that Luther approved of this methodology which Chemnitz also approves and which he uses, with the result that he, Chemnitz, was called a Melanchthonian in contradistinction to Luther who is depicted as rejecting this same error. Perhaps on the basis of Luther's statements, plus those of Chemnitz, Luther himself could also be called a Melanchthonian.

Historians and theologians have tried to build a wall between Luther and Melanchthon on this matter of methodology, which Chemnitz and Luther do not seem to think existed. Chemnitz continues,

Even our adversaries give extravagant witness to this writing [Melanchthon's *LC*]. It is not without cause that they attack this particular book so vigorously. Alphonsus Hispanus writes an entire book in opposition to the *Loci* and argues with great invective against these "philippics." . . . For, because he illustrates his doctrine with proper and fitting words and explains it with such clear and convincing methodology, Melanchthon does more damage to the realm of the pope than all the other writers of the Lutherans. (*LT*, I, 40)

Chemnitz also informs us that Eck had attacked Melanchthon's LC. (*LT*, I, 219) These quotes are important because they show that Luther, Melanchthon, and Chemnitz all looked with favor on the so-called Melanchthonian method (on which Melanchthon certainly had no copyrighted monopoly) and that in the eyes of the Romanists Melanchthon and Luther were on exactly the same side. We could even say much the same with regard to the work of Peter Lombard (d. 1164) and Thomas Aquinas (1224–74), both of whom wrote their theological treatises in thetical style in which points were discussed in an orderly and progressing manner. This was called scholasticism or Aristotelianism, but it was opposed primarily because of the theological errors it contained and the overuse of philosophy rather than because of the method itself. It would seem from the above that there really was no argument over method, but the argument centers in the injection of Aristotelian philosophy into the method, as was the case with Aquinas; but Chemnitz and Luther cannot be accused of injecting Aristotelian philosophy into their theology, despite their approval of the Melanchthonian method. With reference to philosophy itself Chemnitz is well-informed, but he does not say a great deal.

The Use of Schema

Chemnitz frequently uses pictures or schema to illustrate his understanding of theology. One illustration deals with the subject of theology as being the knowledge of God, which is divided into His essence and His will. His essence deals with His unity, the Trinity of persons and the internal works (*opera ad intra*) of God. His will is manifested in creation, and in sustaining man in his fallen state by restoring, converting, justifying, sanctifying, and glorifying him. In a sense this is a summary of Chemnitz' entire *LT*. He has other schema which point out the same things plus several more articles of faith in a slightly more detailed manner, but all are clear and easily comprehended. It is obvious that they were used as teaching devices.

10

The Person of the Son of God

With regard to the person of Christ, the *LT* is but a small part of Chemnitz' extensive writing on this important subject. He wrote more on the doctrine of the person of Christ and the related subject of the Lord's Supper than on any other doctrine, and we may safely say without fear of contradiction that he wrote more on these two matters than any other theologian of his age. No less than 21 out of the 79 items listed in Mahlmann's excellent bibliography [1] deal in whole or in part with one or both of these topics. Some of these works of Chemnitz are enormous, such as his *TNC*, his long epistle to Kirchner (which Leyser had inserted into the *LT* to substitute for the brief and incomplete locus prepared by Chemnitz, who was dying at the time he reached this point in his lectures), the section on the Eucharist in his *ECT*, and his several monographs on the Supper, such as the *Repetitio* and the *Fundamenta*. Even his *Disputatatio* delivered at Rostock on the occasion of his reception of the doctoral degree in 1568 on the work of Christ dealt at great length with the person of Christ. Likewise his 1576 addendum to Urbanus Rhegius' *De Caute Loquendi* begins with two articles on the person of Christ and His ascension into heaven. We shall refer to some of these and other works in this connection.

We begin with a statement from Chemnitz himself that shows how the doctrine became a point of contention in the 16th century together with the precise question that was at issue. It comes from a treatise he wrote in mid-1577 which long remained forgotten and which was only rediscovered by Hermann Hachfeld and published by him in 1865. The title as suggested by Hachfeld is, "A Treatise on the Incarnation of the Son of God and the Work and Majesty of Christ." On the opening page of this work Chemnitz explains how the argument among the German Protestants moved from the Supper to Christology:

> Although it is now more than fifty years ago when, by the special blessing of God, after the very thick darkness of the kingdom of the papacy, worse than that of the Egyptians, the light of the Gospel was kindled and again shone forth, now the spirit of lying and the enemy of the truth in some way either by manifest lies or by some related intermingling of various wild opinions is again trying to extinguish these first sparks and again snatch away the Gospel; and thus among these various fanatical opinions, the old error of Berenger [of Tours] regarding the Lord's Supper is being brought back into the arena of the church by means of an unfortunate controversy, with the leaders of this faction being Carlstadt and Zwingli; and at the very beginning of this contention [during Luther's lifetime] controversies regarding the person of the incarnate Christ who subsists now in two natures, with the divine nature assuming and the human nature being assumed, were mixed into the dispute. For because they could not negate the fact that the words of institution of the Lord's Supper in their natural, proper and genuine sense possess and demonstrate their own meaning, namely, that in the action (*actio*) of the LS there is offered (*exhibetur*) to and eaten by the communicants not only bread and wine, but that very body of Christ which was given for us, and that very blood which is the blood of the New Testament and which was shed for us. Therefore, in order to overturn the proper, natural and genuine meaning of the words of institution they have perverted the doctrine of the two natures in Christ. And because these two natures, the divine and the human, are united in the person of Christ, with the difference of the natures preserved intact and also with the natural or essential properties of each nature kept intact or undisturbed, they contend that the consequence of this is that since it is the natural property of a true human body not to be truly and substantially present at one and the same time in many and different places, thus Christ also in the action of the Supper which is celebrated in the church in different places cannot be present with His body, because through the ascension He has been taken above all the heavens, and thus even though the words of institution sound as if this is the case, that is to say, it is as if the assumed human nature in Christ received absolutely nothing as a result of the union with the divine, and Christ with his body can do or will do or accomplish

258

nothing different from or beyond that which the natural powers of the human body achieve or bear. Further, because vivification or the power to make alive is not a natural property of human flesh, they contend that there is nothing useful, even if the body of Christ in the use (*usus* or *actio*) of the *LS* is present and is received by those who eat. In a shameful way they have misrepresented the fact that the flesh of Christ brings salvation and is life-giving on the grounds that in John 6[:33] it is written, "The flesh profits nothing." And thus our Luther, even though, as he says, the proper sedes and the true foundation regarding the special presence of the body and blood of Christ in the Supper lies in and is constituted by the words of institution, yet he was compelled, as he put it, by this line of reasoning and because of this situation in this controversy regarding the *LS*, also to explain the true understanding of the two natures in Christ and their hypostatic union, as well as the doctrine of the exaltation of the human nature to the right hand of the divine majesty and power; and in the face of these perversions of the sacramentarians [he was compelled] to explain and defend this position on the basis of the Word of God, in order that he might show that the proper and natural meaning of the words of institution of the *LS* are not contaminated or overturned through the doctrine of the two natures in Christ or the article of the ascension, if this is treated and correctly understood according to the explanation of Scripture, but rather it is strengthened and corroborated. Thus, in this controversy there was created a material connection between the doctrine of the *LS* and the personal union of the two natures in Christ, the ascension of Christ into heaven, and His session at the right hand of God the Father almighty.[2]

It is important to hear from Chemnitz himself on this point, because it shows that he was trying to follow carefully in the train of Luther. It also shows why these two doctrines were so intermingled and why so many documents of the era deal with both topics. This is especially true of the Formula of Concord. Although it attempts to keep the two issues distinct, a casual reading of Articles VII and VIII of both the Epitome and the SD shows that despite the best intentions of the writers both articles deal with both subjects at certain points.

To be sure, Chemnitz is constantly aware of the need to deal with the two doctrines separately—at least for the sake of clarity in teaching. Thus, his long treatise on the two natures of Christ (*TNC*) deals almost entirely with the doctrine of Christology, as the title indicates, although it was actually directed against the Wittenberg sacramentarians who in erring on the Supper had fallen into error on Christology. His more concise *Fundamenta* and the *Repetitio* steer away as clearly as they can from a formal discussion of Christology and limit themselves to the Supper. The *LT*, with the exception of a few remarks in the closing quotation from Dithmar Kenkel of Bremen (*LT*, I, 126–27), maintains the distinction between the two doctrines most clearly. This is largely due to the fact that Chemnitz, who while delivering the lectures on Melanchthon's LC was busy writing article after article on both Christology and the Supper, limited himself in his *LT* to a discussion of the ancient controversies on this subject, which had not bridged over into the matter of the Supper. Unlike any of his other writings, the *LT* on the locus in Christology cites the Anathemas of Nestorius against Cyril, Cyril's replies, and the Reprehensiones of Theodoret, who tried to mediate between them at the height of the Christological controversy in the ancient church.

In his *LT* Chemnitz develops the doctrine of Christology in a brief, orderly, and clear way. He divides the locus into three parts: (1) the divine nature of Christ; (2) the human nature of Christ; and (3) the personal union of the two natures in Christ (*LT*, I, 89–128). The same topics form the basis and outline for his entire book, the full title of which is *The Two Natures in Christ, a monograph concerning the two natures in Christ, their hypostatic union, the communication of their attributes, and related questions.* Since the *TNC* deals with the subject much more thoroughly and comprehensively than the *LT*, we shall use the *TNC* rather than the *LT* as the basis for our review of Chemnitz' doctrine of Christology. A review of this remarkable book, often called the most important treatise on Christology ever written within Lutheranism, will be helpful in giving a complete picture of Chemnitz' teaching on this basic doctrine. We can also see in this outstanding book the careful outline and progression that Chemnitz displays as he moves from one point to the next. Although he often appears prolix, when we see his objective and observe the care with which he reaches it, we see that the book is not repetitive or confused, but in a orderly and methodical way goes from point to point until the final goal is reached. In outline form we can demonstrate his thrust and methodology: First, he lays the foundation of the two natures and related concepts. Second, he defines and explains the union of the two natures of Christ. Third, he explores the impact of one nature upon the other as a result of the personal union, otherwise known as the communication of attributes.

THE FOUNDATION

Before discussing the precise question at issue in the doctrine of Christology, Chemnitz carefully lays the foundation in chapters 1–3, upon which he can later discuss the communication of attributes. He opens with a kind of prolegomenon, in which he discusses such terms as essence, person, abstract, concrete, attributes, among others, all of which play a major role in the entire book. After the terminological discussion, Chemnitz proceeds to discuss the two natures of Christ in chapters 2–3, in which he simply confesses and reiterates the decisions of the early church when these issues were addressed at length. As he himself put it, apart from the two natures of Christ, all discussion of a communication of attributes would be useless. "Because the person of the incarnate Christ is made up of two natures, the divine and the human, united into one *hypostasis,* there follows from this a communication of the attributes." (*TNC,* 37) Consequently we cannot discuss this communication unless we say something about the natures themselves.

In keeping with the way in which the creeds had confessed the two natures, Chemnitz first discusses the divine nature of Christ. Here he takes up a number of reasons for affirming the divinity of Christ. First, "Christ Himself clearly establishes that He consists of both a human and a divine nature and that He has existed and subsisted as a person before He was conceived and born of Mary according to the human nature." (*TNC,* 38) Second, "Scripture clearly testifies that the second nature in Christ in addition to the human is the actual, true, and eternal divine essence, not some other spiritual or heavenly substance, nature, or power." (*TNC,* 39) Third, Scripture shows that "only the Son assumed the flesh, but not the entire Trinity." (ibid.)

Chemnitz then takes up the human nature of Christ. After referring to the various heresies that had arisen in the church down through the years regarding this matter, Chemnitz confesses the true humanity of Christ in his own words.

> The true teaching of Scripture is that the Son of God has assumed a true, complete, and total human nature which is of the same substance with us and possesses all the conditions, powers, and desires of our nature as its own normal properties, yet is not wicked, but is without sin, uncorrupted, and holy, but in which are the infirmities that have entered into our nature as the penalties of sin. He has willingly and without blemish assumed this for us in order that He might be made the victim for us (*TNC*, 49).

There is no better definition than this. It contains everything that needs to be said and states it succinctly and adequately.

THE PERSONAL UNION OF THE TWO NATURES

Having defined each nature of Christ distinctively and individually, Chemnitz is ready to proceed with the discussion of the personal or hypostatic union of those two natures. This will in turn lay the basis for him to reach his ultimate goal of dealing with the communication of attributes, especially the communication of majesty to the human nature of Christ.

The Nature of the Personal Union

Chemnitz begins his discussion of the personal union as usual, by taking up the various errors which have crept in regarding this matter. He also sets forth the importance of this teaching for pastoral care by drawing out the comfort that this teaching holds for the Christian.

> It is a great comfort that the surest pledge of our salvation and glorification is the human nature of Christ seated at the right hand of the Father where He appears before the face of God on our behalf (Heb. 7:25), leading us and joining us to the Father (John 17:24), in order that then we may be made to conform to His glorious body (Phil. 3:21). In the very nature by which we are flesh of His flesh and bone of His bones we will come to judgment, in order that we may the more eagerly love His appearing (2 Tim.

4:8). By this tie and bond we shall be joined forever to God in eternal life. The common theological axiom is therefore absolutely true that the human nature which the Son of God once assumed He never lays aside in all eternity, but the union of the divine and the human natures in Christ will remain forever in perpetual connection (ibid., 64).

Chemnitz closes with an excellent definition:

Therefore, in order that we may finally bring this discussion to a close, the true teaching of Scripture concerning the human nature in Christ is this: that the Son of God in the fullness of time joined to Himself, in a perpetual union which shall not be dissolved for all eternity, a human nature, true, complete, entire, of the same substance as ours, possessing a body and a rational soul which contain within themselves all the conditions, desires, powers, and faculties proper to and characteristic of human nature (ibid., 64).

In the chapters that follow he unfolds, defends, and supports this definition on the basis of the Scriptures and corroborated by the church fathers.

The Definition of the Personal Union on Basis of Scripture

With chapter 5 Chemnitz moves to define more precisely the nature of the union of the two natures in the one person based on clear Scripture passages. In typical fashion, and for the sake of clarity and precision, Chemnitz divides his discussion into seven points, each involving various Scripture passages. First, he stresses that Christ does not consist of a union of two persons. He carefully observes the distinction between the person and nature as well as who assumes what.

The human nature did not assume the divine. Nor did man assume God, nor did the divine person assume a human person. But the divine nature of the Logos, or God the Logos, or the person of the Son of God, subsisting from eternity in the divine nature, assumed in the fullness of time a particular individual unit (*massa*) of human nature, so that in Christ the assuming nature is the divine and the assumed nature is the human (ibid., 76).

Second, this union is indissoluble. "The ancient councils say that the natures in Christ are united indivisibly . . . also inseparably. . . . Damascenus adds the word [meaning] . . . 'without . . . interval'" (ibid., 77).

Third, and following on the second point, this means that there is only one person as a consequence of the union:

> By this union the assumed nature was inseparably made the property of the person of the assuming Logos because, although there are and remain two natures in Christ without conversion or commingling, with the difference of both the natures and of their essential attributes intact, yet there are not two but only one Christ . . . one Lord . . . and one Mediator. . . . Likewise, the reconciliation, justification, obedience, grace, and life belong to the one Christ. . . . There are not two sons but one (ibid.).

Note how Chemnitz always brings in the soteriological aspects of the doctrine of Christology.

Fourth, through the incarnation or hypostatic union, the person of the Logos "became . . . a composite person . . . who existed in the divine and human nature and had those two natures personally united and through the union had them mutually present with each other . . ." (ibid., 78).

Fifth, this union has implications for the faith of the Christian. To whom or what is such faith directed? He replies,

> From the preceding it follows that it is also the nature of the hypostatic union that now after the incarnation the person of the Logos cannot and ought not to be considered or made an object of faith outside of, without, or separate from the assumed nature, nor in turn the assumed flesh outside of and without the Logos, if we wish to think reverently and correctly (ibid., 79).

Sixth, despite the unity of the two natures, there is no loss of identity for each. The two natures are joined together by interpenetration or perichoresis, as fire penetrates iron, and yet both retain their own identity and characteristics. Finally, Chemnitz points out several implications that result from this union of natures which he plans to take up in succeeding chapters.

In chapter 6 Chemnitz develops the similes which best describe the personal union, namely, the similes of light and sun, fire and iron, body and soul. For the most part, these similes had been used by the fathers, and they were based, in part at least, on Scriptural analogies. He also refers more fully to the matter of the interpenetration or perichorisis of the two natures.

Description of the Hypostatic Union

In order to describe the personal union more precisely, he distinguishes it from other types of union depicted in Scripture. All told, he discusses 15 different kinds of unions in chapter 7, of which the 15th is unique, namely, the personal union of the two natures in Christ. Chemnitz carefully wends his way through each of them to distinguish them in order to set forth the real purpose of the chapter, a description of the union of the two natures. Among the various types of unions, Chemnitz discusses seven different kinds that refer to the presence and indwelling of the deity: (1) the universal presence of the omnipresent God; (2) the gracious indwelling of the Trinity in all the saints; (3) God's presence with the blessed angels and with men in the life to come; (4) a special appearance of God in corporeal form, as when Jacob saw the Logos and Daniel saw Him in the likeness of the Son of Man; (5) God's presence whereby he is truly present in the church by the external ministry of Word and Sacraments.

> He is present even in the external signs in the use of the sacraments, dispensing and communicating through these visible signs His invisible grace, according to His Word. But the signs themselves, by themselves, add nothing toward this grace. God is not present with them inseparably, but because of the covenant [*pactum*] and according to the Word they are not sacraments apart from their use (ibid., 109).

(6)"God often accomplishes and produces many things through the prophets, apostles, and others, as instruments, [in whom He dwells] when He wishes to use such means" (ibid.). (7) There is a parallel in this to the indwelling of the persons of the Trinity in one another, John 14:10, the Father is in the Son and the Son in the Father, and the Father works and creates through the Son, etc.

Antitheses of the Ancient Church on the Hypostatic Union

Again, in order to avoid falling into error in this most important matter, Chemnitz outlines the parameters for formulating this doctrine by showing where the early church fathers drew the lines for proper and improper speech. The controversies and the refutations by the fathers cast light on this doctrine:

> For when the dangers of the shoals are shown on all sides and carefully observed and solicitously avoided, then navigation can easily and surely hold its correct and untroubled course. And he is the best guide for life who shows the correct path by indicating the deviations and aberrations of which we must beware and from which we must turn (ibid., 111).

For his purposes, Chemnitz discusses in considerable detail the Nestorian, the Eutychian, and the Monothelete controversies in the ancient church. Overall, this chapter gives an excellent picture of how well Chemnitz knew both the history of the church and the theology of the fathers.

Although Chemnitz has made careful distinctions in this matter and has set up the necessary parameters, this does not mean that the personal union of Christ is a matter that one can master and understand with one's mind. In chapter 11 Chemnitz reminds the reader that we are here dealing with a mystery and must avoid curious and subtle arguments, but "rather we must see with our partial understanding on the basis of God's Word how this entire doctrine can be used in the serious and true exercise of faith" (ibid., 147). This doctrine must be applied to faith and life. It is not mere theory. He then proceeds to list seven reasons why the Savior must have a divine nature and seven why He must have a human nature. In each case, Chemnitz is concerned with the consolation of the believer in his struggles against sin.

THE RELATION OF THE TWO NATURES TO ONE ANOTHER

In order to discuss the consequences of the personal union, namely, the effects of one nature upon the other, Chemnitz intro-

266

duces chapter 12 with the subject of the three kinds or categories (*genera*) of relationship which exist between the two natures in the personal union which we today designate as follows: first, the *genus idiomaticum* refers to the communication or ascription of the attributes of the two natures to the person of the Logos, whereby these attributes are communicated to the person, leaving the two natures intact and distinct from one another without confusion or change of essence, while the two natures are united and subsist in one substance (cf. FC SD VIII, 36–45). This genus deals with the sharing or communication of attributes that are properties of the one nature yet are attributed to the person of Christ *in concreto*. According to this distinction it is correctly said *in concreto*: God is man, man is God. On the other hand, it is speaking incorrectly when one says *in abstracto*: Divinity is humanity, humanity is divinity. Second, the *genus apotelesmaticum* refers to the fact that in carrying out his saving work Christ "used the properties of either nature or of both natures appropriate to the act in question."[3] This concerns the sharing or communication of activities which are shared by both natures and which are communicated to the person according to both natures, that is, when each nature performs in communication with the other that which is proper to it. Third, the *genus auchematicum* or *majestaticum* refers to the communication of Christ's majesty to the human nature. The FC VIII, 51 says,

> The Holy Scriptures, and the ancient Fathers on the basis of the Scriptures, testify mightily that, because the human nature in Christ is personally united with the divine nature in Christ, the former (when it was glorified and exalted to the right hand of the majesty and power of God, after the form of the servant had been laid aside and after the humiliation) received in addition to its natural, essential and abiding properties, special, high, great supernatural, unsearchable, ineffable, heavenly prerogatives and privileges in majesty, glory, power, and might above every name that is named. . . .

The development of these genera or categories is actually a contribution of Chemnitz to the theology of the FC. Any cursory reading of the *TNC* will show the close relationship between that book and the FC. (The order of the genera is different in the *TNC* from that in the FC, with 2 and 3 above being reversed in the FC.)

A brief survey of the space devoted to each of the genera will reveal which one was at issue during the Reformation. Chemnitz devotes three chapters to the first genus, the *genus idiomaticum*. He then devotes two chapters to the second genus, the *genus apotelesmaticum*. The longest portion of the book, fully 14 chapters, deals with the *genus maiestaticum*. Of the three genera, this one was the most debated during the Reformation. It is also the crucial one for the theology of Chemnitz. Here Chemnitz gets down to what is the basic purpose of the entire book and the most controverted issue of the day. This particular genus deals with the communication of majesty to the human nature, that

> although nothing is either added to or taken away from the divine nature in itself, yet, because of the hypostatic union with the deity, countless supernatural qualities (*hyperphysica*) and qualities which are even contrary (*paraphysica*) to the common condition of human nature are given and communicated to Christ's human nature (p. 6).

THE COMMUNICATION OF MAJESTY

Chemnitz develops his exposition of the *genus maiestaticum* by stressing in chapters 19–25 that in the communication of majesty no property of either of the two natures in Christ can ever become an essential property of the other nature, that is, an attribute peculiar to that nature in such a way that it belongs to the essence of it. This would violate the ancient rule that the natures are not changed or violated, thus warding off the charge of the Reformed that the Lutherans confused the two natures in their teaching of the *genus maiestaticum*. Here is the real point at issue between Lutherans and Calvinists and it impinges on both the doctrine of Christology and the doctrine of the Lord's Supper. While nearly all of Chemnitz' arguments and points can be traced back to one or more of Luther's statements, and while they are explicit or implicit in the AC and the Apology (Articles III and X), in the SA and the two Catechisms, it is manifest that Chemnitz greatly expands on all of these documents, but in no way contradicts them. Luther had broken a great deal of ground on all aspects of this controversy, of course, long before Chemnitz (see, for example, his *Last Words of David* [AE 15] and his *Councils and the Church* [AE 41],[4] together with his many writings on the Supper for further detail on this.) But the very fact that Luther's teachings on Christology and the Supper are spread among so many writings and deal with both subjects together is one reason for Chemnitz, and later for him and his co-workers on the FC, to try to systematize Luther's teachings and get them into a form in which the entire subject could be looked at at one time and in one locus.

In support of his contention that neither nature is changed into the other nor loses its distinctive qualities, Chemnitz, in chapter 20, distinguishes between two categories of gifts that have been conferred on or communicated to the human nature. Here he discusses the first, namely, the supernatural but finite and created gifts which have been conferred upon and which inhere in the human nature (some of which have also been bestowed upon the saints), but which "are not actually the *essential* attributes of the divine nature," and which remain "intact even in the time of his humiliation," and even while His human characteristics remain intact (ibid., 248–50). For example, Luke 2:52 records that "Jesus advanced in wisdom"; and John 1:14 affirms, "He was full of grace and truth." These bestowed gifts were not in dispute.

In chapter 21 Chemnitz takes up what is really the nub of the whole question, that is, the second category of gifts that have been conferred on or communicated to the assumed human nature. Without touching on the point of the omnipresence or ubiquity of Christ's human nature, Chemnitz states,

> For a simpler, easier, and fuller explanation and understanding of this point we shall take certain passages from Scripture and the Fathers which demonstrate that to Christ have been given in time, not indeed according to the divine but according to the human nature, those gifts which cannot be called created qualities or habitual gifts but which of necessity can be understood only of the attributes belonging to the divine nature of the Logos Himself. And we shall speak later of the mode of communication or bestowal which took place without commingling, conversion, or equation of the natures and the essential attributes of each (ibid., 259).

He cites such passages as Matthew 28:18 where Christ is given "all power in heaven and on earth"; and Hebrews 2:8 where "all

things are subject to him," and John 5:27 where Christ claims authority to execute judgment (ibid., 258–59). Each of these texts indicate
that Christ is given certain divine prerogatives. The adversaries, both
Calvinists and Crypto-Calvinists, had asserted that such a communication of majesty, of necessity, must result in a commingling, conversion, or equating of the two natures. In order to quiet this argument and permit a dispassionate discussion of the true meaning of
the communication of the majesty to the human nature, Chemnitz
concludes,

> Therefore, in order that we may progress in our study of this doc-
> trine in a plainer and simpler way, we shall first remove this
> offense or obstacle from our path by showing that by this teaching
> the natures in Christ are not confounded, abolished, changed or
> equated. Afterwards, when the progress of our journey has
> become more tolerable, we will comment on the testimonies of
> Scripture and the confessions of the ancient church (ibid., 265).

Chemnitz fulfills his promise in the next chapter by taking up
the charge made by his opponents that he had commingled, converted, abolished, or equated the two natures. He heeds Cassian's
ancient warning that we must not give an honor to Christ which
injures Him, and then his own warning that Christ must not be
deprived of honor due Him by commingling the natures or essential
attributes. He re-emphasizes that the communication of "attributes
peculiar to the divine nature. . . . is neither essential or natural, that
is, that they are communicated to the assumed nature neither essentially nor by nature" (ibid., 269). An essential communication
occurred only "when the Father by begetting or through generation communicates to the Son His entire essence and all the essential attributes of His deity, which are [in fact] His very essence . . ."
(ibid.). But the attributes peculiar to the deity are not communicated
to the assumed human nature in this way.

The True Mode of the Communication of the Majesty

Thus far, Chemnitz has affirmed the bestowal of divine attributes
upon the human nature. His opening words in chapter 23 are,

> We have now made it sufficiently certain, manifest, and firm that
> the attributes belonging to the Deity, which (according to Scrip-

ture) have been given or communicated to Christ in time, are not to be understood as having been given to His divine nature in time, but to His person according to His assumed human nature (ibid., 287).[5]

He insists that such communication is not a fanciful theory without any foundation in reality. He devotes several pages to the sacramentarian claim that they cannot see the possibility of the communication of majesty without confusing the two natures. He again uses the simile of body and soul and fire and heated iron to show that even in nature there are examples of similar occurrences where two things are joined without a confusion of them (cf. FC SD, VIII, 19), "For the body and soul, as well as fire and iron, have a communion with each other, not only after a manner of speaking and in a strictly verbal fashion, but in deed and in truth (*vere et realiter*)." See also the Athanasian Creed, "As the rational soul and the flesh or body are one man, so God and man are one in Christ." He recognizes that he is here discussing a mystery, and even if the mystery defies explanation, we can state the *that* of the communication on basis of Scripture, but we cannot explain *how* it takes place.

Chemnitz closes the chapter with a treatment of the words *vere* and *realiter* (ibid., 310). He notes that the sacramentarians could accept Christ's presence in the Supper *vere* or truly, "because they feel that they can conceal their beliefs under this term, but when we say that the body of Christ is really (*realiter*) present with the bread in the Lord's Supper, then the cries arise. . ." (ibid.). They gagged on the word *reale* as referring to a real presence. They could speak of a verbal communication but not a real one. Under the first genus there was a real communication to the person, and under the third a real communication to the human nature, by which "we wish to understand no communication of the natures or the essences [themselves], but rather we are using the term *real* so that we can make it perfectly clear that the communication is not verbal or essential or natural but true (*vera*) or actual, not something false, imaginary, a mere matter of words . . . but rather what truly exists and contains itself in truth and verity, as Athanasius says . . ." (ibid.). For obvious reasons Chemnitz never speaks of a communication of the attributes of the human nature to the divine. In other words, Jesus is not just called God, but is God.

Scripture Passages on the Communication of the Majesty

Chemnitz, anxious to demonstrate that this doctrine is well grounded in the Scriptures, opens chapter 24 with a lovely statement where he says,

> the foremost passage is that remarkable statement of Paul in Col. 2:9: "In Christ dwells the whole fullness of the Godhead bodily." . . . Thus Paul in Col. 1:14–22, having attributed reconciliation, peace with God, and other blessings to the body, flesh, blood, cross, and death of Christ, in order that we may know that those benefits are well established and efficacious and that the restoration which took place in the assumed nature of the Only-Begotten pertains also to us, His brothers, he continues by saying that it pleased God that the whole fullness of the Godhead should dwell in Christ. But in order that we should not understand this as a fullness of created gifts or an indwelling through grace, such as we find in the saints, he adds in chapter 2:9 that the entire fullness of the Godhead dwells bodily in Christ. And the whole fullness of the Godhead means the entire deity of the Logos, . . . that is, the entire, full essence of the deity of the Son (ibid., 313–14).

Especially noteworthy in this connection is Chemnitz' detailed exegesis of the Colossian passages on the subject of Christ's divinity. One of the most prominent passages in Chemnitz' discussion is Matt. 28:18, "all authority has been given to Me." He makes the point that all antiquity understood that this "authority . . . cannot be anything else but divine power" because of the use of the words "in heaven and on earth" (ibid., 317). In addition, "this power showed itself fully and demonstrably in and through the assumed nature. . . and thus the assumed nature was brought into a communion of full and manifest association with the divine power" (ibid.). Under the hermeneutical rubric that Scripture interprets Scripture, Chemnitz states, "we should observe with care in the following Scripture passages how the Holy Spirit Himself interprets this general statement regarding 'all power in heaven and on earth'" (ibid., 319). In the process he lists a host of items which show that this divine power attends this ministry.

All told, Chemnitz categorizes the statement of Scripture under 11 different headings. Of the first nine groupings, seven deal with the various attributes which have been communicated by the divine nature to the human. He discusses such items as the anointing of the Spirit, the wisdom and knowledge of Christ, His vivifying life, the session at the right hand, the glory and majesty attributed to Him and other such items. The ninth category relates to the Lord's Supper, particularly the efficacy of His blood in cleansing us from all sin through the power and grace communicated to His human blood. The 10th category shows the relationship of the *genus majestaticum* and the *genus apotelesmaticum,* asserting that

> the duties of Christ as Redeemer, Propitiator, Mediator, Intercessor, Head, High Priest, King, and Savior are in keeping with His person, not only according to the one but also the other nature; so that in the case of these duties the person has its actions and activities in and through both natures. The divine nature of the Logos acts as the principal agent in these functions in common with the assumed nature as with an immediate organ which cooperates as its own and in unity with it. . . . Therefore, with regard to His church, Christ redeems, makes propitiation and peace, calls, gathers, teaches, converts, justifies, cleanses, gives life, sanctifies, governs, cherishes, sustains, guards, defends, preserves, liberates, and is present with it (ibid., 334–35).

Finally, the 11th category deals with the Christian's worship of this Christ:

> When the church practices the divine worship of Christ, that is, when it believes in Christ as its Redeemer, Head, King, High Priest, and Savior and places its hope and confidence in Him, adores, invokes, worships, fears, serves, praises, and glorifies Him, this refers not only to His divine nature but includes the whole person and thus also the assumed nature. For the works of the Savior pertain to the person according to both natures, and saving faith looks to Christ in His works or offices according to both natures (ibid., 338).

The Terminology of the Church, Ancient and Present

As earnest as Chemnitz is to demonstrate that the Lutheran doctrine is based on the Scriptures, so he is equally anxious to demonstrate that the Lutheran reading of Scripture is neither unique nor new within the church. In chapter 25 he summons and catalogs the testimonies of the ancient church.

> In order that we may not appear to be devising strange interpretations for Scripture passages, creating paradoxes, inventing alien doctrines, or obtruding new terminology into the church, I am noting down some statements from the most ancient and approved writers of the orthodox church concerning the communication of the majesty which we shall now discuss (ibid., 341).

The list provided by Chemnitz reads like a patrology, east and west, from the first century down to Luther. He also cites church councils. Chemnitz deals at such length to prove that not only the Scripture but the church of all ages and all places taught the communication of the divine attributes to the person and to the human nature of Christ. Not surprisingly, this is his longest chapter. In chapter 26, Chemnitz stresses that the doctrine itself is more important than the terminology used to express it, and if the doctrine is correctly upheld, the terminology can vary. But terminology is important because "many people are subtly attacking this doctrine indirectly, gnawing away at the terminology . . ." (ibid., 385). He concludes with a remarkable and helpful statement,

> I have therefore followed other theologians and have called this third classification [or genus] the communication of majesty. This designation is also used by antiquity and comes very close to the terminology of Scripture. Furthermore, it is most satisfactory, since Cyril calls the first category or genus the appropriating (*idiomata*), and the second the communicating (*koinopoiia*) genus, that the third should be called the acquiring (*metapoiia*) genus, from Nyssa's expression, provided only that we add the statement that there is no change or conversion of the natures, but rather the exaltation of the human nature to a better state and a raising of it to the highest sublimity (ibid., 401).

In connection with this Chemnitz discusses at length the terminology employed by the early church fathers.

Consequences and Applications of the Communication of the Majesty

As he discusses the consequences of the communication of

majesty in chapter 28, Chemnitz moves quickly into a new area, namely, the ascension of Christ and His session at the right hand of the Father. This point had come under furious controversy between the Lutherans and the sacramentarians. Although Chemnitz has already briefly touched on the session at the right hand in chapter 24, he devotes much more space to his discussion of the matter. He begins in rather typical style. He does not first attack the current conflict, but begins with a rather obscure controversy on the matter in the ancient church. He contends that the ancient church has always understood the session at the right hand as the reformers understood it, but some ancients, in reacting to a statement of Basil which lent itself to misunderstanding, began to say that "Christ sits at the right hand of the Father only according to His divine nature . . ." (ibid., 407). But, says Chemnitz, "actually, as the Scripture describes the session at the right hand, it refers properly to the assumed nature" (ibid.). He states,

> We have shown . . . that Christ's human nature has been glorified by the divine glory and majesty of God. And thus very properly we should expel from the boundaries of the church the recent error of those who imagine that this majesty is a created, fabricated thing, inferior in divinity, on the throne of which and at the right hand of which Christ has been placed and exalted according to His human nature (ibid., 410).

What Chemnitz says here supports his later contention that the whole Christ, with both the divine and human natures, is present with the church here on earth. The Reformed taught, on the basis of a misunderstanding of the right hand of God, that heaven was a circumscribed place, bounded by spacial boundaries. Consequently, Christ by being there according to His human nature could not be really and truly and substantially present in the Supper when it was celebrated on earth. This was the source of their famous statement that the finite (referring to the body) is not capable of containing the infinite (referring to Christ's omnipresence). This will be discussed more fully later. Chapter 29 deals with the much debated question of the worship of the two natures. Chemnitz has referred in passing to this matter previously, but now he devotes his full attention to it. How is Christ "to be adored, invoked, worshiped, and glorified, and how we are to believe in Him?" (ibid., 411). He replies,

For the purpose of faith, worship, and adoration the name of Christ and His works of salvation are bound together in certain ways. . . . We are therefore discussing nothing less than the remission of sins, salvation, and the other benefits of the Savior which we must lay hold on and retain when we talk about faith in Christ or pray to Him or worship and glorify Him. Thus His person is the object of faith, worship, and prayer. . . . Or to say it more simply, the church worships Christ not only as a person or as natures, but it looks especially to His work and His benefits, that is, the church worships the Logos who assumed our human nature and performs in, with, and through it the works of our redemption and propitiation [note propitiation and not merely expiation], and who still accomplishes His duties or works of salvation, justification, mediation, kingship, priesthood, and headship, not only through His divine nature but also in, with, and through His assumed human nature (ibid., 417, 419).

One can get a glimpse of Osiander's error here. He held that we are justified only by the divine nature, while his opposite, Franciscus Stancarus, held that we are justified only by the human nature. Chemnitz refutes them both and attributes our justification to the whole Christ:

With respect to His human nature, in time, Christ received "a name which is above every name, that at the name of Jesus every knee should bow . . . and every tongue should confess that Jesus Christ is Lord. . . ." For it is beyond controversy that the outward bowing of the knee is a symbol of adoration. . . . The church, both that which is still struggling on earth and that which is already in triumph . . . adores, worships, and invokes Christ, not only with respect to the divine nature, as God the Creator, but also with respect to the assumed human nature, in which . . . He was slain (ibid., 416).

Thus Chemnitz establishes the fact that in the worship of Christ the doctrines of Christology and soteriology are intimately connected. We must worship Him as our Savior according to both natures.

CHRIST IS PRESENT IN THE CHURCH ACCORDING TO BOTH NATURES

In many ways chapter 30 is the goal of all that has been said thus far. Chemnitz begins this important chapter by saying,

> But because the person of the incarnate Christ, our Mediator and
> Savior, consists of two natures which have been united, with the
> divine assuming and the human nature assumed, and in order that
> the doctrine of the presence of Christ in the church can be more
> correctly, clearly, and easily explained, considered, and applied to
> our true comfort, we shall now speak specifically about each of
> His natures, or about the presence of Christ according to each
> nature. There is now no controversy about the divine nature of
> Christ, as to the fact that He is present with His church and with
> all creatures according to this nature. . . . In ancient times, how-
> ever, there were also many disputes on this question. . . (ibid.,
> 423).

He deals directly with the Lutheran-Sacramentarian controversy
concerning the presence of the true body and blood of Christ in
the Supper.

Chemnitz first discusses, rather briefly, the modes of presence of
the divine nature. Then follows a lengthier discussion of the presence of the human nature, which, of course, involves His presence
in the Supper, about which there have been many conflicts. He sets
forth five different modes of presence under five major premises.

Under the first premise Chemnitz describes the circumscribed
form of presence Christ utilized during His stay on earth, saying,
"But this mode of visible existence and this circumscribed and local
form of the presence of His body, according to the conditions and
methods of the life of this world, according to our flesh . . . this He
laid aside through His ascension" (ibid., 427). He corroborates this
statement by citing Jerome, and quoting a statement from Bucer,
on which he intends to expand.

The second premise is that through the ascension Christ's body
has been glorified to the highest glory, but in being glorified He is
not restricted to or imprisoned in heaven. This is the main point of
his entire and lengthy epistle to Kirchner in opposition to Beza, who
had asserted that by the ascension Christ was confined to a local
place (and heaven was a place), and therefore could not be on
earth in the Supper bodily, despite the fact that it was a glorified
body. Beza, a notable textual scholar and the titular successor of
Calvin, had changed the translation of Acts 3:21 in Luther's Ger-

man Bible. Whereas Luther had translated it, "Christ must take possession of heaven," which Chemnitz faithfully follows in FC SD VIII, 119, Beza changed it to read, "Christ must be received by heaven." In his *LT* Chemnitz puts it this way, "But we must also add the point that Christ by that glorious or the earlier natural form is not so restricted and imprisoned in heaven that He cannot, when He wishes, also show and exhibit His presence in that form on earth" (*LT*, II, 430). [6]

Chemnitz concludes,

> I reply, therefore, that Christ, although He ordinarily removed the natural mode of the presence of His body from the earth and will appear at last in glory for judgment, yet in His body, even after His ascension and before the judgment, He can be present or can manifest His bodily presence on earth whenever, wherever, and however He wishes, even in visible form (*TNC*, 431).

He then cites Christ's appearance to Paul in prison as one example of this presence.

Chemnitz asserts that up to this point he and the sacramentarians are agreed, but under the third premise the divergence begins to appear. His third point (ibid., 432–48) is that Christ has given

> an express word and a specific promise . . . that He wills to be present with His body and blood in the observance of His Supper. . . . He is . . . confirming the presence of His complete person in the church on earth, not only according to His deity but also according to His assumed human nature. For He wished the observance of His Supper to be the pledge, sign, and seal of His presence (ibid., 432).

Because there has been a controversy over this matter he separates the points which both parties reject, and then tries to get at the heart of the matter.

First, both sides agree that

> the body of Christ, which is delimited by the attributes of its nature, is not present in the Supper in all places by a local circumspection, or by some mode or condition of human life which is visible, perceptible, or natural, or according to the natural properties of a true body, or through any essential attributes of its own. . . . Nor do we say that this presence of Christ's body in the Supper is of the same nature or condition as the presence of glori-

fied bodies in some observable manifestation. . . . Nor do we in any way teach that the body of Christ is expanded . . . stretched, or extended into all places. . . . Nor do we say that the body of Christ is present in the Supper through some kind of multiplication or duplication, as when the reflection of one body appears in the many pieces of a broken mirror. . . . Nor do we in any way believe that the body of Christ either in the union or in glory has lost its essence and abolished its essential attributes and has been converted or changed into a spiritual, infinite . . . substance which is no longer circumscribed . . . by its essential qualities . . . (ibid., 433–34).

At this point, the two parties diverge. The Crypto-Calvinists insist that Christ is present in the Supper only spiritually and in His divine nature: the Lutherans insist that both natures are present. Chemnitz stresses,

Nor does it agree with the Words of Institution if we attempt to understand the presence of only the merit, power, or efficacy of the body of Christ in the Supper, to the exclusion or separation of His substance (ibid., 434).

At this point Chemnitz states the point at issue or the *status controversiae,*

Now in this whole controversy the question is this: whether the *simple, proper,* and *native* sense of the words of the testament of the Son of God are to be held, believed, retained, and followed, or whether we are to depart from the simple and proper meaning of the words of Christ's testament, reject their native sense, and devise another interpretation from the bookshop of figures of speech (ibid.).

Again, this was not an issue of academic curiosity for Chemnitz. He immediately moves to show why the issue is so important, namely, on account of the Gospel. In a statement that deserves full quotation, he states,

It is certainly a most serious and important matter which is under dispute, namely, the words of Christ's very testament, a doctrine which is so full of consolation, that is, that the Son of God, our Mediator and Savior, according to the words of His testament wills to be present with His church here on earth, which is fighting under the banner of the cross and struggling in this vale of tears.

For He wishes to be present also in and with His assumed nature by which He is of the same substance with us, related to us, our Brother, our very flesh, according to which flesh He does not blush to call us His brothers and in which flesh He was tempted, so that He can share in our sufferings, according to which flesh Christ is our head and we His members. And just as no one hates his own flesh, but nourishes and cherishes it, so also Christ does to His church, since we are members of His body, of His flesh and of His bone" (Eph. 5:29) (ibid., 434–35).

There is nothing theoretical or ephemeral about Chemnitz' work. The Gospel itself is at stake and his concern is both theological and pastoral. Chemnitz proceeds (ibid., 437–48) to list four reasons why we must not accept the thinking of the sacramentarians but must continue to hold that "the Son of God in accord with His divine and efficacious will and power can easily and surely be present with His body (which the words of the testament assert) without thereby destroying the substance of His body or abolishing His essential attributes" (ibid., 437), as derived from the personal union: First, because the simple, proper, and natural meaning of the Words of Institution require us to believe it, and Christ Himself has spoken them. Second, because the personal union itself requires it. Because of the personal union it is not only possible but easy for the Logos to accomplish the presence of His human nature in the Supper, for the human nature subsists in the divine person and not separately or by itself. Because of the personal union the human nature must be where the Logos is. Thus to deny the presence of the human nature in the Supper but to affirm the presence of the divine nature is to deny the personal union. Third, because of His session at the right hand of God. Chemnitz in a sense turns this argument against his adversaries. He argues that because of the personal union the human nature can sit at the right hand of God, thus if the human nature can be in so exalted a position, it follows that it can be present wherever the person is present, and thus it can be in the body and blood in the Supper. He says,

Not that by this exaltation [to the right hand of God] the human nature has become the right hand of God, to be sure, or that through this session it has become infinite or immeasurable in the quality of its nature and essential condition, as God's right hand itself is; but because the right hand of God is not some circumscribed place or enclosed in a certain locale but rather is God's infinite majesty, power, and authority, therefore the Son of God has revealed in His Word that with His body, which He exalted to the right hand of the majesty and power of God, yet, leaving its true nature unimpaired, He can be present wherever He *wills* to be, not according to the natural or essential properties of His body but by reason of and through the efficacy of the majesty and power of God, at whose right hand He sits (ibid., 447).

Note how Chemnitz uses the word *wills* to be present. The argument is not over whether Christ can be present but only over whether He wills to be present or *promises* to be present.

Fourth, since all things have been placed under the authority of Christ's human nature, no interval of space prevents the real presence of His body and blood in the Supper.

Thus, when we begin with the Word and promise concerning the presence of Christ's body and against all objection add His divine power, the personal union, and His session at the right hand to His *will* as it is revealed in the Word, it is surely manifest that the Son of God can accomplish what He teaches and promises in His Word concerning His body, while still leaving its true reality intact; so that with His body He can be present when, how, and wherever He *wishes* (ibid., 448).

In premise four, Chemnitz asserts that Christ is present with the church according to His human nature and not only according to His divine nature. But,

not only at that place and at that moment when and where the Lord's Supper is celebrated in a public service of the church, however, is the whole Christ in both natures present with His church militant on earth, as if as soon as the celebration of the Supper is completed He removes His presence, or as if . . . He were to fly away into heaven, and the members of the church, outside the public service, in their work, in their temptations and tribulations would be deprived of the comforting presence of Christ, their High Priest, their King, their Head, and their Brother. For in the action of the Lord's Supper there is a public, solemn, and peculiar witness and seal that Christ, our Mediator and Savior, *wills* to be graciously present with His church in its struggle here on earth, not with only one portion and part of Himself, that is, with only

His deity, but wholly and completely, that is, with His assumed nature also, by which He is of the same substance with and related to us, our Brother (ibid.).

Thus the presence of Christ with His church on earth is integrally connected with His promised presence in the Supper. Note also the salvific and soteriological aspect of this presence. He is present to save.

Regarding Chemnitz' treatment of Eph. 3:17, "that Christ may dwell in our hearts by faith," Elert says,

Chemnitz clearly expresses his own thought that Christ dwells in the believers "with His essence." . . . This thought is underscored when Chemnitz adds that Paul teaches not only the participation [Koinonia] of the believers in the Spirit (2 Cor. 13:13) but also their participation [Koinonia] in the body and the blood (1 Cor. 10:16). . . . Concerning the indwelling of the Holy Spirit he quotes Luther's exposition of Ps. 51:12, according to which the Spirit dwells in the believers "not only through His gifts but also as to His substance."[7]

Elert goes on to show how the Formula of Concord in SD III, 54 reechoes this same concept. He also calls attention to the fact that in FC SD 3.54 the point is also made that not only does Christ dwell in us but the entire Trinity.[8] Our salvation, including the presence of God and His indwelling, is always for Chemnitz and the FC a trinitarian action.

Finally, under his fifth premise (ibid., 462–65), Chemnitz deals with the difficult problem of the presence of the whole Christ with created things and the related point that all created things are subject to Him according to both natures.

Christ's human nature, therefore, cannot and ought not be removed or excluded from the general dominion which He possesses and exercises over all things, or from the administration of the world, since Scripture expressly affirms that all things, even those which are outside the church have been put under Christ's feet (ibid., 462) [and this must be understood as referring to both the divine and the human natures]. But . . . since Christ is present in the church with each nature and dwells in the individual members, and since His body is in the Supper, . . . the questions center in whether the body of Christ is also in wood and stones, in fruit, in the birds of the air, the beasts of the field, and the fish of the sea, or whether He wishes to be sought and found there. Furthermore, some questions are asked which are foul to hear and abominable to imagine. . . such as whether the divine nature which is everywhere, is found in excreta and sewage (ibid., 462, 463).

Chemnitz continues:

Since we do not have express and definite promise that He *wills* to be sought and found in such places, and since these things add nothing to the edification or comfort of the church and are plain offenses which disturb the weak and give the adversaries occasion for endless controversy, it is safest and simplest to drop all such questions from our discussions and to limit ourselves to the boundaries of divine revelation so that we may seek Christ and lay hold on Him in the places where He has clearly *promised* that He Himself *wishes* to be. And thus we will defer, dismiss, and put off the other questions which people like to ask or argue about for that future heavenly academy, where we shall see face to face the glory of Christ, our Brother, and shall see what it is, what it is like, and how great it is. . . . But let us retain that which is absolutely true, namely, that Christ with His body *can* be present wherever, whenever, and howsoever He *wishes*; but we will judge concerning His *will* only from His clearly revealed Word. . . . Thus also the ancients did not talk about logs, stones, birds, and fish, but about the Lord's Supper, the church, and its members when they discussed the presence and indwelling of Christ (ibid., 463–65).

THE QUESTION OF UBIQUITY

Before completing our summary of the *TNC*, we need to discuss one of the most difficult aspects of this entire matter, the so-called ubiquity question, that is, whether the body of Christ is omnipresent. This became the stumbling point at which some Lutherans refused to subscribe to the FC, and it pointed to a difference of opinion among the authors of the FC with the great John Brenz of Württemberg in the person of his successor Jacob Andreae as his disciple on the one hand, and Chemnitz, Chytraeus, and Selnecker on the other. There is ample documentation to show that both Brenz and Chemnitz, following Luther, did not consider the matter divisive and both viewpoints are set forth in the FC. Andreae in the Epitome's antitheses section (VIII, 30) asserts the Brenzian view that the human nature of Christ is everywhere present (*ubique*) with his body. In his antitheses section to SD VIII, Chemnitz rejects the view that "the human nature in Christ is everywhere present in the same way as the Deity, as an infinite essence, through an essential power or property of its nature" (SD VIII, 90). However, two paragraphs later (VIII, 92), Chemnitz asserts: ". . . through his divine omnipotence Christ *can* be present with his body, which he has placed at the right hand of the majesty and power of God, wherever he desires and especially where he has *promised* his presence in his Word, as in the Holy Communion."

While there is no evidence that the authors of the FC themselves or that Brenz and Chemnitz who knew each other, ever regarded this matter as divisive, yet there was enough difference for various people both to criticize the FC or to refuse to sign it, or for others to take sides between Brenz and Chemnitz, even though they did not take sides against each other, as we shall point out shortly. However, the distinction in the FC is so slight as almost to escape notice. Chemnitz' old ally Heshusius turned against him and, acting under instructions from Duke Julius, used this point as a way of keeping the duchy of Braunschweig from signing. Paul von Eitzen of Schleswig, because of personal animosity against Andreae for other reasons, also kept his territory from subscribing, using the ubiquity question as an excuse, but his territory like Braunschweig remained Lutheran and both ultimately subscribed. The Anhalt theologian Amelung used it as an excuse to pull Anhalt entirely out of the Lutheran orbit and into the Reformed. So the issue was serious.

But the touchstone of Lutheran orthodoxy never became how one stood on the question of ubiquity versus what came to be called the multivoli-presence or the ubivoli-presence as held by Chemnitz, namely, that Christ is present in many places or is present wherever He wills to be. Rather, those who held to the real presence of Christ in keeping with the Words of Institution were regarded as orthodox Lutherans. Melanchthon had been drawn into the matter, of course, because in his constant attempts to make peace with the Calvinists and Crypto-Calvinists on the Supper. He had naturally skated around this controversial issue of ubiquity, and when forced to commit himself on the matter had rejected it. Luther in the early stages of the conflict on the Supper had boldly asserted the omnipresence or ubiquity of Christ's body, as deriving from the communication of the attributes which the human nature had received from the divine; and he had stated that it was impossible to disprove the omnipresence of Christ. But Luther first, last, and always insisted on drawing his doctrine of the Supper from the Words of Institution and rebelled against being dragged into a controversy on Christology.[9] But neither he nor his successors, even Melanchthon, could totally escape. The Calvinists quite cleverly in their contentions against Luther and his followers always raised the spectre of ubiquity as a way of ridiculing them. In fact, all the Lutherans tried to avoid the word *ubiquity* and denied holding to it.

Chemnitz, at the end of his long chapter on Christ's presence in the church according to both natures, cites Luther.

> Luther has also given this advice for simple people as the safest and surest of all. For although he had often disputed concerning the general ubiquity (*ubiquitas*) of Christ, when he later saw into what labyrinths of sophistry the Sacramentarians carried this controversy and how they led it away from the Words of Institution by which the presence of the body and blood of Christ in the Supper is taught and promised, he finally says in his *Vom Abendmahl Christi, Bekenntnis* . . . that although these arguments about ubiquity cannot be refuted, yet he does not wish to argue with anyone as to the mode of the ubiquity by which Christ's body is present in the Supper, since divine wisdom and power can accomplish this in a way unknown to us . . . . Luther advises . . . that we content ourselves with the words of Christ by which in the institution of the Supper He affirms that He is present (*TNC*, 464).

And then Chemnitz does two things. First, he breaks down the definition of ubiquity into two aspects, general or absolute and specific. He accepts specific omnipresence but wants at least to soft-pedal general omnipresence, as the statements cited above demonstrate. Second, he tries to explain Luther's statements as not propounding a general ubiquity but rather that he had stressed Christ's presence in the Supper and in view of the sophistic and labyrinthine questions which began to arise had declared the entire matter of general omnipresence to be kind of an open question.

While one of the quotations Chemnitz used from Luther (ibid., 464) has been declared by virtually every one to be actually a quote from Melanchthon (See *TNC*, 465; *FN*, 54), the other, from his *Vom Abendmahl Christi, Bekenntnis* ("Confession Concerning Christ's Supper"), sometimes called Luther's *Maior Confessio de Coena Domini* (1528) (*AE*, 37.151–372) is indisputably Luther, and corroborates Chemnitz' interpretation of the outspoken Luther. Luther, in answer to impertinent questions concerning other places where the human nature and body of Christ might be (although such questions may be difficult to refute), does not "wish to argue with anyone as to the mode of the ubiquity by which Christ's body is present in the Supper, since divine wisdom and power can accomplish this in a way unknown to us. . . ." [*TNC*, 464]. Instead he points the questioner to the personal union, the session at the right hand, the wisdom and omnipotence of God, and the Lord's Supper. It is of interest also to note that the FC SD, 93ff. cites this same statement from Luther and treats it just as Chemnitz does in his *TNC*, p. 464. Likewise, Andreae in FC Ep. VII, 11–14 cites the passage also and handles it the same way.

Chemnitz also twice (in FC SD VII, 12–16 and 38) quotes the Wittenberg Concord (1536) to establish his position and to secure the approbation of Luther for this position. The Wittenberg Concord (signed by Luther, Melanchthon, and Bucer) marked the closest the Lutherans and their Protestant opponents ever got, but it was never subscribed by the princes and soon disappeared from the scene. But Chemnitz shows that even in this document in which Melanchthon's friend Bucer played a major role "the body and blood of Christ are truly and essentially present, distributed, and received." Transubstantiation was rejected, as was the idea of a local enclosure of the bread or any kind of permanent union with the bread apart from the use of the Sacrament. "Through sacramental union the bread is the body of Christ." The Concord also asserted that the validity of the Sacrament does not depend on the worthiness of the communicant and that unworthy communicants receive the body and blood to their judgment. They also asserted that the union of body and bread is not a personal union like the two natures in Christ, but a sacramental union. They also agreed that the body is "in, with, and under" the bread and rejected a figurative understanding of the words. All of this, says the FC, shows that Luther is the correct interpreter of the AC.

However, the Reformed gradually backed away from the Wittenberg Concord, and nothing came of it, and the differences became wider and wider. It is manifest that the concept of ubiquity was not the cause of the problem between Lutherans and Calvinists; rather, any kind of presence of Christ's body and blood in the Supper other than a purely spiritual presence was the real problem. It would appear that at least one reason the FC includes references to this document is to demonstrate the bad faith of the Calvinists and also to show how close they had once been. The mention of Bucer by name in FC SD VII, 13 would give credence to this opinion. It was extremely important to the authors of the FC to marshall all the allies they could on the difficult point of the real presence. Hence the large number of quotations from Luther, the unaltered AC, its Apology, the Smalcald Articles and Luther's two Catechisms, and the Wittenberg Concord. It is also possible to see the close relationship between and the influence of the earlier writings of Chemnitz on the FC, but in keeping with the agreement made at the beginning that the final document was to contain no documents written by any of the individual writers, no such works were to be cited.

The whole issue shows how delicate matters were just in those years preceding the adoption of the FC and how carefully Chemnitz tried to steer as far over as he could, without denying Luther, or for that matter Brenz with whom he never publicly tangled, in order to win adherents for the FC and not create further divisions among the Lutherans. To a remarkable degree he and his co-workers succeeded.

While some theologians emphasize that there is some difference between Andreae's Epitome and Chemnitz' SD in the FC, we should also note that both parts of the FC follow Chemnitz in putting the ubiquity question last, after all the groundwork has been laid, and both treat this subject as a theological consequence of the communication of majesty.[10] Also the use of Luther's words from his *Vom Abendmahl* in SD VII, 93–103 and VIII, 80–84 which are really the work of Chemnitz, and Ep. VII, 11 and VIII, 30 which was written by Andreae show how close Chemnitz and Andreae really were. Chemnitz, however, correctly distinguished between the general and the specific omnipresence of Christ's body, while Luther, Brenz, and Andreae referred to His general omnipresence. Chemnitz stressed that Christ can be wherever He *wills to be* (multivoli-presence, cf. SD VIII, 78, ". . . so that, also according to and with the same assumed human nature of his, Christ can be and is present wherever He *wills*, and in particular that He is present with His church and community here on earth as mediator, head, king, and high priest.") It would appear that Chemnitz took this slightly varying position not to appease the Calvinists, for this he certainly did not do, and they immediately accused him of holding the hated ubiquity doctrine, but rather to be absolutely faithful to Scripture and not become involved in speculations about things which Scripture does not reveal. Selnecker and Chytraeus followed him in this. Elert states, "The concept of the omnipresence of the body of Christ which was in controversy in the doctrine of the Sacrament was by no means felt to be an integral part of the 'communication of attributes' (*communicatio idiomatum*) and therefore interest in this concept cannot be the real reason for the doctrine."[11]

Luther in the following statement really points up the issue and at the same time puts it in proper perspective as to how seriously the difference between Chemnitz and Andreae should be taken, for one man took hold of one part of Luther's position and the other the other part. Both men could accept this statement of Luther. Luther says,

> Although He is present in all creatures, and I might find Him in stone, in fire, in water, or even in a rope, for He certainly is there, yet He does not wish that I seek Him there apart from the Word, and cast myself into the fire or the water, or hang myself on the rope. For He is present everywhere, but He does not wish that you grope for Him everywhere. Grope rather where the Word is, and there you will lay hold of Him in the right way. Otherwise you are tempting God and committing idolatry. For this reason He has set down for us a definite way to show how and where to find Him, namely the Word.[12]

Both Andreae and Chemnitz accepted this statement, and it supports both of them.[13]

THE COMFORT DERIVED BY THE ANCIENTS FROM CHRIST'S HUMAN NATURE

In chapter 31 Chemnitz has over 30 citations from the fathers, especially from Cyril, which show the comfort that the ancient church derived from the doctrine of Christ's human nature and its participation in the person of Christ. He points out that the "Fathers also teach that He wills to demonstrate His human nature when He deals with us and works in us in His activities as Savior, so that He thereby might bestow His grace and benefits upon us. For the power, grace, efficacy, merits, and blessings of Christ are not communicated to believers outside of or without His person, as if He Himself were not present . . ." (*TNC*, 472). Then he gets to the real purpose of the chapter:

> What sweet comfort this is that the Son of God, our Savior, joins Himself to us and deals with us not with His bare (*nuda*) deity, but in, with, and through the nature in which He is like a head, our kinsman, and of the same substance with us, His members . . . . Here is a most present and certain pledge of our glorification. For how could His members be forever left in their miseries when our Head by the very same nature by which He is our kinsman and of the same substance with us, which is now in the glory of the Father, has joined Himself to us most intimately in the sorrows of this present life? These comforts are weakened and completely lost if we remove the substance of Christ's human nature or exclude it from the Lord's Supper, which is celebrated in the church on earth (*TNC*, 472–73).

Without mentioning the fact, Chemnitz is stressing the *genus apotelesmaticum*, showing that the incarnation relates directly to the saving work of Christ which He accomplished through His human nature. He is always pastoral in his dealing with this subject. It is not merely something academic.

THE DOCTRINE OF THE EXALTATION OF CHRIST'S HUMAN NATURE

We mentioned earlier that these last chapters stress the consequences and results of the communication of the majesty. Note that Chemnitz speaks first of the exaltation rather than the humiliation.

The reason is that the main thrust of the entire book is to demonstrate the fact that the body and blood of Christ in His exalted state are present in the Lord's Supper according to both natures and through the ministry of the Word in the church. His concern is to admonish "as to how this teaching of the exaltation and prerogatives of the human nature in Christ is to be treated and received, so that the reality of His human nature and its essential attributes may not be lost or destroyed" (ibid., 475), since there have always been "those who thought that this wondrous exaltation of Christ's human nature could not take place. . . in the way Scripture describes it, at the same time that the reality of the substance and the essential attributes of His human nature still remain intact" (ibid.). He then describes the error of the Valentinians and others, citing the decisions of the Sixth Ecumenical Council regarding the heretic Severus. The fathers had dealt many times with the question as to whether Christ performed His miracles also according to the human nature, such as walking on water, going through closed doors, etc. He points out that "the testimonies of Scripture concerning Christ's human nature are twofold. Some passages testify as to His essential or natural properties or conditions, while others speak of those things which are added to it beyond its natural properties because of the hypostatic union" (ibid., 482). He shows how even the disciples themselves had doubts about the reality of His body after the resurrection, as when He came through closed doors, when they thought He was a spirit or ghost, and thus it became necessary for Him to command Thomas to reach forth his hand and touch the wounds. Of course, these questions about the actuality of the resurrection of the same body as He had in death still disturb many in the church and are treated with doubt by countless thousands even in a Christian culture.

THE HUMILIATION (*EXINANITIO*)

We now come to the final chapter of Chemnitz' *TNC*—his magnum opus but by no means his only treatise on Christology. Chemnitz almost always in this chapter uses the Latin word *exinanitio* instead of *humiliatio* to describe what we in the modern church constantly call humiliation. Even in the FC the term *exinanitio* occurs; e.g. in Epitome VIII, 16 we see the expression *in statu suae humiliationis sese exinanivit,* which Bente translates "He abstained from it in the state of His humiliation,"[14] and Tappert "in the state of his humiliation he dispensed with it."[15] But in SD VIII, 26 we have *in statu suae humiliationis secreto,* which Bente translates "He kept it concealed in the state of His humiliation,"[16] and Tappert "he kept it hidden during the state of his humiliation."[17] Both *exinanitio* and *humiliatio* are used and are synonymous. Both are used in the ancient church, but *exinanitio* is more common. Dorner makes a great deal out of the use of the term *exinanitio,* but subsequent scholars appear to have ignored him.[18]

Chemnitz asserts that the humiliation began with the moment of Christ's conception in the Virgin Mary. His point in this chapter is that some say that nothing can be attributed to Christ in His humiliated state, even though His human nature was united with the divine Logos, and that thus only finite gifts can be attributed to Him.

> The humiliation (*exinanitio*) mentioned in Philippians 2, therefore, does not indicate a deprivation, removal, robbing, exclusion, taking away, degradation, putting away, lack, absence, loss, bareness, or emptiness of the fullness of the Godhead which dwelt in Christ bodily from the very moment of the conception. But it has to do with the use or exercise of it, that is, the brilliance of Christ did not always shine out in the time of His humiliation, since it was covered with infirmity . . . (*TNC,* 488)

He goes on to say at a later point,

> the principal and most important point regarding the humiliation is that the whole fullness of the Godhead, which dwells personally in Christ's assumed nature, exercises His power, authority, and activity in and through the assumed nature even at the time of the humiliation, although not without means and not always fully and openly (ibid., 490).

He cites several quotations from the fathers to establish his points, and closes his book without any summarization, blessing, prayer, or comment. He has come to the end. He probably was exhausted and had no more to say!

This entire chapter, which is one of the longest in this treatise, is important because it deals with a subject which was a subject of importance at the highest theological level and at the lowliest level of poor uneducated laypeople in their worship life in the congregations.

While many references have been made throughout Chemnitz' *TNC* and also in this feeble effort to summarize and encapsulate his ideas regarding the person of Christ, many readers perhaps by now are wondering if Chemnitz ever in a systematic way dealt with the doctrine of the work of Christ. Indeed he did. This material will be dealt with under his magnificent treatment of the doctrine of justification, but it is always important to stress that Christ did His work in His incarnate state as the God-man. FC SD VIII, 45 puts it this way, in the portion in which Chemnitz plays so important a role, SD VIII, 45 (Bente),

> It is manifest that it is incorrect to say or write that the above-mentioned expressions (*God suffered, God died*) are only *praedicationes verbales* (verbal assertions), that is, mere words, and that it is not so in fact. For our simple Christian faith proves that the Son of God, who became man, suffered for us, died for us, and redeemed us with His blood.[19]

This is as fine a uniting of the doctrines of Christ's person and Christ's work as can be found. Pelikan sums it up well when he says,

> Luther had already set forth a special version of the doctrine of the communication of properties that was intended to safeguard the real presence against the objection that it was precluded by the ascension of the humanity of Christ to the right hand of God. The authors of the *Formula of Concord*, especially Martin Chemnitz, had elaborated and systematized Luther's doctrine, and in the process had compiled an appendix to the *Formula*, entitled "Catalog of Testimonies," intended to demonstrate the continuity of Lutheran christology with that of the ancient church fathers and church councils. . . . With some modifications, largely technical and terminological, the christology of Chemnitz eventually prevailed. . . . the doctrine of the person of Christ was, together with the doctrine of the Trinity, the principal dogmatic heritage of the ancient church and the mark of continuity with it.[20]

11

Justification

In the locus on justification Chemnitz—following Luther, the early Lutheran Confessions, and Melanchthon—comes to the heart of Lutheran theology. Chemnitz himself continually stresses this very point.

> This unique locus in a special way distinguishes the church from all other nations and religions. . . . This locus is the pinnacle and chief bulwark of all teaching and of the Christian religion itself; if this is obscured, adulterated, or subverted, it is impossible to retain purity of doctrine in the other loci. On the other hand, if this locus is securely retained, all idolatrous ravings, superstitions, and other corruptions are thereby destroyed. . . . (*LT*, II, 443)

Right out of Luther! Here we come to the great central teachings of Scripture, dealing with the distinction between Law and Gospel, the promise, faith and particularly saving or justifying faith, the righteousness of faith, grace, justification, and several related points, such as the forensic nature of justification, the imputation of Christ's righteousness, the exclusive particles pertaining to faith and grace which exclude all human works, the doctrine of Christ's atonement, and the basic work of Christ as our only mediator. Chemnitz deals with this doctrine in most of his writings: his *LT*, the *ECT*, his *Enchiridion*, his *Iudicium*, his various confessional writings preceding the FC, the FC itself, all dealing with the subject from much the same viewpoint.

SUMMARY OF JUSTIFICATION

The best introduction to the voluminous writings of Chemnitz on the subject of justification is found in Article III of FC, "The Righteousness of Faith Before God," which well summarizes the entire subject, for while the Osiandrian controversy was the immediate cause for this article, it is manifest that the authors of the *Formula*

wanted to take the opportunity in this and the following three articles to set forth the entire Lutheran doctrine on this matter, which
would seemingly account for the title "The Righteousness of Faith
Before God." For the Formula, justification is only one part of the
entire subject of man's salvation, or to put it another way, the doctrine of justification covers a wide range of topics. A perusal of FC
III will bear this out. After providing a brief synopsis of the controversy that had arisen over this article, namely, the Interim, it proceeds to give a precise definition and a concise summary of the
entire subject. This in turn is followed by a treatment of the vocabulary that best sets forth the doctrine of justification together with
the role of exclusive particles.

It is noteworthy that almost the entire doctrine of justification
and related points as they had been developed up to the time of the
FC is included in the FC. Luther developed his doctrine of justification over several years, and reached his theological pinnacle in his
Lectures on Galatians (1535). Melanchthon also aided and abetted
Luther's development and added a few worthwhile emphases of
his own. In addition, several of the controversies that arose in
Lutheranism, such as the antinomian controversy before Luther's
death and others after his death, impinge in one way or another
on the doctrine of justification. All of this theological development
is reflected in the FC and in the writings of Chemnitz in the years
preceding the FC. Elert makes this important statement,

> Luther finds the change brought about by the Gospel definitely
> expressed in the Pauline concept of justification. . . . It is in this
> concept that the final opposition to the medieval church is devel-
> oped. As Martin Chemnitz showed in his critique of the Trent
> dogma, this concept made it impossible to bridge the opposition.
> In our earliest confessions it is the nucleus; in the later ones it is
> the central point; in the most recent ones it is the assumption that
> can no longer be called in question [1]

The summary given of the FC is in many ways also a summary
both of the mature theology of Luther, of Melanchthon, and Chemnitz. In other words, the doctrine of justification as set forth in the
FC is simply a beautiful distillation of Lutheran theology on this
point stretching back for over 50 years.

Another brief summary of the doctrine of justification is found in Chemnitz' *Formulae recte sentiendi, pie, circumspecte and citra scandalum loquendi. . .* (1575), which was attached to Urbanus Rhegius' *Formulae caute loquendi,* and which achieved confessional status in Braunschweig and Lüneburg. Here he says,

> But this righteousness or merit of Christ, God in His Word and Sacraments offers and sets before us, and wills that by faith which the Holy Spirit through the Word has kindled and worked in us we should lay hold on and receive (Rom. 3). Therefore we are justified before God not without righteousness but by the intervention of that highest and most perfect righteousness which the Son of God our Mediator who was made under the Law has acquired by His obedience, suffering and resurrection. For this alien righteousness [a term which Chemnitz has borrowed directly from Melanchthon in Apology IV, 305], namely, the righteousness of Christ, God out of His gracious mercy through imputation applies and communicates to sinners who in earnest repentance, with true faith, in Word and Sacraments, lay hold on Christ who is made by God righteousness for us and place Him between their sins and the wrath of God. And because of this righteousness or merit of Christ God justifies those who believe in Him, that is, He pronounces them righteous, absolves them from their sins, and the sentence of the curse and eternal death, and receives them into grace, and adoption as sons, makes them heirs of life and eternal salvation. "Therefore, having been justified by faith they have peace with God and access into grace through faith, in the hope of the glory of God" (Rom. 5:[1–2]).[2]

However, because of the enormous importance of this subject both in the theology of Chemnitz and in Lutheran theology in general we shall now follow the order of his complete *LT* and describe in considerably greater detail the teaching of Chemnitz on this basic doctrine. We shall bring in his other writings as further corroboration of the *LT.* Chemnitz begins the locus on justification by referring to what we mentioned earlier as the drama of the way of salvation,

> A consideration of the order shows a great deal. . . . (1) What God is and what His nature is. (2) How man was created in the image and likeness of God. (3) How he fell. (4) What horrible corruption followed, coming upon all human powers. (5) The voice of the Law, which before the judgment seat of God reveals,

accuses, and condemns this depraved nature together with all its fruits. Next in correct and good order follows the locus on justification, dealing with the redemption, restitution, or reconciliation of the human race that has been lost and condemned because of sin (*LT,* II, 443).

Note how the technical terminology appears at once.

Chemnitz approaches the topic in his *LT* much in the same way as he does in the SD of the FC. He begins by first defining the Gospel, particularly as it is distinguished from the teaching of the Law. Chemnitz carefully sets forth the boundaries of each. From there he proceeds to a discussion of the vocabulary that is used in connection with this topic, particularly such terms as *to justify* (*justificare*), *righteousness* (*justitia*), and *to be righteous* (*justus*). Equally important, the terms *freely* and *the grace of God* need to be explained. A major point of contention between the Romanists and the Lutherans centered on the nature and role of faith. Accordingly, Chemnitz deals with this also in his typical thorough fashion.

THE GOSPEL IN CONTRADISTINCTION
FROM THE LAW

Chemnitz then moves into the body of his presentation. First he cites Melanchthon's locus on the Gospel, wherein Melanchthon discusses the concept of the Gospel as promise, a term which he uses constantly as synonymous with Gospel.[3] At almost the very end of his locus Melanchthon makes a statement which created a great deal of trouble. He says, "Christ defines the Gospel in the last chapter of Luke [v. 47] as clearly as an artist when He commands us to teach 'repentance and remission of sins in His name.' Therefore the Gospel is the preaching of repentance and the promise."[4] Actually Melanchthon distorts Luke's words to some degree, for the evangelist is defining the content of the apostolic preaching, while Melanchthon is giving his definition of the Gospel.

The error of Melanchthon in confusing the broad and narrow meanings of the terms *Law, Gospel,* and *repentance,* something which Chemnitz had noted as early as 1561 in his *Iudicium,* was so troublesome that as late as the FC its authors felt the matter needed clarification. This resulted in Article V in the FC on Law and Gospel. Melanchthon and Agricola both were to blame for the confusion, and the framers of the Formula dealt with Agricola and his followers also in FC VI. In a helpful and clear way the FC clears up the confusion on the broad and narrow use of these terms and really settles the controversy at that point. SD V, 27 concludes with an excellent summary,

> For this reason and in order that both doctrines, Law and Gospel, may not be mingled together and confused so that what belongs to one doctrine is ascribed to the other, it is necessary to urge and to maintain with all diligence, the true and proper distinction between Law and Gospel, and diligently to avoid anything that might give occasion for a confusion between them by which the two doctrines would be tangled together and made into one doctrine. Such a confusion would easily darken the merits and benefits of Christ, once more make the Gospel a teaching of Law, as happened in the papacy, and thus rob Christians of the true comfort which they have in the Gospel against the terrors of the Law and reopen the door to the papacy in the church of God. It is therefore dangerous and wrong to make of the Gospel, strictly so called in distinction from the Law, a proclamation of repentance and punishment. Elsewhere, however, when it is generally understood as referring to the entire teaching, a usage that we find occasionally in the Apology too, the Gospel is a proclamation both of repentance and of forgiveness of sins. But the Apology also indicates that, strictly speaking, the Gospel is the promise of forgiveness of sins and justification through Christ, whereas the law is a message that rebukes and condemns sin (Tappert, 563).[5]

Chemnitz' Lutheranism on this point also shows itself in several places in his *ECT*. Obviously the Romanists were acquainted with the concepts of Law and Gospel, but the distinction which Luther and Melanchthon (and which the FC in a few years was to add to the Lutheran testimony) had brought to the church was really almost foreign to the Catholic party. Chemnitz is undaunted by this ignorance, and launches boldly into an excellent discussion of the matter, as, for example in *ECT*, I, 534–37 where he chastises Andrada for a gross confusion of Law and Gospel.

To return to the *LT*, on pp. 445–47, Chemnitz begins with the word *Gospel*, which he defines as that doctrine "of free reconciliation or of the benefits of the Mediator" (*LT*, II, 445).

From this we can understand why Christ and the apostles called the ministry of the new covenant the Gospel. . . . They did not want to designate the public title (so to speak) of their doctrine by the word Law, in order that the difference between the teaching of Moses and the teaching of Christ might be clearer and in order that they might show that these two kinds of teaching must be distinguished even in their very names (*LT,* II, 446).

He continues,

The reasoning behind this designation is abundantly clear. For among the Hebrews the word *basar* and in the Septuagint the word *euangelizesthai* are not used for the indiscriminate announcing of any kind of good and happy news. Rather, when news came that their enemies, by whom they were threatened with a great and dangerous crisis, had fled or been scattered, this announcement of liberation from enemies, restoring peace and tranquillity . . . was designated by this word. . .(*LT,* II, 446).

He cites several Scripture passages to buttress these remarks. Since the Gospel was for all people, he also shows the meaning of the term in secular Greek.

Chemnitz then continues (ibid., 447) with a list of terms which are synonymous with Gospel. The words he uses in treating the heavenly doctrine are emphatic or significant, and there are serious underlying reasons why various names are used for the same concept. "The Gospel is called *the Word,* Is. 2:3; *the doctrine,* Rom. 6:17; 15:4; 16:17; *the Law,* Gal. 2:19 . . . ; *the testimony,* Ps. 19:7; 1 Tim. 2:6. Other terms add a descriptive element, such as *good Word of God,* Heb. 6:5; or *proclamation (kerygma)* in Rom. 16:25. Some terms indicate the divine origin, such as *mystery;* others the subject matter of the Gospel, or its effects, or the instrument which apprehends the Gospel, such as faith. Others are metaphorical (*LT,* II, 447).

DISTINCTION OF LAW AND GOSPEL

The Gospel must be sharply distinguished from the Law. While Chemnitz has touched on this matter several times already both with reference to hermeneutics and in other places, it is in this locus that he really enters into a full discussion of the matter as the central dogma or article of faith of Lutheranism. He says,

> There are many testimonies in Scripture clearly affirming that the doctrine of justification before God must not be taught, learned, or sought in the Law but in the Gospel, e.g. Rom. 1:16–17. . . . The object of justifying faith is not the doctrine of the Law but the voice of the Gospel, which is therefore called the Law and Word of faith. It must therefore be determined, on the basis of clear and firm testimonies of Scripture, what is the proper doctrine of the Gospel, which is to be separated from the Law and which reveals the righteousness of faith before God, upon which faith lays hold unto righteousness and eternal salvation. In this teaching we must seek reconciliation and the forgiveness of sins (*LT*, II, 447).

Chemnitz then proceeds to give several inadequate and erroneous definitions of the Gospel, closing with a quotation of Luther's famous *dictum* from his *Lectures on Galatians* on the theological importance of being able to distinguish between Law and Gospel:

> Whoever knows well how to distinguish between Law and Gospel should give thanks to God and should know that he is a theologian. In temptations I certainly do not know it as I ought. You should distinguish the righteousness of the Gospel from the righteousness of the Law as diligently as heaven is distinguished from earth, light from darkness, day from night . . . and would that we could separate them even farther.[6]

Chemnitz then proceeds to list the main differences by which the doctrine of the Gospel must be distinguished from the Law:

> (1) The doctrine of the Law to a certain degree is known to human reason. But the Gospel is a mystery hidden from the world, revealed only by the ministration of the Spirit. (2) Luther correctly and elegantly says that both the doctrine of the Law and the doctrine of the Gospel deal with the subject of sin, but in a different way. The Law shows sin, accuses, imputes guilt, and condemns sin; but the Gospel remits, covers, and does not impute sin, because it points to "the Lamb of God, who takes away the sin of the world" (3) Paul in Rom. 3:21, 4:5, and 10:5f. shows this difference. The doctrine of the Law is the law of works, which talks about doing: "He who does these things. . . ." It imputes a reward to the one who does the Law. But the Gospel is the law of faith,

because "to one who does not work but believes in Him who justifies the ungodly," He imputes faith for righteousness. (4) The Law prescribes and demands of each individual perfect obedience to all the commandments of God, and it threatens a curse on those who do not have such conformity with the will of God. But the Gospel, because the Law is weakened through the flesh, Rom. 8:3, shows Christ, who was made sin and a curse, "made under the Law," (Gal. 4:4), and is "the fulfillment of the Law for righteousness to everyone who believes" (Rom. 10:4). (5) The promises of the Law are conditional. But the promise of the Gospel concerning the remission of sins is free. (6) "The Law imprisons all under sin" (Gal. 3:22), "makes the whole world guilty before God" (Rom. 3:19), "works wrath" (Rom. 4:15), "puts us under the curse" (Gal. 3:10), "is the ministration of death and damnation" [2 Cor. 3:7, 9 KJV]. But the Gospel is the Word of salvation, peace, reconciliation, etc. It frees from the law of sin and death and is "the ministration" of righteousness and "the Spirit" [2 Cor. 3:8 KJV]. (7) The Law shows what the good works are in which God wants the regenerate to exercise obedience. But the Gospel teaches how they can demonstrate this obedience. For the Gospel contains the promise of the Spirit of renewal, who writes the Law into the hearts of believers (Jer. 31:33). It also teaches how the beginnings of obedience, although imperfect and contaminated in many ways, are pleasing to God in those who are righteous for the sake of Christ. (8) The Law speaks to hypocrites, the secure, the old Adam. The Gospel, however, speaks to the contrite, the broken, the captives, and keeps the new man in a state of grace (*LT*, II, 449–50).

It is important to note that the concept of Law—in Luther, Melanchthon, and Chemnitz, as well as in the Confessions—always refers not to a humanly devised law, but the Law of God as set forth in the Decalog.

As a part of his discussion Chemnitz also moves from the so-called second or accusatory work of the Law to the third use, thus jumping ahead to the next locus, but as something important which must also be said at this point. He refers to the constant confusion of justification and sanctification which so perverted the doctrine of Rome. He says,

Here it is absolutely necessary that the benefits of Christ on account of which we receive remission of sin and are received into eternal life be distinguished from the benefits of sanctification or renewal which follow justification. We are not justified for the sake of the latter, that is, we do not receive remission of sins nor are we received unto eternal life because of this renewal which follows justification, although it is also a benefit of Christ (*LT*, II, 450).

SIMILARITY OF LAW AND GOSPEL

Chemnitz then picks up (p. 455) with additional points on "The Similarity between the Law and the Gospel" (*LT*, II, 455). For example, he says, "The Law has not only material or temporal promises but also the promise of righteousness and eternal life, . . ." to which he adds, "The promise of the Law which speaks of eternal life, because it requires as a condition that the entire Law be perfectly fulfilled, is absolutely useless to us in this flesh, as Heb. 7:18 says" (*LT*, II, 455). That is to say, our failure to keep the Law of God is not the fault of the Law but of our sinful flesh. He continues,

> The Law is not contrary to the promise of the Gospel, Gal. 3:21; nor is the Law destroyed through faith, but rather established . . . . Law and Gospel are so connected that it is impossible to use a mathematical parallel to describe their similarity. . . . The convergence of Law and Gospel consists particularly in this, that the benefits of Christ of which the Gospel speaks are nothing else than satisfaction for the guilt and punishment we owe to the Law and that completely perfect obedience which the righteousness of the Law demands. These two things which the Law requires and demands are given to believers and imputed in Christ for righteousness (*LT*, II, 455).

Therefore,

> there is no way we can understand the greatness of the benefits of Christ unless they are thus compared with the rigor and severity of the Law. This righteousness of which the Law speaks, impossible for us because of the flesh, the Gospel shows and points out in Christ, who was made under the Law, in order that righteousness of the Law might be fulfilled in us (1) by imputation through faith; (2) by the beginning stage when the Law through the Spirit is written in our hearts; (3) in eternal life, when our obedience to the Law of God will be brought to completion. Therefore the righ-

teousness of the Law and of the Gospel is different, and it is also the same. In respect to us it is different, cf. Phil. 3:9, "a righteousness which is not of the Law" (*LT*, II, 455–56).

"But with respect to Christ it is the same; for what the Law demands and requires, this Christ supplies and gives. So also reconciliation is called redemption with respect to Christ, because the compensation has been paid; but with respect to us it is called the gracious remission of sins" (*LT*, II, 456). Here we see the full doctrine of the substitutionary atonement without the actual use of the terminology.

CONTROVERSIES OVER JUSTIFICATION

At this point, Chemnitz himself launches into a lengthy treatise on the controversies associated with the subject of justification and the distinction between Law and Gospel (*LT*, II, 462–73) going back into the OT era, Cain and Abel, and continuing down to the intertestamental period. Then he takes up controversies in the time of Christ and the apostles, the Pharisees, the role of the ceremonial law which of course made its way into the Christian church. Then he deals with the controversies right after the time of the apostles in the early church and handles such groups as the Ebionites, Cerinthus, Simon, Basilides, the Gnostics, the Manichaeans, Valentinus, Marcion, and the Apelles. Without taking up each group, we can simply say that he analyzes the teachings of each of these heretics and their followers. He gives a trenchant analysis of The Shepherd of Hermas and his extravagant works righteousness.

He then devotes a section to unfortunate statements of the fathers who are so often quoted for their orthodox assertions regarding Christology and the Supper. They misused the terms "to justify," "righteousness," etc. They misunderstood the term "faith," and treated it as mere historical faith. They confused Law and Gospel terribly. They confused justification and sanctification, they glorified the idea of merit and righteousness by works, they leaned over backwards to try to win the philosophers, and they had an excessive admiration for outward and severe discipline. In short, the doctrinal deviations picked up by Rome over the centuries in many instances went back to the ancient and largely orthodox fathers.

However, there were some fathers who were helpful in many ways, among whom were Jerome, Ambrose, and particularly Augustine. Chemnitz points out that often the fathers were more scriptural in their devotional writings than in their doctrinal statements.

VOCABULARY

Now, at last, most of the preliminaries have been laid aside, and on p. 475 Chemnitz turns to the vocabulary of justification, which is so beautifully summarized in the FC. He takes up the terms "to justify," "to be justified," "righteous act," "acquittal," and the "righteousness of God and of faith" (*LT*, II, 475). He begins, "Just as the concepts themselves have been revealed in Scripture by the divine voice in the Word, so they cannot properly be understood except from the true and genuine meaning of the words which the Holy Spirit used in handing down the heavenly doctrine" (*LT*, II, 475). Correct terminology is necessary for the correct understanding of the concepts themselves. "We must also add this point, that God has kindled the light of the doctrine of faith by rescuing these terms from the barbarism of the papacy and restoring their true, genuine, and apostolic meaning" (*LT*, II, 476). This in reference to the work of Luther. He summarizes, "There is no doubt that if the linguistic interpretation again falls into neglect or is lost in regard to these terms, the light of this doctrine, even though it is very clear at present, will again be obfuscated and extinguished, just as in the Osiandrian controversy God warned the church with a serious reminder that it should not play games with these words" (*LT*, II, 476).

Justify

Chemnitz begins by dealing with the word "to justify" in secular Greek, showing that here too it has a forensic or declarative or legal meaning. It is never used in secular Greek in the sense of infusing righteousness or justice into a person or with the idea of "expelling one quality and putting in another" (*LT*, II, 477). Chemnitz also contends that "it is manifest and beyond denial or doubt that among the Hebrews the word is a forensic term . . ." (*LT*, II, 477) often used in reference to courts, and often placed in the legal sense in opposition to "condemn," as in Rom. 8:33–34, "It is God who justifies; who is he that condemns?" or Rom. 5:16, "The judgment was by one to condemnation, but the free gift is from many offenses to justification" (*LT*, II, 477). The word *justify* includes three components for Chemnitz,

> (1) It means to absolve the person who has been accused and brought to judgment of the crime with which he was charged, so that he not be condemned by the legal process or that he be restored to his state of innocence. (2) It means to account, pronounce, receive, and accept a person as righteous or innocent. . . . (3) The term also includes the fact that Scripture attributes to those who have been justified the praise, the testimony, and the rewards owed to the righteous and the innocent, and it treats them not as guilty convicts or even as suspects, but as righteous and innocent. . . . This is the forensic or legal meaning of this word (*LT*, II, 478).

Chemnitz also notes that the German *rechtfertigen* has a forensic dimension to it as well.

Chemnitz then takes up a number of synonyms for justification: to impute for righteousness, to be reconciled. Titus 3:5–7 "joins these three expressions: to justify, to save, and to become heirs of eternal life." Peter and John . . . do not use the word *justification*, but used "better known synonyms" (*LT*, II, 483). John had "a particularly long life, so that if he noted any less correct understanding of this matter, he might leave to the church a sure explanation," as, for example, in John 3:16–18, "He who does not believe is condemned already . . . . He who believes shall not be judged. . . . He sent His Son not to judge the world . . . ." "It is clear that these expressions are paraphrases of the word *justification* and have the same meaning we have been speaking about" (*LT*, II, 483). He goes on and on citing both John and Peter and Christ Himself.

He also deals (*LT*, II, 484), with the definition of the expression "the righteousness of God" pointing out that it too has a Law meaning and a Gospel meaning. Luther had said that "although he held to the article of justification, yet he was troubled by the word and did not gladly hear the statement 'In the Gospel is revealed the righteousness of God' [Rom. 1:17], because he understood it as referring to the judicial and severe righteousness by which God enters into judgment with us"[7] (*LT*, II, 484). But Chemnitz cites other examples in which

> it is obvious that "the righteousness of God" can mean nothing else than the goodness and mercy of God, whereby He does not enter into judgment but absolves, receives into grace, redeems, frees, and defends. . . . In these passages the term *the righteousness of God* means the righteousness acceptable before God unto life eternal, and this is the obedience of our Mediator, which God imputes to believers for righteousness if they lay hold on it by faith (*LT*, II, 484–85).

Faith

As is his practice, Chemnitz first gives a brief historical study on how the matter has been perverted, then he shows how we can quite easily investigate Paul's true meaning. Faith is best understood in connection with justification when we state the *status controversiae* thus: "In the dispute about faith the question concerns the application of the merit and obedience of Christ for righteousness and the salvation of everyone who believes" (*LT*, II, 498). In other words, it is clear that the merit of Christ is applied to us by faith, and thus we are absolved and accepted as righteous "not by works but by faith in Christ." For Christ and His work are presented to us in Scripture as "the object with which justifying faith properly is concerned . . . which it grasps and applies to itself" (ibid.). In reply to Roman arguments that this is not the meaning of faith, Chemnitz, following Melanchthon, says, "The point at issue is to show that 'faith' is having in our mind the kind of knowledge that, in the case of true faith, produces an assent in our will and a moving of our hearts, a desire and a trust which lay hold on and apply to oneself the object of faith . . ." (ibid., 492). Here is a clear statement of the knowledge, assent, and trust concept, but note the circumstances involved.

Then Chemnitz proceeds, "Because we are dealing with a matter of great importance, namely what that faith is by which Scripture affirms that we are justified (for 'He who does not believe will be condemned' [Mark 16:16]), and because many are under the persuasion of a false or dead faith, and thus are doing themselves injury of eternal life and salvation; therefore a matter of this importance must not be left only in the hands of those who dispute grammatical points" (ibid., 493). He makes several points on this matter:

> We must carefully consider the weight of the testimonies which clearly show that "faith" in the article of justification must be understood not only as knowledge and general assent, stating in a general way that the promise of the Gospel is true, but that at the same time it includes the activities of the will and the heart; that is, it is a desire and a trust which, in the struggle with sin and the wrath of God, applies the promise of grace to each individual, so that each person includes himself in the general promise given to believers. . . . The very form of the Apostolic Profession of Faith clearly shows that faith is the means by which this application takes place, for we say, "I believe in God . . . ." And this is most definitely proved from the correct use of the Sacraments [individually] (ibid., 493–94).

This concept of distinguishing between general and saving faith appears throughout the writings of both Melanchthon and Chemnitz. Apparently they felt the sting of a charge of some kind of Gospel-reductionism from their Roman opponents, as if in stressing justifying faith they were denigrating the rest of Scripture. On the other hand, they wanted to get away from the Roman concept that faith was merely something historical.

On the other hand, Melanchthon in his definition of faith, which Chemnitz makes his own (See *LT*, II, 486 and 489), stipulates that "faith is to assent to the entire Word of God as it has been given to us" (ibid., 500). He has just previously asserted, "Faith embraces both trust in the mercy of God and knowledge of the historical events . . . . The historical events must be applied to the promise or the effect of His work, as it is set forth in this article, namely, 'I believe in the forgiveness of sins'" (ibid., 486). Chemnitz adopts the same definition of faith and continues,

> Many have debated as to whether this part [about "assent to the whole Word of God"] really ought to be placed in the definition of justifying faith. But there are true and serious reasons why the definition was made up this way, and a consideration of them will teach us much. For justifying faith presupposes and includes general faith, which establishes with a sure conviction and without any doubt that the things revealed in the Word of God are

absolutely true because God Himself is the Author, who is to be praised for His truthfulness because He is beyond all limitation" (ibid., 500).

He continues for some length in this vein.

While discussing faith, in his *ECT,* Chemnitz makes an oblique reference to Melanchthon's definition, "For this reason and with this understanding the men of our party add this little word in the definition of justifying faith: 'Faith means to give assent to the *whole* Word of God that is set before us, and in it to the promise of the gratuitous reconciliation bestowed for the sake of Christ the Mediator" (*ECT,* I, 567). Then he continues, "For we do not approve the opinion of the Marcionite Apelles, who, in Eusebius, argues that it does no harm if someone either simply does not believe or corruptly believes the other parts of the Word of God which belong to the foundation, so long as he believes in Christ crucified" (ibid.). Chemnitz goes after Apelles for the same error again in *ECT* (ibid., 394), and in his *LT* (II, 467 and 501). The argument that the doctrine of biblical inerrancy was a 19th-century import from Reformed Fundamentalism was advanced by those who had not read either Melanchthon or Chemnitz.

Chemnitz then proceeds to point out that the above takes place, but without the Roman concept of faith working through love and without the idea of a general assent. He then sets forth a list of Scripture passages in which various objects of faith are stipulated, such as Hebrews 11, where things like the article of creation, the prediction of the coming flood, the hiding of Moses, the institution of the Passover, the crossing of the Red Sea, etc. are mentioned. Also in regard to Rom. 4:3 "it seems that Gen. 15:5 speaks of physical fertility, of the external or bodily seed" (*LT,* II, 494). The papists use such passages which speak of faith to try to force us back to equating justifying faith with general faith. But the basic question is, "In respect to what object does faith justify?. . . We must allow a distinction. In some places Scripture speaks of the object of faith in a general sense, and in other places it sets up that object with respect to which by grasping it, faith justifies before God" (ibid., 495).

In the next section (ibid., 499), Chemnitz continues with his discussion of faith, this time with reference to the various entities in which faith relies, such as the "general faith, which we commonly call historical faith, not only because it deals with the Biblical stories but because it holds in a general way that the things revealed in the Word of God are true, in the sense of the simple knowledge which historians use. Thus King Agrippa in Acts 26:27 believes the prophets and yet he is not a Christian" (ibid.). There is also faith in miracles. There is a dead faith, or a hypocritical faith, or false or pretended faith. There is a legal faith or an evangelical faith, the catholic faith, faith is hope, etc. He closes with a restatement of Melanchthon's definition of justifying faith as discussed previously.

Yet justifying faith is more than assent. Chemnitz then enters into a rather lengthy discussion of the fact that "what the word 'faith' properly means in the article of justification can most beautifully be gathered and demonstrated from the other names attributed to justifying faith in Scripture" (ibid., 496), "such as 'substance' (*hypostasis*) in Heb. 11:1; 'full assurance' (*plerophoria*) in Rom. 4:21, Col. 2:2, etc.; 'boldness' or 'confidence' (*parresia*), Eph. 3:12, 1 John 2:28, Heb. 3:6, etc.; 'trust' (*pepoithesis*), Eph. 3:12, Ps. 2:11." He goes on to list several similar words, such as 'to keep' or 'to seal.' And in opposition to these terms are concepts of doubting, weak and little faith. He concludes this section with a pastoral note, as he so often does,

> The true meaning of justifying faith is understood best of all in serious exertions of repentance, as the meditations of the ancients show. . . . The doctrine of faith, more than all commentaries, is undertaken chiefly in two ways—either the conscience places itself before the tribunal of God . . . or it finds itself under cross and temptation, in petition and expectation, for both spiritual and corporal things (ibid., 499).

Chemnitz shows why faith is more than an intellectual assent as he moves into "the second part of [Melanchthon's] definition . . . the material principle, that is the proper and principal object in which justifying faith seeks reconciliation, remission of sins, and eternal life" (ibid., 501). This object of our faith is shown us in the Word of God, in Law and Gospel, but "the object of justifying faith is not the Word of God in general, but the promise of the benefits of Christ the Mediator . . ." (ibid.). Though Christocentric, Chemnitz is not Christomonistic. He states,

I think the most expeditious way of doing this is to divide it up according to the article of the Trinity, as Scripture celebrates: (1) the grace, mercy, love, kindness, compassion, and blessing of God the Father; (2) all the benefits of the Son of God in His entire office of Mediator, in the incarnation, the crucifixion, the resurrection, ascension, and sitting at the right hand of the Father—all of which have wide ramification; (3) the fact that the Holy Spirit sets forth these promises, offers, distributes, applies, and seals them by faith, through the Word and the Sacraments, in the hearts of believers" (ibid.).

The same thought is echoed by Chemnitz in his *ECT*, in the chapter on justifying faith,

. . . the following statements of Scripture belong to this subject: first, those which speak of the gratuitous mercy, love, grace, kindness, goodness, etc., of God the Father, sending His Son, choosing, calling, reconciling, adopting receiving to life eternal those who believe, etc. Second, all statements which speak of the office of the Mediator in His incarnation, cross, passion, resurrection, ascension, session at the right hand. Third, that the Holy Spirit sets forth, offers, distributes, applies, seals, these benefits by faith through the Word of the Gospel and through the Sacraments instituted by the Son of God for this purpose. Fourth, here belong also the very numerous statements of Scripture that, by the mercy of God on account of Christ the Mediator, we by faith receive and possess the gratuitous reconciliation, remission of sins, imputation of righteousness, acceptance by God to life eternal, the adoption, liberation from the law of sin and death, liberation from the curse of the Law, the propitiation for sins, peace, joy, hope of the glory of God, the inheritance of salvation and of life everlasting, etc. (*ECT*, I, 569–70).

Note that the close connection of the doctrine of the Trinity (especially as set forth in the Creeds) is re-echoed in modern confessional Lutheran theology. For example, Schlink devotes several pages to the matter under such important headings as "Recognition of the Creator-goodness of God is possible only by faith in the Gospel,"[8] or even more pointedly, "To confess God the Creator means at the same time to confess the cross of Jesus Christ,"[9] and again, "To confess God the Creator means at the same time to confess the Holy Spirit, who makes us alive,"[10] again,

To know God's love means to receive his gracious love. However, the love of God the Creator, Redeemer, and Sanctifier is not given through the demands of the Law, but through the gift of the Gospel. The Triune God, therefore, is known only in the distinction of Law and Gospel, that is, by faith in the Gospel. The train of thought in this chapter has shown that the Creator is known only in the Gospel. The same holds true of knowing God the Sanctifier, for the Holy Spirit is given only through the Gospel. Of every knowledge of God the statement applies: "Thus the entire Holy Trinity, God the Father, Son, and Holy Spirit, directs all men to Christ as to the book of life."[11]

This last quotation is from the confessional writing in which Chemnitz played so major a role, SD XI, 66, the article on divine election. Schlink has correctly analyzed the theology of the Lutheran Confessions—on this point at least.

On p. 501 Chemnitz takes up the part of Melanchthon's definition of faith, where we have "a description of the formal cause or principle, namely, how justifying faith relates to its object" (*LT*, II, 501), that is "in such a way that with a true and earnest desire of the mind, the will, and the heart, it desires, seeks, grasps, receives, and applies personally to individual believers the promise of free reconciliation for the sake of Christ the Mediator, so that it may find rest in it unto righteousness, salvation, and eternal life" (ibid.). He divides the subject as follows:

(1) Scripture calls faith a knowledge or an understanding, (Luke 1:77; Is. 53:11). . . . The decree and history of redemption, the gracious and universal promise that God for the sake of that Victim wants to receive sinners who flee to the Mediator in faith—these teachings are to be shown to faith and inculcated from the Word of God. (2) But because many who hear, understand, and know this either neglect or doubt or reject it. . . . Therefore it is necessary that to this knowledge be added assent . . . that firm persuasion which Paul calls the full assurance of faith . . . whereby each person should determine that the universal promise applies also to him. . . . (3) Then from this knowledge and assent in the mind, by the working of the Holy Spirit, the heart or will conceives a groaning or desire so that, because it feels very earnestly that it is burdened down with sins and the wrath of God, it wills, prays, and seeks that these benefits be given to it which are set forth in the promise of the Gospel. . . . (4) When in this way you turn

away with your mind, your will, and your heart from looking at your sins and feeling the wrath of God and begin to look to the Lamb of God, who takes away the sin of the world, that is, when from the sentence of damnation pronounced upon you through the Law, you flee to the throne of grace, to the propitiation the heavenly Father has set forth in the blood of Christ, it is necessary to add trust (*fiducia*) . . . . (5) Finally, from this faith there follows a confidence (*parresia*) which has access to God, Eph. 3:12; peace of conscience, Rom. 5:1; "the joy of the Spirit," Rom. 14:7, so that the heart, feeling the new life and joy in God, happily rests in the promise of grace, even under the cross, in persecution, finally in death itself; and it has an undoubting "hope of the glory of God," Rom. 5:2 (ibid., 502).

He continues by pointing out that there are different levels of faith, that the light of faith varies from time to time.

We must note the foundations. For we are justified by faith, not because it is so firm, robust, and perfect a virtue, but because of the object on which it lays hold, namely Christ. . . . Therefore when faith does not err in its object, but lays hold on that true object, although with a weak faith, or at least tries and wants to lay hold on Christ, then there is true faith, and it justifies. . . . We must note that these individual grades or levels of faith are not always equally brilliant in believers . . . yet it is still faith, so long as it clings to the true object . . . . We must not determine the status of our faith on the basis of our feeling or comfort or spiritual joy . . . . God often takes away this feeling of peace from believers (ibid., 502).

On p. 505 Chemnitz starts a new chapter, entitled "Faith is a Sure Confidence, Contrary to the Popish Dogma of Doubt." Here he begins in his *LT* with a long quotation from the Decrees of Trent, Session VI, Chapter IX and devotes a long section to this Roman perversion. His main points are that the papists corrupt the nature of the free promise which faith teaches, while their dogma of doubt only corrupts. The very nature of justifying faith renders the dogma of doubt invalid, and the doctrine of the sealing by the Holy Spirit does the same. The sacraments also give persuasive arguments, as does the doctrine of absolution. Chemnitz notes that doubt is condemned in Scripture as a rejection of faith in the mercy and goodness of God and points out that the ancient church held to the assurance of faith and rejected the dogma of doubt. To the papists' claim that Christian humility requires an attitude of doubt, Chemnitz replies,

> But the true and simple answer to this is taken from the distinction between Law and Gospel. For the imaginings of the adversaries have their origins in the idea that God has indeed promised grace, salvation, and eternal life, but that this applies only to those who are worthy either by merits or by attitude. But because the Law always accuses us and convinces us of our unworthiness, nothing can follow from this teaching but perpetual doubt (ibid., 511).

He then goes on to reiterate that if we put our trust in the Law, we should not only have doubt but total despair. Only by faith in the Gospel of God's grace is there deliverance, even from doubt. "Therefore faith does not cling, either with assertiveness or with doubt, to its own worthiness or attitude; but outside itself, in Christ, it seeks the true righteousness which it can safely place in opposition to the judgment of God" (ibid.). He concludes,

> Finally, when all their other bastions have been captured, they take refuge in this, that . . . in regard to present grace there can indeed be certainty, but no one can be sure whether he will persevere to the end. . . . Reply: It is manifest that many do not persevere but fall from grace. But this is not because God does not will that believers, whom He at one time received into grace, should persevere unto the end, but it comes from the fact that many drive out the Holy Spirit and trample their faith underfoot. . . . Therefore, as it pertains to God, the perseverance of the godly is sure; and because it has been revealed in the Word, faith must believe this . . . . Therefore we are commanded to pray for perseverance, because God has promised it. Prayer always requires a promise in order that it may have no cause for hesitancy (James 1:6). But we pray and struggle that the pride of the flesh not stifle the gift of perseverance (ibid., 514).

Chemnitz takes up this dogma of doubt in full detail also in his *ECT* (I, 586–611). The arguments are much the same as noted above.

JUSTIFICATION

Grace

We next come to the word *grace*. Melanchthon begins with a long and important locus, which Chemnitz picks up with an even longer and excellent treatment. Chemnitz begins with his usual definition of terms and reference to the Spirit in the production of the Scripture,

> The Holy Spirit, with singular wisdom, did not wish in the article of justification to use terms taken from the common usage of people, but many terms are of such a nature that they are neither used nor known with this meaning in other kinds of speech, but are idiomatic, proper, and peculiar to Holy Scripture. Just as the content in this article is not known to human reason, so also the words are peculiar; in fact, I might call them sacred, not secular or commonly used. I believe this is the case for two reasons: (1) That the very words might instruct us that there is a difference between the doctrine of the church and the opinions of philosophers, based on reason, regarding justification. Nor should we be surprised that our human reason recoils at the heavenly doctrine of the righteousness before God, since the very words show that there is a mystery here, something placed far above and beyond the purview of human reason. (2) The Holy Spirit wanted not only the contents of this article but also the terms themselves to have a special meaning, distinct from philosophical language, so that . . . the very names of things might serve as warnings that the ideas of philosophy must not be mixed in with the article of justification. . . . The true light of this article was lost when the vocabulary began to lean toward the philosophical meaning of the terms (*LT,* II, 519–20).

Conversely, the purity of teaching was restored when the language was restored.

He begins with a brief overview of the Pelagian controversy, which, of course, had corrupted this teaching. He again cautions regarding confusing the doctrine of justification and the doctrine of sanctification or renewal, for in both articles the Holy Spirit and grace play a pivotal role. He also, typically, makes a word study of the term *grace* and related words, such as the *forgiveness of sins* and the *free gift* in both testaments and in secular literature. He concludes by summarizing regarding the article of justification and the word *grace,*

The main ideas are these: (1) It [the term *grace*] is translated by the word "mercy." (2) It is joined with the concept of showing mercy. (3) It is used in the sense of supplying strength, "because I am weak and loaded down with contempt." (4) Grace is shown although we deserve something else. (5) We must note the correlation with supplication and prayer (ibid., 524).

Then he discusses, again, the relationship between grace and human efforts,

when Paul says: "We are justified freely through the grace of God," . . . we are not to understand that we are justified and saved either entirely by our own newness of life or by a combination of God's mercy and our own newness within us, but that in the article of justification before God the word *grace* means only the mercy of God, which is the remission of sins and free acceptance to eternal life for the sake of the Mediator. Gifts, such as the Spirit of renewal, follow after this acceptance by God, and thus these two matters cannot be torn apart, as John so strongly confirms in his First Epistle, 3:14: "He who does not love remains in death." . . . Therefore we are not rejecting the gifts of renewal when we contend, in keeping with the Scriptural principle, that "grace" in the article of justification means only "the mercy of God." But we do distinguish between these two, and attribute to each the place which Scripture assigns to it, that is to say, to the article of justification the mercy of God, but to the article of renewal [or sanctification] the gifts of newness. We do so for this reason, that faith in the remission of sins and reconciliation with God might not rely on our qualities but solely on the mercy of God, and thus "the promise might be sure," Rom. 4:16 [KJV] (ibid., 525).

He concludes,

"Grace is justifying because God is most kind toward us in Christ Jesus, even when 'dead in sins,' without respect to any quality or works in us, and has 'made us alive together with Christ . . . raised us up . . . and made us sit with Him in heavenly places in Christ Jesus'" (Eph. 2:5–6 [RSV]) (ibid., 526).

Freely

Chemnitz next takes up the word *freely* in order that, as he puts it, "the exclusive aspect of the term *grace* may be seen more clearly and fortified more strongly in the face of all corruptions, Paul in Rom. 3:24 adds the particle 'freely' (*gratis*)" (ibid.). The Lutherans had begun the practice of stressing these so-called exclusive particles, beginning with Luther and his use of the term *sola* in his translation of the NT, continuing with Melanchthon, as in Apology IV, 73; following with Chemnitz at great length in both his *LT* and—boldly—in his *ECT* and the FC itself. Chemnitz, as nearly always, takes up the etymology of the term *freely*, both in the Hebrew and the Greek, as well as the Septuagint and the Vulgate, not to mention Luther, several fathers, and of course in the Scripture itself. He deals with both the negative and the positive side of the meaning.

> Paul adds the particle "freely" ('we are justified "freely" through His grace') in order to show that God in the article of justification does not regard worthiness, merit, cause, form, or anything inherent in us by whatever name you call it as the reason for receiving us into grace. Although He found in us a cause why He could damn us, He by mere free goodness receives us to eternal life. This is what it means "to be justified freely through the grace of God." So these two points cover the things of which we have spoken above: (1) In us there is nothing meritorious, no worthiness or cause for justification and salvation. (2) Because our nature is contaminated in many different ways by sins, we deserve the wrath of God and merit eternal damnation, and yet purely out of the mercy of God for the sake of His Son the Mediator, we have been accepted by God. This is what it means to be "justified freely" (ibid., 528).

Imputation

In the next section Chemnitz takes up the important word *imputation*. While, as indicated above, the concept of God's judgment taking place in a court setting as a forensic act, was by no means a Lutheran discovery, but certainly a Lutheran emphasis, and while Paul uses in several places the picture of God's reckoning, or evaluating, or crediting something to man for the sake of Christ, yet because of the extreme works-righteousness of Rome, when Luther took up these concepts and began to stress them, he was regarded as a heretic.[12] As early as his *Iudicium* (1561), Chemnitz speaks of the imputation of Christ's obedience, which, of course, he had gotten not only from many of Luther's writings but from the AC itself. In his *Iudicium*, which in its section on justification is directly primarily against Osiander, Chemnitz says, "Osiander shamefully attacks, disapproves, rejects, and condemns the doctrine of the Augsburg Confession which affirms that the righteousness of faith before God is the imputation of the obedience of Christ. He calls this doctrine of the Augustana Confession a carnal, physical fantasy, and idolatry."[13]

Chemnitz in his brief and succinct treatment of the doctrine of justification in his *De caute sentiendi* also brings in the doctrine of imputation, where he cites the Apology III, 184, "In this passage to justify signifies, according to forensic usage, to acquit a guilty one and declare him righteous, but on account of the righteousness of another, namely, of Christ." The Apology continues in paragraph 186, "Our righteousness is the imputation of the righteousness of another."[14] In his *Enchiridion*, in the opening statement of the section on justification, he says,

> [In what, then, does justification of man the sinner *before* God consist according to the statement of the Gospel?] [Reply] In this very thing, that God imputes to us the righteousness of the obedience and death of Christ . . . without our works or merits, alone by faith that apprehends the grace of God the Father and the merit of Christ . . . (*Ench.*, 72).

However, to get a full picture of the importance of the doctrine of imputation in Lutheranism, one must consult the *ECT*, which is even more complete and devastating to Rome than is the *LT*. In the latter, Chemnitz much more briefly reviews and actually reiterates what is said in the *ECT*. It is almost as if he is saying, "For the entire subject see my *ECT*." It would appear that he was writing his *ECT* about the same time as he was delivering the lectures which we call his *LT*. Chemnitz devotes scores of pages to this doctrine in his *ECT*, while also here taking a few swipes at Osiander. The Romanists even tried to make the term *imputation* mean infusion, thus taking the entire scene away from the court and placing it in the garden (cf. *ECT*, I, 531). Chemnitz, like Luther and Melanchthon before him, keeps the discussion in the courtroom. He opens the subject in his *ECT* under the question: "What That Righteousness Is Which

316

We Plead Against the Judgment of God in Justification" (ibid., 497).
He says,

> We do not, therefore, teach that believers are justified without
> righteousness, a justification of the ungodly which God pro-
> nounces an abomination in Prov. 17:15 . . . but we say that it is
> necessary that in justification a righteousness should come in and
> intervene, and indeed, not just any kind of righteousness but one
> which is sufficient and worthy in the judgment of God to be
> declared suitable for eternal life. However, our inherent righ-
> teousness, which is begun in the renewal through the Holy Spirit
> is not such on account of the adhering imperfection and impurity
> of the flesh. Therefore a different righteousness is necessary, by
> which, when it enters in and intercedes, we may be justified
> before God to life eternal. This indeed is the satisfaction and obe-
> dience, that is, the righteousness of Christ, the Mediator, which is
> offered through the ministry of the Word and of the Sacraments, is
> apprehended by faith, and is imputed by God to the believers
> . . . so that "covered by it we may now boldly and securely stand
> before the divine tribunal and thus be pronounced righteous to
> life eternal" (ibid., 500–501).

The last words cited are from the Romanist Pighius who is
"compelled by the evidence of the truth to acknowledge and confess this statement as true, godly and in harmony with Scripture"
(ibid).

In an attack on Andrada, *ECT,* pp. 523–37, Chemnitz defines
precisely what our righteousness is:

> (1) that the Son of God became a Mediator for us, being obedi-
> ent to the Father to death; (2) that the Father accepted that satis-
> faction and obedience of the Son for our reconciliation and
> propitiation, which He showed by His resurrection. For this rea-
> son Paul, in the imputation of righteousness, connects the death
> and the resurrection of Christ (ibid., 530).

Chemnitz also attacks the Roman concept that this imputation
"does not mean anything else than that the quality of righteousness is infused" (ibid., 531–32). He cites other Roman authorities
and refutes them all, concluding, "Not because of our righteousness but because of Thy great mercies; not because of deeds done
by us in righteousness, but in virtue of His own mercy He saved
us" (ibid., 537). It is manifest from the above that Chemnitz' Exam-

ination of Trent is not some mere polemic but a carefully thought-through statement both of Roman theology and Lutheran theology. The similarity with the FC and the *LT* as well as the other writings of Chemnitz is manifest. His same serenity of spirit and mild manner of speaking is evident throughout this great work.

Elert has made the observation,

> The tendency to be precise, which dominated the development of the doctrine of justification up to the time of the Formula of Concord, found a definitive expression when later dogmaticians defined justification as a "judicial" (*judicialis*) or a "forensic" (*forensis*) [declarative] "act." . . . Just as the "juridical" element cannot be imagined as being absent from what Paul taught about salvation, so it cannot be imagined as being absent from what Luther taught. Melanchthon had used the expression "forensic usage". . . in the Apology. . . . [15] The forensic doctrine of justification . . . kept alive the realization that even when justification and the forgiveness of sins are equated, the seriousness of the judgment passed on sin dare not be minimized. It is the divine Judge whose verdict faith hears.[16]

The Exclusive Particles

As in the FC, Chemnitz takes up the matter of the Exclusive Particles, something that is reflected in the writings of Luther, Melanchthon, Chemnitz' *ECT*, the Rhegius document, the *Iudicium*, and the Confessions.[17] All focus on the uniqueness and total sufficiency of Christ, but "some of them speak about the cause, some about the merit, and some about the application of justification" (*LT*, II, 538). He then proceeds to list nine words or phrases applying to these exclusive particles: the word *grace*, (*gratia*); the term *freely*, (*gratis*); the word *one* (Rom. 5:19), "through one man's obedience"; the word *Law* (Rom. 3:21), "without the Law"; "without works" (Rom. 4:6); the word *imputation*, used repeatedly in Romans, in three ways: "to impute faith unto righteousness" (*LT*, 539), to impute righteousness without works, and to impute according to grace. "Not imputing their trespasses unto them (2 Cor. 5:19)"; "that we might be made the righteousness of God in Christ" (2 Cor. 5:19); the word *faith*, which Paul uses in several ways, including in an exclusive sense.

318

In the next chapter (*LT*, 540) Chemnitz comes to the nub of the exclusive particle matter, the word *sola*. He repeats the argumentation Luther used in inserting *sola* into his translation. He also shows that even the Vulgate used *sola* when there was no equivalent for it in the original Hebrew, but it fits in both German and Latin. He concludes, "The expression 'by faith alone' in the article of justification was not dreamed up as something new and for the first time by our theologians, but it was always used in the complete consensus of all antiquity in connection with this article, as examples from the writings of the fathers testify" (*LT*, 541). He then proceeds to quote Ambrose, who uses the expression 15 times; along with Basil, Hilary, Chrysostom, and many others. The source for this material is Robert Barnes, the English Lutheran who was put to death by Henry VIII. This topic is not limited to the *LT*. Chemnitz discusses it also in his *Iudicium* (1561).

In his brief *De Caute Sentiendi*, pp. 22–23, he has a paragraph in which he stresses this subject in a remarkable manner, almost to the point of absurdity:

> Therefore in the doctrine of justification we must teach, in such a way that contrary to Pharisaic opinions, the righteousness of faith before God [exact title of Article III of the FC] is attributed only (*soli*) to the free (*gratuitae*) mercy of God, only (*soli*) to the obedience or merit of Christ alone (*solius*), which is offered by the promise of the Gospel, received by faith alone (*sola fide*), and consists alone (*sola*) in the free acceptance, reconciliation, and remission of sins of believers before God, and this takes place that the promise might be certain (Rom. 3 and 4).[18]

ECT 1.582–3 is almost a verbatim quotation of exactly what he has said in the *LT* on the exclusive particles (*LT*, 538–39). He closes his treatment of this matter in the *ECT*, by quoting Luther on Genesis 15:

> "I know that the other virtues are excellent gifts of God; I know that faith does not exist without these gifts. However, the question is what belongs to what. You hold in the hand various seeds. I do not, however, ask which are related to which but what is the peculiar virtue of each. Here say openly what faith alone does, not with what virtues it is connected. Faith alone apprehends the promise; this is the peculiar work of faith alone. The remaining virtues have other things with which they deal." Likewise: "We

know that faith is never alone but brings with it love and other manifold gifts; it is never alone, but things must not for this reason be confused, and what belongs solely to faith must not be attributed to the other virtues."[19]

This is a succinct summary of the chief point at controversy in the Reformation!

THE WORK OF CHRIST

It is noteworthy that with all that Luther, the confessions, and the writings of this era have to say about the person of Christ and the sacrament of His presence, and with all that is said about the nature of man and how he appropriates the work of Christ through faith, yet little is said in special writings or particular loci about the work of Christ itself. Even in Melanchthon's and Chemnitz' loci about the second person of the Trinity the emphasis is entirely on the person, the incarnation, the two natures, and the person but not on the work of Christ. Although a special locus deals with the work of the Holy Spirit, the same is not the case with the work of Christ. The reason, thank God, is obvious, there was no controversy about the historic actions of Christ which brought about the redemption of mankind. All the talk that we have noted above about historic and general faith shows and demonstrates within the pages of his *LT* that all parties, except ultimately the Socinians, were basically in agreement that Christ had come into the world, why He had done so, the circumstances of His conception by the Holy Spirit, birth of the Virgin, His life, His suffering, death and resurrection, and promise of return to judgment. While no locus was set up to describe all of this, there is virtually incessant reference to the work of Christ even in the loci pertaining to God, creation, sin, the nature of the human being, the doctrine of Scripture and the sacraments, the church and ministry, and every other topic which is touched upon.

This is so particularly true in the locus on justification with its special emphasis on the distinction of Law and Gospel and the promise that here, if anywhere, we should make at least a few remarks on Chemnitz' doctrine of the work of Christ. We began the discussion of justification by referring to the FC on this subject. At this point of the work of Christ we shall again point the reader to Articles III–VI of the FC, but also call attention to Chemnitz' locus on justification, where throughout the entire locus reference is made to His work. Note that in nearly every instance the work of Christ is directly attached to our faith in this work, which becomes ours through faith in Him. For example, "The Gospel is preached to those who are repentant [note the lack of reference to historic faith or mere historical facts], and it deals with the gracious promise of reconciliation, remission of sins, righteousness before God, salvation, and acceptance unto eternal life" (*LT*, II, 450)—all things which happen to man because of what Christ did.

The paragraph closes with a similar statement, "This promise is established in God's grace, mercy, and love" (*LT*, II, 450). The Gospel is something which God in mercy offers to man which has been made possible by what Christ has done. He has done it whether man believes it or not. He as our Mediator prays for us before the judgment seat of God. He fulfills the Law for us completely by His perfect obedience to the Law. He redeems us from sin by His own death as our substitute on the Cross. He dies the death we have deserved, thus paying our penalty. He reconciles us to the Father. He sends the Holy Spirit. He intercedes for us with the Father, so that His innocence might be imputed to us and our guilt to Him. He is a servant for our sakes. He is sinless. He humbles Himself. He makes Himself a sacrifice for us. He descended into hell. He rose in triumph leading our captors captive, and sits at the right hand of the Father in eternal glory. He will return to judge, and will take all believers into eternal salvation (see *LT*, I, 79). He alone has made satisfaction. He alone is meritorious and this merit is efficacious. He is our advocate. The final goal of all of Christ's work and our justification is His gift of eternal life (*LT*, II, 550–56).

ELECTION

At the close of his great locus on justification, Chemnitz in a sense takes us back to the beginning, even before the foundation of the world, and says, "Finally, lest speculations about predestination disturb the doctrine of justification, universal statements are to be noted and considered" (ibid., 557). In his *Enchiridion*, which goes back to 1569, he deals with this subject beautifully, and in a highly regarded sermon preached in 1573 at Wolfenbüttel on the account of the wedding of the king's son in Matthew 22 he sets forth this doctrine with utmost clarity. He says it even more succinctly in his *Enchiridion*, to show that the doctrine of election is an integral part of the doctrine of justification:

> This article [of election] excellently confirms the doctrine of free justification by faith, namely that we are justified and saved without our works and merits, freely through grace, for Christ's sake. For before we were born, in fact, before the foundations of the world were laid, before this world began, when we were still nothing, much less could do anything good, we were predestined and chosen to salvation according to God's purpose, on the basis of grace, in Christ, not on the basis of works . . . (*Enchiridion*, 93).

Sola Gratia!

Again, he says, "This doctrine supplies very sweet comfort. For it teaches that our conversion, justification, and salvation was so much in the mind and heart of God, that before the foundation of the world He took counsel and determined and preordained how He wanted to call, lead, and preserve us unto that salvation" (ibid.).

Chemnitz makes these summary points on the subject in his *LT*:

(1) The Son of God, the Mediator, "gave His life as the ransom for all" (1 Tim. 2:6); (1 John 2:2): "He is the propitiation for the sins of the whole world" [universal grace].

(2) It is the will of God the Father "that no one should perish" (2 Peter 3:9), but that all should be saved through Christ (1 Tim. 2:4). He also adds the reason, because "there is one God and one Mediator between God and men . . . who laid down His life as a ransom for all" (vv. 5–6). Therefore, since He wants all to be saved, He did not lay down His life only for certain classes or certain kinds of individuals. It is incorrect to say that the words "He wants all to be saved" means that He wants some out of each of the orders or classes of people [Universal atonement, anti-Calvin].

(3) The Holy Spirit in His ministry universally announces repentance and remission of sins to all. We should note that Paul joins these two concepts together in Rom. 11:32, "For God has imprisoned all under disobedience that He might have mercy on all."

JUSTIFICATION

Therefore in the same way that He wants to have mercy on all, He also has confined all under sin, that is, just as the sins of all are condemned by the Law, and just as the wrath of God accuses all, so also the promise of grace is universal.

(4) It is the universal command of God that all should hear the voice of the Gospel and embrace the promise in faith. Peter also affirms in 2 Peter 3:9 that it is the will of God that "all should come to repentance," and Paul says in 1 Tim. 2:4: " . . . all should come to the knowledge of the truth." Also in Ezek. 33:11 God confirms by an oath that it is His will that "the wicked shall turn from his ways and live."

(5) All who believe in Christ, without discrimination and exception, receive forgiveness of sins and are saved. It is also useful to observe how Scripture sets forth the concept of universality and explains and develops it (*LT,* II, 57). He then cites a dozen Bible testimonies, concluding, "And we should note that just as there is no distinction in the preaching of repentance, so there is none in the promise of grace. And just as there is the same Lord of all, so He is rich toward all" (ibid.).

Chemnitz has been credited with being the first Lutheran to set forth the doctrine of election or predestination in a systematic manner. Note his dealings with the clergy of Göttingen, where he judged that the dispute was over words not doctrine, and where he settled the matter once and for all.[20] Apparently, although the matter was not under debate among Lutherans, the authors of the FC felt that something should be said on this matter, because the quarrel with Calvinism was on the horizon. While the doctrine of election was dealt with much more thoroughly in FC XI, yet it is noteworthy that the basic substance of the doctrine is set forth in the quotation from the *LT.* This is even more evident in the Epitome of the FC.

It is also noteworthy that these paragraphs cited above are added to the locus on justification in Chemnitz' *LT,* for the entire purpose of the Lutherans, every time they discussed this difficult subject, was to stress the comfort of this doctrine, not to snarl people up in questions about whether they are elect or not, but simply to show that from all eternity God has chosen us to eternal life as a result of the saving work of His Son Jesus Christ. This doctrine is part of the Gospel, part of our justification, part of the work of Christ for the salvation of all mankind. The FC SD XI, 87 states this clearly, "This teaching and explanation of the eternal and saving election of the elect children of God gives God His due honor fully and completely" (Tappert, 631). This is said in opposition to Calvin, who insisted that only the doctrine of reprobation really gave God full honor.

> Moreoever, when people are taught to seek their eternal election in Christ and in His Holy Gospel as the "book of life," this doctrine never occasions either despondency or a riotous and dissolute life. This does not exclude any repentant sinner but invites and calls all poor, burdened, and heavy-laden sinners to repentance, to a knowledge of their sins, and to faith in Christ and promises them the Holy Spirit to cleanse and renew them. . . . Hence if anyone so sets forth this teaching concerning God's gracious election that sorrowing Christians can find no comfort in it but are driven to despair, or when impenitent sinners are strengthened in their malice, then it is clearly evident that this teaching is not being set forth according to the Word and will of God . . . (FC SD *XI,* 89–91; Tappert, 631–32).

Conversely, in his *Enchiridion,* he says,

> Thus indeed many are called, but few chosen, because the minority of the called receive and follow that word; the reason for disobedience is not divine predestination but the will of man, perverse and turned away from God; in obstinate wickedness it is not willing to allow or suffer the working of the Holy Spirit through the Word, but by impudent resistance repulses and rejects it (*Ench.,* 92).

In other words, if we are saved it is God's doing beginning with our election; and if we are lost it is the fault of our own rejection, not God's predestination. Herein lies the mystery of election, the insoluable *cur alii, alii non.*

Chemnitz stops short of trying to solve the mystery by simply asserting that there is no cause of our election in us. It is regrettable that as fine a theologian as Hunnius in the next generation tried to solve the problem by asserting the doctrine of election in view of faith (*intuitu fidei*). This solution did not cause much trouble for Lutheran orthodoxy because the real battle at that time was with Calvinism, which all parties within Lutheranism rejected. It was not until Lutheranism came to America, and in the 19th century, that the famous or infamous predestination controversy arose in our midst and real damage was done. Of course, the false doctrine of synergism, as it weaseled its way back into Lutheran Orthodoxy, did real damage to pious souls. It is true that it did not cause a disturbance, but it did cause offense to the lambs of Christ's flock. This was the case because poorly informed and poorly educated Lutheran theologians and pastors, more for political than for theological reasons, insisted on tacking the label of "Calvinist" onto those who held with Chemnitz and the authors of the FC, who did not try (as Hunnius had) to solve the mystery.

Epilog

THE SIGNIFICANCE AND INFLUENCE OF CHEMNITZ

Chemnitz was an enormously talented man. He was in great demand for his learning and wisdom. Note the number of calls he received, to at least three countries and to many places, including the universities of Wittenberg and Tübingen in Germany, and Copenhagen in Denmark. The citations from his writings which have appeared previously in this work bear witness to his intellectual gifts, his deep spirituality, his orthodox theology, and his pastoral heart. He was a great man.

In the foregoing, we have attempted to show examples of his theological and scholarly skills, but there is also a side to Chemnitz that does not receive the attention it deserves. He was truly a pious and godly man. We have made no reference thus far to his remarkable treatise on the Lord's Prayer. We shall make a brief review of this now, in order to demonstrate the high spirituality and piety of this man.

The history of his work *A Substantial and Godly Exposition of the Prayer Commonly Called the Lord's Prayer* is interesting. It was written at an unknown date in Latin. It was translated into English by an unknown translator and published at Cambridge in 1598. George Williams, who has edited the early English version and rendered it into modern English, is totally convincing in demonstrating that the work is from the pen of Chemnitz, although there is no evidence from the time of Chemnitz that he ever wrote such a book.[1] Mahlmann, who is probably the greatest living authority on Chemnitz, lists the work among Chemnitz' genuine writings.[2] The way in which the author handles both the fathers, the Scripture, and the exegetical material, as well as the theological content, is completely congruent with Chemnitz' major writings. One can see the influence of Luther's two catechisms throughout the work.

Chemnitz begins,

> We know indeed that God is ready of his own accord to give good things, especially to those who repent and humble themselves under the mighty hand of God—those who by faith seek, knock, and ask. Therefore, we pour out our prayers before God, not that we doubt His good will, but that we may indeed show ourselves bringing true repentance. He has promised forgiveness of sins to those who repent (Ezek. 18:23). He will lessen His judgments and bestow His blessings (Jer. 18:8). He will give grace unto the humble (1 Peter 5:5). . . . We do this because the Lord has promised all good things to him who knocks and asks (Matt. 7:7). . . . Also spiritual blessings cannot be received any other way than by faith [note his strong Lutheran emphasis on faith]. Indeed, bodily or outward benefits are often bestowed upon the wicked also. But, that these benefits may be profitable for us, it is the will of God that we should wait for them in hope and receive them by faith from His fatherly hand . . . . In our prayers we do in this way lay open our wants and miseries before God, not as though He knew them not, but that by pouring out our cares into the Lord's bosom, we may unburden and ease our own souls.[3]

He continues,

> In this platform of prayer His purpose is to show the following: (1) how small a number of words we must use in prayer, contrary to the vain babbling of the Pharisees and of the heathen; (2) who is to be called upon or to whom we must direct our prayer; (3) with what confidence we must pray; (4) how and for what causes; (5) what things we are to ask; (6) in what order; (7) by what means; and (8) for what end.[4]

Typical Chemnitz! He continues

> Therefore, we do always pray in faith, hope, and charity with a continued desire. Yet at certain times we do with our words entreat the Lord so that we may admonish ourselves how much we have profited in this desire and likewise excite ourselves to do the same more cheerfully. Therefore, when the apostle says, "Pray continually" (1 Thess. 5:17), it is nothing else than this: continually desire a blessed life . . . . As the Creed contains the rule of faith, so this Lord's Prayer is the rule of all prayers . . . . As for

authority, the Son of God Himself, who is our advocate, who brings our prayers unto the Father, who obtains for us the spirit of prayer, who together with the Father hears us, He prescribed unto us this form of prayer.[5]

In discussing the preface "Our Father which art in heaven," he says,

> We are to use words in prayer not so much to move the mind of God by rhetorical insinuations but, by rehearsing and meditating on the words, to stir up in ourselves attention, devotion, confidence, and care to frame our prayers aright. . . . These words, "Our Father," cause us to understand that prayer ought not to be such a bare desire in a wishing manner . . . . [to understand that] prayer or invocation is not to be directed to any creature but only to the heavenly Father . . . . that we must think of God and speak to God in prayer as He has revealed His essence to us in His Word . . . . that He is the Father, the Son, and the Holy Ghost . . . . the Father of our Lord Jesus Christ who sends the Spirit of His Son into the hearts of the faithful whereby we cry, "Abba, Father." . . . We are not to pray in proud and Pharisaical presumption for our own justice or worthiness, for the works or merits either of ourselves or others, but with a humble acknowledgment and confession of our own unworthiness and with the merit and intercession of the only Son of God, our Mediator, for whom the Father has adopted us to be sons and heirs. . . . We not only say "Father" but "Our Father." . . . It serves also to put courage into the weak that they may not think themselves to be excluded from that fatherhood but know that God is no less their Father than the Father of Mary, John the Baptist, and Paul. . . . Finally, this very title puts us in mind of brotherly love; for if there is One who is our Father (Matt. 23:9), then we are brethren and members one to another . . . . This also teaches us to pray not only for our own wants but also to commend unto God in our prayer the necessities of our whole brotherhood and of every member thereof, saying, "Our Father: give us, forgive us."[6]

Proceeding to the qualifying phrase, "which art in heaven," Chemnitz comments,

> When we add, "which art in heaven," we add to the good will of God the following: (1) divine power, that He is able to do and to give those things we ask . . . ; (2) divine providence, that seeing and knowing our wants, He is present to our requests and hears

the same; that He has a care of us; that He orders, disposes, administers, and governs all things and especially all things in His church; (3) divine wisdom, that He knows the way to send help and deliverance; (4) divine rule and dominion, that it belongs to the kingdom and office of Him who dwells in heaven to hear our prayers, to regard our affairs, to help, to deliver, etc. . . . Now specific petitions follow in this prayer. For it is not a true prayer when we only heap up the glorious titles of God; prayer ought to ask something of God or else give thanks for benefits received.[7]

Chemnitz now turns to the first petition, "hallowed be Thy name."

There is no doubt that here is treated the praise, honor, and renown of God. For "name" is often taken for glory and renown. . . . First, in general this petition commends to us the desire of God's glory, that we should chiefly and before all things care for and seek the glory of God. . . . Second, the name of God signifies the properties of perfection, attributes, or virtues God has revealed and declared in His Word concerning His essence, His will, and His works. . . . Third, by relation we desire that the name of God may be hallowed among us, with us, and of us. . . . Fourth, seeing the name of God concerning His essence, His will, His works, and His judgments is made known to us in the Word, we pray that the name of God, that is, His Word, may be given and preached unto us purely, sincerely, in true and sound understanding and in a holy manner, without corruption or deprivation of the Word of God by wolves or hirelings. [Typical Chemnitz and right out of Luther!] Fifth, remembering the above, we must acknowledge the giving of the Word as the holy and singular blessing of God. We must reverently receive it and with diligence and devotion, hear, think, and mediate on it. . . . and adorn the Word with a godly life.[8]

With respect to the second petition, "Let Thy kingdom come," we encounter perhaps for the first time in our study of Chemnitz' theology the old dogmatic division of the kingdom of power, the kingdom of grace, and the kingdom of glory. The kingdom of power includes the concept of providence. "Also there is the kingdom of grace in the Church in this life and the kingdom of glory in the life to come."[9] When we say "Thy kingdom come," this is called "the kingdom of the Father, the kingdom of Christ, and the kingdom of heaven. . . . We should 'first seek the kingdom of God' (Matt 6.33) that we may sit down in the kingdom of heaven and not be cast out (Matt. 8:11). . . . Our prayer is that the kingdom of God may be within us (Luke 17:21) and that Christ may remember us in His kingdom (Luke 23:42)."[10]

On the third petition, "Thy will be done," Chemnitz distinguishes, as a true systematician, between the disposing will of God, and His good will whereby God gives us the Spirit of regeneration and sanctification which creates a new heart in us and takes away our stony heart, counters the will of the devil, and converts us. Then there is also the operative and permitting will of God whereby things which He wills are accomplished and things that He permits come to pass. There is also the optative will of God whereby He shows what He wishes and desires for us.[11]

In his exposition of the fourth petition, "give us this day our daily bread," we see Chemnitz the exegete and the lexicographer. He uses both the Old Testament and the New Testament and the fathers. He devotes considerable attention to the word *epiousion* (daily), the only adjective in the Greek of the Lord's Prayer and a term which has mystified translators and exegetes down through the ages. He concludes with the great majority of fathers and scholars who have studied the question throughout the history of the church that "daily bread" is the best translation we can come up with. The term "daily bread" refers to all our earthly goods. And, of course, the term "our bread" "teaches us to be careful also for the necessities of others, yes, that those things which are given to me and given to you are so bestowed upon us that we should impart thereof unto others (Eph. 4:28). It is not mine nor yours but 'our bread.' Therefore, it is the poor man's bread which you detain when you do not bestow it on the poor."[12] In the handling of the Greek word *epiousion* Chemnitz shows remarkable research and linguistic skills, far exceeding those of most of his contemporaries and many moderns.

On the fifth petition, "forgive us our debts," Chemnitz begins by insightfully saying,

> The asking of daily bread is not put before the remission of sins in the order of prayer as though money were to be sought after in the first place and godliness learned after wealth is gotten. For our Savior Christ bids us to "seek first the kingdom of God" (Matt. 6:33). Because we are naturally carried to seek worldly goods, it is the will of God that His benefits should take footing in us in

earthly things and that through these we may lift up the mind to the knowledge of God and to the desire of spiritual and heavenly blessings.[13]

He shows his Lutheranism a little later, when he says,

This petition also shows that the mercy and pardon we are commanded to seek by prayer is not to be asked of the angels or of the saints but of God Himself in the use of those means [the Word and the Sacraments] by which God will give remission of sins. Because we are commanded to pray for the forgiveness of our debts in this very thing, we humbly confess before God against Popish satisfaction that we cannot make sufficient payment or satisfaction for our sins. We altogether have need of free pardon for our Mediator's sake. Because our sins "have separated between you and your God" (Is. 59:2), we crave in this petition the favor of God, reconciliation and acceptance. . . . Having thus expounded these things, we may easily observe what we are to ask in this petition. We pray therefore because our debts are innumerable, infinite, and unmeasurable that God will not enter into judgment with them and that He will not impute them unto us.[14]

Further,

We ask Him to become and continue to be unto us a gracious and merciful Father and regard us not according to our sins, neither lay upon us the punishment of His curse, nor cast us into prison till we have made satisfaction (Matt. 5:25, 18:25) but pardon both the fault and the punishment of our sins to set us free from the bond or obligation thereto. Through this we may say with Paul, "Who shall lay anything to the charge of God's elect?" (Rom. 8:33). Seeing that they are not general debts or sins but "our debts," therefore everyone that is to pray must consider in each commandment of the Law what sins he has run into and committed. . . . sins of presumption (Ps. 19:13) or sins of infirmity and weakness. So shall we rightly pray for pardon. . . . We must every day pray that our daily sins [reference to venial or daily sins of Luther] may be blotted out, that they be not written with a pen of iron and that we may not "heap up unto ourselves wrath against the day of wrath" (Rom. 2:5). Because God has appointed and ordained certain means whereby He will bestow and whereby we must receive the forgiveness of sins, therefore we likewise pray that God would give us such a mind that we may not condemn [sic, perhaps contemn, or hold in contempt] or neglect but daily exercise the use of the keys of heaven. We ask that by the hearing of the Word, the use of the Sacraments, and other exercise of faith and prayer "God would not give us up unto a reprobate sense void of all grief, not regarding our sins or the wrath of God."[15]

He concludes with reference to a pious death in which we may die forgiven.

His treatment of the expression "as we forgive our debtors,"[16] is reminiscent of his locus on taking revenge. He begins by showing that

> God of His free pleasure has pardoned you. He does not set in opposition our forgiving to God's [forgiving] as any price or desert so that God should forgive us because we have previously forgiven others. But He says, "Be ye kind one to another, and tenderhearted, forgiving one another, even as God for Christ's sake hath forgiven you" (Eph. 4:32).[17]

He continues,

> They will hereafter beware of all sin, amend their lives, and follow after godliness. It is therefore a most weighty admonition by way of a vow or promise in the sight of our heavenly Father that we do not abuse this fatherly gentleness and readiness to forgive by the liberty of sinning. We promise, as it were, a vow, amendment of life. That general doctrine concerning this good purpose of amendment of life Christ propounds in a special example of forgiving one another in a brotherly sort. This very fitly agrees with the words of this petition as we have said, about turning the other cheek (Matt. 5:39). Because the flesh being corrupt with a root of bitterness (Heb. 12:15) and of itself full of impatience, desirous of revenge, and persisting in anger is most far from reconciliation and forgiveness, we also pray that this root of bitterness may be loosened [destroyed], beaten down, and mortified in us by the Holy Ghost. We ask that a love of unity, reconciliation, and forgiveness may be kindled in us. . . . Because we cannot live in this world without many sins against the Lord, neither can converse among our brethren without many offenses one against another, therefore Christ joined both of these together in this fifth petition. So both peace of conscience towards God by the continual forgiveness of sins and brotherly charity, with which God is chiefly delighted, might be preserved among men by continual reconciliation and forgiving one another.[18]

And he concludes,

> Therefore, in heart we forgive our debtors privately, even when they do not repent, neither ask us for forgiveness. Now this brotherly forgiveness contains very much. We should either not conceive anger or hatred against our neighbor which wronged us unjustly or else we should lay aside and put away anger, hatred, and enmity conceived against our neighbor for wrong done unto us. We should neither take revenge, think upon, nor endeavor to take revenge upon our neighbor.[19]

His treatment of the remaining petitions is similar to that cited above. Temptation is from Satan, the world, and our own flesh. Satan is the primary evil, the evil one from whom we pray to be delivered. And, following Luther, deliverance from evil means deliverance also from this evil world into the eternal life to come where there shall be "deliverance from all evil,"[20] "Because every kind of death is not the end of misery, the death of the wicked is the beginning of their torments (Luke 16:22). The death of the godly is their deliverance from all evil and a beginning of everlasting happiness."[21]

His remarks on the conclusion to the prayer reflect his deep faith and firm devotion. Chemnitz brings in his knowledge of the textual problems relating to the doxology of the Lord's Prayer. His linguistic as well as his theological treatment of the word *Amen* is masterful. He concludes his discussion of the entire prayer and of the word *Amen* by saying,

> By this particle faith shows itself not to doubt or to be carried about with the waves of mistrust whether God will hear us and will perform those things which we ask. Instead, it makes sure account that as God has commanded us to ask and has promised that He will hear, so He will faithfully perform and accomplish our requests. Again by this particle faith stirs up itself, upholds, defends, and confirms itself against doubting. For it takes the word "amen" from that promise "Amen, amen, I say unto you, whatsoever ye shall ask the Father in My name, He will give it to you."[22]

In many of his writings, Chemnitz shows his spiritual and devotional side. He is not a mere scientific theologian nor a dry polemicist, despite the abstruseness of some of the topics he discussed. For example, in his *Fundamenta sanae doctrinae de vera et substantili praesentia . . .* he says,

Our faith ought to lay hold on Christ as God and man in that nature by which He has been made our neighbor, kinsman, and brother. For the life which belongs to the deity resides in and has in a sense been placed in the assumed humanity. . . . The proper, simple, and natural meaning of the words of Institution teaches that Christ Himself is present with us in the celebration of the Supper with both His deity and His flesh, and that He comes to us in order to lay hold on us (Phil.3:12) and join us to Himself as intimately as possible. This brings sweetest comfort. . . . And because our weakness in this life cannot bear the glory of His majesty (Matt. 17:2ff.; Acts 9:3ff.) therefore His body and blood are present, distributed, and received under the bread and wine. Nor does He will that we wander around the gates of heaven uncertain in which area of heaven we ought to look for Christ in His human nature or whether we can find Him; but in the Supper He Himself is present in the external celebration and shows by visible signs where He wills to be present with His body and blood. . . . The New Testament is that covenant of grace which is described in Jer. 31:33–34: "I will be merciful toward their iniquities, and their sins will I remember no more. . . . I will be for them a God, and they shall be for Me a people." This covenant toward God the Father is established and confirmed by the shedding of Christ's blood on the cross. But it is necessary for the salvation of individuals that they be brought into this covenant and remain in it. . . . We are received into this covenant by the Spirit through Baptism and preserved in it through the Word. But fearful minds are concerned. . . . Therefore the Son of God willed that in His Supper our faith should be strengthened by a definite pledge and guarantee, so that we might be assured. . . . For He says: "Drink, this is My blood which is the blood of the new covenant."[23]

It is interesting to see how he connects the two sacraments under the one covenant. In his *TNC* he adds more in speaking of the significance of Christ's incarnation, "Furthermore, there is the sweetest comfort in the fact that in all the miseries of this life the body of our humility will not always remain like this, but at a later time will be conformed to the likeness of the glorified body of Christ" (Phil. 3:21). [24]

We shall not quote further, but for a lovely treatise on the blessings of Baptism see his *Enchiridion*.[25] He was more than a theologian. He was a pastor.

EPILOG

With reference to his work on the FC and his death, Pressel says,

> Great was the sorrow over [the death of] Chemnitz in all of Germany, especially in Lower Saxony, and most of all in Braunschweig to which city he had devoted his labors and his prayers with a tireless loyalty beyond any of his generation. He was not a reformatory spirit, he lacked in the originality, the poetic gift, and the lively, creative, and fruitful intuition of Luther; but he is the first and most significant theologian to come out of the German Reformation. . . . Rare depth in research ability, an unmatched clarity of expression, maturity of judgment, gentleness and moderation in contending against those who thought differently from himself . . . The Catholics showed the highest respect for him. While his general method of procedure toward his students was reminiscent of Melanchthon, yet in regard to the content of his teaching he stood in all respects in Luther's doctrine with complete faithfulness and without compromise . . . . a serious and excellent character made a great impression on everyone, so that in his case what had to be done was attributed to his rightness and not to some individual pet idea . . . . He died brokenhearted. It was as if the whole purpose of his life had been disregarded. The unification of the evangelical churches in doctrine and confession had hardly been achieved before new questions arose.[26]

Yet it must be said that the FC not only united Lutheranism: it saved Lutheranism, even in those areas which did not at first adopt the Formula. Despite Pressel's reference to Chemnitz' broken heart, it must be said that as the years went by more and more areas came to look favorably and take confessional action regarding the Formula.[27] Even where it was not accepted at the time, as in Holstein and Prussia, it was largely personal opposition to Andreae, and in the case of Braunschweig it was Duke Julius' pique against Chemnitz himself that prevented its adoption. But ultimately it was adopted in all the territories in Germany that remained Lutheran, including Braunschweig.[28]

Erlandson tells the story of the long and sometimes bitter struggle leading up to the ultimate adoption of the Formula including the entire Book of Concord in Sweden in 1686. We have already mentioned the letter by Chemnitz to the archbishop of Sweden in the interest of introducing the FC to that country. Sad to say, the letter has apparently been lost in a fire in Uppsala.[29]

Skarsten tells the rather dismal story of the fate of the FC in Denmark, Norway, and Iceland, beginning with the burning (an action which Walther denies) of the copy of the Book of Concord sent to King Fredrick II of Denmark (1559–88), whose sister was the wife of the Elector of Saxony, had sent it to him as a gift.[30] Political conditions and the theological climate in Denmark militated against the acceptance or even the use of the book, and to this day the state churches of these three countries have never accepted the FC, making them the only Lutheran churches in Europe which do not accept the entire BC. However, to jump ahead a few years, it is significant that the North American descendents of the Danish-Norwegian-Icelandic immigrants through their membership in the newly created Evangelical Lutheran Church in America (1988), and in the older Evangelical Lutheran Synod of Norwegian ancestry, have all accepted the entire Book of Concord. Skarsten adds the postscript that Finland, which for centuries has been a satellite of Sweden, formally and on its own only in the year 1869 finally "declared the entire Book of Concord to be the symbol of the Church of Finland."[31] It is also the confessional basis for both of the Lutheran churches of Canada. We have not attempted to determine how widespread the acceptance of the FC is in so-called Third World countries, but the entire BC has been translated into Portuguese and is the Confessional basis of the Evangelical Lutheran Church of Brazil. It has also been translated into Korean and the entire BC is the confessional basis for the Lutheran Church of Korea. It has been translated into Spanish. Thus the movement Chemnitz and his coworkers started so long ago still moves forward. He might be much happier today than he was 400 years ago.

CHEMNITZ' PERSONAL IMPORTANCE

Chemnitz' *LT* was used for a century after his death, and to this day his *ECT* is still in use in current dialogs between Lutherans and Roman Catholics. At least one edition of it has been published in every century since it first saw the light of day. He was always ultimately on the right side in theological controversies and thus became normative for all subsequent Lutheran theologians. And he accomplished this feat without much political backing from his duke, without any cronyism among the authors of the FC, without holding a professor's chair, without carrying on the political antics of Andreae or the vicious polemics of Flacius. He just plugged along, said little, kept his counsel, and always spoke the same message to all sides. In his own generation Leyser almost hero-worshiped him, as is proved by his editing of so many of Chemnitz' writings. Note, for example, his description in his dedicatory epistle to Chemnitz' *Iudicium*, where he describes Chemnitz as

> the most outstanding theologian of our age, who ought to be imitated as an example . . . who does not load down his opponents with the errors of their companions, or try to induce others to hate them or try to destroy them by stealth, but leaves their persons out and examines their opinions on the basis of the Word of God, without acrimony but with what is consonant with the divine oracles.[32]

Gerhard borrowed heavily from him, often without giving credit. Hutter praised him highly.

Many modern theologians have spoken in complimentary terms about him, such as Pelikan, who, as previously indicated, praises him for rescuing Lutheranism from Melanchthonianism and Osiandrianism, and for dealing with Rome in such a way as to win the respect of the papalists rather than simply their wrath. On the other hand, Pelikan correctly says that Chemnitz "accused Roman Catholicism of forsaking the tradition in the very act of defending the tradition; for tradition was on the side of biblical authority."[33] Pelikan thinks so highly of Chemnitz' handling of tradition in his *ECT* that he quotes it in full in two of his writings, *Obedient Rebels*[34] and *The Development of Christian Doctrine: Some Historical Prolegomena.*[35]

Another modern theologian who has spoken highly of Chemnitz is Wilhelm Pauck, who says of the *ECT*,

> With great thoroughness and an impressive display of learning in historical theology and without any of the passionate hatred and intemperance that had characterized the polemics of the Reformation age [Chemnitz] endeavored to prove that the Roman Catholic doctrine was against Scripture and the teachings of the ancient Fathers. It was his major purpose to demonstrate that not

> Protestantism but Roman Catholicism could justly be accused of having fallen away from the teachings and practices of the ancient church . . . . Translated into German and French and frequently republished, even in the 19th century, it remained the most useful Protestant criticism of the Council of Trent.[36]

In another place Pelikan makes a statement which perhaps as well as any that could be found summarizes the entire confessional career of Chemnitz. He says,

> Melanchthon's pupil Martin Chemnitz, who helped to make Melanchthon's theology acceptable to later generations by bringing it into line with Luther's, followed him [Melanchthon] in teaching "that Christ rendered satisfaction for all sins, for their guilt and for their punishment, so that nothing remains for our sufferings or satisfactions to do in expiating sins."[37]

We have attempted to show throughout this document that Chemnitz constantly tried to Lutherize Melanchthon in every way he could, and Pelikan's statement supports this position. We have also indicated that Melanchthon in some ways and some very good ways advanced beyond Luther, as in the case of Law and Gospel and the doctrine of forensic justification; and Chemnitz, particularly in the case of Osiandrianism, followed right in the train of the Luther whom Melanchthon had influenced. Pelikan is here demonstrating these points and does so to the advantage of Chemnitz. It was for such reasons that Chemnitz in his attempt to use the best of both Melanchthon and Luther and wedding the two wherever possible, rendered such service in keeping the two main strands of Lutheranism together. But on the points where the two leaders were irreconcilable, Chemnitz came down decisively on the side of Luther, namely, free will and the Lord's Supper.

On the negative side, one of the most virulent opponents of the Lutheran doctrine of the Supper was Rudolph Hospinian (1547–1626), Reformed author of the notorious Concordia Discors (1607) about which we have already commented. Hospinian levels his guns at Andreae, as did many of the Lutherans, but Chemnitz comes off quite well at his very polemic hands. Thus Chemnitz can be called the undisputed father of normative Lutheran theology, the father of Lutheran orthodoxy, and the father of Lutheran unity. We have already indicated the negative attitude of Dorner on both

Chemnitz' Christology and that of the FC, but today few remember Dorner or take him seriously.

As to his person and character, no one says it better than his good friend and admirer, John Gasmer, in his *Oratio* which he delivered in connection with Chemnitz' death. He says,

> He was kindly and calm in character, by nature pleasant and affable, with an earnest and composed face. He was completely alien to haughtiness and ambition, always the author and promotor of beneficial harmony among his colleagues. In settling controversies and in dealing with things which had been whitewashed, and errors which needed to be searched out and refuted, his acumen was as great as his wisdom, so that Mörlin often testified that if he [Chemnitz] had lived in the time of Luther, it would have been a miraculous situation. But because of his constant journeys, vigils, and studies, the powers of his body were gradually weakened. For from the time in which he had returned home from the meeting with the counsellors of the three electors of Palatine, Saxony, and Brandenburg in the year '79 to the journey to Hesse where he also celebrated the wedding of his daughter, he began to fail more and more, like a lamp which was running out of oil. Still, after the wedding was over, he went to Juterbog to a meeting with the theologians and counsellors of the three political electors, and several times after he had returned home, he said that this was going to be the last of his trips and that he was going to turn his thoughts to the last and final journey into his heavenly fatherland with Christ as his leader. But at the end of the year '82 things turned out beyond his hope and expectation, and it turned out that he was invited by the most illustrious electors and by our most clement lord, Duke Julius of Braunschweig-Lüneburg, to attend the colloquium at Quedlinburg[38] because of certain reservations expressed by the theologians of the University of Helmstedt concerning ubiquity.[39] And Chemnitz was summoned in the name of the most illustrious Elector of Brandenburg, even though, because of the weakness of his body and powers, he was not doing well; yet the old man, tired and exhausted, was entirely willing to attend, lest he appear to be trying to stay out of sight. Now it was his habit, when he returned home from such meetings and colloquiums which he had attended, not to keep quiet about things but to inform our ministers about the things which had taken place. But because nothing had been decided and no agreement reached among all the theologians on certain matters, the

orders were given to the individuals that since all the actions had been taken in secret, they were reserving the final report for the further consideration of the electors and princes. Chemnitz reported this to his ministerium and because of the seriousness of the matter, Chemnitz refused to share the outcome with his ministerium, with the result that he offended certain important men when they sought the results from him and when he was unwilling to discuss things with them. Further, he was irritated when the proceedings were made known by his adversaries, so that they might use this information to establish their teachings publicly (although in abbreviated form) against our churches.[40]

Gasmer also adds this point,

I am bringing up these points so that no one get the idea that Chemnitz' silence be interpreted in a wrong sense, when he refused to respond to the criticisms he received from the Pseudo-Wittenbergers [Crypto-Calvinists] in a book which they entitled *Ancoratus* in which they reviled him. His moderation is commendable whereby he was unwilling to fight with sharp language in his disputes against his adversaries, but calmly took up the consideration of the real issues and refused to pursue others with harsh language, and he took pains never to reply with sharp tongue. This is an example which all ought to follow who in their disputings attack the academic standing of their adversaries, or their life, their morals, and their lapses and reply out of their emotions in a hateful manner by piling up insults, so that they fill their minds with a love for criticizing, and add nothing to the substance of the matter but rather poison the minds of men who more fittingly should be concerned about the truth and the studies which go with it.[41]

Also in the same vein is Chemnitz' letter written early in 1570 to Mörlin, in which he speaks about the illusory hopes held out for the coming (May) conference at Zerbst sponsored by Andreae to which Chemnitz was invited and which was of no help in settling the Lutheran conflicts. Chemnitz says,

God give us an understanding heart and fortitude, Amen, that we may do the right thing. On May 7 there will be the meeting at Zerbst, and the princes will send their theologians. And without doubt there will be preparations at the [Imperial] Reichstag against the Flacians who are being proscribed throughout the entire empire. If they throw me out and Prussia does not wish to receive me, God will take me in. And may He bring it about that I am not led astray by false hope or broken down with fear and that I do nothing which does not befit a good pastor.[42]

But despite his mild disposition and his aversion to polemics, in his old age he still received some harsh treatment. John Gude, pastor of St. Martin's church, the congregation which Chemnitz himself had served for so long, picked on the old man and harassed him—probably at the instigation of Duke Julius and the Helmstadt faculty—so that it contributed to his decline. But it is noteworthy that in 1594 after Leyser as superintendent had instigated the *Rettung der Ehren des Glaubens and Bekantnis des weiland Ehrwirdigen unnd Hochgelarten Herrn Martini Chemnitii . . .* against Adam Crato who had slandered Chemnitz, John Gude signed with the other Braunschweig pastors.

Crato had published a diatribe against Chemnitz because of his doctrine of the Lord's Supper in which he had attacked Chemnitz for being mercenary, which may or may not have been the case, since Chemnitz, who as a young man had had to scratch for money for his education, had become quite wealthy over the years. But this charge had not been brought against him during his lifetime. Crato also charged him with cowardice in declining to answer a certain book against Lutheranism written by Lambert Danaeus. The third charge was the worst, the one which elicited the response from the Braunschweig pastors led by Leyser. Crato accused Chemnitz of having lost his faith, so that like Saul and Judas, he was not in heavenly rest. On Oct. 1, 1591, five years after his death, and after the departure of Heidenreich, but only a few weeks after Crato's document had come to their attention, that part of the pastoral Colloquium who had known Chemnitz and worked with him replied defending his honor and his personal Christianity. Crato also accused Chemnitz of being disheartened at the failure of his Apology to the Formula of Concord to gain general acceptance and of having acknowledged at the end the strength of the arguments of his adversaries.

Naturally Chemnitz was disappointed at the fate of the Apology, but he certainly did not in any way take up the position of his adversaries, nor did it cause him to lose his Christian faith. It was common in those days to charge one's opponents with losing the faith on their deathbed. The same charge had been brought against Luther, but in both cases there was no substance to the accusation. The pastors describe Chemnitz' long final illness, the many conversations held with him by friends and colleagues, and the constant assertions by him of his faith and conviction. They spoke of his courage in facing theological opponents in the 30 years he had been among them, and they cited his own will in which he had listed the works which he had left to the city as kind of a heritage.[43] Mager in another article points out that Chemnitz in his will likens his role to that of a prophet (cf. Ezek. 3:17 and 33:6ff.), who sounds the alarm about the approaching enemy, as he also does in his letter to Duke Julius.[44]

In his will, Chemnitz says,

> In the first place and above all I am mindful of the grace of God which has been bestowed on me to live and die in the prophetic and apostolic Scriptures of the Old and New Testaments, as in my committed and high office I have followed truly and without any falsification both in preaching and teaching in this honorable church and in the public confession of which in my dealings with other churches I have set forth and adhered to and confessed in the face of all corruptions (some under my own name and some under the name of other churches), as I have published in my *Enchiridion* or Handbook (*Handbuch*), in the *Repetitio doctrinae de coena*, in *The Two Natures in Christ*, in the Prussian *Corpus Doctrinae*, in the doctrinal content (*doctrinalia*) of the *Ducal Corpus Doctrinae* for Braunschweig [his *Kurzer Bericht* (1569) and the *Wohlgegründeter Bericht* (1576)], in the Appendix to the little book of Urbanus Rhegius which also goes under the name of the Ducal Ministerium of Lüneburg, and finally the Formula of Concord published under the name of many pure churches.[45]

The Braunschweig pastors also praise him for his work as administrator of their church and his leadership in instituting church discipline and the use of the keys. They also expressed appreciation for his support for the work and authority of his pastors. He was "an ornament to this church."

The Braunschweig pastors in their *Rettung* also show their admiration for his work for peace and unity among the German churches. Again quoting Chemnitz' will, the pastors refer to his desire that they remain firm in the faith in all points and that "between both parties there might be continuing unity, so that there may be peace in the chorus and peace in the marketplace (*ut sit pax in choro et pax in foro*), that is, peace in church and peace in society in general.[46]

The pastors also added their own brand of insult, accusing Crato of being like the pigs who root around in a church yard and eat the corpses and like the dogs who gnaw on the bones of the dead people. Obviously this attack on Crato did nothing to diminish Chemnitz' reputation.

We have made mention of Chemnitz' good health during most of his life and his poor health during the last four years. In 1584 he tendered his resignation, but the City Council would not accept it. But they did give much of the workload to Jacob Gottfried, who was the coadjutor and Chemnitz' son-in-law. However, when six months went by and there was no improvement in his health, the Council finally accepted his resignation on Sept. 9, 1584. At this time he made his final speech to the ministerium. The only tasks he retained were his lectures on the LC and his work on *Harmony of the Gospels*, neither of which he ever completed.

His wife survived him by 18 years and passed away on Nov. 29, 1603. Most of his children survived him. His daughters married well and apparently happily. His two sons shared their father's interest in theology and were a credit to him in every way. His posterity for several generations were people of prominence and achievement.[47]

Chemnitz passed away on April 8, 1586 at midnight. He was buried in the chancel of the Martin Church on Sunday, April 10. A large crowd was present, the Council, the ministerium, the students, crowds of prominent citizens, many women. The coadjutor Johann Zanger preached the sermon on the text from Galatians 2, which was also placed on his epitaph in the church, "I through the law am dead to the law, that I might live unto God. I am crucified with Christ, I no longer live, but Christ lives in me . . . and gave Himself for me." Thus passed from the scene one of the great churchmen of all time.

Soli Deo Gloria.

Chronology of the Age of Chemnitz

The chronology below lists only Chemnitz' primary writings.

1415ff
The Council of Constance, which healed the rift in the papacy but curtailed its power. It ushered in the era of Renaissance popes who in turn brought about the downfall of the papacy by their great corruption, thus paving the way for the Reformation. John Hus was burned at this Council.

1453
The fall of Constantinople, marking the beginning of the Renaissance and the rise of humanism in Western Europe.

1456
The publication of the Gutenberg Bible.

1483
The birth of Luther, Nov. 10, Eisleben.

1497
The birth of Melanchthon, Feb. 16, Bretten.

1498
Savanarola burned at the stake at Council of Florence.

1500
The birth of Emperor Charles V.

1503
Tetzel begins sale of indulgences in Germany; renewed the practice in Mainz in 1517.

1517

Luther posts the 95 Theses.

1519

The Leipzig Debate, Eck vs. Carlstadt and Luther. Accession of Charles V as Emperor of the Holy Roman Empire.

1521

The Diet at Worms. Excommunication of Luther.

1522

The birth of Chemnitz, Nov. 9, at Treuenbrietzen in Brandenburg to Paul and Euphemia Chemnitz.

1525–27

The Peasants' War.

1527

John Agricola begins the antinomian controversy, the first controversy within Lutheranism. Not publicly opposed by Luther and Melanchthon until 1537.

1528

Birth of Jacob Andreae at Tübingen. Church in City of Braunschweig reformed by Bugenhagen.

1529

Second Diet at Speyer. Decision of First Diet (1526) rescinded. Evangelicals lodged a protest. This led to Diet at Augsburg in 1530.

1530

The Diet at Augsburg. Presentation of Augsburg Confession.

1531

Melanchthon produced the Apology to the Augsburg Confession.

1536–53

Chemnitz began his formal education, at 14, at Wittenberg, dropping out after 18 months. He continued at the gymnasium in Magdeburg, 1539–42, then in 1542 he became tutor at Calbe; from 1543–45 he studied at Frankfurt on the Oder; returned to Wittenberg, 1545—47. In 1547 he went to Königsberg, where he remained as student and librarian until 1553. He received his M.A. degree in 1548. In 1553 he returned to Wittenberg to continue his studies.

1537

The Smalcald Articles prepared by Luther.

1542

Duchy of Braunschweig captured by Smalcald League and reformed. This lasted until 1547, when the duchy was temporarily regained for Catholicism.

1545–63

The Council of Trent.

1546

The death of Luther at Eisleben, Feb. 18.

1546–48

The Smalcald War, which ended with the Augsburg Interim imposed by the Emperor. Followed by the Leipzig Interim, signed by Melanchthon, Bugenhagen, and Agricola, among others.

1547

The Hardenberg controversy over the Lord's Supper broke out in Bremen. He was supported secretly by Melanchthon, but opposed by Chemnitz from the beginning; cf. Chemnitz' *Anatome* of 1561.

1548

The adiaphoristic controversy began as a result of the Interims and Melanchthon's support of them. The University of Jena was established in opposition to the Crypto-Calvinists at Wittenberg.

1549

The Osiandrian controversy began at Königsberg over the doctrine of justification.

1550

Chemnitz became official librarian at the ducal library in Königsberg. He was called to a public debate with Osiander regarding justification. Chemnitz was considered the winner.

1551

The Majoristic controversy began, dealing with the necessity of good works.

1552

The Peace of Passau, arranged after Charles V's defeat by Maurice of Saxony. This paved the way for the Religious Peace of Augsburg of 1555.

1553

Chemnitz leaves Königsberg after the Osiandrian uproar, and joins the faculty at Wittenberg, and after a few months begins his lectures on the *Loci Communes*. In this year he also wrote his first work, his *Oratio de lectione patrum* (Lecture on the reading of the fathers), first published in 1591.

On July 9, 1553, the Battle of Sievershausen was fought, in which the two older sons of Duke Henry the Younger (Hanswurst, the father of Duke Julius) were killed.

1554

Chemnitz accepts the position as co-adjutor at Braunschweig under Joachim Mörlin. He was ordained at Wittenberg by Bugenhagen.

1555

The Religious Peace of Augsburg, which established the permanent lines of Lutheranism, until the end of the Thirty Years War in 1648. The Synergistic controversy began, involving Melanchthon vs. Amsdorf and Flacius, among others.

Chemnitz marries Anna Yaeger; begins his lectures on the *Loci Communes* at Braunschweig.

1556

Charles V resigned as emperor. Succeeded by his brother Ferdinand.

1557

The Colloquy at Worms. The last serious effort between Catholics and Lutherans to come back together. It failed. It did bring together Chemnitz, Andreae, Melanchthon, Brenz, Marbach, and Mörlin, along with many other Philippists and Gnesio-Lutherans.

1558

The death of Bugenhagen. Chemnitz called as superintendent at Hildesheim, Lüneburg, and Göttingen.

1560

The Flacian controversy begins, dealing with original sin. At first it involved Flacius vs. Strigel. Later it involved Chemnitz, Mörlin, Melanchthon, and almost all of Lutheranism in opposition to Flacius.

Melanchthon died, April 19.

Chemnitz receives invitations to serve as theologian at Lüneburg and Brandenburg.

1561

Chemnitz publishes his first major work on the Lord's Supper, his *Repetitio sanae doctrinae de vera praesentia corporis et sanguinis Domini in Coena* (A repetition of the correct doctrine concerning the true presence of the body and blood of the Lord in the Supper) which grew out of previous less-significant writings on this subject regarding the Hardenberg case.

In the same year he also wrote his *Anatome propositionum Alberti Hardenbergii de Coena Domini* (An analysis of the propositions of Albert Hardenberg regarding the Lord's Supper) as well as his important *De Controversiis quibusdam quae superiori tempore circa quosdam Augstanae Confessionis articulos motae et agitatae sunt Iudicium d. Martini Chemnitii* (An evaluation by Dr. Martin Chemnitz of certain controversies which in earlier times were stirred up and caused disturbances concerning certain articles of the Augsburg Confession).

1562

Chemnitz published his *Theologiae Iesuitarum praecipua* (The main points of the theology of the Jesuits). This was the foreruner to his major work, the *Examen Concilii Tridentini* (English title: *Examination of the Council of Trent*).

1563

The Council of Trent ended.

1564

The death of Calvin at Geneva, May 27. Chemnitz receives call to Copenhagen as professor at the University; and to Halle as superintendent.

1565

Chemnitz receives calls to Göttingen, Wittenberg, Hameln, Küstrin, and Frankfurt. He was called three times to Küstrin.

1566–73

Chemnitz published his *Examen Concilii Tridentini* (English title: *Examination of the Council of Trent*) in four volumes.

1566

He receives the call to Königsberg as superintendent.

1567

Chemnitz receives call to Stettin. Chemnitz and Mörlin make their first public attack on Flacius. They also are invited to Prussia to straighten out the mess left by the Osiandrian controversy and to prepare a new church order for Prussia. Both receive calls to Prussia, Mörlin as Bishop of Samland and Chemnitz as superintendent of Königsberg.

Chemnitz succeeds Mörlin as superintendent of Braunschweig.

The death of Philip of Hesse.

1568

Duke Henry the Younger of Braunschweig-Wolfenbüttel dies and is replaced by his Lutheran son Julius who, on June 11, asks Chemnitz and Andreae to undertake the reformation of the duchy.

Chemnitz receives his earned doctorate at Rostock with a disputation dealing with the "Benefits of the Son of God, our Lord and Savior Jesus Christ." Colloquies at Zerbst, 1568, and Altenburg, 1569, to try to unite the divided Lutherans, Jena vs. Wittenberg. Both failed.

1569

Chemnitz published his *Enchiridion* (English title: *Ministry, Word, and Sacraments*), a book to be used in examining candidates for the ministry.

He also received his first call to Vienna as superintendent.

1570

Chemnitz published his *Fundamenta Sanae Doctrinae de Vera et substantiali praesentia, exhibitione et sumptione corporis et sanginis Domini in Coena* (English title: *The Lord's Supper*), an updating of his work of 1561, against Calvinists and Crypto-Calvinists. He also produced his famous *De Duabus Naturis in Christo* (English title: *The Two Natures in Christ*), also directed against the Crypto-Calvinists. He began his work on the *Harmonia Evangelica* (Harmony of the gospels), later completed by Leyser and John Gerhard.

He also journeyed to Göttingen regarding a controversy on free will. He was approached by Mörlin at Samland to become his coadjutor.

1571

Joachim Mörlin dies at Königsberg after a long illness.

Chemnitz published an attack on the so-called Wittenberg Catechism for its Crypto-Calvinism. He was again invited to Vienna. During this period he was also called to Wittenberg, Swabia, Bavaria, Pfalz, Württemberg, Meissen, and Silesia.

1572

Chemnitz invited by Duke Wilhelm to attend a conference at Gifhorn.

1573

Chemnitz preached his famous sermon on Matthew 22, the parable of the royal wedding, which became a classic for its handling of the doctrine of predestination.

He also wrote his epistle to Timothy Kirchner regarding the Lord's Supper vs. Beza.

He attended a meeting at Salzwedel in Brandenburg at the invitation of his good friend Supt. Andreas Puchenius, regarding the request of the Austrian estates to consult with them concerning an agenda for the Lutheran churches of their territory.

Andreae prepared his famous "Six Christian Sermons," which helped pave the way for the Formula of Concord.

1574

Andreae on the basis of these sermons produced the Swabian Concord, another step toward the Formula of Concord. Chemnitz travelled to Lübeck at the invitation of their senate to discuss the Lord's Supper with them.

1575

Chemnitz twice went to Gifhorn at the invitation of Duke Wilhelm.

Chemnitz and Chytraeus revised the Swabian Concord. The result was the Swabian-Saxon Concord, which later led to the Epitome of the Formula of Concord.

1576

Jan. 19, the Maulbronn Formula was prepared by Lucas Osiander and Balthasar Bidembach on the basis of the Saxon-Swabian Concord.

Meeting at Torgau, May 29–June 7, produced the Torgau Book on the basis of the Swabian-Saxon Concord and the Maulbronn Formula. Meeting attended by Chemnitz, Andreae, Chytraeus, Selnecker, Musculus, and Corner. Produced real agreement.

During the course of this year Chemnitz also attended a meeting at Hannover regarding the Lord's Supper.

Oct. 15, the Julian University of Helmstedt was dedicated. Chemnitz preached the dedicatory sermon.

1577

To shorten the Torgau Book the above-named theologians met twice at Bergen Abbey, near Magdeburg, and after hearing all critics, on May 28 they completed the work and called it the Bergic Book, which we call the Solid Declaration. This is the actual date of the completion of the Formula. The six authors signed it on May 29, 1577.

1578

Aug. 18, the Colloquy at Herzberg, involving all the writers of the Formula, except Chytraeus.

In December Chemnitz had his tragic falling out with Duke Julius.

1579

The Bergic Book and its Epitome were accepted as the Formula of Concord, and the work of securing subscriptions was completed.

At the request of the senate of Halle, Chemnitz helped settle a dispute between theologians of that city. He was called as professor primarius at Heidelberg University.

1580

June 25, the Book of Concord, including the Formula of Concord, was offically presented to the public on the 50th anniversary of the Augsburg Confession.

Chemnitz, at the request of several princes, took part in a visitation at the University of Jena to "promote sound doctrine, good discipline and eduation" (Lentz, p. 255).

1583

The publication of the Apology to the Formula of Concord by Chemnitz, Selnecker, and Kirchner. It included an important history of the Augsburg Confession.

Chemnitz attended the Colloquy at Quedlinberg, the last conference he attended.

1584

Chemnitz retired because of illness and old age. He continued to lecture on the *Loci Communes* for a few months in the sacristy of St. Martin's Church, but on Sept. 9 he called together his co-workers and delivered his final speech to them.

1585

Despite his poor health, he was called upon by several Lutheran princes of the evangelical estates of the empire to assist them in replying to a request from King Henry of Navarre, also called Henry IV of France, who had written them requesting an alliance of all Protestants against the pope and the emperor. They took his advice, namely, that the Swiss and the French subscribe to the Book of Concord.

1586

April 18, Chemnitz died. His wife Anna survived him by 17 years.

1591

Leyser edits and publishes Chemnitz' *Loci Theologici* (1592).

1593

Leyser edits and publishes Chemnitz' *Harmonia Evangelica*.

Notes

Preface

1. Charles P. Krauth, *The Conservative Reformation and its Theology* (Philadelphia: The United Lutheran Publication House, 1913), 306.

2. Ibid., 310

3. Inge Mager, "Das Corpus Doctrinae der Stadt Braunschweig im Gefüge der übrigin niedersächsischen Lehrschriften-sammlungen," in *Die Reformation in der Stadt Braunschweig, Festschrift 1528–1978,* ed. Hans-Walter Krumwiede (Braunschweig: Gesammtherstellung Druck und Verlagshaus Braunschweig, 1978).

4. St. Louis: Concordia, 1970, vol. 1, 47–49.

5. Clyde L. Manschreck, *Melanchthon: The Quiet Reformer* (New York: Abingdon, 1958). An exception is the book by the Lutheran, Michael Rogness, *Philip Melanchthon: Reformer without Honor* (Minneapolis: Augsburg, 1969).

Acknowledgments

1. P. G. Barton, *Um Luthers Erbe, Studien und Texte zur Spatreformation, Tileman Heshusius* (1527–1559), (Wittenberg, 1972).

Chapter 1

1. Barbara W. Tuchman, *The March of Folly* (New York: Knopf, 1984). Tuchman entitles her colorful chapters thus: (1) "Murder in the Cathedral": Sixtus IV, 1471–84; (2) "Host to the Infidel": Innocent VIII, 1484–92; (3) "Depravity": Alexander VI, 1492–1503; (4). "The Warrior": Julius II, 1503–13; (5) "The Protestant Break": Leo X, 1513–21; (6) "The Sack of Rome": Clement VII, 1523–34.

2. Cf. Scott H. Hendrix, *Luther and the Papacy* (Philadelphia: Fortress, 1981), 159.

3. James M. Estes, *Christian Magistrate and State Church: The Reforming Career of Johannes Brenz* (Toronto: University of Toronto Press, 1982), 19.

4. *Luther's Works,* American Edition 44:115–217.

5. Philip J. Rehtmeyer, *Antiqvitates Ecclesiasticae Inclytae Urbis Brunsvigae, oder, Der berühmten Stadt Braunschweig Kirchen-Historie,* part 3 (Braunschweig: Christoph Friedrich Zilligers, 1710), 535.

6. Andrew L. Drummond, *German Protestantism Since Luther* (London: The Epworth Press, 1951), 181–83.

7. Cf. C. F. W. Walther's essay on "Church and State" in *Essays for the Church,* vol. 1, trans. R. E. Smith (St. Louis: Concordia, 1992), 64–68, where he compares and contrasts the advantages and disadvantages of the church in Germany and America and concludes that it is better off in the new country.

8. Estes, 29–32. The episcopacy continues at present to be a major item of discussion within the ELCA. Cf. "A Study of Ministry: Report of the 1991 Churchwide Assembly," study edition, pp. 20ff. This concern stems, seemingly, from the dialogs of the past 20 years with the Episcopal church in the United States.

9. Jaroslav Pelikan, *From Luther to Kierkegaard* (St. Louis: Concordia, 1950), 36.

10. Ibid., 37–38.

11. Chemnitz, *Loci Theologici,* vol. 2, trans. J. A. O. Preus (St. Louis: Concordia, 1989), 381–85.

12. Ibid., 696, 698, 702, 704.

13. FC, SD XII. 27.

14. Cf., e.g., the introduction to the Kirchner letter re Beza, and Theodor Mahlmann, "Bibliographie Martin Chemnitz," in *Der zweite Martin der Lutherischen Kirche,* ed. Wolfgang A. Jünke (Braunschweig: Ev.-luth. Stadtkirchenverband und Propstei Braunschweig, 1986), 411, as well as Leyser's introductions to the *Loci Theologici,* vol. 1, 17–24.

15. Cf. Hermann Hachfeld, *Martin Chemnitz nach Seinem Leben und Wirken, insbesondere Nach Seinem Verhältnisse zum Tridentinum* (Leipzig: Breitkopf and Härtel, 1867) on the Supper.

16. For a popular treatment, see James M. Kittelson, *Luther the Reformer: The Study of the Man and His Career* (Minneapolis: Augsburg, 1986). For a more thorough and detailed account, see the three volume set by Martin Brecht in German, all three volumes in English. *Martin Luther: The Road to Reformation, 1483–1521, Martin Luther: Shaping and Defining the Reformation, 1521–1532,* and *Martin Luther: The Preservation of the Church, 1532–1546,* trans. James L. Schaff (Minneapolis: Augsburg-Fortress, 1985–1993).

17. Edmund Schlink, *Theology of the Lutheran Confessions,* trans. Paul F. Koehneke and Herbert J. A. Bouman (Philadelphia: Muhlenberg, 1961), 71–72.

18. WA 17 II, 179–80; translation in Ewald M. Plass, *What Luther Says: An Anthology,* vol. 2 (St. Louis: Concordia, 1959), 573.

19. Mark Edwards, *Luther's Last Battles* (Ithaca, NY: Cornell University Press, 1983), 208.

Chapter 2

1. J. E. Sandys, *A Short History of Classical Scholarship* (Cambridge, 1915), 233–34.

2. Jaroslav Pelikan, *From Luther to Kierkegaard: A Study in the History of Theology* (St. Louis: Concordia, 1950), 29–48. Compare Richard R. Caemmerer's "The Melanchthonian Blight," *CTM* 18 (May 1947): 321–38, which basically echoes Pelikan. To Caemmerer the blight consisted of Melanchthon's humanism, his emphasis on the intellect, his stress on the natural law, his system of ethics

NOTES

based on the law and not on love, which produced the concept of obedience to the minister as one of the marks of the church, the latter point a notion that is entirely absent in Chemnitz. The other points mentioned here are dealt with by Chemnitz in a more restrained manner.

3. Will Durant, *The Reformation, A History of European Civilization from Wycliff to Calvin: 1300–1564* (New York, 1957), 441.

4. Theodore Schmauck tells us that upon the delivery of the Augsburg Confession to the emperor, Melanchthon wrote to Luther that "he was plunged into the deepest woe, and his eyes were *fountains of tears*." Theodore Emanuel Schmauck and C. Theodore Benze, *The Confessional Principle and the Confessions of the Lutheran Church as Embodying the Evangelical Confession of the Christian Church* (Philadelphia: General Council Publication Board, 1911), 436.

5. Theodor Kolde, "Die Älteste Redaktion der Augsburger Confession," in Schmauck, 221–82.

6. Schmauck, 197–98, footnote 16.

7. George J. Fritschel, *The Formula of Concord, Its Origin and Contents: A Contribution to Symbolics* (Philadelphia: The Lutheran Publication Society, 1916), 40, footnote 1.

8. See Robert Kolb, *Confessing the Faith: Reformers Define the Church, 1530–1580* (St. Louis: Concordia, 1990), 36–38.

9. Schmauck, 627.

10. Michael Rogness, *Philip Melanchthon: Reformer Without Honor* (Minneapolis: Augsburg, 1969), 123.

11. Friedrich J. Stahl, *Die Lutherische Kirche und die Union* (Berlin: Wilhelm Hertz, 1859), 108f., cited from Juergen L. Neve, *A History of Christian Thought,* vol. 1 (Philadelphia: The United Lutheran Publication House, 1943), 260.

12. Pelikan, 44–45.

13. WA 10. ii, (175–80) 180–222, and 227–62.

14. Barnes had studied at Wittenberg and frequently acted as messenger between Henry and Luther at the time of Henry's divorce, which Luther treated as he treated the bigamy of Philip of Hesse, something not proper but permissible. In 1540 poor Barnes, as a sign from Henry of gratitude and esteem, was burned at the stake for his opposition to Henry's basically Roman "Six Articles." Luther eulogized him as a martyr.

15. Manschreck, *Melanchthon on Christian Doctrine* (New York: Oxford Press, 1965), p. xx. An interesting historical footnote is that Archbishop Cranmer, who was Henry's religious adviser for a lengthy period, was secretly married to the niece of Andreas Osiander, during his strong Lutheran days (Schaff, *Creeds,* 1.300). Queen Elizabeth I in the time of Chemnitz even made efforts to thwart the adoption of the Formula of Concord in Germany.

16. *Corpus Reformatorum,* vol. 31, 334.

17. Ibid., 339–40.

18. Werner Elert, *The Structure of Lutheranism,* trans. Walter A. Hansen (St. Louis: Concordia, 1962), 290f.; Cf. *CR,* vol. 9, 922–23.

19. F. Guizot, *History of France,* vol. 3 (1872), 15.

20. George J. Fritschel summarizes the situation very well in *The Formula of Concord, Its Origin and Contents: A Contribution to Symbolics,* 19–25.

21. Ibid., 26.

22. Fritschel, 28–29.

23. Friedrich Bente, *Historical Introduction to the Symbolical Books* (St. Louis: Concordia, 1921), 99.

24. *CR,* vol. 8, 839–44; Cf. Fritschel, 72.

25. Bente, 101; *CR,* vol. 41, 593.

26. Neve, vol. 1, 260.

27. Fritschel, 50.

28. Philip Schaff, *The Creeds of Christendom,* vol. 1 (New York: Harper and Brothers, Publishers, 1919), 300; quoted in Schmauck, 592.

29. Robert Kolb, "Dynamics of Party Conflict in the Saxon Late Reformation: Gnesio-Lutherans vs. Philippists," *The Journal of Modern History Supplement,* 49.3 (1977): p. D1299.

30. See Robert Kolb, "Matthaes Judex's Condemnation of Princely Censorship of Theologians' Publications," *Church History* 50 (1981): 401–14.

31. Fritschel, 40–41.

32. Cf. Timothy J. Wengert, "Casper Cruciger (1504–1548): The Case of the Disappearing Reformer," *The Sixteenth Century Journal* 20 (1989): 417–41. He informs us that Melanchthon enjoyed preparing learned papers so much that he even prepared them for others who then fobbed them off as their own. In this way, down through the years almost all of the writings of Cruciger came to be credited to Melanchthon, and Cruciger almost disappeared.

33. E. G. Schwiebert has a full and excellent treatment of this matter in his *Luther and His Times* (St. Louis: Concordia, 1950), 643–63.

34. Few of the voluminous works of Melanchthon have been rendered into English. In addition to the 1944 translation of the *Loci Communes* of 1521 by Charles Leander Hill (Boston: Meador Publishing Company, 1944), we have *Melanchthon Selected Writings* also translated by Hill and edited posthumously by Elmer E. Flack and Lowell J. Satre, 1960 (Minneapolis: Augsburg, 1962), containing several significant but short works by the preceptor. We also have the 1965 translation by Clyde Manschreck of the 1555 German edition of the *Loci Communes.* But much remains to be done, and much of it would be valuable to the church and its historians.

35. *Loci Theologici,* trans. J. A. O. Preus (St. Louis: Concordia, 1989).

36. Philip Melanchthon, *Loci Communes, 1543,* trans. J. A. O. Preus (St. Louis: Concordia, 1992).

37. James M. Kittelson, *Luther, the Reformer* (Minneapolis: Augsburg, 1986), 249.

38. Melanchthon, *Loci Communes, 1521,* trans. Charles L. Hill, 117–68; J. A. O. Preus II, "Chemnitz on Law and Gospel," *Concordia Journal* 15 (October 1989):406–22.

39. Pelikan, 42–43.

40. Ibid., 43.

41. Seeberg, 373.

42. *LT,* 475–84.

NOTES

43. For an additional picture of Chemnitz' view, see his *De Caute Sentiendi* of 1575 or its German translation of 1576, *Ein Wolg. Bericht von den fürn. Artikeln Christliche Zere* . . .

44. See Kolb, *Confessing the Faith*, 1990.

45. Something that even the greatly liberalized Rome of the 20th century has not been willing to do either although the question was initially broached by Cardinal Ratzinger in 1974 out of whose suggestion came a great deal of literature. Cf. *A Joint Commentary on the Augsburg Confession by Lutheran and Catholic Theologians*, eds. George Wolfgang Forell and James F. McCue (Minneapolis: Augsburg, 1982) and Joseph A. Burgess, ed., *The Role of the Augsburg Confession: Catholic and Lutheran Views* (Philadelphia: Fortress, 1980).

46. E.g., see his *Iudicium* of 1561.

47. Cf. Seeberg, 379ff.

48. *LC,* 41–46; *CR,* vol. 21, 651–65.

49. Manschreck, xiii.

50. *CR,* vol. 21, 376.

51. *LC,* 44; as cited by Chemnitz, *LT,* vol. 1, 224; Cf. *CR,* vol. 21, 659.

52. *LT,* vol. 1, 250.

53. See *LT* at very end of book 3, p. 222 in standard late editions (e.g., *Loci Theologici* (Frankfurt: Johannes Spies, 1591), Appended Theses, p. 11, 14).

54. Pelikan, 44.

55. See Theodor Mahlmann, "Bibliographie Martin Chemnitz," in Jünke, 393 for details. See also Rehtmeyer, *Antiqvitates Ecclesiasticae Inclytae Urbis Brunsvigae, oder, Der berühmten Stadt Braunschweig Kirchen-Historie,* "Beylagen Des Dritten Theils Nemlich der Reformationshistorie der Stadt Braunschweig," 239–44 [The Beylagen are a part of Rehtmeyer's history, but are paginated separately], dated August 28, 1576, where he refers to his dealings with the church of Göttingen on this matter.

56. Manschreck, xii–xiv; but cf. his reference to the subject in his second version of the *Loci Communes* in *CR,* vol. 21, 330–32 and a slightly longer version, still under the second aetas, *CR,* vol. 21, 450–53.

57. *LC,* 82; Cf. Chemnitz *LT,* vol. 2, 445.

58. *LT,* vol. 2, 450–51.

59. Manschreck, xv.

60. Reinhold Seeberg, *Text-Book of the History of Doctrines,* vol. 2, trans. Charles E. Hay (Grand Rapids, Michigan: Baker Book House, 1952), 342. In footnote 3 on the same page Seeberg adds very correctly, "Strictly speaking, Melanchthon cites Vulgarius (Theophylact) only to prove that the Greeks also teach the presence of the body of Christ. He by no means thereby commits himself to their *mutari.* . . . But we dare not deny a fatal diplomacy in the choice of the citation." Apparently the Romanists were fooled for a time, and that even modern Lutherans can also become confused: see how Bjarne W. Teigen handles this point in his book *The Lord's Supper in the Theology of Martin Chemnitz* (Brewster, Massachusetts: Trinity Lutheran Press, 1986), 52–53, where he vainly seeks support for a consecrationist position on the moment of the real presence of Christ in the Supper in Melanchthon's peculiar statement

in Apology 10.2. This is in direct contradiction to Seeberg, who appears to have the better of the argument. Nor does Chemnitz support consecrationism.

61. Manschreck, xv.

62. *CR*, vol. 31, 871.

63. Robert Kolb, *Nikolaus von Amsdorf* (1483–1565) (Nieuwkoop: B. DeGraaf, 1978), 87.

64. See Robert Stupperich, *Der Unbekannte Melanchthon; Wirken und Denken des Praeceptor Germaniae in neuer Sicht* (Stuttgart: W. Kohlhammer, 1961).

65. Pelikan, 44–45.

Chapter 3

1. Cf. Günter Chemnitius, "Eine Theorie zur Entstehung des Namens Chemnitz" in *Der zweite Martin der Lutherischen Kirche,* ed. Wolfgang A. Jünke (Braunschweig: Ev.-luth. Stadtkirchenverband und Propstei Braunschweig, 1986), 253–58. Related to this is also another article in the same Festschrift, pp. 328–52, this by Margarete Staude, "Einige bedeutsame Nachkommen der Familiae Chemnitz," which deals with the many illustrious descendants of Chemnitz. There is also an important city in Saxony, the third largest in the territory, which previous to the Communist takeover in eastern Germany was called Chemnitz, the name of which is traced back to the settlement of Wends who had made the area their home. Ironically the Communists renamed the city Karl Marx Stadt. It has since resumed its previous name.

2. Philip J. Rehtmeyer, *Antiqvitates Ecclesiasticae Inclytae Urbis Brunsvigae, oder, Der berühmten Stadt Braunschweig Kirchen-Historie,* part 3 (Braunschweig: Christoph Friedrich Zilligers, 1710), 275–76.

3. Manfreid P. Fleischer, "Melanchthon as Praeceptor of Late-Humanist Poetry," *The Sixteenth Century Journal* 20 (Winter 1989):559–80. Fleischer suggests that Chemnitz was drawn to Sabinus just because of their mutual interest in poetry.

4. Chemnitz, "An Autobiography of Martin Kemnitz," trans. August L. Graebner, in *Theological Quarterly* 3 (October 1899): 473. Much of the following is based on information found in this writing.

5. J. Gasmer, *De Vita, Studiis, et Obitu Reverendi et Clarissimi Viri D. Martini Chemnitii . . . .* (Braunschweig: 1588).

6. Chemnitz, "An Autobiography of Martin Kemnitz," 481–82. This Latin word, transliterated into German as *inclinierte,* is very uncommon and has been interpreted by some as a reference to Chemnitz' interests in astrology. But when he says that this inclination is toward theology and godliness, it is doubtful if this instance has reference to astrology. In fact, the German word occurs often enough in Chemnitz' writings, and since it was common in Latin which he often interspersed with German, we may simply assume that it was a word in common use with Chemnitz and make no speculations as to any connection with astrology.

7. Rehtmeyer, part 3, 216.

8. Chemnitz, "An Autobiography of Martin Kemnitz," 483.

9. See Reinhold Seeberg, *Text-Book of the History of Doctrines,* vol. 2, trans. Charles E. Hay (Grand Rapids, Michigan: Baker Book House, 1952), 372–74.

10. Michael Rogness, *Melanchthon: Reformer without Honor* (Minneapolis: Augsburg, 1969), 165, footnote 389.
11. Martin Stupperich, "Martin Chemnitz und der Osiandrische Streit," in Jünke, 231.
12. *LT,* vol. 2, 553.
13. Ibid., 548.
14. Ibid., vol. 1, 90.
15. Ibid., 146.
16. Ibid., 306.
17. Ibid., vol. 2, 479.
18. Pelikan, *From Luther to Kierkegaard: A Study in the History of Theology* (St. Louis: Concordia, 1950), 42–43.
19. Ibid., 43.
20. Seeberg, vol. 2, 372–73, footnote 2.
21. Chemnitz, "An Autobiography of Martin Kemnitz," 484.
22. See Robert Kolb, "Martin Chemnitz, Gnesio-Lutheraner," in Jünke, 115–29.
23. Gasmer, 23.
24. Seeberg, vol. 2, 381.
25. This church today is Roman Catholic, having been given in the last century to refugee Catholics who were coming to the city. All of the other ancient churches are still Lutheran, all in a beautiful state of repair.
26. Chemnitz, "An Autobiography of Martin Kemnitz," 487.

Chapter 4

1. For details see Werner Spiess, *Geschichte der Stadt Braunschweig im Nachmittelalter* (Braunschweig: 1966), 89ff.
2. See Spiess, 48–61.
3. Virtually all of the following is based on Philip J. Rehtmeyer, *Antiqvitates Ecclesiasticae Inclytae Urbis Brunsvigae, oder, Der berühmten Stadt Braunschweig Kirchen-Historie,* part 3 (Braunschweig: Christoph Friedrich Zilligers, 1710), 207–73.
4. J. Gasmer, *De Vita, Studiis, et Obitu Reverendi et Clarissimi Viri D. Martini Chemnitii . . .* (Braunschweig: 1588), 23.
5. Rehtmeyer, part 3, 227–28.
6. Ibid., 230.
7. Ibid., 231–34.
8. See Ernst Koch, "Striving for the Union of Lutheran Churches: The Church-Historical Background of the Work Done on the Formula of Concord at Magdeburg," *The Sixteenth Century Journal* 8, no. 4 (1977): 105–21.
9. See Theodore G. Tappert, trans. and ed., *The Book of Concord* (Philadelphia: Fortress, 1959), 9.
10. Ibid., 5, footnote 5.
11. Ibid., 3–16.

THE SECOND MARTIN

Chapter 5

1. Jobst Ebel, "Die Herkunft des Konzeptes der Konkordienformel: Die Funktionen der fünf Verfasser neben Andreae beim Zustandekommen der Formel," *Zeitschrift für Kirchengeschichte* 91 (1980): 240, footnote 36, in reference to *CR* 9, 962, where Melanchthon accuses Mörlin of coming very close to transubstantiation.

2. Ibid., 246, footnote 73.

3. We must distinguish between this 1561 work of Mörlin and a 1569 work by Chemnitz of nearly the same name (*Kurzer Bericht*) that became part of the Braunschweig city *corpus doctrinae* and the ducal *corpus doctrinae* of 1569 and 1576, a document that achieved confessional status in the area.

4. See *Die Evangelische Kirchenordnungen des XVI Jahrhunderts*, vol. 6.1, Niedersachsen, ed. Emil Sehling (Tübingen: J. C. B. Mohr [Paul Siebeck], 1955), 92–139 where the Lüneburg Articles, or the *Erklerung*, are included in the 1569 edition of the ducal Braunschweig *corpus doctrinae*. On pages 89–92 of the same document are listed as confessional writings of this duchy also the three creeds, the Augsburg Confession "as presented to Emperor Charles in the year [15]30 and printed the next year '31" and its Apology, the Smalcald Articles, and the catechisms of Luther. Note that thus by 1561 all the Confessions except the Formula of Concord were being included in the various *corpora doctrinae* of the Lower Saxon cities.

5. *De Controversiis quibusdam, quae superiori tempore circa quosdam Augustanae Confessionis articulos motae et agitatae sunt. Iudicium d. Martini Chemnitii . . .*,ed. Polycarp Leyser (Wittenberg, 1594).

6. Manschreck, *Melanchthon on Christian Doctrine*, xv.

7. Inge Mager, "Das Corpus Doctrinae der Stadt Braunschweig im Gefüge der übrigin niedersächsischen Lehrschriften-sammlungen," in *Die Reformation in der Stadt Braunschweig, Festschrift 1528–1978*, ed. Hans-Walter Krumwiede (Braunschweig: Gesammtherstellung Druck und Verlagshaus Braunschweig, 1978), 115.

8. Theodor Mahlmann, "Martin Chemnitz," in *Gestalten der Kirchengeschichte*, vol. 6, *Die Reformationszeit II*, ed. Martin Greschat (Stuttgart: W. Kohlhammer, 1981), 317.

9. Mager, "Das Corpus Doctrinae der Stadt Braunschweig im Gefüge der übrigin niedersächsischen Lehrschriften-sammlungen," p. 115, footnote 41 where she cites as her source the *Bekenntnis des ministerii Braunschweigs*, p. 466 and Heppe a.a.O., p. 133; also see her footnote 43, where she cites Heppe, p. 134.

10. Mahlmann, 319.

11. Philip J. Rehtmeyer, *Antiqvitates Ecclesiasticae Inclytae Urbis Brunsvigae, oder, Der berühmten Stadt Braunschweig Kirchen-Historie*, part 3 (Braunschweig: 1710), 263.

12. Inge Mager, "Erbe und Auftrag nach dem Testament von Martin Chemnitz," in *Der zweite Martin der Lutherischen Kirche*, ed. W. A. Jünke (Braunschweig: Ev.-luth. Stadt Kirchenverband und Propstei Braunschweig, 1986), 154.

13. Ibid., 153–54.

14. Ebel, 246; Cf. footnote 74.

NOTES

15. J. Gasmer, *De Vita, Studiis, et Obitu Reverendi, et Clarissimi Viri D. Martini Chemnitii . . .* (Braunschweig, 1588), 24.
16. Rehtmeyer, part 3, 269.
17. Gasmer, 24.

Chapter 6

1. See James M. Estes, *Christian Magistrate and State Church: The Reforming Career of Johannes Brenz* (Toronto: University of Toronto Press, 1982) for an example of how things developed in Württemberg; also Pauck, pp. 155ff.
2. *Luther's Works,* American Edition 40:313–14. Cf. *Luther's Works,* American Edition 40:266, where we are told, "Melanchthon was the author of the *Instructions,* but Luther's ideas underlie the whole and some passages reflect his pen. Because of the endorsement of it by Luther, and the fact that he not only wrote the preface but made revisions in later editions, the work is generally included in the works of Luther."
3. Cf., e.g., Jodi Bilinkoff, *The Avila of Saint Teresa: Religious Reform in a Sixteenth-Century City* (Ithaca, NY: Cornell University Press, 1989), 108–51.
4. Cf. Estes, 33, 39.
5. For the total document see Rehtmeyer, *Antiqvitates Ecclesiasticae Inclytae Urbis Brunsvigae, oder, Der berühmten Stadt Braunschweig Kirchen-Historie,* part 3, Beylagen, 122–36. For a summary see *Examination of the Council of Trent,* vol. 1, trans. Fred Kramer (St. Louis: Concordia, 1971), 19–20. For a longer summary see *Examen Concilii Tridenti,* ed. Eduard Preuss (Berlin: Gustav Schlamitz, 1861), 932–34, which we shall use here, all in words of Chemnitz.
6. Cf. Inge Mager, "'Ich habe dich zum Wächter gesetzt über das Haus Israel': zum Amstverständnis des Braunschweiger Stadtsuperintendenten und Wolfenbüttelschen Kirchenrats Martin Chemniz," *Braunschweigisches Jahrbuch* 69 (1988): 67–69.
7. Rehtmeyer, part 3, 316–35 is the chief source for our information on this era. He tells us that he got most of his material from one of Julius' courtiers, a Francis Algermann, a layman who published his work in 1598 and again in corrected and edited form in 1608. Also see Mark U. Edwards, *Luther's Last Battles* (Ithaca: Cornell University Press, 1983), 115ff. See also Chemnitz' letter of December 1578 to Julius in Kurt Kronenberg, "Die Reformation im Lande Braunschweig," in *Vier Jahrhunderte Lutherische Landeskirche in Braunschweig,* Festschrift, ed. Landeskirchenamt Wolfenbüttel (Braunschweig: Georg Westermann, 1968), 9–11 and Horst Reller, "Die Auseinandersetzung zwischen Herzog Heinrich d.J. und Herzog Julius von Braunschweig-Lüneberg in den Jahren 1553–1568," in *Jahrbuch der Gesellschaft für niedersächsische Kirchengeschichte* 67 (1969): 91–106.
8. Rehtmeyer, part 3, 316.
9. *Luther's Works,* American Edition 41:179–256.
10. Edwards, 149
11. Ibid.
12. Rehtmeyer, part 3, 318.

13. Horst Reller, "Die Auseinandersetzung," 93–106.

14. Rehtmeyer, part 3, 321.

15. Ibid., 323.

16. Kronenberg, 9–10.

17. Ibid., 10.

18. Rehtmeyer, part 3, 325.

19. See Rehtmeyer, part 3, 83 and Kronenberg, 7.

20. See his *Christian Magistrate and State Church: The Reforming Career of Johannes Brenz*, 66–70.

21. Kronenberg, 13.

22. *Luther's Works*, American Edition 40:265, 271–72.

23. Jobst Ebel, "Die Herkunft des Konzeptes der Konkordienformel: Die Funktionen der fünf Verfasser neben Andreae beim Zustandekommen der Formel," *Zeitschrift für Kirchengeschichte* 91 (1980): 247–48; Cf. Rehtmeyer, part 3, 338–39, and Beylagen, 243.

24. Kronenberg, 14.

25. Rehtmeyer, part 3, 326.

26. Kronenberg, 14.

27. Pauck, 106ff.

28. Ibid., 140.

29. Kronenberg, 11.

30. *Luther's Works*, American Edition 53:68–69.

31. See Kronenberg, 15–16, 19; also Ebel, 247–48.

32. See Melanchthon's and Chemnitz' Loci for rather extended discussions of this matter.

33. Kronenberg, 16.

34. Ibid., 16.

35. Pauck, 138.

36. *LT,* vol. 2, 698–706.

37. Wolfgang A. Jünke, "Martin Chemnitz, Bischof der Stadt Braunschweig," in *Der zweite Martin der Lutherischen Kirche,* ed. Wolfgang A. Jünke (Braunschweig: Ev.-luth. Stadt Kirchenverband und Propstei Braunschweig, 1986), 283.

38. See Jodi Bilinkoff, *The Avila of St. Teresa: Religious Reform in a Sixteenth-Century City* (Ithaca: Cornell University Press, 1989), 15–52.

39. See *LT,* vol. 2, 698.

40. Rehtmeyer, part 3, Beylagen, 142.

41. Pauck, 143.

42. *Die Evangelische Kirchenordnungen des XVI Jahrhunderts,* vol. 6.1, Niedersachsen, ed. Emil Sehling (Tübingen: J. C. B. Mohr [Paul Siebeck], 1955), 83–89.

43. Inge Mager, "Das Corpus Doctrinae der Stadt Braunschweig im Gefüge der übrigin niedersächsischen Lehrschriften-sammlungen," in *Die Reformation in der Stadt Braunschweig, Festschrift 1528–1978,* ed. Hans-Walter Krumwiede

NOTES

(Braunschweig: Gesammtherstellung Druck und Verlagshaus Braunschweig, 1978), 112–15.

44. *Die Evangelische Kirchenordnungen des XVI Jahrhunderts*, 83–89.

45. Mager, "Das Corpus Doctrinae der Stadt Braunschweig im Gefüge der übrigin niedersächsischen Lehrschriften-sammlungen," 113.

46. As cited by Mager, "Das Corpus Doctrinae der Stadt Braunschweig im Gefüge der übrigin niedersächsischen Lehrschriften-sammlungen," 115, note footnotes 34–35 which refer to the statements of Chemnitz as recorded in the minutes of the ministerium of Braunschweig.

47. See Theodor Mahlmann, "Bibliographie Martin Chemnitz," in *Der zweite Martin der Lutherischen Kirchen,* ed. Wolfgang A. Jünke (Braunschweig: Ev.-luth. Stadt Kirchenverband und Propstei Braunschweig, 1986), 382–83; Sehling, vol. 6.1, 83–280; Inge Mager, "Erbe und Auftrag nach dem Testament von Martin Chemnitz," in *Der zweite Martin der Lutherischen Kirchen,* ed. Wolfgang A. Jünke (Braunschweig: Ev.-luth. Stadt Kirchenverband und Propstei Braunschweig, 1986), 155–57.

48. Sehling, vol. 6.1, 92, footnote 31.

49. Mager, "Das Corpus Doctrinae der Stadt Braunschweig im Gefüge der übrigin niedersächsischen Lehrschriften-sammlungen," 115.

50. Ibid.

51. Almost all of this is from Rehtmeyer, part 3, 342–44.

52. Rehtmeyer, part 3, 343.

53. Ibid., 352.

54. Mager, "Erbe und Auftrag nach dem Testament von Martin Chemnitz," 159–66.

55. See Annelies Ritter, "Über die Lehrschriften in den Fürstentümern Wolfenbüttel und Lüneburg am Ende des 16 Jahrhunderts," in *Jahrbuch der Gesellschaft für Niedersächschische Kirchengeshichte* 50 (1952): 83.

56. Hans-Walter Krumwiede, "Vom reformatorischen Glauben Luthers zur Orthodoxie, Theologische Bemerkungen zu Bugenhagens Braunschweiger Kirchenordnung und zu Urbanus Rhegius formulae quaedam caute et citra scandalum loquendi" ("From the reformer's faith of Luther to Orthodoxy, Theological Notes on Bugenhagen's Braunschweig Church Order and Urbanus Rhegius' Formula Caute Loquendi"), *Jahrbuch der Gesellschaft für Niedersächsische Kirchengeschichte* 52 (1955): 43.

57. Mager, "Das Corpus Doctrinae der Stadt Braunschweig im Gefüge der übrigin niedersächsischen Lehrschriften-sammlungen," 118.

58. Ibid.

59. Cited in Mager, "Das Corpus Doctrinae der Stadt Braunschweig im Gefüge der übrigin niedersächsischen Lehrschriften-sammlungen," 121, from the Foreward to the *Corpus Doctrinae Julium.*

Chapter 7

1. Jobst Ebel, "Die Herkunft des Konzeptes der Konkordienformel: Die Funktionen der fünf Verfasser neben Andreae beim Zustandekommen der Formel," *Zeitschrift für Kirchengeschichte* 91 (1980): 253.

THE SECOND MARTIN

2. Theodore R. Jungkuntz, *Formulators of the Formula of Concord* (St. Louis: Concordia, 1977), 146–54.

3. Arthur C. Piepkorn, "Andreae, Jakob" in *The Encyclopedia of the Lutheran Church*, vol. 1, ed. Julius Bodensieck (Minneapolis: Augsburg, 1965), s.v.

4. Philip J. Rehtmeyer, *Antiqvitates Ecclesiasticae Inclytae Urbis Brunsvigae, oder, Der berühmten Stadt Braunschweig Kirchen-Historie*, part 3 (Braunschweig: Christoph Friederich Zilligers, 1707–20), 351.

5. Cf. Theodor Mahlmann, *Das neue Dogma der lutherischen Christologie* (Gütersloh: Gütersloher Verlagshaus Gerd Mohn, 1969).

6. Chemnitz, *The Two Natures in Christ,* trans. J. A. O. Preus (St. Louis: Concordia, 1971), 24.

7. Cf. Mahlmann.

8. Klaus Schreiner, "Rechtglaubigkeit als 'Band der Gesellschaft' und 'Grundlage des Staates.' Zureidlichen Verpflichtung von Staats und Kirchendienern auf die 'Formula Concordiae' und das 'Konkordienbuch,'" in *Bekenntnis und Einheit der Kirche: Studien zum Konkordienbuch,* eds. Martin Brecht and Reinhard Schwarz (Stuttgart: Calwer Verlag, 1980), 351–80.

9. Lewis W. Spitz, "Introduction: The Formula of Concord Then and Now," in *Discord, Dialogue, and Concord: Studies in the Lutheran Reformation's Formula of Concord,* ed. Lewis W. Spitz and Wenzel Lohff (Philadelphia: Fortress, 1977), p. 1, footnote 1.

10. See Spitz and Lohff, pages 7–8 for a succinct summation of these conflicts.

11. For a complete and useful bibliography of the literature relative to the Confessions and the Formula of Concord see Edmund Schlink, *Theology of the Lutheran Confessions,* trans. Paul F. Koehneke and Herbert J. A. Bouman (Philadephia: Fortress, 1977), 318–44. See also David P. Daniel and Charles P. Arand, "A Bibliography of the Lutheran Confessions," *Sixteenth Century Bibliography,* vol. 28 (St. Louis: Center for Reformation Research, 1988).

12. Jobst Ebel, "Jacob Andreae (1528–1590) als Verfasser der Konkordienformel," *Zeitschrift für Kirchengeschichte* 89 (1978): 78–119; Cf. pp. 85–86, footnote 32.

13. George J. Fritschel, *The Formula of Concord: Its Origin and Contents* (Philadelphia: The Lutheran Publication Society, 1916), 92.

14. See Ebel, "Jacob Andreae (1528–1590) als Verfasser der Konkordienformel," pp. 87–88 and footnotes 42–48.

15. Ibid., 87; Cf. p. 92.

16. Robert Kolb, "Martin Chemnitz, Gnesio-Lutheraner," in *Der zweite Martin der Lutherischen Kirche,* ed. W. A. Jünke (Braunschweig: n.p., 1986), 115–29.

17. Friedrich Bente, *Historical Introductions to the Book of Concord* (St. Louis: Concordia, 1965), 245.

18. See Ebel, "Jacob Andreae (1528–1590) als Verfasser der Konkordienformel," 111.

19. Ibid., 113.

20. It apppears that the practice of Lutheranism at this time was that ordination was reserved for those who served a congregation in some capacity. Those, like Melanchthon and Chytraeus, who spent their entire lives in teaching as the

doctors of the church, even though they might preach, were not ordained. Likewise Chemnitz, although he was engaged to serve on the Wittenberg faculty, was not ordained until he received and accepted the call to Braunschweig, which did involve the pastorate of Martin Church.

21. Ebel, "Die Herkunft des Konzeptes der Konkordienformel," 257.

22. For a brief biography see Jungkuntz, *Formulators of the Formula of Concord,* 69–88. See also Ebel, "Die Herkunft des Konzeptes der Konkordienformel," 254–64. Ebel considers Chytraeus to have played a more substantive role in the Formula than even Selnecker.

23. See Chemnitz, *Loci Theologici,* vol. 2, trans. J. A. O. Preus (St. Louis: Concordia, 1989), 593–630.

24. See Rehtmeyer, part 3, 577–81.

25. Ernst Koch, "Striving for the Union of Lutheran Churches: The Church-Historical Background of the Work Done on the Formula of Concord at Magdeburg," *The Sixteenth Century Journal* 8, no. 4 (1977): 114.

26. Ebel, "Jacob Andreae (1528–1590) als Verfasser der Konkordienformel," 114.

27. Ibid., 115.

28. Ebel, "Die Herkunft des Konzeptes der Konkordienformel," 253.

29. Gerhard Müller, "Alliance and Confession: The Theological-Historical Development and Ecclesiastical-Political Significance of Reformation Confessions," trans. Herbert J. A. Bouman, *The Sixteenth Century Journal* 8, no. 4 (1977): 138.

30. Chemnitz, *LT,* vol. 1, 284–89.

31. Cf. his *The Two Natures in Christ,* trans. J. A. O. Preus (St. Louis: Concordia, 1971), chapter 25, pp. 341–94, which has 313 patristic citations from 32 Greek and Latin fathers and closes with 18 citations from Luther. The same is the case in chapter 15, pp. 181–95, which has 76 citations from about 18 fathers, with the last 10 from Luther, the last church father. There are several other chapters that show the same pattern. There is a very interesting display of pictures in the Brüdern-Ulrici Church in Braunschweig unlike anything I have ever seen elsewhere. In the choir of this lovely 12th-century church, which was once attached to a monastery of "brothers," there is a series of 46 portraits, 38 of which are pre-Reformation. They were all painted about 1597 and depict church fathers from the second to the 16th centuries, beginning with Ignatius of Antioch and continuing down through the pre-Constantinian period, the great fourth-century fathers, those of the fourth to the seventh centuries, then notables of the period of the Middle Ages and the pre-Reformation. In trying to determine the criteria for selecting these 38 fathers, I discovered that they do not match the names in the Catalog of Testimonies of the Formula of Concord or the Book of Concord, but it can be demonstrated that every one of them is quoted in a writing of Chemnitz, *Loci Theologici, Two Natures in Christ,* or *The Examination of the Council of Trent.* They are his list of fathers, by no means all he cites, but the primary ones. Then after the 38 come eight others of the post-Reformation era, but all fathers in their own right: Luther; Melanchthon; Bugenhagen, who brought the Reformation to the city of Braunschweig; the three greatest superintendents of the city, Mörlin, Chemnitz, and Leyser; and finally two notable professors, Hunnius and Mylius. It is interesting to speculate that perhaps the great and learned Dr. Chemnitz may have

been consulted as to which fathers should have their pictures in the choir, and he picked those whose writings he perhaps knew best or whom he considered most important. We perhaps will never be sure, but it is interesting to speculate.

32. See William Russell's Ph.D. thesis on the Smalcald Articles, due to be published by Augsburg Fortress.

33. Cf. the list of Luther citations from *Loci Theologici* above.

34. It is interesting that at the Convention of Lichtenberg, held in 1576, called by the elector of Saxony to establish peace among the Lutherans and which resulted in the Formula of Concord and the Book of Concord, when the participants, including Chemnitz, discussed what documents belonged in such a book in addition to the already-accepted confessional writings, the suggestion was made that Luther's *Lectures on Galatians* be included. It was not done, but it indicates the esteem in which the work was held.

35. *Luther's Works,* American Edition 25:50–56.

36. Chemnitz, *ECT,* vol. 1, 33.

Chapter 8

1. Inge Mager, "'Ich habe dich zum Wächter gesetzt über das Haus Israel': zum Amstverständnis des Braunschweiger Stadtsuperintendenten und Wolfenbüttelschen Kirchenrats Martin Chemnitz," *Braunschweigisches Jahrbuch* 69 (1988): 66.

2. Theodore R. Jungkuntz, *Formulators of the Formula of Concord* (St. Louis: Concordia, 1977), 64.

3. Chemnitz' letter is cited in part by many authors, but it has been difficult to find a complete copy. However, the letter is quoted in full in J. G. Leuckfeld's *Antiquitates Groningensis* (Quedlinburg, 1710), addenda IV, 59ff.

4. WA 51.219f. Cf. Mager, "Wächter." Mager has caught the situation precisely. Chemnitz speaks as a spiritual watchman.

5. Theodor Pressel, *Martin Chemnitz. Nach Gleichzeiten Quelle,* Leben und Ausgewählte Schriften der Väter und Begründer der lutherischen Kirche, vol. 8, eds. J. Hartmann et al. (Elberfeld: R. L. Friderichs, 1862), 66–67.

6. Ibid., 66.

7. *Die Evangelische Kirchenordnungen des XVI Jahrhunderts,* vol. 6.1, ed. Emil Sehling (Tübingen: J. C. B. Mohr [Paul Siebeck], 1955), 83–89.

8. Pressel, 66.

9. Pressel, 69.

10. Ibid.

11. Ibid.

12. Philip J. Rehtmeyer, *Antiqvitates Ecclesiasticae Inclytae Urbis Brunsvigae, oder, Der berühmten Stadt Braunschweig Kirchen-Historie,* part 3 (Braunschweig: Christoph Friederich Zilligers, 1707–20), 368.

13. Ibid.

14. Theodor Mahlmann, "Martin Chemnitz," in *Gestalten der Kirchengeschichte,* vol. 6, *Die Reformationszeit II,* ed. Martin Greschat (Stuttgart: W. Kohlhammer, 1981), 325–26.

15. Rehtmeyer, part 3, 385–86; Beylagen, 219–20.

16. Rehtmeyer, part 3, 499–500.

17. Ibid., 501.

18. Rehtmeyer, part 3, Beylagen, 276–81.

19. See Christoph Hartknock, *Preussische Kirken-Historia* (Frankfurt am Main: Simon Beckenstein, 1686), 458ff., Chapter V 1686, regarding the strife between bishops Heshusius and Wigand regarding the terms *abstract* and *concrete,* in which young Mörlin was also involved and on the losing side.

20. For the later role of the Formula in the Lutheran church see Robert D. Preus, "The Influence of the Formula of Concord on the Later Lutheran Orthodoxy," in *Discord, Dialog, and Concord,* eds. Lewis W. Spitz and Wenzel Lohff (Philadelphia: Fortress, 1977), 86–101. See also Trygve R. Skarsten, "The Reaction in Scandinavia," ibid., 136–49 and Johannes Wallman, "Die Rolle der Bekenntnisschriften," in *Bekenntnis und Einheit der Kirche: Studien zum Konkordienbuch,* eds. Martin Brecht and Reinhard Schwarz (Stuttgart: Calwer Verlag, 1980), 381–91.

PART 3

1. Note that the first five questions on the subject of Scripture all cite Chemnitz' *Examination of the Council of Trent,* vol. 1, trans. Fred Kramer (St. Louis: Concordia, 1971). Leonhard Hutter, *Compendium Locorum Theologoricum,* ed. Wolfgang Trillhaas, no. 183, Kleine Texte für Vorlesungen und Übungen, ed. Kurt Aland (Berlin: Walter de Gruyter and Co., 1961), 1–2.

2. Johann Gerhard, *Loci Theologici,* vol. 3, ed. Eduard Preuss (Berlin: Gustav Schlawitz, 1865), 142.

3. His *ECT* (all references are to vol. 1); his *The Two Natures in Christ,* trans. J. A. O. Preus (St. Louis: Concordia, 1971); his *Fundamenta Sanae Doctrinae De Vera et substantiali praesentia...corporis et sanguinis Domini in Coena, The Lord's Supper,* trans. J. A. O. Preus (St. Louis: Concordia, 1979), LS; his *Ministry, Word, and Sacaraments: An Enchiridion,* trans. Luther Poellot (St. Louis: Concordia, 1981), Ench.; his Theses attached by Leyser to Chemnitz' LT Theses, *Loci Theologici,* ed. Polycarp Leyser (Frankfurt: Johannes Spies, 1591), Appended Theses, 1–32. We also include here Melanchthon's *Loci Communes,* LC.

Chapter 9

1. The term "churches" in the Augsburg Confession refers to the territorial churches of the signers. In Chemnitz the term "churches" is also used in this sense and also with reference to the various city churches of the New Testament. The term indicates an increasing number of churches, as the reformation spread, but the church, in the singular, is one, still to be reformed, and always in need of careful attention and protection as to its faith and its life. And it is

in that context that we must regard and judge Chemnitz. Cf. Luther, Melanchthon, the AC, Grane p. 92, and Chemnitz.

2. Chemnitz, *LT,* "Appended Theses" [Thesis 1:6], p. 1.

3. See also Tappert, FC, SD 2.26, p. 526; also Apol. 4.108, p. 122.

4. Chemnitz, *LT,* "Appended Theses" [Thesis 1:4], p. 1.

5. For a fuller treatment of this subject see J. A. O. Preus, "The New Testament Canon in the Lutheran Dogmaticians," *The Springfielder* 25 (Spring 1961): 8–33; cf. also Robert D. Preus, *The Inspiration of Scripture: A Study of the Theology of the Seventeenth Century Lutheran Dogmaticians* (Mankato, Minnesota: Lutheran Synod Book Co., 1955), 93–108.

6. See J. A. O. Preus, "The New Testament Canon in the Lutheran Dogmaticians," 12.

7. Edmund Schlink, *Theology of the Lutheran Confessions,* trans. Paul F. Koehneke and Herbert J. A. Bouman (Philadephia: Fortress, 1977), p. xvi. For a further description of the Lutheran confessional view see Ralph A. Bohlmann, *The Principles of Biblical Interpretation in the Lutheran Confessions* (St. Louis: Concordia, 1983).

8. See John F. Johnson, "Authority and Tradition: A Lutheran Perpective," *Concordia Journal* 8 (September 1982): 179–86, for an excellent discussion of this matter with its implications for 20th century Lutheranism in its "ecumenical relations" with other Protestestants and Rome. The article summarizes Chemnitz' position on the distinction between tradition and traditions and its relevance in the modern era.

9. Ibid., 183.

10. Johann Gerhard, *Loci Theologici,* vol. 1, ed. Eduard Preuss (Berlin: Gustav Schlawitz, 1863), 237–40.

11. C. G. H. Lentz, *Dr. Martin Chemnitz, Stadtsuperintendent in Braunschweig, Ein Lebensbild aus dem 16 Nachrichten* (Gotha: Friedrich Andreas Perthes, 1866), 107, footnote 4.

12. See Melanchthon's words in the preface to his 1543 edition of his *Loci Communes,* as cited in Chemnitz' *LT,* vol. 1, 35.

13. In fact, while we cannot speak definitively, yet the *Oxford English Dictinary,* 2nd ed., prepared by J. A. Simpson and E. S. C. Weiner, vol. 7 (Oxford: Clarendon Press, 1989), 169, indicates that the concept of the interpretation of Scripture, or hermeneutics, as a separate discipline from exegesis or dogmatics appears only once in the 18th century, and the word *hermeneutics* did not come into common use in English until the 19th century. One could hazard the guess that the same situation prevailed in Germany. The word is very rare in Latin, and often is written in Greek letters.

14. For a fuller treatment of this matter see my article, "Chemnitz on Law and Gospel," *Concordia Journal* 15.4 (October 1989): 406–22.

15. *Luther's Works,* American Edition 25:416.

16. *Luther's Works,* American Edition 27:346.

17. Wilhelm Pauck, ed., *The Library of Christian Classics,* vol. 19, "Melanchthon and Bucer" (Philadelphia: The Westminster Press, 1969), 71.

18. The Swedish theologian Holsten Fagerberg in his *A New Look at the Lutheran Confessions (1529–1537),* trans. Gene J. Lund (St. Louis: Concordia, 1972), has

caught this point on hermeneutics very clearly. He states on p. 35, ". . . seemingly good reasons can be adduced to the effect that the Confessions have provided us with a key to the interpretation of Scripture by their distinction between Law and Gospel." In his footnote 4 Fagerberg quotes R. Josefson, "Kirkosyn och Kyrkorätt: Kommentar till bekännelses Krifternas teologi," *Forum Theologicum* 17 (1960): 53, "[Law and Gospel] cannot and must not be looked upon as one form of interpretation alongside of the others. They rather constitute the basic presupposition of the Biblical and theological work of the reformation." Fagerberg continues, "The entire Bible, both the Old Testament and the New, can be studied from the point of view of Law and Gospel (Ap IV, 5). Justification is the article which 'alone opens the door to the entire Bible' (Ap IV, 2 German). Schlink, who here represents a large number of theologians, has seized upon these and other similar expressions and has concluded that Law and Gospel are not only the keys which open the door to the secrets of Scripture, but also that the Gospel is that which is normative in Scripture. . . ." Then Fagerberg, speaking a little more precisely than Schlink's last sentence, adds another point which must also be stressed. On p. 38 he says, "If Law and Gospel had provided a general rule of interpretation, the Confessions should have limited the questions they put to the Scriptures [as many Gospel-reductionists do today], confining them to matters directly concerned with this rule. But such is not the case. Nothing daunted, they go on to ask what the Bible says about the Lord's Supper, about the ministry and its various ranks and responsibilities, about marriage and clerical celibacy, about good works. One can find no basic limitation to questions directly connected with the distinction between Law and Gospel." From what has been said above, we may assert that this very fairly represents the position of Martin Chemnitz on Law and Gospel and the hermeneutical principle. Melanchthon in both the 1521 and the 1542 version of his *Loci* has lovely statements on Law and Gospel, which Chemnitz eagerly echoes.

19. Robert D. Preus, "The Hermeneutics of the Formula of Concord," in *No Other Gospel: Essays in Commemoration of the 400th Anniversary of the Formula of Concord 1580–1980*, ed. Arnold J. Koelpin (Milwaukee: Northwestern, 1980), 330–31.

20. See Robert Preus, "The Unity of Scripture," *Concordia Theological Quarterly*, 54 (January 1990): 14–16.

21. Cf. *Luther's Works*, American Edition 37:305.

22. For a fuller discussion of this point see Robert Preus, "The Hermeneutics of the Formula of Concord," 319–35, footnote 20.

23. See Robert Preus, "The Unity of Scripture," 1–23.

24. *Luther's Works*, American Edition 1:196.

25. Note also Melanchthon's Apology, Tappert 106.46 and FC SD Tappert 562.23, under the locus on Law and Gospel.

26. J. Gasmer, *De Vita, Studiis, et Obitu Reverendi, et Clarissimi Viri D. Martini Chemnitii . . .* (Braunschweig, 1588), 39.

27. Ibid.

28. Ibid.

29. *Luther's Works*, American Edition 41:3–178.

30. It is of interest that John Gerhard cites almost the entire *Oratio* in his *Patrologia, sive De Primitivae Ecclesiae Christianae Doctorum Vita ac Lacubrationibus Oposculum posthumum . . .,* 4th ed. (Jena: Johannes Theodore Fleischer, 1673) {posthumously published in 1653}.

31. Peter Fraenkel, *"Testimonia Patrum: The Function of the Patristic Argument in the Theology of Philip Melanchthon,"* Travaux D'Humanisme et Renaissance, vol. 46 (Geneva: E. Broz, 1961), 7. This well documented treatise should serve as a basis for a similar study of Chemnitz and the fathers, a study which would lead us far beyond the confines of this volume, and yet it is something that should be undertaken soon.

32. Note *LT,* vol. 2, 469 where Chemnitz tries to put the best construction on some unfortunate statements of the fathers.

33. Fraenkel, 7.

34. Ibid., 16.

35. Ibid., 17.

36. Ibid., 36–41.

37. Ibid., 266–69.

38. Ibid., 267.

39. *LT,* vol. 1, 35–37 and *CR,* vol. 21, 603–6.

40. *LT,* vol. 1, 40. See also footnote 36 on same page.

Chapter 10

1. Theodor Mahlmann, "Bibliographie Martin Chemnitz," in *Der zweite Martin der Lutherischen Kirchen,* ed. Wolfgang A. Jünke (Braunschweig: Ev.-luth. Stadtkirchenverband und Propstei Braunschweig, 1986), 368–424.

2. Chemnitz, *De Incarnatione Filii Dei Item De Officio et Maiestate Christi Tractatus,* ed. Hermann Hachfeld (Berlin: Gustav Schlawitz, 1865), 1–3.

3. Theodore G. Tappert, trans. and ed., *The Book of Concord* (Philadelphia: Fortress, 1959), 598, footnote 6. As the FC SD says (8.47, Tappert, 600), "Thus Christ is our mediator, redeemer, king, high priest, head, shepherd, and so forth, not only according to one nature only, either the divine or the human, but according to both natures. . . ."

4. *Luther's Works,* American Edition 15:3–178.

5. While he begins this chapter with the teaching of Scripture on this point, it is significant that he has over 100 citations from church fathers, from Ignatius to Luther, to back up his points, and in chapter 25 dealing with other aspects of the same point he has nearly 300 citations.

6. Strange to say, while Luther's translation is just as possible grammatically as Beza's, nearly all modern versions follow Beza, including some purporting to be "Lutheran" Bibles. Cf. *The Holy Bible: An American Translation,* ed. William F. Beck (New Haven, Missouri: Leader Publishing Co., 1976), 152, "whom heaven had to receive," and the *God's Word to the Nations, New Testament* (Cleveland: Biblion Publishing, 1988), 224, which reads "whom heaven must receive."

7. Werner Elert, *The Structure of Lutheranism*, trans. Walter A. Hansen (St. Louis: Concordia, 1962), 159–60.

8. Ibid., 160.

9. See Martin Luther's "Confession Concerning Christ's Supper," 1528, in *Luther's Works*, American Edition 37:151–372, esp. 207, 214, 227–35; "That These Words of Christ, 'This is My Body' . . . Still Stand Firm Against the Fanatics" in *Luther's Works*, American Edition 37:1, 13, 15, 17, and 56–66.

10. See Francis Pieper, *Christian Dogmatics*, vol. 2, trans. Theodore Engelder and John Theodore Mueller (St. Louis: Concordia, 1951), 198–205.

11. Elert, 232.

12. *Luther's Works*, American Edition 36:342.

13. Only a few more comments need our attention in regard to the ubiquity question. Pieper in his monumental *Christian Dogmatics*, vol. 2, 198–205, deals with the Brenz-Chemnitz matter at some length. He points out that any attempt to magnify the difference between Brenz-Luther and Chemnitz was due to the efforts of Rudolph Hospinian (1547–1626), a Reformed adversary of the Formula of Concord, against which he had written a *Concordia Discors* (1607) to which Leonhard Hutter (1563–1616) had written his much more famous defense of the FC, called *Concordia Concors* (1614). Pieper is very astute in pointing out that the mark of the Reformed is their insistence that "the finite is incapable of the infinite," while the mark of a Lutheran is to reject this notion. Having established that both Brenz and Chemnitz held firmly to the Lutheran position, there is no way a person can make any serious division between Luther-Brenz as over against Chemnitz or the other authors of the FC. Chemnitz was in no way trying to cozy up to the Crypto-Calvinists, as some Reformed have tried to assert. The mere fact that he wrote his monumental *TNC* against them suffices to settle that point. But it does appear that Chemnitz was trying to draw the line a little tighter, to leave less reason for his adversaries to ridicule the Lutherans, and to make certain that the Lutherans said no more and no less than the Scripture required. Thus it was wiser to avoid the subject of general ubiquity with the consequent comments about sewers, gallows, excreta, fish, birds, and stones. Chemnitz certainly made his position clear, as the criticisms of Hospinian make manifest. Likewise, the Wittenberg Crypto-Calvinists were not impressed with Chemnitz' work, but he was not as vulnerable to their attacks as Luther had been, and Chemnitz' work, along with his other publications did a great deal to instruct the rest of German Lutheranism, outside of Wittenberg, as to what the facts were and what the truth was.

Pieper is warring against Dorner and Frank, two 19th century German theologians, who had picked up this point about ubiquity, and he is reacting to them quite strongly, e.g. p. 200, where he says, "The assumption that in the Formula of Concord there is either a deliberate (Dorner) or an unintentional (Frank) compromise of the teachings of Luther and Chemnitz must be rejected as utterly without foundation. Chemnitz was able to subscribe to the words of Luther and Brenz: 'All things are through and through full of Christ, also according to the humanity' without a compromise because he himself so taught. . . . Just so Luther, had he not died in 1546, could have signed the Formula of Concord without compromising his stand, because, besides the omnipresence of Christ's human nature, he also taught the 'voli-presence,' that

is, the volitional presence, in the Lord's Supper." This is an interesting statement and accurate, because it asserts the obvious fact that Christ, as Chemnitz always contended, could be present where He willed to be, something
which neither Luther nor Brenz could possibly refute (nor would they want
to), because if Christ can be omnipresent according to His human nature, He
certainly must have willed it, so that there could not be any effort on the part
of Luther or Brenz to charge with error a person who held the voli-presence.
And the fact is that Brenz, who died in 1570, could certainly have known of
this distinction and objected to it, had he desired to do so. Andreae, who
was his spiritual and theological son, makes no known objection to Chemnitz' position; and it is well known that these two men, working closely as
they did on the FC, expressed in a quiet way both positions, and Chemnitz
voiced no objection to the Brenz-Andreae position. But, as we have just said,
and as is obvious throughout the *TNC,* Chemnitz shied away from these discussions about excreta, sewage, etc, and said that we should not argue about
such matters, but simply take the Scripture at its word and teach that Christ is
present where He wills or promises to be. Further, especially on p. 464 of his
TNC, Chemnitz is very anxious to cite Luther in a way which supports the voli-
presence and shows a retreat from his former stronger position, and, perhaps
even more significantly, Chemnitz in no way repudiates anything Luther had
said and he never mentions Brenz at all. He saw no need to because Luther
had previously declared the matter an open question, which Chemnitz obviously held also. Pieper seems to be anxious about the use of the word "compromise," but we are really here speaking about an open question, not a divisive point of doctrine.

Pieper, however, does to a degree pit Luther against Chemnitz, pp. 204–5,
but later he seems to be saying almost exactly what Chemnitz says, p. 240,
"Omnipotence and omnipresence are ascribed to Christ's human nature
directly when Scripture informs us that Christ in time, and especially after His
exaltation, has all things under His feet and fills the universe, in particular
the Church, as we read in Eph. 1:20–23; 4:10." Chemnitz says the same thing
on pp. 449 and 455. Then Pieper continues, ibid., "In this way not only the
later Lutheran dogmaticians, but also Chemnitz and his contemporaries show
the reason from Scripture why not all divine attributes are predicated of
Christ's human nature in the same manner, though with the fullness of the
Godhead all divine attributes were joined to Christ's human nature." He then
has a long quotation from Chemnitz (the location of which is not indicated)
in which Chemnitz expands on this point, seemingly with Pieper's full
approval, and which appears to support Chemnitz fully. So, in summary, the
issue never became a point of real concern, and should not be one today. It
is noteworthy that in this and the concluding chapter of the *TNC* Chemnitz
stresses the importance of taking our reason captive to the Scripture.

Perhaps we need to add the point that Dorner (J. A. Dorner, *History of the
Development of the Doctrine of the Person of Christ*, vol. 4, tr. D. W. Simon
(Edinburgh: T. and T. Clark, 1876), 198–219), is no less critical of Chemnitz
than of the FC. He is not impressed with either. He is critical of both Brenz and
Chemnitz for their "false spirit of compliancy," p. 212, toward each other and
for their failure to take into consideration the psychological aspects of Christology. But perhaps the most telling point of his critique is p. 207 where he

says, "The inner conciliation of these two points of view [the Suabians represented by Andreae, and the Wittenbergers of Melanchthon], with which the
German Reformation had been inoculated by its fathers, would have been
the birth-hour of a new, higher Christology, analogous in form to the Lutheran
doctrine of justification: - nay more, it would have led also to the substantial
reconciliation of the Reformed and Lutheran Christology, as indirectly to that
of the Reformed and Lutheran doctrine of the Supper. To such a result, however, it would have been necessary for the two points of view, the Suabian
and the Lower Saxon, to engage in a long struggle with each other. Instead
whereof, by premature concessions, a unity was improvised which was desti-
tute of inner reality. The Christological antagonism between the Suabians and
the Low Germans, with Chemnitz at their head, was put into the background,
and concealed by palliatives, in order that the opponents of the Lutheran
doctrine of the Supper, or those who were deemed its opponents, might be
met with the fact of a realized concord; whereas, logically, the doctrine of
the Supper depended for being brought to a satisfactory completion on Christology."

This is the worst indictment of Chemnitz I have ever read. Historically speaking, Brenz knew of Chemnitz' position which came out as early as his Repetitio in 1561. Brenz said nothing. Nor did he say anything regarding the error
of his old friend Osiander. Andreae had demonstrated his ability to adjust to
the position of those with whom he disagreed, but he did take some strong
positions, and one of them dealt with the ubiquity matter. Yet he and Chemnitz worked together for about a decade leading up to the FC, and seemingly
did not come to blows over this matter, despite at least Chemnitz' strong dislike of Andreae. Selnecker, likewise, schooled in the Melanchthonian school,
found no fault with Chemnitz' position, nor did Chytraeus with the same viewpoint, nor either of them with the Suabian position. Chemnitz, in trying to
keep peace with both Brenz and Luther and the Melanchthon supporters
within Lutheranism, went about as far as anyone could, and he was not faulted
by any except extreme Gnesio-Lutherans who seem to have been motivated as
much by dislike for the Suabian Andreae as by doctrinal concerns, and
attacked him more than they did Chemnitz. Even Heshusius had gone along
with the FC until Julius influenced him, and there is no indication that Julius
had any interest in the Suabian position. What Dorner is asking in stating that
they moved too fast and should have taken more time was utterly impossible
in view of the inroads of Calvinism, the situation among the princes, and for
that matter the attitudes within the Lutheran clergy. Had Lutheranism followed
Dorner's advice, there would have been no FC and probably today no
Lutheranism at all. The idea that given time to reconcile Chemnitz and the
Suabians would have led to reconciliation between Lutherans and Calvinists
is foolish. The Lutherans and the Reformed would have been even farther
apart. Neither Brenz, Luther, Andreae, nor Chemnitz considered this matter
of ubiquity important or even a matter of theological controversy. Recall that
at the Colloquium at Herzberg in 1578, involving all but Chytraeus of the
authors of the FC, in a debate with Amelung of the still-officially Lutheran
Anhalt, Amelung was equally critcal of both Andreae's position and Chemnitz'.
Amelung had become a Calvinist and as such could endure no concept of
the real presence of the true body and blood of Christ in, with, or under the
elements. And whether a "substantial reconciliation of the Reformed and

Lutheran Christology" would have resulted is really ridiculous. Efforts have been made down through the past four centuries, beginning with such meetings as Herzberg, continuing under such great syncretists as Calixtus and Danaeus, the Prussian Union of Dorner's own enlightened era—down to our own time with the ill-fated Leuenberg Theses. Still no "substantial" genuine doctrinal agreement between the two groups has taken place. Even the advent of Higher Criticism has not obliterated the problem despite Dorner's hopes, as long as any respect at all is paid to the theology of the Supper and of Christology. Bengt Hägglund, *History of Theology*, trans. Gene J. Lund (St. Louis: Concordia, 1968), 367, writing a century after Dorner says, "Dorner (d. 1884) . . . with the aid of Hegelian thought forms attempted to present a new exposition of Christology. . . . [He] found it difficult to combine the picture of the historical Jesus, as created by modern research, and the old doctrine of the two natures, and this formed the background of his Christological study. . . . Generally speaking, this concept represented a surrender of the traditional view of the Incarnation." Chemnitz lives on. Thank God.

14. Friedrich Bente, ed., *Concordia Triglotta, The Symbolical Books of the Ev. Lutheran Chuch* (St. Louis: Concordia, 1921), 821.
15. Tappert, 489.
16. Bente, *Concordia Triglotta,* 1025.
17. Tappert, 596.
18. Dorner, 207.
19. Bente, *Concordia Triglotta,* 1031.
20. Jaroslav Pelikan, *The Christian Tradition: A History of the Development of Doctrine,* vol. 4, "Reformation of Church and Dogma (1300–1700)" (Chicago: The University of Chicago Press, 1984), 352.

Chapter 11

1. Werner Elert, *The Structure of Lutheranism,* trans. Walter A. Hansen (St. Louis: Concordia, 1962), 73.
2. Chemnitz, *Formulae recte sentiendi . . .,* (De Caute Sentiendi) (1575).
3. See Elert, 65–66, on Gospel as promise—excellent; also see *LT,* 224, 450, 501.
4. Philip Melanchthon, *Loci Communes.*
5. Cf. Apol. 4.62, trans. and ed. Theodore G. Tappert, *The Book of Concord* (Philadelphia: Fortress, 1959), 115, where this statement occurs, a statement which probably accounts for the very existence of FC 5.
   Cf. also Edmund Schlink, *Theology of the Lutheran Confessions,* trans. Paul F. Koehneke and Herbert J. A. Bouman (Philadephia: Fortress, 1977), 71, "If, then, God's law is correctly understood only when we know the Gospel, i.e., the work of Christ, it follows that the rediscovery of the Gospel is also the rediscovery of the divine law. It would be an erroneous possibility to try to know the law of God in truth *apart from the Word of Scripture*" (see above p. 49ff).
6. *LT,* vol. 2, 449; *Luther's Works,* American Edition 26:115.
7. *Luther's Works,* American Edition 34:33.

8. Schlink, 56.

9. Ibid., 58.

10. Ibid., 59.

11. Ibid., 66.

12. Lowell C. Green, "Faith, Righteousness and Justification: New Light on Their Development Under Luther and Melanchthon," *The Sixteenth Century Journal* 4, no. 1 (April 1973): 81, asserts that Melanchthon may even have preceded Luther in stressing the doctrine of the imputation of Christ's righteousness. He quotes Melanchthon in a writing of Sept. 9, 1519, in which he says, "Therefore righteousness is the benefaction of Christ. All our righteousness is the free imputation of God [SA, I, 24]." Green describes this as "the first clear statement of the Melanchthonian doctrine of justification through the imputation of the merits of Christ" (p. 82), even prior to Luther's statements. It was not of interest to Chemnitz to speculate on whether Luther or Melanchthon had the idea of justification being by imputation first; he is interested in showing that Luther had these ideas, that the Lutheran Confessions picked them up, and that the FC should accept them.

13. Chemnitz, *Iudicium,* 1561.

14. Friedrich Bente, ed., *Concordia Triglotta, The Symbolical Books of the Ev. Lutheran Chuch* (St. Louis: Concordia, 1921), 205, 207; Cf. also p. 23b of Chemnitz' *De Caute Sentiendi.*

15. See Apol. 4.305–307, Tappert, 154, or Apol. 3.184–86, Bente, 205–207. (Bente preserves the use of the term "forensic" which Tappert does not.)

16. Elert, 104–5.

17. The use of the exclusive particle, of course, goes back to Luther himself, see his Lectures on Genesis 15, in *Luther's Works,* American Edition 3:24–25, which Chemnitz cites in the *ECT,* vol. 1, 585 and in the *LT,* vol. 2, 544, and it becomes a confessional matter as early as 1531 in the Apol, 4.77–78, Tappert, 117, where Melanchthon says, "We obtain the forgiveness of sins only by faith in Christ. . . . Therefore we are justified by faith alone. . . ." Andreae in Epitome 3.10, Tappert, 474, makes special reference to the *particulas exclusivas*; and the SD in 3.7, Tappert, 540, says, "Therefore he [Paul] stresses the exclusive terms, that is, the terms by which all human works are excluded. . . ." The next several paragraphs continue this point. Also see SD 3.36, 43, 53, and 4.2, Tappert 545, 547, 548, 551.

18. Chemnitz, *Formulae recte sentiendi . . ., (De Caute Sentiendi)* (1575), 22–23.

19. *ECT,* vol. 1, 585; Cf. *Luther's Works,* American Edition 3:24–25.

20. See Rune Söderlund, *Ex praevisa fide, Zum Verständnis der Prädestinationslehre in der lutherischen Orthodoxie,* Arbeiten zur Geschichte und Theologie des Luthertums, New Series, vol. 3, eds. Bengt Hägglund and Heinrich Kraft (Hannover, Lutherisches Verlagshaus, 1983).

21. From a private conversation with Robert Kolb.

Epilog

1. D. Georg Williams, "A New Edition of Martin Chemnitz's 'A Substantial and Godly Exposition of the Prayer Commonly Called the Lord's Prayer,'" unpublished STM thesis, Concordia Theological Seminary, Ft. Wayne, Indiana, 1982.

2. Theodor Mahlmann, "Bibliographie Martin Chemnitz," in *Der zweite Martin der Lutherischen Kirche,* ed. Wolfgang A. Jünke (Braunschweig: Ev.-luth. Stadtkirchenverband und Propstei Braunschweig, 1986), 419–20.

3. Williams, 15–16.

4. Ibid., 19.

5. Ibid., 22–24.

6. Ibid., 27–33.

7. Ibid., 38–39.

8. Ibid., 43–47.

9. Ibid., 48.

10. Ibid., 48–50.

11. Ibid., 52.

12. Ibid., 64.

13. Ibid., 68.

14. Ibid., 70–71.

15. Ibid., 72–73.

16. Ibid., 75–80.

17. Ibid., 75.

18. Ibid., 76–77.

19. Ibid., 79–80.

20. Ibid., 92.

21. Ibid.

22. Ibid., 101.

23. Chemnitz, *The Lord's Supper,* trans. J. A. O. Preus (St. Louis: Concordia, 1979), 187, 191–92.

24. Chemnitz, *The Two Natures in Christ,* trans. J. A. O. Preus (St. Louis: Concordia, 1971), 51.

25. Chemnitz, *Ministry, Word, and Sacraments: An Enchiridion,* trans. Luther Poellot (St. Louis: Concordia, 1981), 112–20.

26. Theodor Pressel, *Martin Chemnitz. Nach gleichzeitigen Quellen,* Leben und ausgewählte Schriften der Väter und Begründer der lutherischen Kirche, vol. 8, eds. J. Hartmann et al. (Elberfeld: R. L. Friderichs, 1862), 70–71.

27. Friedrich Bente, *Historical Introductions to the Book of Concord* (St. Louis: Concordia, 1965), 247–256; C. F. W. Walther in an excellent series of articles prepared for the 300th anniversary of the adoption of the FC, 1877 (see "Vorwort zu Jahrgang 1877," *Lehre und Wehre* 23, nos. 1-2-3 (1877): 1–5, 33–54, 65–76, English translation Everette Meier, 1990); Theodore E. Schmauck and C. Theodore Benze, *The Confessional Principle and the Confessions of the Lutheran Church as Embodying the Evangelical Confession of the Christian Church* (Philadelphia: General Council Publication Board, 1911), 700–45; and

NOTES

Arnold J. Koelpin, *No Other Gospel: Essays in Commemoration of the 400th Anniversary of the Formula of Concord 1580–1980* (Milwaukee: Northwestern Publishing House, 1980) (note particularly Seth Erlandsson, "The Formula of Concord in the History of Swedish Lutheranism," 67–102, on the ultimate adoption of the FC in Sweden); together with many others, all tell the story of the adoption of the FC, the hindrances placed in its way, the political struggles, and the ultimate, almost complete acceptance in Lutheran Germany.

28. While Heshusius had for years been oppposed to the ubiquity emphasis which had been injected into the FC by Andreae and the Swabians, Walther cites several expressions from Heshusius in which prior to Duke Julius's quarrel with Chemnitz he had heartily endorsed the document, Swabians and all (See Walther, Meier translation p. 11).

29. Erlandsson, 78–80.

30. Trygve R. Skarsten, "The Reaction in Scandinavia," in *Discord, Dialogue, and Concord*, eds. Lewis W. Spitz and Wenzel Lohff (Philadelphia: Fortress, 1977), p. 136ff.

31. Ibid., 149.

32. Polycarp Leyser, "Introduction to the *Iudicium* of Chemnitz."

33. Jaroslav Pelikan, *The Riddle of Roman Catholicism* (Nashville: Abingdon Press, 1952), 52.

34. Jaroslav Pelikan, *Obedient Rebels: Catholic Substance and Protestant Principle in Luther's Reformation* (New York: Harper and Row, Publishers, 1964), 50–51.

35. Jaroslav Pelikan, *The Development of Christian Doctrine: Some Historical Prolegomena* (New Haven: Yale University Press, 1969), 220.

36. Pauck, *The Heritage of the Reformation*, 161.

37. Pelikan, *The Christian Tradition: A History of the Development of Doctrine*, vol. 4, "Reformation of Church and Dogma (1300–1700)" (Chicago: The University of Chicago Press, 1984), 162.

38. The conference at Quedlinburg was called by the three Lutheran electors (Dec. 1582–Jan. 1583) to finalize arrangements regarding the FC, to defend it against accusations that only six men had participated in its production, and to work on the so-called Apology or Defense of the FC; see Schmauck, 663–64 and 838.

39. While it is known that Heshusius, who was now at Helmstedt, had always had problems with ubiquity, we must balance off this fact against his previous complimentary remarks about the FC, and also the fact that he was now very much under the influence of Duke Julius. It ought also to be said before we close that the quarrel with Duke Julius never really died, even though at the end Julius gave his consent to the FC. But the way in which the University of Helmstedt was established put all power into the hands of the Duke, whose son, Heinrich Julius, became the first official rector at the time the school was opened. Heinrich Julius after the death of his father and after the firing of Timothy Kirchner came under the influence of a more serious opponent of Chemnitz and Kirchner than Heshusius, the rascally Daniel Hofmann. Hofmann was a strong opponent not only of Chemnitz, but he was even more of a Melanchthonian for his use of philosophy, and he tilted the school in that direction, so that when the greatest syncretist of them all, Georg Calix-

tus, began his unionizing endeavors about 1615 to get together with both Rome and the Reformed, he was compared with Melanchthon. See Hans-Walter Krumwiede, *Zur Entstehung des landesherrlichen Kirchenregiments in Kursachsen und Braunschweig-Wolfenbüttel,* Studien zur Kirchengeschichte Niedersachsens, vol. 16, ed. Hans-Walter Krumwiede (Göttingen: Vandenhoeck and Rupprecht, 1967), 260.

42. *Fortgesetzte Sammlung von alten und neuen theologischen Sachen,* 1737, Beytrag. Altes, p 132–36, Leip., p. 22.

43. For reference to his will see Pressel, 71–73; Inge Mager, "Erbe und Auftage nach dem Testament von Martin Chemnitz," in *Der zweite Martin der Lutherischen Kirche,* ed. Wolfgang A. Jünke (Braunschweig: Ev.-luth. Stadtkirchenverband und Propstei Braunschweig, 1986), 148–71.

44. Inge Mager, "'Ich habe dich zum Wächter gesetzt über das Haus Israel': Zum Amstverständnis des Braunschweiger Stadtsuperintendenten und Wolfenbüttelschen Kirchenrats Martin Chemniz," *Braunschweigisches Jahrbuch* 69 (1988): 57–61, 66–69.

45. Chemnitz, "Will," in Pressel, 71.

46. Rettung (see p. 504)

47. For a description of his family tree and posterity see Margarete Staude, "Einige bedeutsame Nachkommen der Familie Chemnitz," in *Der zweite Martin der Lutherischen Kirche,* ed. Wolfgang A. Jünke (Braunschweig: Ev.-luth. Stadtkirchenverband und Propstei Braunschweig, 1986), 328–52.

Bibliography

We shall put in parentheses the name by which an author/title shall appear in the body of this text.

I. PRIMARY SOURCES

Rather than print a full list of the some 79 items listed in Mahlmann's (Mahlmann) bibliography, I shall simply refer the reader to this work of Mahlmann which is included in Wolfgang Jünke's *Der zweite Martin der Lutherischen Kirche*, Ev.–luth. Stadtkirchenverband und Propstei Braunschweig, 1986, p. 368–425, (Jünke), where every work, except presumably those in which Chemnitz was only a partial author, as, for example, the FC, is listed. This bibliography is particularly valuable in that it contains Mahlmann's helpful descriptions of the works, their chronological date of publication, and remarks to identify the contents of the works. It also includes translations.

Another large but incomplete bibliography has been prepared by Georg Williams and placed on file in the libraries of Concordia Seminary, St. Louis and Concordia Theological Seminary, Ft. Wayne.

II. SECONDARY SOURCES

A. Biographical

Adam, M. "Martinus Chemnitius." In *Vitae Germanorum Theologorum.* . . . Frankfurt: J. Rosae, 1620. (Adam)

Baur, Jörg. "Martin Chemnitz." In *Einsicht und Glaube: Aufsätze*, 154–72. Göttingen: Vandenhoeck und Ruprecht, 1978.

————. "Martin Chemnitz, Luthertum und Bilderfrage im Fürstentum Braunschweig–Wolfenbüttel und in der Stadt Braunschweig in Reformationsjahrhundert." *Jahrbuch der Gesellschaft für niedersächsische Kirchengeschichte* 67 (1969): 7–23.

Chemnitius, Günter. "Eine Theorie zur Entstehung des Namens Chemnitz." In *Der zweite Martin der Lutherischen Kirchen*, ed. Wolfgang A.

Jünke, 253–58. Braunschweig: Ev.-luth. Stadtkirchenverband und
Propstei Braunschweig, 1986.

Chemnitz, Martin. *An Autobiography of Martin Chemnitz.* The original German of this autobiography may be found in Rehtmeyer, vol. 4, part 8.1,
p. 273 ff. An English translation of this by A. L. Graebner is found in
the *Theological Quarterly* 3, no. 4 (October 1899): 472–87. The work
seems to have been written in 1555, but a few additions are made at
the end, listing the births and deaths of his children, with the last entry
of 1579. (Autobiography)

Gasmer, J. *De Vita, Studiis, et Obitu Reverendi, et Clarissimi Viri D. Martini Chemnitii* . . . Braunschweig: n.p., 1588. (Gasmer)

Hachfeld, Hermann. *Martin Chemnitz nach Seinem Leben und Wirken,
insbesondere Nach Seinem Verhältnisse zum Tridentinum.* Leipzig:
Breitkopf and Härtel, 1867.

Jünke, Wolfgang A. "Martin Chemnitz, Bischof der Stadt Braunschweig."
In *Der zweite Martin der Lutherischen Kirche,* ed. Wolfgang A. Jünke,
283–327. Braunschweig: Ev.-luth. Stadtkirchenverband und Propstei
Braunschweig, 1986.

———. "Zum 400. Todestag von Martin Chemnitz." *Diakrisis* (May 1986):
63–64.

Koch, Ernst. "Solange er lebte, lebte er Christus—Bemerkungen zu eini-
gen Portraits von Martin Chemnitz." In *Der zweite Martin der
Lutherischen Kirche,* ed. Wolfgang A. Jünke, 130–45. Braunschweig:
Ev.-luth. Stadtkirchenverband und Propstei Braunschweig, 1986.

Kramer, F. "Martin Chemnitz." In *Shapers of Tradition in Germany, Switzer-
land, and Poland, 1560–1600,* edited and with an introduction by Jill
Raitt. Foreword by Robert M. Kingdom. New Haven: Yale University
Press, 1981.

Kunze, J. "Chemnitz, Martin." In *Realenzyklopädie für protestantische Theologie und Kirche,* 3d edition, ed. J. J. Herzog, vol. 3, 796–804. Leipzig:
1896–1913.

Lentz, C. G. H. *Dr. Martin Chemnitz, Stadtsuperintendent in Braunschweig. Ein Lebensbild aus dem 16 Nachrichten.* Gotha: Friedrich
Andreas Perthes, 1866. (Lentz)

Mager, Inge. "'Ich habe dich zum Wächter gesetzt über das Haus Israel':
zum Amtsverständnis des Braunschweiger Stadtsuperintendenten und
Wolfenbüttelschen Kirchenrats Martin Chemnitz." *Braunschweigisches
Jahrbuch* 69 (1988): 57–69.

———. "Das Testament des Braunschweiger Stadts Superintendenten Martin Chemnitz (1522–1586)." *Braunschweigisches Jahrbuch* 68 (1987):
121–32. (Mager Testament)

BIBLIOGRAPHY

Mahlmann, Theodor. "Chemnitz, Martin." In *Theologische Realenzyklo-pädie*, vol. 7. Berlin: Walter de Gruyter, 714–21.

Müller, G. "Martin Chemnitz (1522–1586). Ein Reformator der Zweiten Generation." *Lutherjahrbuch* 57 (1986): 119–27.

Müller, John Theodore. "Der 'andere Martin' und seine hohe Bedeutung für uns lutherische Theologen in Amerika." *Concordia Theological Monthly* 7, no. 9 (September 1936): 661–70.

Preachers of Braunschweig. *Rettung der Ehren des Glaubens und Bekenntnis des weiland Ehrwürdigen und Hochgelarten Herrn Martini Chemnitii . . . Welcher unverschampt und lugenhafft in offenem Truck von einem freuelbosen Menschen gelestert worden als wenn er für seinem Ende von seiner Bekentnuss abgefallen were.* Braunschweig: Gestellet und publiciret von den Predigern der Loblichen Stadt, 1592. (Rettung)

Pressel, Theodor. *Martin Chemnitz. Nach Gleichzeiten Quelle.* Leben und Ausgewählte Schriften der Väter und Begründer der lutherischen Kirche, vol. 8, eds. J. Hartmann et al. Elberfeld: R. L. Friderichs, 1862. (Pressel)

Preuss, F. R. Eduard. "Vita Martini Chemnicii." In *Examen Concilii Tridentini . . .*, 925–58. Berlin: Gustav Schlawitz, 1861. (Preuss)

Staude, Margarete. "Einige bedeutsame Nachkommen der Familiae Chemnitz." In *Der zweite Martin der Lutherischen Kirche*, ed. Wolfgang A. Jünke, 328–52. Braunschweig: Ev.-luth. Stadtkirchenverband und Propstei Braunschweig, 1986.

Volk, E. "Der Andere Martin. Eine Erinnerung an der lutherischen Theologen Martin Chemnitz." *Lutherische Theologie und Kirche* 10 (1986): 81–95, 145–55; 11 (1987): 16–23.

B. Background in German Ecclesiastical History and Theology

Adam, M. "Martinus Chemnitius." In *Vitae Germanorum Theologorum. . . .* Frankfurt: J. Rosae, 1620. (Adam)

Barton, Peter F. *Um Luther's Erbe: Studien und Texte zur Spätreformation, Tilemann Hesbusius (1527–59).* Untersuchungen zur Kirchengeschichte, vol. 6. Witten: Luther–Verlag, 1972.

Bertram, J. Georg. *Der evangelische Lüneburg oder Reformations–und–Kirchen–Historie der Alt–berühmten Stadt Lüneburg.* Braunschweig: Schröder, 1719. (Bertram)

Beste, Johannes. *Geschichte der Braunschweig Landeskirche von der Reformation bis auf unsere Tage.* Wolfenbüttel: n.p., 1889. (Beste)

Bornkamm, Heinrich. *Luther's World of Thought.* Trans. Martin H. Bertram. St. Louis: Concordia, 1958.

Brecht, Martin. *Martin Luther.* 3 vols. Trans. James L. Schaff. Minneapolis: Augsburg Fortress, 1985–1993.

Caemmerer, Richard R. "The Melanchthonian Blight." *Concordia Theological Monthly* 18 (May 1947): 321–38.

Dedeken, Georg. *Thesauri Consiliorum et Decisionum . . . .* 3 vols. Jena: Zachariah Hertels, 1671. (Deddeken)

Dorner, Isaak A. *A History of the Development of the Doctrine of the Person of Christ.* 5 vols. Trans. William L. Alexander and D. W. Simon. Clark's Foreign Theological Library, 3d. ser., vols. 10, 11, 14, 15, 18. Edinburgh: T. and T. Clark, 1863–1878.

Drummond, Andrew L. *German Protestantism Since Luther.* London: The Epworth Press, 1951.

Durant, Will. *The Reformation, A History of European Civilization from Wyclif to Calvin: 1300–1564.* The Story of Civilization, vol. 4. New York: Simon and Schuster, 1957.

Edwards, Mark U. *Luther's Last Battles: Politics and Polemics, 1531–46.* Ithaca, NY: Cornell University Press, 1983. See also his "Luther's Last Battles." *Concordia Theological Quarterly* 48, nos. 2 and 3 (April–July 1984): 125–40.

Elert, Werner. *Eucharist and Church Fellowship in the First Four Centuries.* Trans. Norman E. Nagel. St. Louis: Concordia, 1966.

——— . *The Structure of Lutheranism.* Trans. Walter A. Hansen. St. Louis: Concordia, 1962. (Elert)

Estes, James M. *Christian Magistrate and State Church: The Reforming Career of Johannes Brenz.* Toronto: University of Toronto Press, 1982.

Fagerberg, Holsten. *A New Look at the Lutheran Confessions (1529–1537).* Trans. Gene J. Lund. St. Louis: Concordia, 1972. (Fagerberg)

Fleischer, Manfred P. "Melanchthon as Praeceptor of Late-Humanist Poetry." *The Sixteenth Century Journal* 20 (Winter 1989): 559–80 [editor unknown]. *Forgesetzte Sammlung von alten und neuen theologischen Sachbern.* 1737. Many letters to and from Chemnitz are contained in this collection.

Fraenkel, Peter. *Testimonia Patrum: The Function of the Patristic Argument in the Theology of Philip Melanchthon.* Travaux D'Humanisme et Renaissance, vol. 46. Geneva: E. Broz, 1961. (Fraenkel)

Gerhard, Johann. *Loci Theologici.* 10 vols. Ed. F. R. Eduard Preuss. Berlin: Gustav Schlawitz, 1863–1885.

BIBLIOGRAPHY

Green, Lowell C. "Melanchthon, Philipp." In *The Encyclopedia of the Lutheran Church*, vol. 2, ed. Julius Bodensieck, 1517–27. Minneapolis: Augsburg, 1965.

Hägglund, Bengt. *History of Theology*. Trans. Gene J. Lund. St. Louis: Concordia, 1968. (Hägglund)

Hartknock, Christoph. *Preussische Kirchen Historie*. Frankfurt am Main: Simon Beckenstein, 1686.

Hauschild, Wolf–Dieter. "Corpus Doctrinae und Bekenntnisschriften." In *Bekenntnis und Einheit der Kirche: Studien zum Konkordienbuch*, eds. Martin Brecht and Reinhard Schwarz, 235–52. Stuttgart: Calwer Verlag, 1980. (Brecht–Schwarz)

————. "Zum Kampf gegen das Augsburger Interim in norddeutschen Hansestädten." *Zeitschrift für Kirchengeschichte* 84 (1973): 60–81.

Hutter, Leonhard. *Compendium Locorum Theologoricum*. Ed. Wolfgang Trillhaas. Kleine Texte für Vorlesungen und Übungen, ed. Kurt Aland, no. 183. Berlin: Walter de Gruyter and Co., 1961.

Kittelson, James M. *Luther the Reformer: The Study of the Man and His Career*. Minneapolis: Augsburg, 1986. (Kittelson)

Kolb, Robert. "Dynamics of Party Conflict in the Saxon Late Reformation: Gnesio-Lutherans vs. Philippists." *The Journal of Modern History Supplement* 49, no. 3 (1977): D 1289ff.

————. "Martin Chemnitz, Gnesio–Lutheraner." In *Der zweite Martin der Lutherischen Kirche*, ed. Wolfgang A. Jünke, 115–29. Braunschweig: Ev.-luth. Stadtkirchenverband und Propstei Braunschweig, 1986. (Kolb)

————. "Mathaes Judex's Condemnation of Princely Censorship of Theologians' Publications." *Church History* 50 (1981): 401–14.

————. *Nikolaus von Amsdorf (1483–1565)*. Nieuwkoop: B. DeGraaf, 1978.

Koldewey, Friedrich, ed. "Neun bisher nicht gedruckte Briefe Melanthons über und an Martin Kemnitz." *Zeitschrift für die historische Theologie* 36, no. 1 (1872): 3–23.

Krauth, Charles Porterfield. *The Conservative Reformation and its Theology: As Represented in the Augsburg Confession, and in the History and Literature of the Evangelical Lutheran Church*. Philadelphia: J. B. Lippincott, 1871. (Krauth)

Kronenberg, Kurt. "Die Reformation im Lande Braunschweig." In *Vier Jahrhunderte Lutherische Landeskirche in Braunschweig, Festschrift*, ed. Landeskirchenamt Wolfenbüttel, 8–32. Braunschweig: Georg Westermann, 1968. (Kronenberg)

Krumwiede, Hans–Walter. *Zur Entstehung des landesherrlichen Kirchenregimentes in Kursachsen und Braunschweig-Wolfenbüttel. Studien zur Kirchengeschichte Niedersachsens, vol. 16, ed. Hans–Walter Krumwiede. Göttingen: Vandenhoeck and Ruprecht, 1967.

———. "Vom reformatorischen Glauben Luthers zur Orthodoxie, Theologische Bemerkungen zu Bugenhagens Braunschweiger Kirchenordnung und zu Urbanus Rhegius formulae quaedam caute et citra scandalum loquendi." Jahrbuch der Gesellschaft für Niedersächsische Kirchengeschichte 52 (1955): n.p.

Lentz, C. G. H. Dr. Martin Chemnitz, Stadtsuperintendent in Braunschweig. Ein Lebensbild aus dem 16 Nachrichten. Gotha: Friedrich Andreas Perthes, 1866. (Lentz)

Mackinnon, James. Luther and the Reformation. 4 vols. London: Longmans, Green, and Co., 1925–1930.

Mager, Inge. "Erbe und Auftrag nach dem Testament von Martin Chemnitz." In Der zweite Martin der Lutherischen Kirche, ed. Wolfgang A. Jünke, 146–71. Braunschweig: Ev.-luth. Stadtkirchenverband und Propstei Braunschweig, 1986. (Auftrag)

Mahlmann, Theodor. "Martin Chemnitz." In Gestalten der Kirchengeschichte, vol. 6, "Die Reformationszeit II," ed. Martin Greschat, 315–31. Stuttgart: W. Kohlhammer, 1981.

Melanchthon, Philipp. Epistolae, Iudicia, Concilia, Testimonia Aliorumque ad Eum Epistulae quae in Corpore Reformatorum desiderantur. Reprint of 1874 edition. Ed. Heinrich E. Bindseil. New York: G. Olms, 1975.

———. Loci Communes, 1521. Trans. Charles Leander Hill. Boston: Meador Publishing Company, 1944.

———. Loci Communes, 1543. Trans. J. A. O. Preus. St. Louis: Concordia, 1992.

———. Melanchthon on Christian Doctrine: Loci Communes, 1555. Trans. and ed. Clyde L. Manschreck. New York: Oxford University Press, 1965.

———. Melanchthon Selected Writings. Trans. Charles Leander Hill. Eds. Elmer E. Flack and Lowell J. Satre. Minneapolis: Augsburg, 1962.

Noth, Gottfried. Grundzüge der Theologie des Martin Chemnitz. Erlangen: [s.n.], 1930.

Olivier, Daniel. Luther's Faith: The Cause of the Gospel in the Church. Trans. John Tonkin. St. Louis: Concordia, 1982.

Pauck, Wilhelm. The Heritage of the Reformation. Rev. ed. Glencoe, IL: Free Press of Glencoe, Inc., 1961. (Pauck)

Pelikan, Jaroslav. The Christian Tradition: A History of the Development of Doctrine. Vol. 2, "The Spirit of Eastern Christendom (600–1700)," vol. 4, "Reformation of Church and Dogma (1300–1700)." Chicago: The University of Chicago Press, 1984.

BIBLIOGRAPHY

———. *From Luther to Kierkegaard: A Study in the History of Theology.* St. Louis: Concordia, 1950. (Luther to Kierkegaard)

———. *Obedient Rebels: Catholic Substance and Protestant Principle in Luther's Reformation.* New York: Harper and Row, Publishers, 1964. (Rebels)

Peterson, Luther D. *The Philippist Theologians and the Interims of 1548: Soteriological, Ecclesiastical, and Liturgical Compromises and Controversies within German Lutheranism.* Ph.D. diss., University of Wisconsin, 1974.

Petersen, W., et al. "1985 Bethany Lutheran College Reformation Lectures." In *The Lutheran Synod Quarterly* 25, no. 4 (December 1985): 1–7 [Wilhelm Petersen. "A Biographical Sketch of the Life of Martin Chemnitz 1522–1586."]; 8–35 [Eugene F. Klug. "Chemnitz and Authority."]; 38–86 [J. A. O. Preus. "Martin Chemnitz on the Doctrine of Justification."]

Pieper, Francis. *Christian Dogmatics.* 3 vols. Trans. Theodore Engelder and John Theodore Mueller. St. Louis: Concordia, 1950–1953. (Pieper)

Plass, Ewald M. *What Luther Says: An Anthology.* 3 vols. St. Louis: Concordia, 1959.

Preus, J. A. O. "Chemnitz and the Book of Concord." *Concordia Theological Quarterly* 44, no. 1 (October 1980): 200–212.

———. "The Use of the Church Fathers in the Formula of Concord." *Concordia Theological Quarterly* 48, nos. 2 and 3 (April–July 1984): 97–112.

Preus, Robert D. *The Theology of Post-Reformation Lutheranism.* Vol. 1, "A Study of Theological Prolegomena." vol. 2, "God and His Creation." St. Louis: Concordia, 1970–1972. (Prolegomena)

Rehtmeyer, Philip J. *Antiquitates Ecclesiasticae Inclytae Urbis Brunsvigae, oder, Der berühmten Stadt Braunschweig Kirchen-Historie.* Chapter 8 of Part 3, 273–536. Braunschweig: Christoph Friedrich Zilligers, 1710. (Rehtmeyer)

Reller, Horst. "Die Auseinandersetzung zwischen Herzog Heinrich d.J. und Herzog Julius von Braunschweig-Lüneberg in den Jahren 1553–1568." *Jahrbuch der Gesellschaft für niedersächsische Kirchengeschichte* 67 (1969): 91–106.

Ritter, Annelies. "Über die Lehrschriften in den Fürstentümern Wolfenbüttel und Lüneburg am Ende des 16 Jahrhunderts." *Jahrbuch der Gesellschaft für Niedersächsische Kirchengeschichte* 50 (1952): 82–95.

Roensch, Manfred. "Die Kontrovers–theologische Bedeutung des Examen Concilii Tridentini von Martin Chemnitz." In *Der zweite Martin der Lutherischen Kirche.* ed. Wolfgang A. Jünke, 190–200. Braunschweig: Ev.-luth. Stadtkirchenverband und Propstei Braunschweig, 1986.

THE SECOND MARTIN

Rogness, Michael. *Philip Melanchthon: Reformer Without Honor.* Minneapolis: Augsburg, 1969. (Rogness)

Rupp, E. Gordon. "The Old Man Luther." *Baptist Quarterly* 32, Supplement, "Faith, Heritage and Witness," ed. J. H. Y. Briggs (1987): 21–33.

Saarnivaara, Uuras. *Luther Discovers the Gospel: New Light upon Luther's Way from Medieval Catholicism to Evangelical Faith.* St. Louis: Concordia, 1951.

Sandys, J. E. *A Short History of Classical Scholarship.* Cambridge: n.p., 1915.

Schaff, Philip. *The Creeds of Christendom.* 3 vols. New York: Harper and Brothers, Publishers, 1919.

Schmauck, Theodore Emanuel, and C. Theodore Benze. *The Confessional Principle and the Confessions of the Lutheran Church as Embodying the Evangelical Confession of the Christian Church.* Philadelphia: General Council Publication Board, 1911. (Schmauck)

Schorn–Schütte, Luise. "'Papocaesarismus' der Theologen? Von Amt des evangelischen Pfarrers in der Frühneuzeitlichen Stadtgesellschaft bei Bugenhagen." *Archiv für Reformationsgeschichte* 79 (1988): 230–61.

Schwarz, Reinhard. "Lehrnorm und Lehrkontinuität. Das Selbstverständnis der lutherischen Bekenntnisschriften." In *Bekenntnis und Einheit der Kirche: Studien zum Konkordienbuch,* eds. Martin Brecht and Reinhard Schwarz, 253–69. Stuttgart: Calwer Verlag, 1980.

Schwiebert, Ernest G. *Luther and His Times.* St. Louis: Concordia, 1950.

Seeberg, Reinhold. *Text-Book of the History of Doctrines.* 2 vols. Trans. Charles E. Hay. Grand Rapids, Michigan: Baker Book House, 1952.

Sehling, Emil, ed. *Die Evangelische Kirchenordnungen des XVI Jahrhunderts.* Vol. 6.1, "Niedersachsen." Tübingen: J. C. B. Mohr [Paul Siebeck], 1955.

Spiess, Werner. *Geschichte der Stadt Braunschweig im Nachmittelalter.* Braunschweig: 1966.

Stupperich, Robert. *Der Unbekannte Melanchthon: Wirken und Denken des Praeceptor Germaniae in neuer Sicht.* Stuttgart: W. Kohlhammer, 1961. (Stupperich)

Volkmann, Rolf. "Martin Chemnitz und die Gründung der Universität Helmstedt." In *Der zweite Martin der Lutherischen Kirche,* ed. Wolfgang A. Jünke, 353–67. Braunschweig: Ev.–luth. Stadtkirchenverband und Propstei Braunschweig, 1986.

Wengert, Timothy J. "Casper Cruciger (1504–1548): The Case of the Disappearing Reformer." *The Sixteenth Century Journal* 20 (1989): 417–41.

C. Confessional Involvements

1. Confessions in General and Book of Concord

Bohlmann, Ralph A. *The Principles of Biblical Interpretation in the Lutheran Confessions.* St. Louis: Concordia, 1983.

Die Bekenntnisschriften der evangelisch–lutherischen Kirche. Göttingen: Vandenhoeck and Rupprecht, 1986.

The Book of Concord: The Confessions of the Evangelical Lutheran Church. Trans. and ed. Theodore G. Tappert. Philadelphia: Fortress, 1959. (Tappert)

Burgess, Joseph A., ed. *The Role of the Augsburg Confession: Catholic and Lutheran Views.* Philadelphia: Fortress, 1980.

Concordia Triglotta. The Symbolical Books of the Evangelical Lutheran Church. Ed. and Historical Introductions by Friedrich Bente. St. Louis: Concordia, 1921. (Bente HI)

Daniel, David P., and Charles P. Arand. "A Bibliography of the Lutheran Confessions." *Sixteenth Century Bibliography.* Vol. 28. St. Louis: Center for Reformation Research, 1988.

Fagerberg, Holsten. *A New Look at the Lutheran Confessions (1529–1537).* Trans. Gene J. Lund. St. Louis: Concordia, 1972. (Fagerberg)

Forell, George Wolfgang, and James F. McCue, eds. *A Joint Commentary on the Augsburg Confession by Lutheran and Catholic Theologians.* Minneapolis: Augsburg, 1982.

Grane, Leif. *The Augsburg Confession: A Commentary.* Trans. John H. Rasmussen. Minneapolis: Augsburg, 1981. (Grane)

Hutter, Leonhard. *Concordia Concors: De Origine und Progressu Formulae Concordiae Ecclesiarum Confessionis Augustanae, ...* Frankfurt: J. Christopher Föllginer, 1690.

Johannsen, J. C. G. "Die Unterschrift der Concordienformel in Sachsen." *Zeitschrift für die Historische Theologie* 17, no. 1 (1847): 3–69.

Mager, Inge. "Aufnahme und Ablehnung des Konkordienbuches in Nord–, Mittel– und Ostdeutschland." In *Bekenntnis und Einheit der Kirche: Studien zum Konkordienbuch,* eds. Martin Brecht and Reinhard Schwarz, 271–302. Stuttgart: Calwer Verlag, 1980.

Maurer, Wilhelm. *Historical Commentary on the Augsburg Confession.* Trans. H. George Anderson. Philadelphia: Fortress, 1986. (Maurer)

Müller, Gerhard. "Alliance and Confession: The Theological-Historical Development and Ecclesiastical-Political Significance of Reformation Confessions." Trans. Herbert J. A. Bouman. *The Sixteenth Century Journal* 8, no. 4 (1977): 123–40.

388

THE SECOND MARTIN

Schlink, Edmund. *Theology of the Lutheran Confessions*. Trans. Paul F. Koehneke and Herbert J. A. Bouman. Philadelphia: Muhlenberg, 1961. (Schlink)

Wallman, Johannes. "Die Rolle der Bekenntnisschriften." In *Bekenntnis und Einheit der Kirche: Studien zum Konkordienbuch*, eds. Martin Brecht and Reinhard Schwarz, 381-91. Stuttgart: Calwer Verlag, 1980.

2. Formula of Concord

Brandy, Hans C. "Jakob Andreaes Fünf Artikel von 1568/69." *Zeitschrift für Kirchengeschichte* 98 (1987): 338-51.

Daniel, David P. "The Acceptance of the Formula of Concord in Slovakia." *Archiv für Reformationsgeschichte* 70 (1979): 260-76.

Ebel, Jobst. "Die Herkunft des Konzeptes der Konkordienformel." *Zeitschrift für Kirchengeschichte* 91, no. 1 (1980): 237-81. (Ebel Herkunft)

———. "Jacob Andreae (1528-1590) als Verfasser der Konkordienformel." *Zeitschrift für Kirchengeschichte* 89 (1978): 78-119. (Ebel Verfasser)

Fritschel, George J. *The Formula of Concord, Its Origin and Contents: A Contribution to Symbolics*. Philadelphia: The Lutheran Publication Society, 1916.

Gensichen, Hans-Werner. *We Condemn: How Luther and 16th-Century Lutheranism Condemned False Doctrine*. Trans. Herbert J. A. Bouman. St. Louis: Concordia, 1967. (Gensichen)

Hägglund, Bengt. *History of Theology*. Trans. Gene J. Lund. St. Louis: Concordia, 1968. (Hägglund)

Hauschild, Wolf-Dieter. "Corpora Doctrinae und Bekenntnisschriften. Zur Vorgeschichte des Konkordienbuches." In *Bekenntnis und Einheit der Kirche: Studien zum Konkordienbuch*, eds. Martin Brecht and Reinhard Schwarz, 235-51. Stuttgart: Calwer Verlag, 1980.

Heppe, Heinrich L. J. *Geschichte der lutherischen Concordienformel und Concordie*. Marburg: Elwert'sche Universitäts Buchhandlung, 1857.

Jungkuntz, Theodore R. *Formulators of the Formula of Concord*. St Louis: Concordia, 1977. (Jungkuntz)

Kingdom, Robert M., ed. "The Formula of Concord Quadricentennial Essays." In *The Sixteenth Century Journal* 8, no. 4 (1977): 1-140.

Klug, Eugene F. *Getting into the Formula of Concord: A History and Digest of the Formula*. Epitome translated by Otto F. Stahlke. St. Louis: Concordia, 1977.

Koch, Ernst. "Striving for the Union of Lutheran Churches: The Church-Historical Background of the Work Done on the Formula of Concord at Magdeburg." *The Sixteenth Century Journal* 8, no. 4 (1977): 105-21.

BIBLIOGRAPHY

———. "Der Weg zur Konkordienformel." *Fuldaer Hefte* 24, "Vom Dis-
sensus zum Konsensus: Die Formula Concordiae von 1577" (1980):
10–46.

Koelpin, Arnold J., ed. *No Other Gospel: Essays in Commemoration of the
400th Anniversary of the Formula of Concord 1580–1980*. Milwaukee: Northwestern, 1980. (Koelpin)

Kolb, Robert. "Jakob Andreae 1528–1590." In *Shapers of Tradition in Germany, Switzerland, and Poland, 1560–1600*, edited and with an
introduction by Jill Raitt, p. 53ff. Foreword by Robert M. Kingdom. New
Haven: Yale University Press, 1981.

———. *Andreae and the Formula of Concord: Six Sermons on the Way to
Lutheran Unity*. St. Louis: Concordia, 1977.

———. *Confessing the Faith: Reformers Define the Church, 1530–1580*.
St. Louis: Concordia, 1991.

Lohff, Wenzel, and Lewis W. Spitz. *Widerspruch, Dialog and Einigung:
Studien zur Konkordienformel der Lutherischen Reformation*. Stuttgart:
Calwer Verlag, 1977. All of the essays in this volume are of particular
interest to this treatise. Also interesting is the English companion volume:

———. *Discord, Dialogue, and Concord: Studies in the Lutheran Reformation's Formula of Concord*. Philadelphia: Fortress, 1977. Nearly all
of the essays are relevant.

Lohse, Bernhard. "Das Konkordienwerk von 1580." *Kirche und Bekenntnis*. Wiesbaden: GMBH, 1980, 194–222.

Mager, Inge. *Die Konkordienformel im Braunschweig–Wolfenbüttel. Die
Entstehung–Rezeption–Geltung*. Theol. Habil. Göttingen, 1986. This
work is noteworthy not only for its very complete history of the treatment of the FC in the duchy of Braunschweig–Wolfenbüttel, and also
for its very helpful footnotes and its list of sources and related literature and also for its chronological table of pertinent letters and publications, which surpass anything I have seen in this area.

Mager, Inge. *Die Konkordienformel im Fürstentum Braunschweig–Wolfenbüttel*. Göttingen: Vandenhoeck & Ruprecht, 1993. A major work,
which unfortunately arrived too late to be included in this study.

Neve, Juergen L. *A History of Christian Thought*. Vol. 1. Philadelphia: The
United Lutheran Publication House, 1943. (Neve)

Preus, Robert D. *Getting into the Theology of Concord: A Study of the Book
of Concord*. St. Louis: Concordia, 1977.

Preus, Robert D., and Wilbert Rosin, eds. *A Contemporary Look at the Formula of Concord*. St. Louis: Concordia, 1978. (Preus–Rosin)

Scaer, David P. *Getting into the Story of Concord: A History of the Book of
Concord*. St. Louis: Concordia, 1977.

Scheiner, Klaus. "Rechtgläubigkeit als 'Band der Gesellschaft' und 'Grund-lage des Staates.' Zureitlichen Verpflichtung von Staats und Kirchen-dienern auf die 'Formula Concordiae' und das 'Konkordienbuch.'" In *Bekenntnis und Einheit der Kirche: Studien zum Konkordienbuch*, eds. Martin Brecht and Reinhard Schwarz, 351–80. Stuttgart: Calwer Verlag, 1980.

Selnecker, Nikolaus. *Recitationes aliquot de consilio scripti libri Concordiae, et de modo agendi, qui in subscriptionibus servatus est.* Leipzig: 1582.

Skarsten, Trygve R. "The Reaction in Scandinavia." In *Bekenntnis und Einheit der Kirche: Studien zum Konkordienbuch*, eds. Martin Brecht and Reinhard Schwarz, 136–49. Stuttgart: Calwer Verlag, 1980.

Walther, C. F. W. "Vorwort zu Jahrgang 1877." *Lehre und Wehre* 23, nos. 1, 2, 3 (Jan–Feb–Mar, 1877): 1–5, 33–54, 65–76. Translated by Everette Meier, 1990.

3. Other Confessions

Gensichen, Hans–Werner. "Die Lehrverpflichtung in die Hannoverschen Landeskirche." *Jahrbuch der Gesellschaft für niedersächsische Landeskirche* 48 (1950): 96–108.

Jedin, Hubert. *A History of the Council of Trent.* 2 vols. Trans. Ernest Graf. St. Louis: B. Herder Book Co., 1957.

Kolb, Robert. "The German Lutheran Reaction to the Third Period of the Council of Trent." *Lutherjahrbuch* 51 (1984): 63–95.

McNally, Robert E. "The Council of Trent and German Protestantism." *Theological Studies* 25, no. 1 (March 1964): 1–22.

Mager, Inge. "Das Corpus Doctrinae der Stadt Braunschweig im Gefüge der übrigin niedersächsischen Lehrschriften–sammlungen." In *Die Reformation in der Stadt Braunschweig. Festschrift 1528-1978*, ed. Hans–Walter Krumwiede, 111–22. Braunschweig: Gesamtherstellung Druck und Verlagshaus Braunschweig, 1978.

Piepkorn, Arthur Carl. "Martin Chemnitz' Views on Trent: The Genesis and the Genius of the Examen Concilii Tridentini." *Concordia Theological Monthly* 37, no. 1 (January 1966): 5–37.

Seebass, G. *Schrift und Tradition in der Diskussion zwischen dem Tridentinum und Martin Chemnitz, Wissenschaftliche Haus zur Ersten Theologischen Prüfung der Evangelischen Kirche der Pfalz.* Heidelberg: n.p., 1987.

Stupperich, Robert. "Die Reformatoren und das Tridentinum." *Archiv für Reformationsgeschichte* 47 (1956): 20–63.

Uckeley, Alfred. "Urbanus Rhegius: Wie Man Forsichtlich und ohne Arg-erniss Reden Soll Von Den Furnemesten Artikeln Christlicher Lehre . . . Nach der Deutschen Ausgabe von 1536 nebst der Prediganweisung Herzog Ernst Des Bekenners von 1529." In *Quellenschriften zur Geschichte des Protestantismus* . . . , vol. 6, ed. J. Kunze and C. Stange, 1 ff. N.p.: 1908.

D. On Individual Doctrinal Points

1. God

Piepkorn, Arthur Carl. "The Two Natures in Christ by Martin Chemnitz in English Translation: A Review Article." *Concordia Theological Monthly* 44, no. 3 (May 1973): 218-26. A review article.

2. The Lord's Supper

Baur, Jörg. "Abendmahlslehre und Christologie der Konkordienformel als Bekenntnis zum menschlichen Gott." In *Bekenntnis und Einheit der Kirche: Studien zum Konkordienbuch*, eds. Martin Brecht and Rein-hard Schwarz, 195-218. Stuttgart: Calwer Verlag, 1980.

Frank, G. L. C. "A Lutheran Turned Eastward: The Use of the Greek Fathers in the Eucharistic Theology of Martin Chemnitz." *St. Vladimir's Theo-logical Quarterly* 26, no. 3 (1982): 155-71.

Gozdek, Frank-Georg. "Der Beitrag des Martin Chemnitz zur lutherischen Abendmahlslehre." In *Der zweite Martin der lutherischen Kirche*, ed. Wolfgang A. Jünke, 9-47. Braunschweig: Ev.-luth. Stadtkirchenver-band und Propstei Braunschweig, 1986.

Hoaas, Bryniolf. *The Bestowal of the Benefits of the Real Presence: The Early Eucharistic Works of Martin Chemnitz as a Contribution toward the Formula of Concord Article VII.* Th. D. diss., Concordia Seminary, St. Louis, 1990. His bibliography is extremely valuable.

Mahlmann, Theodor. *Das neue Dogma der lutherischen Christologie.* Güter-sloh: Gütersloher Verlagshaus Gerd Mohn, 1969.

Mörlin, Joachim. *Contra Sacramentarios, Disputationes duae, prima de Coena Domini, Altera de communicatione idiomatum.* Eisleben: n.p., 1561.

Neuser, Wilhelm. "Hardenberg und Melanchthon. Der Hardenbergishe Streit (1554-1560)." *Jahrbuch der Gesellschaft für Niedersächsische Kirchengeschichte* 65 (1967): 142-86.

Oftestad, B. T. "'Historia' and 'Utilitas'. Methodologische Aspekte der Abendmahlstheologie bei Martin Chemnitz." *Archiv für Reformationsgeschichte* 77 (1986): 186–225.

Petri, Friedrich. *Num Fides Possit supra coelos, & illic ipsam carnem Christi comprehendere contra Sacramentarios . . .* Wittenberg: n.p., 1584.

Quere, R. "Melanchthonian Motifs in the Formula's Eucharistic Christology." In *Discord, Dialogue, and Concord: Studies in the Lutheran Reformation's Formula of Concord*, eds. Lewis W. Spitz and Wenzel Lohff, 58ff. Philadelphia: Fortress, 1977.

Sasse, Hermann. *This Is My Body: Luther's Contention for the Real Presence in the Sacrament of the Altar*. Adelaide: Lutheran Publishing House, 1977.

Teigen, Bjarne W. *The Lord's Supper in the Theology of Martin Chemnitz*. Brewster, MA: Trinity Lutheran Press, 1986.

———. "Martin Chemnitz und Solida Declaratio VII, 126." In *Der zweite Martin der Lutherischen Kirche*, ed. Wolfgang A. Jünke, 242–52. Braunschweig: Ev.-luth. Stadtkirchenverband und Propstei Braunschweig, 1986.

3. Scripture

Johnson, John F. "Authority and Tradition: A Lutheran Perpective." *Concordia Journal* 8 (September 1982): 179–86.

Klug, Eugene F. *From Luther to Chemnitz: On Scripture and the Word*. Grand Rapids, MI: William B. Eerdmans Publishing Co., 1971. (Klug)

Lossner, Arthur B. *Martin Chemnitz and his locus De Sacra Scriptura against Roman Errors*. B.D. Thesis, Concordia Seminary, St. Louis, 1947.

Oftestad, Bernt Torvild. "Traditio und Norma: Hauptzüge der Scriftauffassung bei Martin Chemnitz." In *Der zweite Martin der Lutherischen Kirche*, ed. Wolfgang A. Jünke, 172–89. Braunschweig: Ev.-luth. Stadtkirchenverband und Propstei Braunschweig, 1986.

Olson, A. L. *Scripture and Tradition in the Theology of Martin Chemnitz*. Cambridge: n.p., 1965.

Pelikan, Jaroslav. *The Development of Christian Doctrine: Some Historical Prolegomena*. New Haven: Yale University Press, 1969.

———. "Tradition in Confessional Lutheranism." *Lutheran World* 3, no. 3 (December 1956): 214–22.

Preus, J. A. O. "The New Testament Canon in the Lutheran Dogmaticians." *The Springfielder* 25 (Spring 1961): 8–33.

BIBLIOGRAPHY

Preus, Robert D. *The Inspiration of Scripture: A Study of the Theology of the Seventeenth Century Lutheran Dogmaticians.* Mankato, Minnesota: Lutheran Synod Book Co., 1955.

4. Original Sin

Mörlin, Joachim. *Themata De Imagine Dei in Homine Autore D. Ioachimo Miorlino Episcopo Sambiensi, &c. et de Eadem Materia brevis tractatus D. Doctoris Martini Chemnitii Superintendentis Brunschuicensis, contra impiam et absurdam propositionem: Peccatum esse substantiam, uel ipsam etiam animam rationalem.* Wittenberg: n.p., 1570.

5. Predestination

Chemnitz, Martin. "A Sermon on the Gospel in Matthew 22, about the king who gave a wedding for his son, in which the great article of God's providence is explained in all simplicity." Trans. Ralph Rokke from the German original "Eine Christliche Predige von der Verschung or Wahl Gottes zur Seligkeit ause dem Evangelio Mattei 22. Am zwanzigsten Sontag nach Trinitatis. Gethan in Furstlichen Capellen zu Wolfenbuttel." 1987.

Söderlund, Rune. *Ex praevisa fide, Zum Verständnis der Prädestinationslehre in der lutherischen Orthodoxie.* Arbeiten zur Geschichte und Theologie des Luthertums, New Series, vol. 3, eds. Bengt Hägglund and Heinrich Kraft. Hannover: Lutherisches Verlagshaus, 1983.

6. Conversion

Green, Lowell C. "The Three Causes of Conversion in Philipp Melanchthon, Martin Chemnitz, David Chytraeus, and the 'Formula of Concord.'" *Lutherjahrbuch* 47 (1980): 89–114.

Hoaas, Brynjulf. *The Doctrine of Conversion in the Theology of Martin Chemnitz: What Conversion Is and How It Is Worked.* STM Thesis, Concordia Theological Seminary, Ft. Wayne, IN, 1985.

Schmidt, Kurt. "Der Göttinger Bekehrungsstreit 1566–1570." *Zeitschrift der Gesellschaft Niedersächsische Kirchengeschichte* 34 (1929): 66–105.

7. Justification

Green, Lowell C. "Faith, Righteousness and Justification: New Light on Their Development Under Luther and Melanchthon." *The Sixteenth Century Journal* 4, no. 1 (April 1973): 65–86.

Hoffmann, Gottfried. "Die Rechtfertigung des Sünders vor Gott nach dem Examen Concilii Tridentini von Martin Chemnitz." In *Der zweite Martin der Lutherischen Kirche*, ed. Wolfgang A. Jünke, 60–92. Braunschweig: Ev.–luth. Stadtkirchenverband und Propstei Braunschweig, 1986.

Kolb, Robert. "'Good Works are Detrimental to Salvation': Amsdorf's Use of Luther's Words in Controversy." *Renaissance et Reforme* (1977): 136ff.

Mullet, Gerhard. "Die Rechtfertigungslehre: Geschichte und Probleme." In *Studienbucher Theologie: Kirchen und Dogmengeschichte*. Gütersloh: n.p., 1977.

Roth, Dr. "Ein Braunschweiger Theologe des 16 Jahrhunderts: Mörlin und seine Rechtfertigungslehre." *Jahrbuch der Gesellschaft für Niedersächsische Kirchengeschichte* 50 (1952): 59–81. [Contains full text of the "Supplik der Königsberger Frauen für Mörlin"—cf. p. 106 to this in text.]

Stupperich, Martin. "Martin Chemnitz und der Osiandrische Streit." In *Der zweite Martin der Lutherischen Kirche*, ed. Wolfgang A. Jünke, 224–41. Braunschweig: Ev.–luth. Stadtkirchenverband und Propstei Braunschweig, 1986.

_____. *Osiander in Preussen 1549–1552*. [Chapter B, "Der Streit um Die Rechtfertigungslehre," part 1, "Die Ansätze des Streits um die Rechtfertigungslehre."] In Arbeiten zur Kirchengeschichte, vol. 44, eds. Kurt Aland, Carl Andresen, and Gerhard Müller, 110–36. Berlin: Walter de Gruyter, 1973.

_____. "Zur Vorgeschichte des Rechtfertigungsartikels in der Konkordienformel, [this is chapter 3 for preceding].

8. Law and Gospel

Elert, Werner. *Law and Gospel*. Trans. Ed Schroeder. Facet Books Social Ethics Series, vol. 16. Philadelphia: Fortress, 1967.

Preus, J. A. O. "Chemnitz on Law and Gospel." *Concordia Journal* 15 (October 1989): 406–22.

9. Free Will

Hägglund, Bengt. "Wie hat Martin Chemnitz zu Luthers De servo arbitrio Stellung genommen?" In *Der zweite Martin der Lutherischen Kirche*, ed. Wolfgang A. Jünke, 48–59. Braunschweig: Ev.-luth. Stadtkirchen-verband und Propstei Braunschweig, 1986.

10. Adiaphora

Keller, Rudolf. "Im Konflikt über die Adiaphora: Martin Chemnitz auf dem Weg zum zehnten Artikel der Konkordienformel." In *Der zweite Mar-tin der Lutherischen Kirche*, ed. Wolfgang A. Jünke, 93–114. Braun-schweig: Ev.-luth. Stadtkirchenverband und Propstei Braunschweig, 1986.

Mehlhausen, Joachim. "Die Streit um die Adiaphora." In *Bekenntnis und Einheit der Kirche: Studien zum Konkordienbuch*, eds. Martin Brecht and Reinhard Schwarz, 105–28. Stuttgart: Calwer Verlag, 1980.

11. Creation

Secker, Philip J. *The Goodness of Creation and the Natural Knowledge of the Goodness of God in Nicholas Selnecker, David Chytraeus, and Mar-tin Chemnitz*. STM Thesis, Concordia Seminary, St. Louis, 1967.

E. Other Specific Writings

Bilinkoff, Jodi. *The Avila of Saint Teresa: Religious Reform in a Sixteenth-Century City*. Ithaca, NY: Cornell University Press, 1989.

Hendrix, Scott H. *Luther and the Papacy*. Philadelphia: Fortress, 1981.

Mumm, Reinhard. *Die Polemik des Martin Chemnitz gegen das Konzil von Trient*. Naumberg: Lippert and Co., 1905.

Pelikan, Jaroslav. *Obedient Rebels: Catholic Substance and Protestant Prin-ciple in Luther's Reformation*. New York: Harper and Row, Publish-ers, 1964.

——. *The Riddle of Roman Catholicism*. Nashville: Abingdon Press, 1952. (Riddle)

Tuchman, Barbara W. *The March of Folly*. New York: Knopf, 1984.

Index

THE SECOND MARTIN

INDEX

INDEX